"With the goal of reconciling widely divergent and often divisive views on the biblical creation account, Ben Smith revives the interpretation of Genesis 1 first proposed by British physicist Alan Hayward. Smith argues for seven consecutive 24-hour days during which God proclaims, in a topical rather than chronological order, what he will do over billions of years to prepare Earth for human existence and redemption."

Hugh Ross, astronomer, author, pastor, and president of Reasons to Believe

"Will anyone ever show Christianity a way out of our battles over Genesis 1 and 2? It's a crucial question for the sake of our unity and our witness. This much I have known for sure: it could only happen through a firm commitment to the authority and truth of Scripture, coupled with competent attention to all of the many biblical and scientific arguments. This much I have also wondered: whether it would also require a fresh perspective on the intended meaning of the biblical text. Ben Smith's work in this book is indeed competent, thorough, and above all Scripture-affirming; and he may have also supplied us with that missing final ingredient: a way to interpret the text literally (according to its intended meaning) that resolves any need for controversy or disunity. His work deserves careful review."

Tom Gilson, Senior Editor for TheStream.org and author of ***True Reason****: Confronting the Irrationality of the New Atheism*, **Critical Conversations**: *A Christian Parents' Guide to Discussing Homosexuality with Teens* and *A* ***Christian Mind***

"Ben Smith is committed to digging into Scripture to decipher the truth related to young-Earth vs. old-Earth creation, that today causes a chasm of division in the church and in families. He is passionate about knowing the truth from a *literal* reading of Scripture, so that the church can be a credible witness to the gospel of Jesus Christ, the Creator. He spent some years committed to a young-Earth view and concluded: 'The YEV has big holes. We need a boat that floats.' He has developed a Prophetic Days View that is biblically based. Its five points '...can be discerned *from the text of Genesis alone and are more literal to the text than the Young-Earth View*.' Chapter 2 clearly describes his straightforward literal interpretation of Genesis."

Ken Wolgemuth, Ph.D., petroleum consultant, founder of **Solid Rock Lectures**, and contributing author to ***The Grand Canyon****: Monument to an Ancient Earth*

"*Genesis, Science, and the Beginning* contributes to the ongoing dialogue and debate over the proper approach to interpreting the biblical account of creation. All thinking Christians understand that the primary purpose of the Bible is to relate transcendent theological truths, not to serve as a textbook on science. But whether or not the Bible is scientifically reliable is neither a secondary nor a tangential matter. Ben Smith has devoted years of study to the topic, and the scope of the book provides ample evidence of both the breadth and the depth of his research. Written in an informal and conversational style for the non-specialist, the book makes a valuable contribution to our understanding of the controversy as it is currently framed. A sensible and hermeneutically-sound concept of the biblical creation story is something that all serious Christians should aspire to understand. This book is not the final word on the controversy, but it moves the debate along and opens up new avenues of thought that all serious students of the Bible and apologetics would benefit from considering. Highly recommended."

Jefrey D. Breshears, Ph.D. founder and president of **The Areopagus** in Atlanta, Ga. and author of *An Introduction to Bibliology* and *The Absolute Truth About Relativism*

"*Genesis, Science, and the Beginning* is a well-researched presentation about the age of the Earth controversy. Chapters two and five are, in themselves, sufficient to allow a person adhering to the 24-hour day interpretation of the days of Genesis to reconcile that view with an old earth and an old universe as evidenced by science."

Rodney Whitefield, Ph.D., author of *Reading Genesis One*

"Ben Smith's book *Genesis, Science, and the Beginning* is a clear and careful look at what the Bible and the book of nature say about creation. It honors both science and scripture and will contribute to the needed dialog about Genesis in today's world. From the introduction onward, I found it very straightforward, open, with proper humility and excellent clarity. Ben's criticism of the Young Earth Creationist position was certainly straightforward and clear, but also showed proper restraint. Overall, I think the work in the book is outstanding, and will be useful to me in discussing these ideas."

Rod Nave, Ph.D., Department of Physics, Georgia State University, and author of **HyperPhysics**

"Apologetics books can sometimes have great evangelistic potential and when I began to read this one, that's the first thing that came to mind. Ben's insistence on rightly interpreting the Word of God and being honest with scientific fact brings about a convincing argument, that in my opinion, successfully marries true science with the Bible on matters of creation. In that sense, it should silence the skeptics of the Word, as well as those who blindly assert that science is wrong just because of wrong assumptions of what the Bible says and means. Read this book with an open heart and mind. You may discover a new confidence in the Bible, a new respect for scientific facts and a new appreciation of the Creator."

Marc Limbaugh, Pastor of Renew Church, Carrollton, Ga.

GENESIS, SCIENCE, AND THE BEGINNING

*Evaluating Interpretations
of Genesis One
on the Age of the Earth*

BENJAMIN D. SMITH JR.

GENESIS, SCIENCE, AND THE BEGINNING
Evaluating Interpretations of Genesis One on the Age of the Earth

Copyright © 2018 Benjamin D. Smith Jr. All rights reserved. Except for brief quotations in critical publications or reviews, no part of this book may be reproduced in any manner without prior written permission from the publisher. Write: Permissions, Wipf and Stock Publishers, 199 W. 8th Ave., Suite 3, Eugene, OR 97401.

Wipf & Stock
An Imprint of Wipf and Stock Publishers
199 W. 8th Ave., Suite 3
Eugene, OR 97401

www.wipfandstock.com

PAPERBACK ISBN: 978-1-5326-4331-6
HARDCOVER ISBN: 978-1-5326-4332-3
EBOOK ISBN: 978-1-5326-4333-0

Manufactured in the U.S.A.   08/07/18

Unless otherwise indicated, Scripture quotations are from the New American Standard Bible, © copyright THE LOCKMAN FOUNDATION, 1960, 1962, 1963, 1968, 1971, 1972, 1973, 1975, 1977, 1995, A Corporation Not for Profit, La Habra, CA. All rights reserved.

Scriptures marked NIV are from The Holy Bible, New International Version, Copyright © 1973, 1978, 1984 by the International Bible Society. All rights reserved.

Scriptures marked ESV are from The Holy Bible, The English Standard Version. Copyright © 2001 by Crossway Bibles, a division of Good News Publishers. All rights reserved.

Scriptures marked NKJV are from The Holy Bible, New King James Version, Copyright © 1990 by Thomas Nelson, Inc. All rights reserved.

Contents

Abbreviations	v
Acknowledgements	vii
Introduction	1
Part I – Presenting the Prophetic Days View	
1 – The Big Pictures	7
2 – The Prophetic Days View	17
3 – A Beautiful Picture of our Creator	43
4 – The Beginning and you – What now?	53
Part II – Defending the Prophetic Days View	
5 – Objections to the Prophetic Days View	59
6 – Death *Before* the Fall	93
7 – The Top Ten Views of Genesis 1	127
8 – Why I Repented of the Young-Earth View	139
9 – Evaluating other Old-Earth Views	153
10 – Biblical Scientific Inerrancy?	187
Appendices	
A – Defending Definitions: Word Studies in Genesis One	209
Translation of Genesis 1:1 – 2:4a	229
B – The Meaning of רקיע (*raqîa'*) in Genesis: Expanse or Firmament? And what are those "waters above" the expanse?	231
Bibliography	249
Footnotes	257
Indices	
Scripture Index	285
Subject Index	291

Abbreviations

ADV	–	Analogical Days View
AiG	–	Answers in Genesis
CJB	–	Complete Jewish Bible
CMI	–	Creation Ministries International
CRI	–	Christian Research Institute
CTV	–	Cosmic Temple View
DAV	–	Day-Age View
EC	–	Evolutionary Creation
ESV	–	English Standard Version of the Bible
FV	–	Framework View
GV	–	Gap View
HCSB	–	Holman Christian Standard Bible
ICR	–	Institute for Creation Research
IDV	–	Intermittent Days View
JPS	–	Jewish Publication Society
KJV	–	King James Version of the Bible
LCV	–	Limited Creation View
LXX	–	the Septuagint
MT	–	Masoretic Text
NASB	–	New American Standard Bible
NIV	–	New International Version of the Bible
NKJV	–	New King James Version of the Bible
NRSV	–	New Revised Standard Version of the Bible
NT	–	New Testament
OEC	–	Old Earth Creationist
OEV	–	Old Earth View
OT	–	Old Testament
PDV	–	Prophetic Days View or Proclamation Days View
RDV	–	Revelatory Days View
RSV	–	Revised Standard Version of the Bible
RTB	–	Reasons To Believe
TE	–	Theistic Evolution
YEC	–	Young Earth Creationist
YEV	–	Young Earth View
YLT	–	Young's Literal Translation of the Bible

Scripture Abbreviations

Old Testament

Gen.	–	Genesis	Eccl.	–	Ecclesiastes
Ex.	–	Exodus	Song	–	Song of Solomon
Lev.	–	Leviticus			
Num.	–	Numbers	Is.	–	Isaiah
Dt.	–	Deuteronomy	Jer.	–	Jeremiah
Josh.	–	Joshua	Lam.	–	Lamentations
Jdg.	–	Judges	Ezek.	–	Ezekiel
Ruth	–	Ruth	Dan.	–	Daniel
I Sam.	–	I Samuel	Hos.	–	Hosea
II Sam.	–	II Samuel	Joel	–	Joel
I Kgs.	–	I Kings	Amos	–	Amos
II Kgs.	–	II Kings	Ob.	–	Obadiah
I Chr.	–	I Chronicles	Jon.	–	Jonah
II Chr.	–	II Chronicles	Mic.	–	Micah
Est.	–	Esther	Nah.	–	Nahum
Neh.	–	Nehemiah	Hab.	–	Habakkuk
Ezra	–	Ezra	Zeph.	–	Zephaniah
Job	–	Job	Hag.	–	Haggai
Ps.	–	Psalms	Zech.	–	Zechariah
Pr.	–	Proverbs	Mal.	–	Malachi

New Testament

Mt.	–	Matthew	I Tim.	–	I Timothy
Mk.	–	Mark	II Tim.	–	II Timothy
Lk.	–	Luke	Tit.	–	Titus
Jn.	–	John	Phil.	–	Philemon
Acts	–	Acts	Heb.	–	Hebrews
Rms.	–	Romans	Jms.	–	James
I Cor.	–	I Corinthians	I Pet.	–	I Peter
II Cor.	–	II Corinthians	II Pet.	–	II Peter
Gal.	–	Galatians	I Jn.	–	I John
Eph.	–	Ephesians	II Jn.	–	II John
Phlp.	–	Philippians	III Jn.	–	III John
Col.	–	Colossians	Jude	–	Jude
I Th.	–	I Thessalonians	Rev.	–	Revelation
II Th.	–	II Thessalonians			

Acknowledgments

Gratitude is so difficult to express adequately to the many people who have helped make the vision of publishing this book possible.

Scientific thanks go out to Rod Nave whose physics and astronomy expertise kept me from overextending my science evidence. Ken Wolgemuth has been a tremendous blessing with his knowledge of geology, corrections, suggestions, passion, and support.

Reasons To Believe (RTB) is an exceptionally valuable science resource no apologist should go without and I highly recommend anything from them. Despite my disagreement with the Day-Age View, my appreciation goes out to the scholar team of Hugh Ross, Fuz Rana, Ken Samples, Jeff Zweerink, and AJ Roberts who all set tremendous examples of excellence and Christ-like behavior in the face of much opposition. They have helped me more than they know.

Philosophical thanks go to the much deserved Dr. Richard G. Howe whose knowledge, humor, humility, help, and friendship are an encouragement. I wish all YEC were like him. Also, Russ Crawford, with his razor sharp philosophical mind, always challenges me to keep my arguments solid.

Theological thanks go to Rodney Whitefield who helped greatly with his knowledge of Hebrew and his corrections and additions to the manuscript. He was one of the few people who graciously took the time to read the early manuscript and offer helpful suggestions and encouragements. Appreciation also goes to Joshua Stewart of Luther Rice College and Seminary who assisted with some Hebrew corrections.

Author and Editor Tom Gilson was especially helpful toward successfully launching the book and I greatly appreciate his encouragement and willingness to share his expertise.

Tom Griffin, Ratio Christi Syndication Manager for *Truth Matters*, is a great friend and I thank him for his support and conversations related to the topic of this book. Ratio Christi is an awesome organization in which to be involved. Their stand for the truth of Christ on college campuses inspires me, and their vision to plant apologetics clubs on as many college campuses as possible will bear fruit for the Kingdom of God. Please support your local chapters and their leaders. And if your local college does not have a chapter, pray about starting one.

The RTB Atlanta apologetics forum is a special group of people. Thanks go to Rod (president) and Brenda Nave, Jefrey Breshears (of the

Areopagus), Eric and Andrea Smith, Bruce and Pamela Phillips, Butch Johnston, Colin and Tracy Green, and Mark Tabladillo for their commitment to making the meetings highly informative and fun. The spirit of humility and maturity rests in that place and it is a joy.

All the members of our apologetics discussion groups in my local community and at my church deserve more credit for this work than I could possibly ever give them. Randy Pierce deserves special recognition from that group because of his support, desire for truth, and faithfulness. He is a major reason this book is available. The Woodward boys (Adam, Noah, Isaac, and Ezra) were some of my early victims, but they have taught me plenty also (Rainbow Falls forever guys!). Drew Boon and the Hitchcock twins Blake and Brent are additional exceptional assets whose discussions contributed to the manuscript.

Marc Limbaugh, my pastor of 20 years amazes me with his wisdom, openness, and fearlessness of the truth. He is a man who makes you want to be closer to God. I wish all pastors and church leaders had his humility and discernment when it comes to complicated controversial matters. Thank you, Marc, for your prayers, support, and counsel.

Iron sharpening iron friends are a blessing no one should be without. Much gratitude is owed to Matthew Piquette, Tom Woodward (not the one you may be thinking of), Russ Barnes (R.I.P.), James Gross, and Kelly Cook for simply being great friends and all that entails.

The joy of having children who have endured their father's intellectual prompting and probing has been great, and to see them join in is even better. My wife and I have three awesome mature young adults (Duran, Lanae, and Lauren) who love the Lord, respect their parents, and have a hilarious good time together. Duran contributed several good arguments to this book.

The love and support from my wife Carissa deserves special honor. She has supported me through the highs and lows, through the failures and successes, and my appreciation for her has not been near good enough. I love you my dear.

Finally, God is the One who deserves all the praise, honor, and glory for all that we do and His guiding hand has been obvious to me in the production of this work. My prayer is that He will use this book to move the church closer to the truth of His word, and then convey that truth to the world that desperately needs Him. To God be the glory!

Introduction

For the last 30 years I have been intently interested in the old Earth versus young Earth controversy. Among evangelical Christians, this issue is one of the most divisive issues of our day even though many Christians do not realize it. However, Young-Earth Creationists (YEC – those who believe the Earth is only about 6,000-10,000 years old) and Old-Earth Creationists (OEC – those who accept modern science's age of billions of years) both deserve commendation for taking a stand and defending the Bible against the onslaught of naturalistic evolution, atheism, secularism, and postmodern relativism rampant in our world. *Both* YEC *and* OEC are creationists, not evolutionists. Conservative scholars exist on both sides who believe the Bible is the inerrant Word of God. On those issues and many more both sides stand united.

But on the age of the universe and Earth and the interpretation of Genesis YEC and OEC differ widely and accusations fly. OEC are accused of leading a generation down a slippery slope toward unbelief and compromising the infallible Word of God to the fallible word of man because of their agreement with science the universe and Earth are billions of years old. Or worse, OEC are accused of worshipping a different god who would allow the death of animals before sin. On the other hand, YEC are accused of making Christians look like idiots, fundamentalist zealots who know nothing of science and who turn a blind eye toward the facts. Or worse, YEC are accused of being deceivers by deliberately ignoring facts they cannot explain.

Compromiser or idiot? I do not like either choice and I can sympathize with anyone who has wrestled with the issue because I have wrestled with it for a long time. After studying the reconciliation of the Bible and science for so long I have at least settled the issue to my own satisfaction and that wasn't easy. This book is written to help fellow searchers settle it for themselves.

I became a Young-Earth Creationist shortly after becoming a Christian in 1985 and found that position was not popular at Georgia Tech where I was attending college, but I was willing to endure that for the sake of truth. I quickly immersed myself in the writings of Henry Morris and Duane Gish from the Institute for Creation Research (ICR – a YEC organization) and in a debate I could defend YEC even to this day; but *I no longer believe it*.

I was converted to being an OEC primarily by the writings of Hugh Ross (astronomer and founder of Reasons To Believe – RTB, an OEC organization) and Alan Hayward (physicist). But, even after accepting what I now consider to be overwhelming evidence the universe and Earth are billions of years old, there were still many Biblical issues I needed to work out in detail. For example, does Genesis allow for an old Earth? I believe it does and this book is about how. If I had found that Genesis was wrong and the Bible was unsupported by good science then I can honestly say I may not be a Christian today, or I would be a liberal one at best. That may sound like a strong statement, but Christianity, or anything else for that matter, should not be accepted on blind unsubstantiated faith, or purely on some religious experience or feeling. Nor do I believe God expects blind faith of believers. If something is true there should be evidence to support it if we are to believe it.

Here is the main problem this book addresses

The Bible is perceived by many people to say that the universe and Earth were created in six 24-hour days about 6,000 years ago. *It does not!* In fact, I will plainly say that the traditional Young-Earth View (YEV) is flatly wrong about its interpretation of Genesis 1. As is often the case, the Bible does not say what many people think it says. Careful study should be made to determine what Genesis really says. I believe Genesis 1 was simple to the original audience, but we are a long time since then and are left struggling to understand how they would have understood it. And, of course, we now have those science issues (like age) to deal with. In the end I hope you will see Genesis does not force us to take a side on the age of the universe and Earth. Genesis simply does not tell us.

Why is this issue important? Why not avoid controversial issues?

I hear these questions asked frequently. Some people think Christians should avoid controversy because it causes divisions. They say we should concentrate on unity and our agreements. However, I believe *controversy is unavoidable* and it is the attitude with which it is handled that should set Christians apart as different from the world, not running from disagreement. If we can show respect and love for those with whom we differ, that will have a much greater impact than being afraid to confront controversy.

Ultimately, YEC and OEC are both working toward converting people to Christianity. At the very least, Christianity can be defined as *believing and following the teachings of Jesus Christ.* The teachings of Jesus are found in the Bible and if the Bible is not seen as a trustworthy testimony of Jesus then people are less likely to follow Him. The problem is the Bible is not taken seriously and one reason for that is people believe it is an old mythological book with little basis in scientific fact. This belief in a lack of scientific accuracy becomes a major intellectual hurdle to many people accepting the truth of Christianity, and even causes serious doubts among those who call themselves believers. And hence, the young Earth/old Earth controversy is unavoidable because when Biblical accuracy is questioned science is where it begins.

The book of Genesis is foundational for the entire Bible. It is no wonder then that controversy, ridicule, and passion are dragged along behind it like cans tied to the bumper of a newlyweds' vehicle. The noise Genesis creates should be understandable. If the story it tells is true then the Bible should be taken seriously. If it is false then the power of the Bible is undermined.

I believe the Bible is true, which is abundantly clear even from its first chapter. If we Christians are to reach the generations of people who have grown up in ignorance of the Bible we will have to answer some tough questions, but the Bible has those answers. The stakes are high therefore, and I, for one, need to know the truth to know with which side to be aligned. Since you are reading this book I believe you must feel the same way.

The Big Questions

No one wants to be wrong about their foundational philosophy of life, their worldview. The existence of God is certainly a belief most people accept and it has profound effects on one's worldview, but the question quickly arises as to how we can know anything about this God. What is He like? Does He care about me? Does He have a purpose for my life? Can He help me? Can I just live my life the way I want and in the end it does not matter? Does God expect something from me? These types of questions are on everyone's mind but the answers people come up with vary so widely one can wonder if there is any way to objectively find real answers. Am I left with only my opinion and you with yours?

What if...? And this question deserves a serious attempt to answer. *What if God actually spoke to us and revealed what He is like and what His purposes are?* What if God cared enough to give us an objective revelation of Himself so we would not be left with just opinions? The Bible claims to be that revelation from our Creator. If God wrote down

His will and purpose for creating the universe, then the question shifts from "How can I know anything about God?" to "What does it say?"

Now I will not deny that there are disagreements about what the Bible means. In fact, the main topic of this book revolves around differences of opinion on the interpretation of Genesis. Because there are differences it takes an honest effort to sort through the options and determine which one you believe. The answer could have eternal consequences. *Is there anything more important than that?*

Perhaps no chapters of the Bible are more studied and commentated than Genesis 1-3. I suspect more volumes have been written on these three chapters than have been written on any other part of the Bible. The importance of the subject matter in these three chapters cannot be overstated. The authority and validity of the whole Bible rests on them. Everything Scripture has to say is built upon the foundation laid in the opening chapters of Genesis. All that is most important about our existence traces its origins to the story told in these brief three chapters. Starting with where we came from, to why we are here, to how humanity got in the mess we are in, and what must be done about it, these all originate in the first three chapters of Genesis. Ultimately, the reason for Christ's death on the cross goes back to the Fall of man recorded in Genesis 3. The very foundation and essence of the Gospel message is completely lost without an understanding of Genesis 1-3. Skeptics often understand what is at stake better than many Christians, as atheist George H. Smith says,

> To claim, as does the demythologizer, that the Bible is not to be regarded as historical, is to undercut the historical basis of Christianity – and ultimately to destroy the concept of Christianity as such… Once the Bible is conceded to be factually incorrect, there is – from the atheist point of view – nothing further to argue.[1]
>
> If the Bible is conceded to be mistaken or based on superstition in some instances, what is to prevent us from rejecting all of the supernatural accounts in the Bible – including the life and Resurrection of Jesus – as myths?[2]

The validity of Jewish and Christian truth claims stand firm or collapse in Genesis.

Because the importance of how Genesis is interpreted has such a profound effect on crucial subjects, is it any wonder that the controversies surrounding these verses are so intense? Humility is a must in these situations and the Bible warns that "God resists the proud, but gives grace to the humble" (I Pet. 5:5b). And "Knowledge puffs up, but love edifies. And if anyone thinks that he knows anything, he knows nothing yet as he ought to know." (I Cor. 8:1b-2) The ability to admit when we are wrong and change our mind in the face of good evidence is a quality sorely lacking among many people, including Christians. We should be careful about what we "know" we know. It is not that we cannot know anything; it is just that we should seek the truth, be humble and loving and willing to hear what others say, and be willing to change our own mind if we are wrong. That attitude will reach more people for Christ than all the arguing over theology and science in the world.

Proper attitude withstanding, a theologically sound coherent interpretation of Genesis is necessary to reach some people and helpful in providing a solid support for the faith of many others, including me. So, to endeavor to be correct about what Genesis says is commended by God. "Be diligent to present yourself approved to God, a worker who does not need to be ashamed, rightly dividing the word of truth." (II Tim. 2:15) So this book's intention is to humbly understand the truth and rightly divide Genesis 1, a worthy but difficult goal.

Let us see if it is possible to remain faithful to a literal historical interpretation of Genesis *and* the sciences of geology and astronomy on the age of the universe and Earth.

And so we begin.

Part I – Presenting the Prophetic Days View

1

The Big Pictures
(Wading into the shallows)

Anyone who has read Genesis 1:1-2:4 can plainly see it is a highly structured story with repeated phrases, a simple and generic narrative, and an overall pattern centered around a work week of six days and a seventh day of rest. Evangelicals unanimously agree on two overall themes of Genesis 1: God is our Creator and He created the Earth as a "good" place for humanity to live and worship Him. However, one should not simply dwell upon these two themes, despite their significance. God gave us much more in Genesis 1 and this information is not irrelevant. The details are important because I do not think God would have given them otherwise.

The author of Genesis 1 obviously intended us to believe what he wrote really happened sometime in the past. That is, it is making a claim to be accurate history in some sense. The question then becomes, "Is it true?" The conclusion of this book is, "Yes!" But, let us get the big pictures first and then go diving in the deep water later. Six structural elements of Genesis 1 make a good start.

First – Genesis 1 is unique and memorable

Genesis 1 is like no other section of Scripture in the Bible. Nowhere else do we find a historical narrative as highly structured as this one. In fact, because the account is so highly structured many advocate the account is poetry. However, many others see that there are big differences between Hebrew poetry and Genesis 1. Rather than get into a lengthy discussion of Hebrew grammar and poetic styles, hopefully we can all agree that even if Genesis 1 was written poetically it was still written with the intent to present a true account of God creating the heavens and Earth. Therefore, it is not pure symbolism, metaphor, or allegory, though it may contain them. Instead, it matter-of-factly presents a historical account of what God did, but in a highly structured format.

I submit to you that the reason it was written that way was to make it easy to memorize. If someone wanted an important story to be remembered amongst people who could not read or write it would make sense to tell it in a format that is easy to remember. In fact, when I point out the structure of the account below it is likely you may never forget it.

Second – Seeing Patterns

An overall chart of Genesis 1 (see figure 1.1) reveals a general layout of the account that is symmetrical, but not perfectly so because it has some deviations. The general pattern is what makes the whole account easy to remember and the deviations are meant to draw our attention to certain aspects the author wanted to emphasize. Those emphases will be shown as they appear along the way. The creativity behind the layout is awe inspiring alone.

Anyone can see the main layout of the account centers around God proclaiming something, then giving us more information related to that proclamation, and then tagging it with an ending (the evening and morning phrase plus a numbered day). More specifically, each of the 6 Days contains:

1. A proclamation (although 4 out of the 6 Days have more than one)
2. A fulfillment phrase (a statement God's proclamation was fulfilled)
3. Action phrases (a description of various actions that occurred)
4. The evening and mo ning phrase
5. A numbered Day

These five are present within the text of each of the 6 Days, but the 7th Day is completely different. Also, another important note related to the five-fold pattern is that sometimes actions are listed *before* the fulfillment phrase, meaning 2 and 3 are not always in the same order but 1, 4, and 5 are.

Third – The account intentionally uses common broad generic terms

The terms used in the account are very generic. They have specific definitions, but they cover a broad semantic range. (See figure 1.2 for a glossary.) The account refers to categories of which *everyone* is familiar regardless of education or culture, and the categories are broad enough to be universal in nature. That is, the account is exhaustive in regard to normal human experience. Nothing we would *normally experience* is left out and God is said to be the originator of it all.[1]

Broad generic definitions also imply the account should be seen as written to humanity in general and not to an exclusively Jewish audience. In fact, the account is free from specifying or embellishing any particular civilization, race, or culture. It portrays humanity in its innocence before any of those distinctions began. The revelation given by the account was apparently meant to be for all humanity, everywhere, at all times, and is even revelation Adam and Eve would have wanted to know.

Therefore, *Genesis 1 was written to all humanity to declare the origins of ALL major features of the creation common to everyone.*

Fourth – The subject arrangement of the Days is topical not chronological

Despite the strong desire of many for the arrangement of the 6 Days to match the scientific order of appearance on Earth of the various features and creatures listed in the account, the account *cannot* be made to accomplish the task (See chapter 9 for more). The reason is because the 6 Days in Genesis 1:3-1:31 are very generic and arranged topically, not scientifically chronological. Many commentators have pointed out the arrangement as:

Day 1 – Light	Day 4 – Source and purpose of the lights
Day 2 – Waters and sky	Day 5 – Creatures in the water and sky
Day 3 – Dry land and plants	Day 6 – Land creatures and humanity that eat plants

Because this topical arrangement is apparent in the account some have suggested the Days were not literal Earth days.[2] However, that conclusion does not follow. Just because the Days are arranged topically does not mean they could not be a real Earth week. Some have countered their argument by denying the topical arrangement above[3], but the topical arrangement looks very obvious and serves as a powerful memorization tool which is what I believe it was designed to do. However, the topical arrangement in no way eliminates the historical nature of the account. The Days still can and should be taken literally and chronologically.

That the parallel Days arrangement was intended by the author is also evidenced by the other parallel structures of the account (again, see figure 1.1). Notice for example, there is one proclamation on Days 1 and 4,[4] two on Days 2 and 5, and three on Days 3 and 6. Also, two common phrases repeated on most Days are missing from Days 2 and 5. These are not coincidences and show the intricate planning someone put into the story to make it easy to remember.

Genesis, Science, and the Beginning

Figure 1.1 – Outline of Genesis 1:1-2:4a

1:1 – God creates the heavens and the earth *before* the 6 Days of the main narrative (1:3-31).
1:2 – The account then moves to a time just *before* Day 1 when Earth was desolate, lifeless, dark, and wet.

Day 1 – Light – **1:3-5**
  God said
    Let there be light
      Light was
      God saw
      God separated
      God called
  Evening and morning, <u>one day</u>

Day 2 – Waters and sky – **1:6-8**
  God said
    Let there be an expanse
    Let it separate
      God made
      God separated
      It was so
      God called
  Evening and morning, a 2nd day

Day 3 – Dry-ground and plants – **1:9-13**
  God said
    Let the waters below gather
    Let dry-ground (land) appear
      It was so
      God called
      God saw
  God said
    Let the earth sprout

      It was so
      The earth brought forth (produce)
      God saw
Evening and morning, a 3rd day

Day 4 – Lights – **1:14-19**
  God said
    Let there be lights in the expanse of the heavens for…[4]
      It was so
      God made
      God placed (set)
      God saw
  Evening and morning, a 4th day

Day 5 – Animals in water and sky – **1:20-23**
  God said
    Let waters abound
    Let flyers fly
      God created
      God saw
      God blessed
  Evening and morning, a 5th day

Day 6 – Land animals and man – **1:24-31**
  God said
    Let the earth bring forth (produce)
      It was so
      God made
      God saw
  God said
    Let Us make man
    Let them rule
      God created
      God blessed and said
      God informed
      It was so
      God saw
  Evening and morning, <u>the 6th day</u>

2:1-4a – The heavens and the earth and all their hosts are finished and God rested on the 7th Day.

Notice six parallels in the structure: 1. The subjects of Days 1 and 4, 2 and 5, and 3 and 6 match. **2.** There are four phrases after the proclamations on Days 1 and 4. **3.** There are two proclamations after "God said" on Days 2 and 5. **4.** A common phrase on most of the Days is missing from Days 2 and 5. "God saw that it was good" is missing from Day 2 and "And it was so" is missing from Day 5. **5.** There are two "God said" on Days 3 and 6. On Day 3 the first one is followed by two proclamations. On Day 6 the second one is followed by two proclamations. **6.** There are three proclamations each on Days 3 and 6.

Also notice the five complete patterns (items every Day contains except Day 7): 1. A proclamation **2.** A fulfillment phrase **3.** An action phrase or two or more **4.** The evening and morning phrase, and **5.** A numbered day

And the four partial patterns (items that are repeated but not every time): 1. God saw it was good, **2.** God called or named something, **3.** And it was so, and **4.** God blessed.

Chapter 1 – The Big Pictures

Figure 1.2 – Glossary of important terms as used in Genesis 1:1 – 2:4a (NASB)
(See Appendix A for a defense of these definitions)

English	Hebrew[5]	Verses used	Definition
Account	*toledoth*	2:4a	account, history, or generations
Beast	*chay*	1:24-25, 28, 30	*any* wild animal or relatively large "living thing", often carnivorous
Beginning	*reshith*	1:1	the first or chief *part* of the whole of something
Birds	n. *'owph*	1:20-23, 26, 28	*any* flying creature, not just birds (see fly)
Bring forth	*yatsa*	1:12, 24	to go out, bring out, bring forth, produce
Cattle	*behemah*	1:24-26	*any* large animal usually herbivorous, livestock
Created	*bara*	1:1,21,27,2:3-4	to make a new thing
Creeping things	n. *remes*	1:24-26, 30	the verb means to crawl or move with short steps
Creeps	v. *ramas*		the noun refers to *any* small moving creature on the ground: insect, reptile, mammal, etc.
Day	*yom*	throughout	the daylight portion of a 24 hour period
Deep	*tehôm*	1:2	a deep place like a sea
Dry land	*yabbâshâh*	1:9-10	dry-ground, not the same as "earth" or "land"
Earth	*erets*	throughout	all land, land above water (dry-ground)
Evening	*'ereb*	throughout	the lighted part of 24-hours *after* sunset, dusk
Expanse	*raqia*	1:6-8,14-17,20	the expanding clear space of the sky (See App. B)
Fly	v. *'uwph*	1:20	verb form of the noun for "birds", i.e. to fly
Formless	*tohu*	1:2	desolate, uninhabitable, wasteland, unproductive
Fruitful	*parah*	1:22,28	to bear that which is beneficial for mankind
Gathered	*qavah*	1:9	to gather together, potentially slowly
God	***Elohim***	throughout	**God, the most frequent word in the account**
Good	*towb*	throughout	beneficial for mankind but ultimately for God
Govern	*memshalah*	1:16, 18	having control by being given power, not taken
Heavens	*shamayim*	throughout	the heights above the land
Image	*tselem*	1:26, 27	resemblance as a representative
Kind	*miyn*	throughout	in a similar category or classification
Light	*'owr*	1:3-5,15,17,18	light
Lights	*ma'owr*	1:14, 15, 16	light-bearers or luminaries
Likeness	*demuwth*	1:26	resemblance as in having similar qualities
Living creature	*nephesh chayah*	1:20, 21, 24	a living soul/creature, "soulish" creatures locomote and avoid pain (i.e. fear)
Made	*'asah*	throughout	to do, or cause something to happen
Man	*'adam*	1:26. 27	man or mankind
Monsters	*tanniym*	1:21	large animals feared by man
Morning	*boqer*	throughout	the lighted part of 24-hours *before* sunrise, dawn
Moves	*ramas*	1:21,26,28,30	same as creeps, not to be confused with "moving"
Moving	*rachaph*	1:2	hovering or brooding in the sense of nurturing
Multiply	*rabah*	1:22, 28	to increase in quantity
Placed	*nathan*	1:17	to appoint or give for a purpose
Plants	*'eseb*	1:11, 12, 29, 30	very generic word for wild or cultivated plants
Rule	*radah*	1:26, 28	to rule by taking or maintaining control
Separated	*badal*	1:4,6,7, 14,18	to separate or set apart for a special purpose
Spirit	*ruwach*	1:2	Spirit (of God), spirit (of man), wind, or breath
Sprout	v.*dasha*	1:11	to begin any plant's growth (see vegetation also)
Subdue	*kabash*	1:28	to take authority by force – resistance implied
Surface	*paniym*	1:2, 20, 29	the face or front side of something
Swarms	n.*sherets*	1:20	an abundant variety of kinds of animals (see teem)
Teem	v.*sharats*	1:20, 21	to abound-with or move in large numbers
Trees	*'ets*	1:11, 12, 29	any plant *with wood* one might call a tree or bush
Vegetation	n.*deshe*	1:11, 12	any newly sprouted plant or vegetation
Void	*bohu*	1:2	empty of life, lifeless
Waters	*mayim*	throughout	all waters no matter what form they take
Work	*melakah*	2:2, 3	to do the task one was sent to do

11

A problem arises with the order as it relates to established paleontology however. According to Genesis God proclaimed:

1. All plants (including fruit trees and grains – Day 3) before sea creatures (Day 5) and insects (Day 5 and/or 6)
2. Birds (Day 5) before land animals (Day 6) which would include reptiles
3. Whales (Day 5) before land mammals (Day 6)

According to paleontologists, sea creatures and insects were before fruit trees and grains, reptiles were before birds, and land mammals came before sea mammals. Some people at this point write off Genesis as scientifically contradictory, but I will show you soon how this is easily resolved. For now, let me make the problem worse.

One particular attempt to get around the scientific order issue has been to define some words above much narrower or wider to make the scientific order fit. For example, there are some who claim insects and reptiles were not included in the "creeping things" proclaimed on Day 6.[6] I would simply ask the reader to look at what Genesis says and see if that idea pops out at you. Genesis 1:25 says, "God made the beasts of the earth after their kind, and the cattle after their kind, and everything that creeps on the ground after its kind…" Does not "everything that creeps on the ground" sound like it includes *everything*? If this verse does not include insects and reptiles, are we to believe the author of Genesis excluded telling us the origin of those creatures? I think not and prefer simple interpretations and the simple reading of the text is that God spoke of all land animals on Day 6, *all of them*, thus the scientific order issue remains. (See Chapter 9 for more.)

Now that the problem is worse please do not give up. As I said, there is a simple solution, and it is coming in the next chapter.

As for this fourth point that Genesis 1 was written topically rather than scientifically, one more point needs to be made. The topical arrangement means *the author was more concerned about emphasizing the structure of the account than the chronology of events*. However, that does not mean the account is missing chronological elements. It most certainly is not, but it does have some serious chronological issues.

Fifth – Some statements in the account are out of chronological sequence

Most people read through Genesis 1 without ever noticing any chronological problems. However, there are two blatant examples:

Gen 1:14 says, "Let there be lights in the expanse of the heavens..."
Then 1:15 adds, "and it was so."
Then 1:16 adds, "God made the two great lights..."

and

Gen 1:24 says, "Let the earth bring forth living creatures..."
Then 1:24 adds, "and it was so."
Then 1:25 adds, "God made the [living creatures]..."

In both cases, how can it be "so" the proclamations were fulfilled *before* God made the lights and animals necessary to fulfill the proclamations? Or put another way, why did God have to make the lights and animals when the proclamation was already said to be "so" (fulfilled)?

These out-of-sequence statements are not some haphazard mistake or variety of arrangement. They are this way *on purpose*. How do I know? Because the order is different on Day 2:

Gen 1:6 says, "Let there be an expanse..."
Then 1:7 adds, "God made the expanse..."
Then 1:7 adds, "and it was so."

And the second proclamation on Day 6:

Gen 1:26 says, "Let Us make man in Our image..."
Then 1:27 adds, "God created man in His own image..."
Then 1:30 adds, "and it was so."

Genesis 1:14-16 and 1:24-25 *did not have to be written out of chronological order.* They could have been written like Day 2 or the second proclamation on Day 6. *Why then were they written out of sequence?* Again, the next chapter will reveal the answer. For now, just know *the account is not entirely in chronological order* and ponder why.

This lack of concern over time sequence is not unusual for the Hebrew mind. *All commentators* of Hebrew grammar I have read agree the Hebrew language is not preoccupied with chronology the way English is. English verb tenses can be very specific on the order of events, but Hebrew is not. In Hebrew there are basically two verb tenses usually explained as describing actions that are either complete or incomplete.[7] Completed actions describe events that are already done, and thus in English are usually translated in the past tense, but in Hebrew it is impossible to determine by tense alone what order a series of

13

completed events took place. Incomplete actions are often translated in the present or future tense because they represent actions that were continuing at or beyond the time it was written. Because of these aspects of the Hebrew language, *the sequence of Biblical events must be determined by logical means based on the context and/or time indicators in the account.* Hebrew is a language that forces one to think logically.

Sixth – The 7 Days represent a chronological sequence

Despite containing dischronologies, the account also clearly contains time indicators, a fact that is curious to say the least. How can it be both in chronologic order and not? The answer to that question is the key to reconciliation with science, but again, the next chapter awaits.

Reconciling the Genesis week with the scientific age of the universe and Earth is our issue of contention. However, in the realm of all possible scenarios, the possibility exists the two are contradictory. My main goal is to determine what Genesis says (a good interpretation straight from the text) and then see if it matches well established science. In other words, Biblical truth claims will be tested against modern scientific discoveries. As a side note, reconciliation with science *does not necessarily mean complete agreement.* The Bible could be right and some scientists wrong.

Some YEC vehemently object here and say we should not test the infallible Word of God by fallible human methods. But, my response is, "How else are we to know whether it is true or not?" If it is supposed to be accepted by pure blind faith, or a presupposed *a priori* belief in its truth, or an ambiguous good feeling, then *I* would vehemently object. That would put Christianity in the same category as any religion or cult that encourages its followers to seek a religious feeling or experience to determine truth, but one person's blind faith is as bad as the next. Christianity is different than other religions however. God has provided us a text that makes many truth claims that can be tested and the very fact that some of these claims *can* be tested indicates that God is inviting and encouraging us to do just that. Test them. "Test all things; hold fast what is good" (I Th. 5:21). We should not fear testing the Bible to see if it is true. If it is true it will pass the tests, and if it passes the tests then those who believe it is a fairy-tale are the ones with a problem.

What about those Days?

Are the Days of Genesis 1 normal 24-hour days? And if so, how do we reconcile that with geology on the age of Earth? Or do we reinterpret science? Let us keep it simple for now. I believe the Genesis account was written to be simple. If we take it that way the answer to the question of whether the Days are normal Earth days is easy to answer.

In reference to Day 1 Genesis 1:3-5 says:

> Then God said, "Let there be light"; and there was light. God saw that the light was good; and God separated the light from the darkness. God called the light day, and the darkness He called night. And there was evening and there was morning, one day.

I will have much more to say about these verses, but for now, notice one very simple thing. *Genesis is defining "day" here for us.* We do not have to contemplate deeply to understand "God called the light day..." What light is this? In Chapter 2 I will show conclusively it is the light on the surface of Earth. Everyone who is not completely blind understands what daylight is. Thus, in its very first use of the word, Genesis defines "day" as *the lighted portion of a normal day on the land.*

What about that second use of the word, "And there was evening and there was morning, one day"? My question is simply this: Is there *any contextual reason* to believe *within two sentences* that the author of Genesis has used "day" to mean something else? No, the simplest most natural way to understand the Days of Genesis is to see them as *the lighted portion of a normal Earth day.*

In addition to this are the uses of the words "evening" and "morning". Notice "evening" is mentioned *first* and the most natural way to understand why is to see that God worked during the daylight hours of Day 1, and then it became "evening" (the lighted portion of the day *after sunset*[8]), and then it became night (the time *between* evening and morning), and then it became "morning" (the lighted portion of a day *before sunrise*[8]), and thus one daylight passed on Earth. And then God did something else on Day 2, the next daylight (day) on Earth.

As discussed under the fifth point above, time sequence in Hebrew must be determined by the logic of the context and time indicators. Here in Genesis 1:3-5 logic and context lead to the Days being normal Earth days in chronological sequence with evenings and mornings *in between* day and night respectively, and the time indicators (a numbered day and the evening and morning phrase) point to the same conclusion. Those who believe the Day-Age View (the idea the Days were long periods of time) obviously object here. Their Biblical objections will be discussed in depth in Chapter 9 and some in Chapter 2.

From a contextual standpoint, the meaning of "day" in Genesis is simple. It refers to the *daylight* portion of a normal Earth day, *not the whole 24 hour period*, which is additionally supported because "day" is contrasted with "night", like this:

<u>Day 1</u>→ evening→ <u>night</u>→ morning→ <u>Day 2</u>→ evening→ <u>night</u>→ morning→ <u>Day 3</u>...

In conclusion then we are left with these six simple structural elements to the Genesis 1 account and I believe *any overall view of Genesis must incorporate all of them in any attempt to reconcile with modern science.*

First – Genesis 1 is a unique and memorable *historical* account.
Second – Each of the 6 Days are highly structured containing a five-fold pattern.
Third – The account intentionally uses common broad generic terms to be *exhaustive* in regards to the origin of the features and creatures most commonly related *to humanity.*
Fourth – Though scientifically reconcilable (as we will soon see), God's proclamations over 6 Days were in topical order, not scientifically chronological order.
Fifth – Some statements in the account are logically out of chronological sequence.
Sixth – The 7 Days of Genesis are a chronological sequence of a normal Earth week of seven days.

Does our task of reconciling Genesis with modern science on the age of the universe and Earth look daunting and hopeless? Allow me to show you how simple I believe the solution is.

2

The Prophetic Days View
(Trying to stay in the shallows)

A Personal Note

Before I present what I believe to be the correct interpretation of Genesis I want to tell you how I got here. As I said in the introduction I began my Christian walk as a Young-Earth Creationist with a hunger for the truth. I also had a strong desire to teach others what I learned. In the process of wanting to convince someone of the truth I wanted to be able to answer any question or objection they might have raised against what I believed so I began to read viewpoints different from my own to better understand what all sides say and anticipate arguments in advance. When I read what others were saying about the YEV a surprising thing happened; I became convinced *I was the one who was wrong.*

However, I was still not convinced any of the other interpretations of Genesis I had read were correct. Then I read about a little-known view known as the Days of Divine Fiat View.[1] I was very impressed by its simplicity and always kept it in the back of my mind as my preferred view of Genesis, but I still had many questions about specific details.

When an opportunity arrived years later for me to teach on Genesis I decided to take all the books, commentaries, and reputable internet articles I could find and make an outline of every major view of Genesis with their strengths and weaknesses. I wrote down *every* point made by each view and the evidence they used to support them, and I wrote down every argument against each view and responses to objections when I could find them. I tested each point against the text and looked for any internal inconsistencies, even in my own preferred view. My intent was to take Genesis at face value and come to a conclusion about what it says, *regardless of science*. Then I was going to proceed from there to whatever conclusion it led and advocate my conclusion.

While teaching what I had lea ned to a small group we had an hour and a half conversation on Genesis 1:1 alone, and *didn't exhaust the subject!* After seeing the glazed-over looks of the people in the group, amazed that so much could be said about one verse, I realized if we were

17

going to make it through Genesis this century I was going to have to compartmentalize what I believed so I set out to write down the main points of my view, and so this book was born. Five points distinguished themselves and since that time when discussing this subject I usually limit myself to these five which I now present to you.

This chapter is a presentation of five major points that differ considerably from the Young-Earth View. I did not invent these five points so my view is not brand new, but to my knowledge the five points are not developed in this format in any other book or website. Point one I realized on my own from reading Genesis, but all OEC views agree with it. Point two came from John Sailhamer[2] (advocate of the Focus on Palestine View). Point three I first read from Hugh Ross[3] (advocate of the Day-Age View) though many of the specific applications of it I added myself. Point four I got from Alan Hayward[4] and it is the main point of the Prophetic Days View (PDV), but Hayward called it the Days of Divine Fiat View, and he did not give it as much Biblical support. Point five is a logical conclusion from points one, two, and four, but all OEC views agree with it for different reasons.

Now the question in my mind is: can I convince you these five points are correct? I do not know. The Holy Spirit is the guide into all truth (John 16:13) and hopefully He will use this book to guide people in that direction, or correct me if necessary. It is my hope that the Prophetic Days View will contribute to the church body regaining a reputation of being champions of truth, rather than being seen as ignorant people of blind faith with no relevant message for the world. Also, it is my hope this book will serve to unify OEC under one view, and convert some YEC along the way.

The Important Question

What does Genesis 1 actually tell us about the origin of the universe? Scholars and laymen alike have been trying to answer that question for thousands of years and many people think they know it well, but what you are about to read may surprise you.

On our journey we should let the text speak for itself. Priority must be given to the way the original audience[2] would have understood it. Because Genesis 1 is the first chapter of the Bible, it should contain clues within itself as to its meaning. Genesis takes the lead to interpret and define the rest of the Bible rather than the other way around. We should also not add details to the text and speculation should be avoided.

With all of that in mind here are the reasons I believe the Prophetic Days View is the correct view of Genesis, what the author really meant.

The Five Points of the Prophetic Days View

Genesis 1:1-5
[1] In the beginning God created the heavens and the earth. [2] The earth was formless and void [desolate and lifeless[6]], and darkness was over the surface of the deep, and the Spirit of God was moving over the surface of the waters. [3] Then God said, "Let there be light"; and there was light. [4] God saw that the light was good; and God separated the light from the darkness. [5] God called the light day, and the darkness He called night. And there was evening and there was morning, one day.

These first five verses of Genesis are so simple a child can understand the main themes they are meant to convey: that God created the universe, and He transformed it by His words into a place fit for us to live. The profound and simple nature of the text stands out as an awe inspiring testimony to the genius of the Author.

However, with one question I can show you how difficult these verses can quickly become. **Is the first verse part of the narrative sequence of the story, or is it only a summary of the whole story?** To help answer the question understand that today most Hebrew scholars agree that the phrase "the heavens and the earth" is a figure of speech for "the all" or "the universe". Biblical Hebrew has no word to compare to the English word "universe" so when Biblical writers referred to everything that exists they used the phrase "the heavens and the earth" which is a human perspective of the universe.

As a result of that meaning some see verse one as a summary of the whole account, something like, "In the beginning God created everything, and then here are more details about how He did that." But Genesis 1:1 cannot be a summary of the whole account because if that were true we would be left with an interesting problem that is addressed in the first point of the PDV.

The simplest and most natural way to understand verses 1-5 is that some unspecified time ago "in the beginning" God created the heavens up there and the land down here. Sometime after the land's creation it was desolate, lifeless, dark, and wet. Then God spoke over the waters and His first proclamation was for light to come to be on the surface. God saw that the light was good, made a holy separation of light and darkness, defined "day" and "night", and then the evening came and light dawned just before the next day. And that was one daylight time on Earth. Viewed that way, verse one is part of the story, not a summary of it. Here is why I believe that is the correct way to look at it.

Point 1: The Earth existed *before* the 7 Days started.

We begin with a good question to ask about the Genesis 1 account, and the answer helps us answer my previous question. **On which of the 7 Days did God create the Earth?** The answer is none of them. *The Earth was already there before the 7 Days started*. How do I know that? Genesis 1 gives us five *strong* reasons and Job adds a sixth.

First, the 6 Days are each bounded by the opening phrase "Then God said…" and the ending phrase "And there was evening and there was morning, the [nth] day". *Nowhere* on any of the Days *between those phrases* is there anything about the creation of the Earth. The Days are bounded by what God said at the beginning, and the evening and morning formula at the end. *That is the pattern*. Because the creation of the Earth is not mentioned between the opening and closing phrase of any Day, the Earth was not created on any of the Days. The only place where the origin of the Earth is mentioned is in Genesis 1:1, which then must be before the 7 Days start.

Second, Genesis 1:2 explicitly says, "The earth was…" meaning *it already existed before the opening phrase of the first Day* in the four conditions described in the rest of the verse: desolate and lifeless[6], wet and dark. God was about to change the condition of the whole Earth from desolate to inhabitable. He was going to change it from being void of life to being full of life. He was going to change it from being dark to having light. And He was going to change it from being wet to having dry ground. *The proclamations on the Days match the conditions of the Earth in verse 2 that needed changing for life to exist*, thus connecting the 7 Days with the primeval Earth. But, the changes those proclamations initiated took place on an Earth that was already there before God spoke.

Third, the proclamations that God said on each of the 6 Days are specifically said to be fulfilled within the text of that Day. For example, on Day 1 God said, "Let there be light" and then the text says, "and there was light". *Each Day records the fulfillment of that Day's proclamation*, but nowhere do we find God saying, "Let there be a heavens and an earth" on any of the 7 Days or anywhere else. The absence of a proclamation and fulfillment of the creation of the Earth within the text of a Day implies it was not done on any of the Days, because it does not match the pattern.

Fourth, Day 1 began with the light appearing. You cannot have any Days without a light source. But verse 2 says "darkness was over the surface of the deep", meaning the Earth was there with no light on the surface, which means it was there *before a Day could be measured*. The light had to be there before the 7 Days could be measured, and the Earth was there in darkness before the light, and the text specifically says Day 1's evening and night *followed* its day (night is between evening and morning – 1:5), therefore the Earth had to be there before the 7 Days.

Fifth, Hebrew verb structure shows the main narrative is in verses 3-31 and verses 1 and 2 stand outside that narrative with a different verb structure. Hebrew scholar C. John Collins says, "Since the backbone of the narrative... uses [a particular Hebrew verb structure], and since Genesis 1:1-2 does not... we conclude that these verses stand outside the main stream of the narrative."[7] If verses 1-2 stand outside the 6 Day main narrative, and verses 1-2 are what specifies the creation of the Earth, then the creation of the Earth must have been before the 7 Days began.

Sixth, Job 38:4, 9, and 12-13 add additional testimony, "Where were you when I laid the foundation of the earth? ...When I made a cloud its garment And thick darkness its swaddling band... Have you ever in your life commanded the morning, And caused the dawn to know its place, That it might take hold of the ends of the earth...?" Notice the order of events is in the same order as Genesis. The land's foundations were laid (Earth created), Earth was covered in darkness, and the morning dawned. Earth was there first, before the dawn, therefore, before the 7 Days.

For those reasons we can conclude the Bible says the Earth was in existence *before* the 7 Days of Genesis. The evidence is strong for that conclusion.

We can also answer whether Genesis 1:1 is a summary of the whole account or whether it is part of the account. It must be part of the account because otherwise the account does not tell us when God created the Earth. If it is only a summary then it would be summarizing information not provided in the more detailed story, namely, what Day God created the Earth. But, if it is part of the account then it is telling us God created the heavens and Earth first "in the beginning" and then afterward began to transform a lifeless planet by a work done over the next 7 Days.

Why does it matter that the Earth was there before the 7 Days? The reason is because it shows that *everything was not created within 6 Days*. Namely, the heavens and Earth were created *before* the 7 Days, and because the Young-Earth View insists *all* was finished within the 7 Days this puts their interpretation at odds with what Genesis says and *makes the PDV more literal to the text than the YEV*. Their objections to this interpretation will be covered in Chapter 5 in great detail.

How long was the Earth there before the 7 Days? Genesis does not tell us. All it says is the heavens and the Earth were created "in the beginning". When was that? The Bible does not specify. According to astronomy the universe began approximately 13.7 billion years ago. Does that contradict Genesis? No, it does not.

Point 2: The "beginning" in Genesis 1:1 was an unspecified *block of time*, not a moment, in which God initially created "the heavens and the earth".

This point further develops the idea the Earth was there before the 7 Days, but it goes beyond that and says the heavens and the Earth were not created instantaneously *just before* the 7 Days. The "beginning" refers to a *significant block of time*, not a moment. A timeline illustration may help understand what Genesis 1:1 means by "In the beginning".

First moment of time   The Beginning   Earth in Gen 1:2   7 Days to present

⇩   ⟺   🜨   ⟹

How do I know that? The Bible gives us three reasons.

First, the overall meaning one gets from all the uses of the Hebrew word *reshith* (beginning) is that it refers to *the first part of the whole of something, sometimes the best or chief part.*[8] Biblical support for this is found in Job 8:7 and 42:12 which speak of Job's early life, "Though your beginning was insignificant, yet your end will increase greatly" and "the Lord blessed the latter days of Job more than his beginning…" The end (latter days) of Job's life has a longer period of time in mind than just his death. This longer "end" is contrasted to his "beginning" which must also have a longer period of time in mind than just the moment of his birth. Jeremiah 28:1 is another example, "Now it came to pass… in the beginning of the reign of Zedekiah king of Judah, in the fourth year, in the fifth month…" The significance is that almost 4½ years into Zedekiah's 11-year reign is still the beginning of his reign.

If those references are not convincing enough "the beginning" was a block of time and not a moment of time, please refer to the footnotes.[8] Hebrew scholar John Sailhamer defined the word this way, "The Hebrew word *reshith*, which is the term for 'beginning'… has a very specific sense in Scripture. In the Bible the term always refers to an extended, yet indeterminate duration of time – *not* a specific moment. It is a block of time which precedes an extended series of time periods."[9] Because *reshith* is used in Gen. 1:1, "the beginning" *must* refer to the first *part* of the whole of time.

Second, if "beginning" referred to the first moment of time there are two other Hebrew words, *rishon* and *techillah*, which would have been more appropriate than *reshith* in Genesis 1:1. These other two words "…differ from [*reshith*] in that they mark a 'beginning' of a series in opposition to the 'second' or 'next' member of the series [see Gen 13:3-

4]. [*Reshith*], on the other hand, marks the 'beginning' in opposition to the 'end'..."[10] Genesis 13:3-4 reads, "And he [Abram] went on his journeys from the Negev as far as Bethel, to the place where his tent had been at the beginning [*techillah*], between Bethel and Ai, to the place of the altar, which he had made there formerly [*rishon* - "at the first" - KJV and RSV]..." Had either of these two words been used in 1:1 it could have been translated, "At the beginning God created..." or "At first God created..." Instead, because *reshith* is used, it is translated "In the beginning" and sometime *in* that beginning block of time "God created the heavens and the earth." *Every* major translation of the Bible has the first three words of Genesis as "In the beginning".

Third, Proverbs 8:22-27 adds additional testimony:

> The LORD possessed me [Wisdom] at the beginning [*reshith*] of His way, Before His works of old. From everlasting I was established, From the beginning, from the earliest times of the earth. When there were no depths I was brought forth, When there were no springs abounding with water. Before the mountains were settled, Before the hills I was brought forth; While He had not yet made the earth and the fields, Nor the first dust of the world. When He established the heavens, I was there...

Notice, Wisdom is said to be possessed at the "beginning" *before* God's works of old, from the earliest times of the Earth, before there was an ocean, spring, mountain, hill, or field. The establishment of the heavens is even considered as part of the beginning. If Wisdom was there "at the beginning" before those geographical features, then the block of time called "the beginning" began before them also, and because the 7 Days caused them, the beginning was before the 7 Days.

As a side note, it is worth noting the order of events in this passage listed in reverse order: established the heavens [Big Bang and formation of galaxies?] – the first dust of the world [Matter left over from the explosion of stars?] – made the earth and fields [formation of the planet and land?] – brought forth hills [buckling of strata?] – settled the mountains [as they have been during human history] – and then springs abounding with water [establishing underground water?]. *That is an amazing correlation to our modern astronomical history of the universe and Earth that also correlates to the story told in Genesis!*

For the three reasons above we can conclude the heavens and Earth were created in an unspecified block of time called "the beginning" before the condition of Earth described in 1:2. Genesis *defines* "the beginning" as the time from the first moment of time until the whole land was uninhabitable, empty, dark, and wet. In the first part of time God created the heavens and the earth before the 7 Days started.

Is this point of the PDV the same as the traditional Gap View? No, it is not. The traditional Gap View attempts to explain the age of the Earth and the existence of fossils by saying Earth was created a long time ago (1:1), then judged and destroyed (1:2), and then re-created in six days a short time ago. While the Gap View and the PDV agree there was a gap of time before the condition of the Earth in verse 2, they disagree significantly on what happened during that block of time. Neither the text of Genesis, nor the whole Bible, show any cause whatsoever to postulate a previous creation and destruction during that time, and science gives no indication of a re-creation 6-10,000 years ago. For more on the Gap View and its Biblical and scientific problems see Chapter 9.

Point 3: The creation account is given by God to humanity from our perspective, as if we were watching what God was doing from the surface of the Earth.

Stories are written and told from a specific perspective and Genesis 1 is no different. It paints a picture for the reader of what God was doing, but it is not visualized from outer space looking down on Earth. In modern times since space travel and photography have become common we have tended to think of Earth as a planet floating in space orbiting the Sun. For the ancients it is likely no such perspective was possible. That the account is written from a perspective that *anyone at any time* could understand should surprise no one then. It is written as if we were an observer on the surface of Earth observing God's work unfold. From that perspective Genesis 1:2, and particularly the events of Days 1, 2, and 4, take on a meaning that many Bible readers have never considered. But before I get into that, how do I know the view from the surface is the perspective of the account? Genesis gives us five very clear indicators.

First, the word "surface" is emphasized by its use twice in verse 2, "...darkness was over the *surface* of the deep, and the Spirit of God was moving over the *surface* of the waters." (my highlights) "Surface" is used *twice* here for no other reason except to make sure we understand that is the perspective of the account. It could not be much clearer.

Second, as I mentioned at the beginning of this chapter, the phrase "the heavens and the earth" is a figure of speech in Hebrew used to mean "the all" or "the universe". The phrase itself is stated from a human perspective of the universe viewing "the heavens" (all that is up there) and "the earth" (all that is down here). The Hebrew word for "heavens" is *shamayim* and refers to *the heights* above the Earth.[11] The Hebrew word for "earth" is *erets* and refers to *all land*, even underwater, but it is most commonly used of dry land.[11] When both words are combined it has the effect of describing the universe as everything up there and everything down here, *from the perspective of the surface*.

Third, many words and phrases used in Genesis 1 only make sense from the surface of the Earth. Examples include: day, night, morning, evening, waters above and below the expanse, and heavens.

Fourth, the phrase "on the earth" is used seven times in Genesis 1 (verses 15, 17, 22, 26, 28, 29 and 30). Is "on the earth" clear enough?

Fifth, the events recorded on Day 3 (dry-ground and plants), Day 5 (sea and flying creatures) and Day 6 (land animals and humanity) are clearly only applicable to the Earth. Therefore, it makes the most sense to say all 7 Days refer to events from the same perspective.

This earthly perspective affects our understanding of the text in four significant places. If we *let the text speak specifically for itself and not go beyond what is written* we will see the condition of the heavens and Earth in verse 2, and what happened as a result of the Day 1, 2, and 4 proclamations, are not what many people think. *If you will get a grasp of this perspective, along with Point 4, your understanding of Genesis 1 will be transformed.*

The human perspective of viewing what God did from the surface of the Earth affects our understanding of Genesis 1 primarily in four places:

First, Genesis 1:2 pictures a desolate, lifeless, and dark place. "The earth was formless and void, and darkness was over the surface of the deep, and the Spirit of God was moving over the surface of the waters." My questions to you are this: **Where and why was it dark?**

The "where" is answered directly from the text, "darkness was over the surface of the deep." *The text specifically tells us it was dark on the surface of the waters.* But do not miss what the text is not telling us. It *is not telling us anything* about whether it was dark in the whole universe, so *it would be wrong to go beyond the text on this*. People have been assuming for hundreds of years that Genesis says the whole universe was created in complete darkness. It does not. One must go beyond what the text actually says to get that interpretation from Genesis 1:2. From the human perspective of the account Genesis is only telling us it was dark on the surface of Earth.

So, why was it dark? Genesis gives us only one clue for the answer. On Day 2 God proclaims for an "expanse" to come to be *between* the waters above and the waters below. Prior to that proclamation there was no "expanse". The expanse is equated with the heavens (Gen. 1:8), meaning it is all that is up there above the land. The reason the word "expanse" is used on Day 2 is because it refers to an *expanding transparent space* between the ocean (the waters below) and the clouds/rain (the waters above).[12] Before there was a clear space between the waters, the waters above came all the way down to the surface of Earth. This would have had the effect of making it darker on the surface, the way a dense fog would do today, only according to Genesis 1:2, the fog must have been thick enough to shield the surface from all light.

Job 38:8-9 is an additional witness to this and says, "Or who shut in the sea with doors when it burst out from the womb, when I made clouds its garment and thick darkness its swaddling band." (ESV) From Job it should be clear that a "garment" made of clouds "swaddled" the sea and was the cause of the "thick darkness". Thick enough cloud cover is certainly capable of blocking all sunlight and causing darkness on the surface of the Earth.

Even some Young-Earth Creationists are in agreement with part of this textual conclusion.

> Apparently, before this [expanse] existed, the earth waters on the surface of the earth and the cloud waters as we now know them were contiguous without an intervening clear air space. It was a situation like a dense fog upon the surface of the waters. Clear vision of all except the very nearest objects must have been impossible. Free activity unhampered by the fog blanket would have been impossible. Man would not have had an appropriate sphere for activity, nor could sunlight have penetrated freely to do its beneficent and cheering work.[13] [Leupold]

The Bible specifically tells us it was dark on the surface of the deep because the Earth was covered with thick clouds. It does not tell us it was dark in the whole universe. Such expansion of the meaning of the text of the Bible should be avoided, and it is scientifically inaccurate.

Second, on Day 1 God said, "Let there be light" (1:3). My question to you is this: **Let there be light where?** What light is this talking about? Does light appear for the first time in the universe because of this proclamation, or only on the surface of Earth? From a human perspective *we can only say the text says it became light on the surface of Earth.*

The proclamations on the 6 Days were meant to remedy the condition of Earth as it was in verse 2. *Earth* was uninhabitable (formless); God was going to change it to being inhabitable. *Earth* was empty of life (void); it was going to be full of life. *Earth* was wet; dry ground was going to appear. The *surface of Earth* was dark. Light was going to appear *in the whole universe*? No, light was going to appear *on the surface of Earth*. The other three conditions apply to Earth only. God was not going to make other planets habitable, or make other planets full of life, or make land appear on other planets. Therefore, the light was to come to be for the first time on the surface of Earth only. That is what the text says despite decades of commentators making statements like, "The exigencies of the text... require the first day's work to be the original production of light throughout the universe, and in particular throughout our planetary system."[14] The text says nothing about light appearing in the whole universe. It is only talking about light appearing on the surface of Earth.

That this has to be the correct interpretation is supported by the fact that God called that light, "day". That only makes sense from a human perspective on Earth. It is *never* day and night in outer space. The "light" proclaimed on Day 1 is called "day". *The light is the day on Earth*. God calls it that to define for us what "light" He is referring to so we will not misunderstand. I do not see how it can be any clearer than God directly telling us what light he is talking about. *The light is the day on Earth, not light in the entire universe.*

John Walton drives this point home by noting that the text of Genesis 1 is referring to the *function* of light here. He asks a very good question, "Why didn't God simply call light 'light'?"[15] In reference to God calling the light "day" he adds, "[Day] is not what light is... If something connected with light is named 'day' we can deduce that it is not light itself, but the period of light, for that is what 'day' *is*... In this case then, the author intends for us to understand the word 'light' to mean a period of light." A *period of light* to the ancients, and us, only makes sense from the perspective of the surface of the land.

The text should be allowed to say what it says and no more. From the original readers' perspective, they simply would have understood Genesis 1 teaches that it was dark on the land in the beginning and God made it light on Day 1. How God did it is not specified in the text. Also, whether this was the very first light ever to exist anywhere is not spelled out in the text either. So *no one should speculate and emphatically insist that it was*. The clues *from the text* show the light on Day 1 is *only* referring to light on the surface of Earth.

Third, on Day 2 God said, "Let there be an expanse in the midst of the waters, and let it separate the waters from the waters." **What are these waters "below" and "above" the expanse?** (Gen. 1:7) From the perspective of the surface of Earth they are none other than the ocean and rain.[17] Some YEC have suggested that "...the 'waters above' are at the

27

outer limits of the universe..."[18] or are at the "...perimeter of the solar system..."[18] because they are attempting to solve the problem of how old the universe looks. But, the text of Genesis says nothing like the "waters above" were so far off the Earth they were not visible. The waters above the expanse are talked about as if they were what all people know, the water that falls from the clouds. YEC attempts to make them otherwise are examples of trying to make Genesis fit *their* science, which usually ends in an exegetical nightmare, like in this case. Ironically, some YEC are hypocritically doing what they often accuse OEC of doing, reading science into the text.

Anyone can observe that water falls from the clouds, as did the writers of scripture (Pr. 3:20, Eccl. 11:3, Is. 5:6). And it is clear Biblical authors understood the water cycle of the Earth to some degree (Gen. 2:6, Ps. 135:7, Eccl. 1:6-7). From the simple perspective of the surface of Earth the "waters above" are rain.

Fourth, on Day 4 Genesis 1:14-19 reads:

[14]Then God said, "Let there be lights in the expanse of the heavens to separate the day from the night, and let them be for signs and for seasons and for days and years; [15]and let them be for lights in the expanse of the heavens to give light on the earth"; and it was so. [16]God made the two great lights, the greater light to govern the day, and the lesser light to govern the night; *He made* the stars also. [17]God placed them in the expanse of the heavens to give light on the earth, and to govern the day and the night, [18]and to separate the light from the darkness; and God saw that it was good. [19]There was evening and there was morning, a fourth day.

I quoted more of Genesis here because, more than any other, Day 4 is the Day YEC run to as one of the fortresses of their view. The reason is because the Bible is perceived to say the Sun, Moon, and stars were made on Day 4.

I can honestly say, *if the Bible says the Sun was made on Day 4 after the Earth then all hope of reconciling Genesis to astronomy is lost*. But, I am about to show you *from the text of the Bible* that *Genesis does not say the Sun, Moon, and stars were made on Day 4*. If you have never seen this before I believe you are in for a serious eye-opener. Very close attention must be paid to what the Bible actually says here. Unfortunately many people do not want to hear too many details or study verses deeply, but it is necessary in this case. Fortunately, it will not be necessary to appeal to the Hebrew text to show you what I hope you are about to understand. The NASB translation above is sufficient for my case.

Chapter 2 – The Prophetic Days View

The fact that Genesis 1 is written from the perspective of the surface of Earth should be clear by now. However, it is entirely possible that God could have made the Sun, Moon, and stars on Day 4 and a hypothetical observer on Earth could have watched them appear suddenly in the sky. Just because the account is written from a human perspective does not guarantee any particular conclusion about when God made the Sun, Moon, and stars.

What God actually proclaimed on Day 4 is really important to see. Please look closely again, "[14]Then God said, 'Let there be lights in the expanse of the heavens to separate the day from the night, and let them be for signs and for seasons and for days and years; [15]and let them be for lights in the expanse of the heavens to give light on the earth.'"

"Let there be…" means God proclaimed for something to come to be that did not exist before, but notice the proclamation does not stop with "Let there be lights." It says, "Let there be lights *in the expanse of the heavens…* [emphasis mine]" The last part, "in the expanse of the heavens", is overlooked or scarcely mentioned by *every author and commentator I have ever read.*[19] I even glossed over it myself for years until I saw an important component of the verses. The phrase is repeated *three times* in the text of Day 4 (verses 14, 15 and 17). Why is a phrase that looks so insignificant and redundant repeated three times within four verses? God does not repeat something three times without a reason; therefore, the phrase cannot be insignificant. So, I began to meditate on it until I saw what I hope you will see.

But before I saw it, to make matters worse, I asked myself, "Why does the phrase use *both* words 'expanse' and 'heavens' when the 'expanse' was called (named) 'heavens' in verse 8?" If the two are equated, why didn't verse 14 say, "Let there be lights in the heavens?" Or, "Let there be lights in the expanse?" Or simply, "Let there be lights?" *Why use both words?*

My answers and breakthrough came when I added three simple letters, "ing", to the phrase. "Let there be lights in the *expanding* of the heavens." Aha! There was the meaning and purpose of the phrase. What God actually proclaimed on Day 4 was not for the lights to come to be for the first time. *He proclaimed for the lights to come to be in a new location from the perspective of the surface of Earth.* The lights were to come to be in the expanding-clear-space (expanse) of the heavens.

Prior to the fulfillment of the proclamation on Day 4 the heavens, as seen from Earth, did not contain the cause of the light on Earth. Originally in verse 2, complete darkness was on the surface, no light. Then light appears, but there is no expanse (a clear space between the waters), only a perpetual fog. Then a transparent space (the expanse)

29

appears *between* ("in the midst of") the fog (clouds) and the surface waters. The clear space continues to expand until the clouds are well above the land, like an overcast day. That expanding clear space from Day 2 was *limited* to being *only* the space between the surface waters and the clouds. Then, as a result of the proclamation on Day 4, the clear space continued to expand until the sources of the light were *in the expanse* (the clear space). Then it could be said, "and it was so" (15b), *the lights have come to be for the first time in the expanding clear space of the heavens where they have never been.*

I am pressing this point because it is too easy to miss, like I did for many years. For a long time I thought God had proclaimed for the Sun, Moon, and stars to come into existence on Day 4, but that is *not* what God proclaimed.

What expanded? A good way to think about Day 2 and 4 is to ask yourself what Genesis describes expanded. The Hebrew word many Bible versions translate "expanse" means "an expanded thing" (See Appendix B for further detail). If something expanded, what was it? Was it the atmosphere? No, the modern concept of a gaseous atmosphere around a planet would have been completely foreign to the ancients. Was it the universe or space that expanded? Though astronomers today observe that space is expanding, and expanding space could be continuing fulfillment of the proclamation, again, that modern concept would have been foreign to the original audience. I think Genesis is saying something much simpler. What expanded was the view (clear space) from the perspective of the surface of the land.

So why did God use the phrase three times? He did it to call our attention to it so we would not miss its significance and the real meaning of what He proclaimed on Day 4.

Why did God use both words in the phrase after He called the expanse "heavens"? It was the way He chose to convey the idea the heavens as seen from Earth *expanded*. How else could He have said the clear space of the heavens expanded? If He had said, "Let there be lights" or "Let there be lights in the heavens" then it could be misunderstood to mean the lights themselves came to be for the first time as a result of the proclamation, but the proclamation on Day 4 was not to *make* the lights. Also, if He had said, "Let there be lights in the expanse" then Genesis could be interpreted to mean the lights were *below* the clouds because Day 2 limits the expanse to between the waters.

How can it be said something new came to be as a result of the proclamation? If, as a result of God's proclamation on Day 4, the sky cleared enough for the Sun to become visible from the surface of Earth for the first time, could it be said that the Sun came to be "in the expanse of the heavens"? Yes, God said, "Let there be lights *in the expanding clear space of the heavens*" and that is what happened, the clear space expanded to include the lights. What needs to be understood is that prior to the proclamation on Day 4, and from the perspective of the surface of Earth, the lights *were not in the clear space* (expanse). After the proclamation, what did not exist (the Sun, Moon, and stars *in* the expanding clear space) came to be, but the lights could have existed before the expanse. The lights themselves are not coming to be, it is the *location* of the lights *in the expanse* that is coming to be. Were the lights *in the expanse* prior to the proclamation of Day 4? No. Were the lights in existence prior to Day 4? The text does not say, but *something* was lighting the Earth, so they could have been. We should let God's word define "the expanse" and it did on Day 2. The expanse *was* the clear space *between* the surface waters and the clouds, meaning the expanse was limited to what could be seen. Now, as a result of the proclamation on Day 4, the clear space includes the Sun, Moon, and stars.

With all that in mind consider another oddity of Day 4's text. Many commentators have noticed that the statements listed on Day 4 are *not in chronological sequence* (as I mentioned in Chapter 1), but most people who read the account do not notice it. Look at the sequence: verse 14 says "Let there be lights in the expanse of the heavens..." (proclamation), then 15b says "and it was so" (fulfillment), then 16 adds "God made the two great lights ..." (action). If it was already "so", why did God have to make the lights? Or, how could it have been "so" before God made the lights? Either question shows the sequence cannot logically be chronological. However, if the order of the last two statements had been reversed (proclamation, action, and *then* fulfillment) we would not be having this conversation. But *that is not how the text reads*. God put it in the non-sequential order for a reason. (I promised in Chapter 1 to tell you why.)

Why are there deliberate non-chronological sentences on Day 4? God listed verse 16 out of sequence because *it is not what fulfilled the proclamation*. Each of the 6 Days follows a pattern. Each Day has a proclamation, a fulfillment phrase, an action phrase or two, the evening and morning phrase, and a numbered Day. If you will look at *each* phrase, *after* each fulfillment phrase, on each Day, you will see that in *every* case the phrases *after* the fulfillment phrases *do not fulfill the proclamations*. Because the fulfillment has already been mentioned it makes perfect sense the text does not say any more about how the fulfillment was done. Most people believe verse 16 fulfills the proclamation of Day 4, or gives more detail to the fulfillment, but it does not. That is an all too common misunderstanding of the text of Day 4.

31

If "And God made two great lights…" (v.16) is not the fulfillment of the proclamation on Day 4, then why is it even mentioned? The answer is really quite simple. After the proclamation for the expanse to expand to include the lights was fulfilled, the next obvious question *from a hypothetical observer on the surface of Earth* (or hearer of the story) would be, "Well where did those lights I can now see come from?" The fulfillment (v.15b) of the proclamation (v.14) prompts the question of where the now visible lights originated. So God told us *He* made them (v.16). That is why it is in that order.

So, *when* did God make the Sun, Moon, and stars? I do not mean that as a science question. I am looking for a textual answer. Does the text tell us? The text is very clear the Sun, Moon, and stars were made by God. Consider the following in determining an answer as to *when*:

1. Evidence from the text shows the perspective of the account is from *the surface of Earth*. The light on Day 1 refers to light on the surface only, not in outer space. Day 4 could then be referring to when the source of the light on Day 1 became knowable from the surface.

2. The source of the light on Day 1 *could not have been seen* by a hypothetical observer on Earth on Day 1 because there was no expanse between the waters. The waters above came all the way down to the surface. The surface was perpetually foggy, but visible.

3. Though God can make light apart from the Sun (Revelation 22:5), *nowhere in the Bible* does it explicitly say what the source of the light was on Day 1, but everyone knows the Sun is Earth's light source.

4. Verse 16 *is not* a more detailed account of the fulfillment of the proclamation on Day 4. It is non-chronologically after the fulfillment. The fulfillment of the first part of the proclamation occurred when the expanding of the heavens occurred, not when the lights were made.

5. Everyone can see verse 16 is *intentionally* out of sequence (it did not have to be) so where to place it in sequence must be determined *logically*.

6. An account written from the perspective of the surface of Earth would not logically tell us the origin of the source of the light until the lights could be seen from the surface so listing "God made the lights" on Day 4 *makes sense* even if that action predates the proclamation.

7. Because the proclamation was for the lights to come to be in a new location (from the perspective of Earth), and not into existence, the text is assuming the lights (Sun, Moon, and stars) already existed before the Day 4 proclamation.

8. The use of the phrase "to separate the day from the night" (1:14) *equates the source of the light on Day 1 and Day 4*. That reference on Day 4 clearly points back to Day 1 by using the same words, two of

which were named by God on Day 1 (1:4-5). The reference back to Day 1 must have been done for a reason.

9. The coming to be of light on the surface of Earth on Day 1 from an unspecified source, *calling it good*, and then replacing it three days later with a different source, especially when the source could not be seen on Day 1 anyway, seems unlike the actions of an *all-wise* God.

10. Job 38:4 and 7 say, "Where were you when I laid the foundations of the earth? ...When the mo ning stars sang together And all the sons of God shouted for joy?" These verses indicate that morning stars sang for joy when the foundations of the land were laid, i.e. when Earth was created. Though "mo ning stars" references angels, because it is in parallel with "sons of God" (Job 1:2, 2:9), why would stars be used as a metaphor for angels if stars did not already exist? Also, how did the angels see to rejoice without light? Therefore, if stars existed, then light existed before Earth, and so could the Sun (it is a star after all).

After considering all of this it should be noted no direct evidence in the text of Genesis, or the whole Bible, absolutely concludes the source of light on Day 1 was the Sun, but no direct evidence exists against that conclusion either. The Bible does not specify, but there is a strong circumstantial case the Sun was the source of light on Day 1.

Therefore, believing the Sun, Moon, and stars were made before Day 1 "in the beginning" would not be unfaithful to the Bible. That being the case, and the fact the Bible is ambiguous on the subject, scientists can be left to answer the question, and their answer matches well with Genesis 1:1, "In the beginning God created the heavens and the earth." The heavens were created in a block of time called the "beginning" which was before the 6 Days. The existence of the Sun before Earth is not contradictory to Genesis. As I told you, *Genesis does not say the Sun, Moon, and stars were made on Day 4.*

The overall conclusion of Point 3: Genesis 1 was written from the perspective of the surface of Earth. From that perspective, the text tells us it was dark on the surface only. Light came to be only on the surface as a result of the proclamation on Day 1. The waters above the expanse are those seen from the surface only, i.e. rain. As a result of the proclamation on Day 4 for the expanse to expand to include the Sun, Moon, and stars, the cause of the light on Day 1 became visible from the surface only. The lights were made prior to Day 4. These are textual conclusions and what Genesis actually says. Genesis does not say the whole universe was dark, or that the light proclaimed on Day 1 was the first light in the whole universe, or that the waters above the expanse are out in space unseen from Earth, or that the Sun, Moon, and stars were made on Day 4. *Genesis does not make those errors!*

Point 4: The fulfillments of the proclamations (prophecies) that God said on the 6 Days were not all meant to be understood as fulfilled or initiated *within* the Day they were given.

This point is the defining point of the Prophetic Days View. The first three points, or parts of them, are shared by some of the other Old-Earth Views of Genesis, but Point 4 is not. Because this point is unique to the PDV, and because of the way people have been thinking about Genesis for so long, it is perhaps the most difficult point to accept. I must therefore develop it as exhaustively as I can.

A simple (?) question: Did God fulfill His proclamations *on the Day He gave them*? Point 4 is essentially the idea the proclamations God said on the 6 Days were not meant to be understood as fulfilled *on those Days*. That is not difficult to understand and I think it is the way the original audience understood it. God said the proclamations over six normal days[20] at a time when Earth was in the condition described in verse 2, and then carried out their fulfillments over an unspecified amount of time after that. This is no different than the way God normally works. Isaiah 46:9-10 says:

> Remember the former things long past, for I am God and there is no other; I *am* God, and there is no one like Me, declaring the end from the beginning and from ancient times things which have not been done, saying, 'My purpose will be established, and I will accomplish all My good pleasure...'

Isaiah says God declares "the end from the beginning" meaning, at the beginning God declares the end. The word "beginning" here is the same as Genesis 1:1. It would not have been unlike God's character to prophesy the end product of His creation long before He fulfilled it. He is the only one who can do that. God often prophesies an event well in advance of its fulfillment, and I believe the text of Genesis 1 is specifically telling us that is exactly what God did on the 6 Days.

How do I know that? Genesis 1:1-2:4a gives us seven reasons, which I present in the order the text gives them, not necessarily in the most persuasive order.

First, the first proclamation on Day 3 says, "'Let the waters below the heavens be gathered into one place, and let the dry land appear'; and it was so." (1:9) Are we to believe the text of Day 3 teaches God caused millions of square miles of land to spring from the ocean, all the water gathered together, and the ground dried out all over the Earth, all in one day? The problem is not that God cannot do it that way; it is that the text does not say it that way. "Be gathered" is *qavah* in Hebrew and is rarely used in the OT in this form. It most commonly means *to patiently wait on*[21] and gives the connotation of *a slow process*. God commanded the waters to gather and the land to appear so they would not have done so by themselves. The Hebrew should also be understood as God acting upon the waters and land, but nowhere in the text of Day 3, other than a proclamation, is God mentioned doing anything to fulfill what He said. In fact, a unique feature of Day 3 is that it does not contain a statement about *any* action God did other than speaking and seeing.[22] Every other Day contains God doing something else, i.e. separating, making, placing, creating, etc. This omission of God's direct action implies God's use of secondary means here, i.e. a mediated secondary cause.

According to Psalm 95:5, "The sea is His, for it was He who made it, And His hands formed the dry land." Psalms says God made the sea and formed the dry land, but Genesis suggests it was done by slow processes. God was responsible for fulfilling His proclamations, but the question is whether He used a method whereby all was accomplished in one day or whether He used a longer process. The activities in the first part of the text of Day 3 are the first evidence all was not completed on that Day, but the second part of Day 3 emphasizes it even more.

Second, the second proclamation on Day 3 says, "'Let the earth sprout vegetation, plants yielding seed, *and* fruit trees on the earth bearing fruit after their kind with seed in them'; and it was so. The earth brought forth vegetation…" (1:11) Two points should be noted.

First, *the land is the agent* proclaimed to sprout plants. Even though supernatural intervention is necessary for the land to do its part, i.e. God must make the seeds that sprout, *God is still not said to be the one accomplishing the verbs in the sentences.*

Second, the verb changes from "sprout" (v.11) to "brought forth" (v.12) and not every Bible translation makes that clear[23]. The land *sprouts new growth* (the meaning of the verb in v.11)[24]. Then the proclamation is fulfilled ("it was so"). Then the land *produces* plants (brings forth more).[25] If *the land* is doing it then it is happening slowly like today. The text gives *no indication* of any hyperactive growth, or trees being made full grown. There is no way to look at, "And the earth brought forth vegetation…" and say it happened in one day because the land cannot do that. If plants experienced accelerated growth or instantaneous appearance then God would have to have done it, which means the land would not have done it unlike what the text says. If the land does something then it is done naturally. So, if we *follow the text* and believe *the land did it*, then it happened naturally the way we see plants grow today, and that takes longer than a day.

Genesis 2:8-9 gives additional testimony to that and says, "The LORD God planted a garden toward the east, in Eden; and there He placed the man whom He had formed. Out of the ground the LORD God caused to grow every tree that is pleasing to the sight and good for food." God *planted* a garden. If words mean anything this cannot be taken as highly accelerated growth. The words "caused to grow" in verse 9 simply mean to grow. A noun derived from that Hebrew verb means a branch or bud (Is. 55:10), meaning the plants God planted budded and grew. This is no different than saying, "Farmer Brown grew a garden." God grew a garden that He planted and He even walked among it (Gen. 3:8) possibly implying He may have *physically* done some of the work. Hyperactive growth is not meant here any more than in Ps. 147:8, "… [God] makes grass to grow on the mountains" (same verb as 2:9).

The main point here is that the proclamations on Day 3 could not have happened in a day. The land cannot bring forth plants in a day. The text says *the land* produced vegetation, *not God*. God started it and allowed the land to bring it forth. I am not suggesting God is incapable of making mature trees in a day (Jonah 4:6). I am only saying *Genesis does not say He did*, so let no one force it to say so.

Third, on Day 4 one of the purposes for the lights is stated like so, "Let there be lights in the expanse of the heavens… and let them be for signs and for seasons and for days and years…" (1:14) God proclaimed for the lights to be used for marking time and for signs. Signs point humanity to God[26], like the star of Bethlehem. We all agree whatever God proclaims will happen, so it should come as no surprise then to read "and it was so" in verse 15. But wait a minute. **What was so?** The proclamation was fulfilled. The lights came to be in the expanse of the heavens and were used for their purposes to measure time and act as signs. Is that a problem? Yes, how could it be "so" *on Day 4* that the lights were used for their purposes *before* anyone was there to use them? God said, "Let them be for signs…" but the lights cannot be a sign, or be used to *measure* time, *until someone uses them* for that purpose.

The Hebrew verb *hayah* (let them be) is used three times in the proclamation of Day 4. The verb demands that something that *was not* came *to be* in order for that part of the proclamation to be fulfilled. The first part of the proclamation was fulfilled when the lights came to be in the expanding clear space of the heavens. The second part can only be fulfilled by something new happening too. In order for something new to happen to fulfill the lights' proclaimed purpose, *someone must use the lights for their purposes*. Therefore, this part of the proclamation can *only be fulfilled after the second proclamation on Day 6 is fulfilled* and humans use the lights for their purposes.

This is a clear indication the proclamation on Day 4 cannot have been fulfilled on Day 4. In fact it would have taken at least a year after humanity was created to fulfill this proclamation. So, why does it say "it was so" in the text of Day 4 when it did not happen on Day 4? Simple, the phrase is a parenthetical past tense statement informing us the proclamation was fulfilled, but it should not be understood as strictly chronological.[27] We have already seen there are non-chronological statements in the Genesis 1 account. This is another one, but the main points are this proclamation *cannot* be fulfilled *on Day 4* and took longer than a day to be fulfilled.

Fourth, on Day 5 God blessed the water and flying creatures "…saying, 'Be fruitful and multiply, and fill the waters in the seas, and let birds multiply on the earth.'" (1:22) Notice, God did not create the seas and skies *full* of sea creatures and flying creatures. He let *them* fill the seas and skies on their own, which would have taken a long time. Though this does not show the proclamation took longer than a day (because it is not the proclamation), it does show the account speaks of natural processes operating and statements in the text are *definitely* not intended to be understood as accomplished in a day. Sea creatures cannot reproduce, increase, and *fill the seas*, nor can birds multiply on the land, in a day. Who filled the seas with fish? The fish did.

In Genesis 1 God intended for us to understand some processes on Earth happened naturally and thus slowly. He did not make fully functioning ecosystems. He planted seeds and let them sprout and grow. He made many different kinds of animals in small quantities and let them populate the Earth on their own. Animal reproduction, plant growth, ecosystem equilibrium, and the geologic processes of continental uplift and water drainage are examples of natural processes at work in the Biblical picture painted by Genesis 1. God proclaimed for natural processes to begin to work on Earth.

Fifth, the first proclamation on Day 6 says, "Then God said, 'Let the earth bring forth living creatures after their kind: cattle and creeping things and beasts of the earth after their kind'; and it was so. God made the beasts of the earth after their kind, and the cattle after their kind, and everything that creeps on the ground after its kind…" (1:24-25) By now I would bet you are beginning to see the text better and can already guess what I am about to say about this proclamation.

The verb "bring forth" is the same as in verse 12 referring to plants. The land brought forth more plants after plants sprouted; meaning plants grew by natural processes. The huge difference here on Day 6 however is that *this is part of the proclamation*. God proclaimed for *the land* to produce animals. The land only operates by natural processes so what

God proclaimed was for natural processes to begin working with land animals. In order for this proclamation to be fulfilled *all animals* in all three categories of land animals proclaimed would have to reproduce: beasts (like elephants), cattle, and creeping things (all kinds of animals that move along the ground).[28] But natural processes work slowly, especially when it comes to mammal reproduction. The gestation period for an elephant is about 22 months. A cow's is about 9½ months.

This Day 6 proclamation could not possibly have been fulfilled in a day. God did *not* proclaim for *Him* to make land animals in the same way that He proclaimed the existence of humanity, "Let Us make man in our image…" God proclaimed for *the land* to do the producing. If God had intended to do the producing He would have said it that way.

However, someone might object, "The text says *God made* the animals." Yes, but notice again, the statement is non-chronological *after* the fulfillment phrase. The land could not produce animals until God made them so how can the text say "it was so" before God made them? The proclamation could not be fulfilled until the animals existed so God had to make the animals first. **The really important point to notice is:** *God making the animals is not the same as the land producing animals and is not what fulfilled the proclamation.* The proclamation was fulfilled after the land produced animals, not when God made them. The actual sequence would logically be: God spoke the proclamation; God made the animals; The animals reproduced on the land; The proclamation was fulfilled. But, the text is not in that order, because if it was, one could get the mistaken idea it was fulfilled that day, and that is not what the author intended to say.

That sequence is no different than Day 4. God had to make the lights before the proclamation could be fulfilled, but the making of the lights is not what fulfilled the proclamation. Remember that the pattern of the 6 Days shows the phrases *after* the fulfillment phrase *do not fulfill the proclamation.* They are parenthetical extra information out of chronological sequence. If God meant this Day 6 proclamation was completed in a day the text could have been made much simpler by putting the first proclamation in the same order as the second proclamation like so, "Then God said, 'Let Us make land animals.' And God made the land animals. And it was so." Sadly, most people think Genesis says the proclamations were completed on the Day they were spoken, but it does not. Every word from God is exactly as He wanted it. Thus, if we let God's word mean what it says, *it is impossible for this proclamation to have been fulfilled in a day.*

Sixth, the second proclamation on Day 6 says, "Then God said, 'Let Us make man in Our image, according to Our likeness; and let them rule over the fish of the sea and over the birds of the sky and over the cattle and over all the earth, and over every creeping thing that creeps on the earth.'" (1:26) What part of this proclamation cannot be fulfilled in a day? The second half says, "Let them rule over the fish... the birds... the cattle and over all the earth [land], and over every creeping thing..." How could humanity rule over *all that* in a single day? *God is not just putting humanity in charge here.* It does not say, "Let them be rulers [noun]." "Rule" is a *verb* in the proclamation. God proclaimed humanity will rule and bring these animals and the land into subjection. Verse 30 says, "it was so", but they could not all be subjected in one day.

Adding evidence to this conclusion is the blessing God gave to Adam and Eve. In the blessing God tells them to "rule". If it was already true that they ruled those creatures as soon as they were created then there would be no need for God to tell them to do it. Truth is, the subduing and ruling of Earth was something God intended to train them to do and something *they were going to have to accomplish*. The proclamation was going to take time to fulfill and therefore could not have been fulfilled on Day 6.

Seventh, in the text of the 7th Day it says, "Then God blessed the seventh day and sanctified it..." (2:3) My question is: **When did God bless the 7th Day?** Did He do it *on* the 7th Day? The text does not say so and implies the blessing came afterward mainly because God did not do any work on the 7th Day. Also, the text of Day 7 is odd in that the words of the blessing are not recorded the way the blessings to the sea and flying creatures (1:22) and humanity (1:28) are recorded. According to Genesis 1, God's proclamations are the work God did *on* the 6 Days. The most likely reason the actual wording is not recorded is to avoid the appearance that God worked on the 7th Day. If God had blessed the 7th Day *on* that day it could be confused for work (i.e. one of His proclamations). Also, because the Sabbath was made for humanity (Mk. 2:27), the blessing was not done on the 7th Day because humanity was not on Earth yet. The second proclamation on Day 6 had not been fulfilled so no humans were there to whom God could speak. God would have waited to bless it after He created humanity because it was *for us*. Thus, we have another item that did not happen on the Day listed.

The Overall Conclusion of Point 4: Any interpretation of Genesis must be able to give us good reasons why the structure of Genesis 1 contains phrases that are out of chronological order. The account did not have to be written that way, but it was, so God must have had a good reason for doing it. One reason offered by the PDV is: the statements made after the fulfillment phrases do not describe the fulfillment of the proclamations. They are simply extra information God included because we needed to know them, but they are not necessarily sequential, and in some cases impossibly so. Misunderstanding the purpose for the out-of-sequence phrases has contributed to generations of people believing God fulfilled His proclamations instantaneously on the Day He gave them.

In contrast, God's proclamations were *purposefully* worded in a way that required longer than a day to fulfill. Genesis lists statements that cannot be done in a day. Genesis lists events that did not happen within the 7 Days. Genesis contains statements that are clearly and intentionally out of chronological order. Genesis tells us God created the heavens and the Earth in a block of time called the "beginning"; then God did a six-day work of proclaiming, *in topical order*, what was going to happen to an desolate, empty, dark, and deluged planet; and then the fulfillments of those proclamations became "so" over an unspecified period of time after the 7 Days with His guiding hand. *We are not meant to understand the proclamations to have all been fulfilled in one week.* And we are not told how long it took.

Point 5: Because the "beginning" was an unspecified block of time before the 7 Days (Point 2), and the prophecies given on those Days were not all completely fulfilled on the Days given (Point 4), *Genesis does not tell us the age of the universe and Earth.*

Point 5 is a simple logical conclusion from Points 2 and 4. The 7 Day work God did stands as a dividing point between two unspecified periods of time: the "beginning" block of time, and the time it took to fulfill His proclamations (prophecies). Because both time periods are unspecified we can conclude that Genesis does not tell us the age of the universe or Earth, nor does it even allow any kind of *textual* speculation on the subject. One cannot even get an estimate or "ballpark" figure. God has apparently allowed humanity to answer that question on our own. Therefore, whatever age scientists verifiably assign to the universe (currently 13.7 billion years) or the Earth (4.5 billion) *does not contradict Genesis*. Christians should not fear these figures. Every Old-Earth View of Genesis agrees with that conclusion.

As a side note, by not specifying an age for the universe or Earth God was very wise as He always is. Without a specified age, the Bible removes the age issue from being an issue at all. *Genesis can be reconciled with any age of the universe and Earth because Genesis does not tell us their age.* Someone could even accept the Prophetic Days View and maintain a young Earth position. The only philosophies or religions Genesis blatantly contradicts on the age of the universe are any that advocate an eternal universe, like Atheism, Buddhism, Hinduism, and various forms of new-age philosophy because Genesis clearly indicates the universe and Earth are finite with a beginning. But, on the age of the universe and Earth the Bible is silent.

Concluding the Prophetic Days View

To summarize what I believe Genesis says about the prehistoric account of the universe and Earth goes like this: *First*, God created the universe (Gen. 1:1) with its vast array of galaxies, stars, planets, and moons (including the Earth) during an unspecified amount of time called the "beginning" before the 7 Days of Genesis began. *Second*, Genesis 1:2 continues the story from a human perspective on the surface of the Earth at a time when Earth was dark, wet, uninhabitable, and empty of life. *Third*, God did a six-day work designed to change those conditions wherein He proclaimed (prophesied) what He was going to do to the Earth thereby causing our human perspective of the heavens and Earth. *Fourth*, God ceased activity on the 7th Day as a pattern for mankind to follow later. *Fifth*, God fulfilled all His proclamations over an unspecified amount of time after the 7 Days culminating in the creation of Adam and Eve in the Garden of Eden.

Six last emphases of the Prophetic Days View:

First, the PDV is Biblically based. It is not based on forcing science on Genesis. The five points of the PDV can be discerned *from the text of Genesis alone and are more literal to the text than the Young-Earth View*. Tell that one to your young-Earth friends.

Second, the Days of Genesis 1 are taken as normal historical chronological Earth days, just like the text most naturally reads. This eliminates any squabbling over the length of the Days. They can be seven 24-hour periods and still allow for an old universe and Earth.

Third, the whole Genesis creation account is a historical account of what actually happened. Though every statement is not absolutely sequential, the account is not an analogy, metaphor, or poetry.

Fourth, the PDV helps explain the structure of Genesis 1. The out-of-sequence phrases are explained as extra information God wanted us to know, and they are not what fulfilled the proclamations. Also, the parallel structure[29] of Days 1-3 with 4-6 is explained without having to resort to a metaphorical framework (the Framework View) or a poetical myth. Instead, the account is a true chronology of a historical week with six days of prophesying *in a general topical order* (as a tool for easier memorization), and a day of ceased activity, sandwiched between two unspecified periods of time: "the beginning" wherein God created the universe and Earth before the 7 Days, and the time it took to fulfill the proclamations after the 7 Days.

Fifth, by not specifying an age for the universe and Earth the PDV is reconcilable with modern astronomy and geology (or *any age*).

Sixth, though allowing for old age, the PDV is a creationist view. It does not advocate the evolution of all living creatures from a common ancestor. It advocates the miraculous instantaneous creation of a historical Adam and Eve from whom the whole human race descended. However, it is worth noting that the issue of whether Genesis allows evolution is a separate issue from interpreting the Days of Genesis 1 on the age of the universe or Earth.

After years of doing my best to diligently evaluate every major view of Genesis, and doing my best not to allow my interpretation to be influenced by current scientific ideas, I have concluded the Prophetic Days View is the correct interpretation of the account. In this entire chapter I have concentrated solely on the text of the Bible and Genesis to arrive at this conclusion. If I am wrong I gladly welcome any rational person to gently and reasonably show me where.[30] However, if I am right it is time the entire Christian body renounce the Young-Earth View. The ship is sinking Biblically and scientifically so quit trying to row it and abandon ship!

Also, if the PDV is correct, the other Old-Earth Views should become extinct. And maybe the body of Christ can move past the age of the Earth issue and unify to show the Bible is demonstrably true to a world that has abandoned it as an outdated irrelevant unscientific book. Jesus and His mission are what people really need, and His story for us begins in Genesis. Genesis is the most relevant story of origins that has ever, or ever will, exist.

Before I proceed to defend my interpretation of Genesis – the Prophetic Days View (PDV) – now is a good time to reflect on the conclusions afforded by the PDV that follow from the discovery that Genesis and science do not contradict one another on the age of the universe and Earth. In the intellectual realm of Christian Theology forgetting why we are even pursuing a defense of the authority and inerrancy of the Bible is too easy. I do not simply wish to convince someone the Bible is from God; I sincerely seek to introduce people to the God of the Bible. The next two chapters conclude the primary section of the book and will hopefully encourage the faith of believers and spark a response to God's call upon unbelievers. The remaining six chapters and appendices are a defense of my position and are not for the weary minded.

3

A Beautiful Picture of Our Creator
(*Why* did God draw the map (Genesis) the way He did?)

Chapter 1 outlined the overall layout of Genesis 1:1-2:4a and Chapter 2 presented the positive case that the scientific age of the universe and Earth are not a problem for Genesis. God knew what He did and how it happened and He told us a glimpse of it, but Genesis is more than a miraculous revelation of our origins supporting the authority of the Bible. It is also about our purpose (a subject of the next chapter) and more importantly, *Genesis is a revelation of God Himself.*

Everyone must face the fact that a God capable of creating this incomprehensibly vast universe is also Himself incomprehensibly vast and powerful beyond understanding (infinite in fact). Just for a minor comparison, consider that if the Sun were the size of a basketball, the Earth would be about half the size of a bb and Jupiter would be no larger than a ping pong ball. The Sun's energy output is enough to turn the whole Earth into ashes almost instantly if we were close enough to it. *And God is more powerful than that!* Compared to the universe, our star is tiny and one of billions of billions. *And God is bigger still!*

Yet, He chose to reveal Himself to humans and we are said to be created in His image. Far from being an uncaring God who remains uninvolved in His creation, God has given us a picture of Himself so we would know Him. Knowing Him begins with knowing about Him, but we cannot know anything about God He does not want us to know. Therefore, whatever God has revealed to us must be important to know.

As I studied Genesis it could have become easy to forget the ultimate purpose why I was doing it, just as this book could become one more useless file of knowledge in your brain if you miss increasing your faith in God through it. Reconciling Genesis and modern science is not an important end by itself. The real goal here is to know God better, love Him more, and trust Him more by seeing the evidence He has given us. The more you are convinced it is true, the more it will affect your relationship with God and your behavior.

That brings me back to Genesis. Genesis 1 is a revelation *of God*: what He is like, what He does, and why He does it. The account begins with a declaration that God's existence was *before* His creation. This automatically makes God transcendent, sovereign, and more powerful than all the universe contains. Genesis assumes those facts to be understood, in the same way Paul does in Romans 1:18-23, but God is more than just our Ruler and Creator, though those are certainly important enough to humble us. He continues in Genesis past verse one because there is much more to know.

After looking at patterns in Genesis 1 for a long time and trying to understand why God arranged it in its particular order, it suddenly occurred to me that *each Day has an emphasis about God*. Beyond telling us He is our Creator I believe God had more in mind for the structure of the Days than just proclaiming what He was going to do to Earth. He structured the text of each Day to emphasize something about Himself and His purposes and this helps explain what might look like a semi-random ordering of the text. Chapter 1 showed Genesis has a fivefold pattern on each Day: a proclamation, a fulfillment phrase, action phrases, the evening and morning phrase, and a numbered day. However, only the beginning and ending of a Day's text is identical. The fulfillment and action phrases are in what might look like random order.

Notice that the structure of each Day sometimes contains a *repeated* phrase, or something is *omitted* that appears on the other Days, or in some cases something new is *added*. These repeats, omissions, and additions are intentional and identify the emphasis God intended for that Day. By emphasis I do not necessarily mean the subject of each Day. For example, light is the main subject of the activities of Day 1, but not necessarily its emphasis. The emphasis of each Day is the revelation of God's character on each Day. God wants us to see something *about Himself* on each Day.

What is even more amazing to me is that not only is there an emphasis about God on each Day, but *all six emphases apply to each Day of Genesis and every day!* When I saw that, I was astounded that the text of Genesis 1 is arranged so meticulously. *Nothing* should be taken for granted about it. No word is insignificant or can be removed without doing damage to the text.

Day 1 – Genesis 1:3-5

What is special about the order of the text of Day 1? What stands out on Day 1 from other Days is, "Then God said, 'Let there be light'; and there was light." No other Day is structured like that. Instead, the other Days have a phrase that states God, or a secondary agent, did some action in relation to His proclamation to bring it to pass. For example, on

Day 2 God says, "Let there be an expanse..." and then the text says, "And God made the expanse..." However, on Day 1 God simply proclaims light and light happens. No phrase says something like, "And God made the light." That a phrase of this nature appears on *each of the other Days*, but is omitted here is surely not a mistake. The omission is evidence that on Day 1 *God wanted to emphasize the power of His spoken word.*

So, the **Emphasis of Day 1** is: God speaks what He desires and it comes to pass and absolutely nothing can stop it. God is faithful and true to His word. Whatever He says or promises is sure to happen.

Day 2 – Genesis 1:6-8

What is special about the order of Day 2? Two things stand out, the first of which has nothing to do with the emphasis of Day 2, but is worth noting.

The first odd thing about Day 2, recognized by many commentators for several thousand years[2] now, is the absence of God seeing the results of Day 2 as "good". Day 2 is the only Day of the 6 Days where the "and God saw that it was good" phrase is absent. Why? I asked this question in my apologetics discussion group at my church and from a humorous perspective one man quipped it was because Day 2 is Monday. Apparently even God is not fond of working on Monday. But seriously, the most common answers commentators have suggested for God omitting the phrase are that there was nothing particularly good for humanity proclaimed on Day 2, or that the work begun on Day 2 is not finished until Day 3 where God does see that it is good. I do not like those answers mainly because the use of the word "separated" on Day 2 involves a holy vs. common distinction that is good for humanity.[3] Nor do I think humanity living on a perpetually foggy Earth was what God intended, so the making of a clear space *was* "good" for man. Also, the text gives no indication the work of Day 2 was completed on Day 3.

So, why did God leave the phrase out of Day 2? One possibility that was suggested to me in a discussion online was that the clear space (expanse) is invisible and that is why God did not say He saw it. Despite the cleverness of that observation I do not think it is correct because the effects of an expanding clear space are visible so God could have seen the effects of His proclamation.

The best suggestion I have for the absence of the phrase is to call our attention to it. By leaving it out it has forced commentators and Bible scholars to wonder why, and this naturally calls our attention to a phrase in Genesis that might otherwise be overlooked or under-emphasized. Let us not forget Who is the source and definer of goodness. By omitting the phrase our attention is directed to the fact it is missing and causes us to think of God's goodness, *something we frequently need to remember*. God's goodness calls to my mind Hebrews 11:6, "And without faith it is impossible to please Him, for he who comes to God must believe that He is and that He is a rewarder of those who seek Him." In order to come to God, we must believe He exists *and* He is good (a rewarder) to those who seek Him. There are many who believe He exists, but few who seek Him personally as the good rewarder. That God is good is certainly a revelation of His character but it would be ironic the emphasis of Day 2 would be identified by not mentioning it.

The second unique thing about Day 2 is the addition of God *saying and doing* the same thing. God *proclaims* an expanse, and then God *makes* an expanse, and then the text says it came to pass. Why is this threefold wording necessary? To emphasize a point: Day 2 has added something different than Day 1. It is no longer only God said it and it comes to pass. Now, it is God said it, *God does it,* and it comes to pass. The addition of the action phrase is new to Day 2 and brings us to its emphasis.

The **Emphasis of Day 2** is: God alone is responsible for bringing to pass (making or causing) what He speaks. Not only does God speak something and it happens, whatever He says He will *do*.

Day 3 – Genesis 1:9-13

What is special about the order of Day 3? The order of Day 3 is very different than Days 1 and 2. It uses "Then God said..." twice and the number of events needed to completely fulfill the proclamations on Day 3 was far more than Days 1 and 2. Also, for the first time in the order of the text, the fulfillment phrase occurs *before* the action phrase. The first part of Day 3 does not contain an action phrase. The second half contains "The earth brought forth..." but the first half does not have a phrase like "And God caused the land to rise and the waters to gather" or "And the land appeared and the waters gathered." But these peculiarities do not emphasize anything about God Himself.

Most significant though, conspicuously missing from Day 3 is *God's actions of any kind* related to His proclamations.[4] *This is the only Day like that.* Day 1 has "God separated". Day 2 has "God made". Day 4 has "God made" and "God placed". Day 5 has "God created". Day 6 has "God made" and "God created". But Day 3 only has "The earth brought forth". This can be no accident. But why? Why are God's actions missing from Day 3?

Day 3 introduces the idea of God's use of secondary causes. Meaning, God is not always the direct cause of an event; sometimes, if not most times, He is the indirect cause of an event.[5] That is the clear case here. *Day 3 does not have God as the subject of any actions related to His proclamations.* Instead, it has the waters doing the gathering, the dry-ground doing the appearing, and the earth doing the sprouting and producing. *The clear emphasis of Day 3 is on natural processes*, i.e. secondary indirect causes (and, as I pointed out in Chapter 2, that means *slow processes*). God's actions missing from the text of Day 3 surely must emphasize something. This is not to say God did nothing to fulfill His proclamations on Day 3. He proclaimed them to be, so He is ultimately the originator who caused the existence of land, seas, and plants. They would not have existed had God not proclaimed them to be, but God allowed nature to run its own course just as He allows us to run ours. God made the Earth and then land appeared from the waters, and then the waters ran off (gathered), and the land dried out. God then let the dry-ground sprout plants (after presumably creating seeds and planting them – Gen 2:19) and the resources of the Earth caused the plants to grow (produce). God originates, nature follows.

The **Emphasis of Day 3** is: God frequently accomplishes His purposes through secondary causes by relinquishing direct control of His creation. That means we are responsible for our actions and can be held accountable for them.

Day 4 – Genesis 1:14-19

What is special about the order of Day 4? There are two additions and one repetition that are very important about Day 4.

First, Day 4 repeats the phrase "in the expanse of the heavens" three times. Surely a threefold repetition is meant to draw some attention. As we saw in Chapter 2, this repetition is there to emphasize what God *actually proclaimed* on Day 4. He did not proclaim for the lights to come into *existence* for the first time; He proclaimed for the lights to come to be in a new location from the perspective of the surface of the Earth – in the expanding-clear-space of the heavens. Important as that is to understand, it does not say anything particular about God Himself.

Second, Day 4 is the first Day that adds *undisputable* out-of-sequence phrases to the text and everyone, YEC and OEC alike, agrees that is the case. Verse 16 (God making the lights) cannot be in sequence with the fulfillment phrase, "and it was so" (verse 15), because God had to have made the lights before the proclamation could be fulfilled. Also, God making the lights is not a description of the fulfillment of the proclamation; it is a parenthetical statement that God made the lights that have now become visible in the expanding-clear-space of the heavens. Day 4 is clear testimony that the proclamations were not fulfilled on the Day proclaimed because the Day 4 proclamation could not have been completely fulfilled until after Day 6 (See Chapter 2). But again, this does not emphasize anything about God Himself.

Third, Day 4 is the only Day God specifically includes in His proclamation the *purposes* for what He proclaimed. God gives three purposes for the lights: (1) To separate day from night – This is an obvious reference back to Day 1 equating the now visible lights to the same causes of the light on that Day. It also represents a cycle that is good for life. (2) For signs, seasons, days, and years – This means God intended the lights to be used as time keepers, but this part of the proclamation could not have been fulfilled until at least a year after mankind arrived. (3) For giving light on the Earth – This may sound like an obvious "duh" statement. Of course they are for the purpose of lighting the Earth. However, the statement is more profound than first appearance. The lights are not gods to be worshipped, they are merely lights. Proclaiming not only the location of the lights, but also their purposes, clearly says something about the character of God.

The **Emphasis of Day 4** is: God has purposes for all He does.

That sounds simple because it is, but it can be profound when considering why God created anything at all, especially us. We all have a deep emotional longing for a purpose, but in order to know our purpose God must tell us. This longing is not a feeling we must abandon as an impossible dream. Each of us actually has a purpose because God would not have created us without one. *You are not worthless. You are not a mistake.* Every person on the planet has the capacity and purpose to love God and love others and thus fulfill the reason we are here.

Day 5 – Genesis 1:20-23

What is special about the order of Day 5? Three things stand out but only one emphasizes anything about God's character.

First, Day 5 is missing "and it was so", but it still has a fulfillment phrase similar to Day 1. In verse 21 the statement that God created an abundant variety of living creatures in the waters and air is the fulfillment phrase of the proclamation in verse 20, so "and it was so" is not necessary.

Second, Day 5 is the first time the word "create" is used in the main narrative of verses 3-31. "Create" was first used in verse 1 and will appear again on Day 6, but here its use is significant because it is the second time God creates something new. God had to do something different to fulfill this proclamation than He did to fulfill the others. Apparently, creating living creatures *that move* involved God doing something so completely different than He had already done that the word "create" is used to describe it.

Third, for the first time God pronounces a blessing on the living creatures to be fruitful and multiply. The omission of "and it was so" does not appear to point toward any main emphasis for Day 5, nor does the second use of the word "create". But, God blessing His creatures shows God's care and intimate involvement in His creation. God is not the god of Deism who is uninvolved in his creation after winding it up and letting it go. God stays active in it and blesses it.

The **Emphasis of Day 5** is: God caringly designs, blesses, and stays active in His creation for the benefit of life. We are not alone and God has blessed us to be fruitful and multiply. We can flourish if we live God's way.

Day 6 – Genesis 1:24-31

What is special about the order of Day 6? The order of Day 6 is not any different than any other Day. There are two proclamations, but that is the same as Day 3. There are out-of-sequence phrases, but that was true of Day 4. There are phrases that cannot be fulfilled in a day, but that was true of Days 3, 4, and 5. God creates and blesses in the text of this Day, but that is true of Day 5.

However, one thing makes this Day so special that the text refers to it as "the" sixth day[6]. The answer is no secret and is obvious to just about everyone: Humanity was created as a result of the second proclamation on Day 6. The Earth exists for us. That may seem arrogant, but it is what God is telling us. God intended a special purpose for humanity which is evident from the uniqueness of our creation. We are created in His image (representing God on Earth carrying out His instructions with His authority[7]) and His likeness (bearing a resemblance having similar qualities[8]), and have the ability for a relationship with Him no other creature on Earth can have. Day 6 contains the crescendo of the account. Verse 27 says, "And God created man in His own image, in the image of God He created him; male and female He created them." This threefold repetition of the word "created" within one verse *screams* for attention and calls for us to contemplate what it means to be created in God's image.

And that brings us to the **Emphasis of Day 6** but before I list it relook at the previous emphases of each Day:

Day 1: God speaks what He desires and it comes to pass and absolutely nothing can stop it.
Day 2: God alone is responsible for bringing to pass (making or causing) what He speaks.
Day 3: God frequently accomplishes His purposes through secondary causes by relinquishing direct control of His creation.
Day 4: God has purposes for all He does.
Day 5: God caringly designs, blesses, and stays active in His creation for the benefit of life.
Day 6: God works and creates with humanity's benefit and purpose in mind.

As I stated earlier, what struck me as so amazing about the Days having an emphasis is twofold. *First*, it helps explain why the text of each Day is arranged in its particular order with all the additions, omissions, and repeats. And *second*, each emphasis applies to every Day and every day. What an amazing literary accomplishment is Genesis 1! Its details are planned meticulously for us to ponder. Genesis' age, accuracy, and ability to speak to every human generation is testimony to its Divine inspiration.

One last comment concerning the emphasis of Day 6 needs to be made. The importance of humanity is not being emphasized over the glory of God. God forbid! God ultimately does everything for His own glory (Eph. 1:9-12) and that is true because *nothing is greater or more glorious than God*. The greatest gift God has given to humanity is Himself, His presence, a relationship with Him. He can give nothing greater because nothing *is* greater. Because God is ultimately about His own glory, it makes perfect sense that He would invest Himself in activities that would glorify Him, which includes creating humanity as a creature capable of glorifying God in a special way. Therefore, having humanity's benefit and purpose in mind ultimately glorifies Him, and benefits us. As John Piper has so aptly and succinctly put it:

…God is most glorified in me when I am most satisfied in Him…[9]

You should repeat that several times until its meaning sinks in, and then ask yourself just exactly how satisfied are you in your Creator.

Day 7 – Genesis 2:1-4a

The 7th Day should not be ignored, but it is very different than the others. Everything that is true of the other Days is omitted from the 7th

Day except that God blesses it. God blessing something is not unusual at this point however. What really calls for attention on Day 7 is that God "rested". The Bible writers knew God did not need rest and yet God tells us He ceased work on the 7th Day. The question that screams to be answered at this point is, "Why?" Why did God do that?

After the Israelites left slavery in Egypt and were in the desert, God gave them manna to eat daily, but He gave them twice as much on the sixth day so they would not have to gather it on the seventh (Ex. 16:22-30). From that time on it became known as the Sabbath Day, "a holy sabbath to the LORD" (v. 23). Considering that some people disobeyed the command to not gather manna on the seventh day (v. 27), the people must not have been familiar with resting on a day or treating any day as a special day to the Lord. It was an unusual command for these people who were used to a slave's lifestyle in Egypt.

After the Exodus however, the progressive revelation of God indicated that the seventh day of the week was to be a special worship day for the people of God and no work was to be done on that day. That is what gives us an idea of why God ceased activity on the 7th Day. It was to set an example for mankind to follow. The possibility exists that Adam and Eve were told of the blessed 7th Day and maybe even observed it, but time and the increase of human depravity slowly caused a blessed seventh day to be forgotten. However, such an idea is only speculation. There is no indication that anyone between Adam and Moses regularly practiced a seventh day observance. Regardless of when mankind found out about God blessing the 7th Day, it seems clear God rested on it to set the pattern He designed for mankind.

As mentioned above, one should remember that God does all things for His own glory and pleasure which, to an unenlightened mind, may sound very selfish. However, one must understand that God is pure goodness and that whatever is good for God (His own glory) is also good for us as creatures in His image. Therefore, the Sabbath is good for us and was always meant to be so. God gives us the absolute best thing He can give us and that is Himself. We are created to enjoy a relationship with God and He has given us a day that is intended to help us understand that gift, a day to rest and worship Him.

For today, the Sabbath is still more than rest; it is a day unto the Lord, a special day for corporate worship and fellowship with fellow believers. Obviously, our relationship with God and relationship with people are not ignored the rest of the week, but just as God expects us to give at least a tenth (tithe) of our financial increase to Him, He commands us to set aside a day of worship for Him. Some complain about being made to feel guilty for not attending church by saying they can worship God anywhere anytime, so why do they need to go to a special place to worship Him? Two reasons: First, God wants us to regularly be involved and influenced in a body of believers to minister to one another. Second, people who do not follow God's commands to observe a special day of worship generally do very little worship of Him any other time, and especially not weekly.

So, I return to my question. Why did God cease work on the 7th Day? He did it as an example for us to follow. We are also to do all our labor on six days and consecrate a day to Him. Those who obey are blessed.

God's revelation of Himself in the very first pages of a story He inspired should be no surprise and should not be missed. From Genesis 1:1-2:4a we learn our Creator is: transcendent (outside of and above all of creation), immensely powerful, sovereign, vastly intelligent, creative, a Spirit (immaterial), authoritative, immanent (working in His creation), purposeful, living, caring (loving), relational, and good. All that is just in the first chapter, and I am sure it is not an exhaustive list of what can be gleaned from Genesis 1 about God. Some good ol' preachers in the Bible-belt would say, "That'll preach!"

Amen!

4

The Beginning and you – What now?
(Now that we are at our destination, *why am I here*?)

Are we there yet?

Yes, we are now at a place where science causes no problems with the Bible on the age of the universe and Earth, a place where the Bible can be taken literally and scientifically without error, thus giving good reason to believe it is inspired by God and authoritative for our lives. Here is a quick summary of conclusions drawn from the Prophetic Days View *literal* interpretation of Genesis and modern science. You can then be the judge as to whether you agree.

One: Genesis 1:1 says this universe in which we reside had a beginning. Scientists have arrived at the same conclusion.[1] Non-Christian mathematical physicist Paul Davies admits, "Nearly all cosmologists now accept that we live in a universe that had a definite beginning in a big bang, and is developing toward an uncertain end."[2] That is an astounding statement to make because of its theistic implications, but it has come about because the preponderance of evidence points to a beginning of time, space, energy, and matter originating out of a singularity (a space of mathematically infinite compression). The Bible said the universe and Earth had a beginning long before science verified it. What caused the universe to expand and form at an extremely fine-tuned rate? Who or what determined its initial conditions and the constants and forces that govern its behavior? Genesis says God did in the beginning. Unfortunately, many Christians ignorantly think scientists describe the Big Bang as a random explosion somewhere in space long ago in the past. *That is not what scientists have shown!* Cosmologists have shown that *time, space, energy, and matter all began in the event.* Big Bang cosmology is a friend to the Bible, not its enemy, even if it involves billions of years.

Two: Genesis 1:2 says the Earth was once uninhabitable, empty of life, dark, and wet. Scientists have arrived at the same conclusion.[3] Toward the end of an age in Earth history known as the Hadean era approximately four billion years ago, after intense bombardment from space debris remaining from the formation of the solar system and a likely collision with a Mars sized planet forming our Moon, Earth would have been inhospitable for life and indeed was lifeless. The cooling of the planet and the condensation of the water in the atmosphere would have left the surface of Earth dark from thick cloud cover (Job 38:9), and Earth's speed of rotation (being faster then) and its proximity to the Moon (being closer then) would have inundated any land above sea level on a regular basis by extremely high winds and tidal movements. The Earth was indeed uninhabitable, lifeless, dark, and wet in its early days just as the Bible said. I find it compelling of Divine inspiration Genesis could be so accurate about the conditions of a specific time in Earth's early history long before humanity could verify it.

Three: The texts of Days 1, 2, and 4 make it clear that the view from the surface of the Earth into the heavens was to progressively become clearer. God proclaimed for the coming to be of an expanding clear space that would eventually expand to include the objects that were causing light on the surface. Just such an expanding clear view of the heavens is exactly what scientists say happened.[4] It went from an opaque atmosphere, to translucent, to transparent.

Four: The text of Day 3 says that God proclaimed for plants to sprout on the land and Day 5 says God proclaimed for life to swarm in the oceans. According to the Bible life would not exist were it not for the word and hand of our Creator. Though many scientists believe life originated naturally on Earth they have utterly failed to explain how. Neil DeGrasse Tyson says, "Although we can state approximately when life began on Earth, we don't know where or how this marvelous event occurred."[5] One could of course argue that the absence of evidence for a natural explanation for abiogenesis does not mean it did not happen. However, I would counter with the fact that the more scientists have discovered about the immense complexities of life, the more a natural explanation of life's origin evades them.

One would expect that if life began naturally scientists would be able to duplicate it rather simply in a lab, but they are not getting closer to an answer, rather, it is moving away from them. That is exactly what one should expect to find if the origin of life was not natural. *If God really did create life then the origin of life has no natural explanation.* So, despite our advances in knowledge of how life operates, a natural explanation for life's origin should be nowhere in sight, and that is exactly what we find.[6] But, keep looking.

Life is far too complex to assemble itself by natural law, even given billions of years. Yet, geologic evidence suggests that life appeared on Earth within a 50-100 million year window just as Earth's conditions were able to support it. Ward and Brownlee report, "One of the most telling insights we have gleaned from the fossil record is that life formed on Earth about as soon as environmental conditions allowed its survival."[7] That means that not only did nature have to align all the right chemicals in exactly the right place under the right conditions, but at just the right time also. In every other circumstance where coincidence becomes too improbable to explain an event people suspect design, like casino security knowing someone is cheating when they win too much. But, for atheists, when the conclusion leads to an Intelligent Designer, i.e. God, suddenly astronomically improbable natural coincidences become the answer. I am continuously amazed at how anyone can be an atheist in light of the complexity of life and the utter lack of any plausible naturalistic means for life's origin.

Five: Day 5 limits flying creatures to flying across the front side (face) of the expanding clear space above the Earth, meaning the writer of Genesis knew flying creatures could not fly to the Sun or Moon and were restricted to the lowest part (face) of the sky, which is not entirely obvious to an ancient observer. Though this is only a small detail, it shows that accurate details were not an unconcern for the author, or his Inspirer. The information Genesis contains was ahead of its time.

Six: Genesis 1:1, 1:21, and 1:27 use the word "create" in a progressive way to describe three important events. This three-fold use of a Hebrew word, only used for Divine actions, implies that a fundamental difference exists between the substance of the universe, animate life, and humanity. The creation of the universe speaks of God creating the general stuff of which all is made (1:1), but animate life is more than just an arrangement of the general stuff of the universe and so required God creating something new (1:21). Animate life has a form of locomotion, hence motivation to seek what it wants, and a sense of fear to move away from harm. These "soulish" emotional-like qualities required something new beyond the structure of plants which appear more mechanical. Also, humanity is more than star dust plus animate life with a soul. We are created in the image of God (1:27). We have a spirit analogous to God's Spirit which has similar qualities and represents God's desires on Earth. We have been given authority to rule and a mandate to subdue the land. The difference between animals and humans is more than quantitative, it is qualitative.[8]

Seven: Though a more developed version of my ideas on Genesis vs. evolution will have to wait for another book expounding Genesis 2:4b-5:1, the evidence from 150 years of testing Darwinism have done more to disprove it than support it. As one example, Phillip Johnson says, "Today, just as when Darwin first published *The Origin of the Species* in 1859, the fossil record as a whole is something that has to be explained away."[9] Scientific problems with evolution abound and many authors have obliged us with multiple examples.[10] Basically, no naturalistic mechanism has demonstrated the ability to increase useful genetic complexity in living creatures. An Intelligent Designer is necessary.

Eight: God rested and is finished. The incredible complexity exhibited in the fine-tuning of the universe for life's existence, and the existence of life itself, took input from a highly superior supernatural intelligent source we call God. Without that input we would not exist, so when God discontinues additional input, it only makes sense that, in the case of a finite creation, all begins to break down. The universe is running down. It is using up its energy sources. The complexities of life are decaying and mutations are creeping in. No new animals are being formed. Animals are becoming extinct far faster than they ever appeared on Earth. The natural resources available to us are being depleted. However, despite all of that, God is in control and He created planet Earth for humanity. Therefore, we need not worry about what humanity's future will be (though this should not encourage waste). God has promised a new heavens and new earth (Rev. 21:1) with imperishable bodies (I Cor. 15:42) when the time comes. Because the first chapter of the Bible proves trustworthy, we can expect these other promises to come to pass as well. One day, "And so it came to pass" could be written over the entire Bible.

Nine: And finally, Genesis makes no commitment on the age of the Earth or universe. Though many interpret the 6 Days to be the time it took God to complete His creation, we have seen that interpretation is incorrect. God proclaimed what He was going to do to the Earth over a period of six days, but the time it took for Him to fulfill His proclamations is not specified because in many cases the text makes it clear the proclamations could not have been fulfilled on the Day they were proclaimed. The 7 Days of Genesis 1:1-2:4a were a real week sandwiched between two unspecified periods of time, the "beginning" which was before the 7 Days, and the time it took for God to fulfill His proclamations after the 7 Days. Thus, from a Biblical perspective, we do not know how old the Earth is and its actual age does not affect the accuracy of Genesis or the inerrancy of the Bible. This allows us to openly discuss the scientific data for the age of the universe and Earth free from the constraints of a poor Young Earth View interpretation.

I think it was quite wise of God to leave the question unanswered. If the Bible leaves the age of the universe and Earth unanswered, Christians should quit arguing about it. Instead, let us unify in our common salvation and begin contending with the world, not each other, following the instruction of Jude 3:

> Beloved, while I was making every effort to write you about our common salvation, I felt the necessity to write to you appealing that you contend earnestly for the faith which was once for all handed down to the saints.

The exegetically sound Prophetic Days View combined with an old-Earth progressive creationist position (like Hugh Ross's organization Reasons To Believe – RTB) makes a formidable offense and defense as a scientifically accurate literal reading of the Bible, and it dispenses with the untenable arguments of the Young Earth View, many of which will be answered in the chapters that follow. I believe the best apologetic for contending for Genesis is RTB and Discovery Institute *science* combined with the Prophetic Days View *interpretation*.

Why are you here then?

I believe the Bible and science are easily reconciled with modern astronomy and geology. I hope you agree. For the Christians reading this I hope it has strengthened your faith and that it motivates you to deepen your relationship with your Creator, Jesus Christ. Genesis reports that God created the heavens and the earth in the beginning, but John 1:1-3 identifies God as Jesus, "In the beginning was the Word, and the Word was with God, and the Word was God. He was in the beginning with God. All things came into being through Him, and apart from Him nothing came into being that has come into being." If it had a beginning then Jesus was its cause, and thus, He is our God. Let us love Him with all our heart, mind, soul, and strength.

For those of you who are not Christians, please allow me to share some good news, but it starts with some bad news. According to Genesis God created everyone (including you) to have a relationship with Him. Sadly, the fellowship that humanity enjoyed with God was broken when Adam and Eve sinned by disobeying God's command not to eat from the tree of the knowledge of good and evil. Since that time disobedience to God has been the norm and the effects of sin are tragic.

If you are honest with yourself, I am sure you will agree you have not always lived a life obedient to what God desires, and that is called sin. Because of your sins you have not enjoyed fellowship with your Creator. God told Adam and Eve that in the day they ate of the tree they would surely die (Gen. 2:17). As a result of humanity's disobedience, spiritual death (separation from God's fellowship) was the effect of the Fall that all humanity has experienced. Also, by God's pronouncement, physical human death became the penalty for sin (Gen. 3:19). Therefore, the penalty that must be paid for your sins and mine is death. The problem is we cannot pay the penalty ourselves and thus we are condemned. Only a pure sacrifice can atone for sin and we are not pure, thus we are condemned. That is the bad news.

The good news is, God knew our predicament ahead of time and made provision for us. Jesus Christ came to Earth to die for our sins, "just as the Son of Man did not come to be served, but to serve, and to give His life a ransom for many." (Mt. 20:28) The question is, how is the payment that Jesus paid applied to your account? Romans 3:22-24 explains that it comes to you through "faith in Jesus Christ for all those who believe; for there is no distinction; for all have sinned and fall short of the glory of God, being justified as a gift by His grace through the redemption which is in Christ Jesus." If you will believe in what Jesus did for you, you can be "justified as a gift." That means you can be declared righteous (without sin) as a gift (free – you cannot earn it) through what He did. Romans 10:9 adds, "if you confess with your mouth Jesus *as* Lord, and believe in your heart that God raised Him from the dead, you will be saved." Confessing Jesus as Lord means you commit your life to serving Him.

The good news is, your sins are forgiven if you believe in who Jesus is and what He did for you, and you can have a relationship with your Creator, Jesus Christ. The more you realize the depth of your sin and the value of the gift God has given, the more it will cause you to love Him, and thus fulfill the very purpose for which you were created. Pray to Him now, confess your sins, believe in what He did for you, confess Him as the Lord of your life, begin the journey of becoming like Christ, and you will be saved from sin and death, and begin to know God.

Concluding Part I

That concludes my case for reconciling science and the Bible on the age of the universe and Earth. After years of searching for a solution to the science/Genesis problem, I believe the Prophetic Days View is the best answer and the intended meaning of the Author. I hope your faith has been strengthened, or has begun, as a result.

On the other hand, questions and disagreements sparked by these four chapters are certainly rolling around inside the head of many. The rest of this book is intended to be a reference work defending my position presented in Chapters 1 and 2. Now it is time to go deep-sea diving for those who need it.

Part II – Defending the Prophetic Days View

5

Objections to the Prophetic Days View
(Grab your scuba gear it's about to get deep)

Of course people object to my view of Genesis. I object to theirs. People are not easily persuaded to change their minds about major doctrines, which is to be expected. I wasn't either. Just as the Bereans were commended and called "noble-minded" because they were "…examining the Scriptures daily to see whether these things [Paul said] were so" (Acts 17:11), the Scriptures should be examined to see if the PDV is in line with the whole Bible. If it is not it should be scrapped in the same way I think the other views of Genesis should be.

In an effort to be thorough I am going to give my answers to *every* objection to the PDV that I have found in print or that I could come up with on my own. This will be carried out in *reverse order* from Chapter 2 because objections to Point 4 are more specific to the PDV. Then Chapter 6 will answer the biggest objection Young-Earth Creationists apply to nearly every Old-Earth Creationist view: the existence of death and disease before the Fall.

Objections to Point 4: The fulfillments of the proclamations (prophecies) that God said on the 6 Days were not all meant to be understood as fulfilled or initiated *within* the Day they were given.

If there are verses in the Bible that say everything was fulfilled or completed in 6 or 7 days then the PDV is wrong. The question is whether such verses exist. Opponents of the PDV believe strongly that they do. I believe that when those verses are examined closely they do not say what many people think they say. There are three passages most often cited to prove all was completed in 7 days. And there are four more arguments after that.

For those who do not like scuba diving in deep water the structure of this chapter is such that after stating the various objections I will give a short answer first *if a deep dive is coming*. If the short answer is sufficient for you feel free to jet-ski over the deep water to the next sandbar (bold type numbered objection).

The First Objection to Point 4: The text of the 7th Day

The text of the 7th Day stands as potentially the greatest challenge to the PDV. "The Church has long understood that God's creation work was completed by the original Sabbath… The Bible teaches…that the seventh day signaled the end of God's creation work."[1] Those who believe the Young-Earth

View (and other views too) believe the Bible says the heavens and Earth and everything that had to be done to them were completed in six days (even if the days were ages, God's days analogous to ours, or metaphorical days). Many people do not believe God worked by creating or making land, plants, animals, or humanity *after* the 7th Day. Understandably, this belief causes some to dismiss the PDV quickly, but please give me a chance to explain. The PDV says God prophesied on the 6 Days, but fulfilled the prophecies over an unspecified period of time later. So, which one is it: completed in six days or not? It's *both*.

The Short Answer: While I agree God did a work that was completed in six days, people have been *assuming* that work was *everything* listed in the Genesis 1 account rather than *let the text define what the work was*. Instead, Genesis 2:2 says God completed a work in seven days *and* Genesis 2:2-3 tells us God *created work* for Him to do *after the seven days*. The work God completed in seven days was to proclaim what He was going to do to change the desolate and lifeless condition of the Earth. God worked by speaking over six days *and* by fulfilling his proclamations after the 7 Days, but the *fulfillments* of the proclamations were *not* part of the work God completed within seven days, they were work God did after the initial six-day work. God did both: *He did work by creating* (proclaiming), and *He created work to be done* (the fulfillments).

A good way to show this is to look at Genesis 2:2 laid out in a parallel format. This is the ESV translation rearranged slightly to better match the order of the Hebrew text. Can you see the crucial difference between the two lines?

    God completed on the seventh day   His work that He had done,
and He rested   on the seventh day from all His work that He had done.

Why does the second line add the word "all"? Is there a difference between "His work" in the first line and "all His work" in the second line, as if the work in the second line was more than the first? I think so; otherwise there is *no reason* to add "all" to the second line (or verse 3). The work in the first line is what was completed in six days (as it says), which was proclaiming what He was going to do. "All" the work God rested from in the second line is everything He did in proclaiming *and fulfilling the proclamations* He made on the 6 Days.

The Deep: Now it gets more analytical and technical.

Genesis 2:1-2 – What was the work God did on the 6 Days? In formulating a response, I am going to let Genesis 1:1-31 guide my interpretation of 2:1-3 rather than the other way around. We should let the text define the work God did. The text of Genesis 1 has already clearly said God created the heavens and Earth before the 7 Days began so *their creation cannot be a part of the work God did on the 6 Days*. (See objections to Points 1 and 2 below.) And the text has given us proclamations and statements that could not have been fulfilled or completed in six days so they cannot be part of the work God completed on the 6 Days either.

Genesis 2:1 says, "Thus the heavens and the earth were completed, and all their hosts." This statement serves as the final "and it was so" phrase of the account, meaning that when this was written all had been fulfilled. God is finished creating this world and fulfilling His proclamations. He is no longer working on them. He still works and creates other things, but not on creating living creatures or our habitat. Notice that this verse is tagged with "and all their hosts" which means it is referring to more than Gen. 1:1. The heavens and the earth of 1:1 did not include all the work God did to fill them. The filling resulted from work God did after their initial creation.

The Hebrew word for "work" refers to *the task of one who was sent*.[2] In the case of employment, an employer "sends" an employee to do a task and the task is their work or job. But God is the only one who can send Himself to do something, so for the Bible not to be misunderstood as another god sending *Elohim* (God) to accomplish a task, Genesis tells us God created His own work.

Genesis 2:2 plainly says God completed a work within 7 Days, *but the verse by itself does not explain what that "work" was*. One should not *assume* the completed work was *everything* in the text prior to this. The one clue Genesis 2:2 gives us to define the work is that the work was whatever God did on the 6 Days because God completed that work within that time. If we can determine what God did on the 6 Days then we know what the work was.

What does the text say God did within the 6 Days? From Gen. 1:1-31 there are two occurrences we know *must* have happened *within* the 6 Days. *First*, God spoke. He proclaimed what was going to happen. The text specifically says, "And God said..." on each of the 6 Days so we know God spoke within the 6 Days. "And God said..." *marks the beginning of each day* and the evening and morning mark the end. That is the pattern. *Second*, light appeared on Day 1. We know this because the text specifically says "there was morning" on six days which can only be true if there was at least some light. A separated day and night is necessary to mark out the first discernible week on the surface of the Earth. Within the six days God spoke and light came to be on Day 1. Therefore, the work God finished within the 7 Days was to proclaim (prophesy) what was going to happen to a desolate and empty Earth.

What was "all His work" that God did? If the work God completed in the 7 Days was proclaiming what He was going to do, then it makes perfect sense to say "all His work" included both the proclamations and their fulfillments. Notice Genesis 2:2 does not say God completed "all His work" on the 7th Day.

Some will disagree by saying the text says that all the statements made within the text of each Day must have been fulfilled that Day, but it does not say that. The heavens and the earth were done *before* the 7 Days and the proclamations are stated in ways that cannot be completed in a day. Also, remember that the account is arranged topically (as discussed in Chapter 1), not entirely chronological. Logic dictates, and *everyone* agrees (even YEC), some statements in the account are out of chronological order. Genesis 1:15, 16, and 25 are obviously out of sequence as we saw in Chapters 1 and 2. Because they are out of sequence it is possible that others are too. The others are just not as obviously out of sequence as 1:15, 16, and 25.

Why are there non-chronological statements in the account? The statements between the proclamations and the refrain are simply parenthetical past tense completed actions that are not necessarily in exact chronological order, nor are they always occurrences within the 6 Days. They are information God needed to give us, and they had to be inserted somewhere. Since they are related to the proclamations on the 6 Days it makes sense to insert them in the texts of those Days, but they are listed out of sequence so we would know they were not necessarily completed on that Day.

Genesis 2:3 – Consider a host of translations of the latter half of Genesis 2:3 and pay particular attention to the differences at the end of the verse:

NASB (1977)
   He rested from all His work which God had created and made
NASB footnote at Bible Gateway[3] (1995)   (created to make)
KJV (old)
   he had rested from all his work which God created and made
KJV 1611 margin note[4]   (created to make)
NKJV (1990)
   He rested from all His work which God had created and made
ESV (2001)
   God rested from all his work that he had done in creation
NRSV (1989)
   God rested from all the work that he had done in creation
NIV (1984)
   he rested from all the work of creating that he had done
JPS[5] (1917)
   He rested from all His work which G-d in creating had made
HCSB[6] (2009)
   He rested from His work that God created to make
Green[7] (1986)
   He rested from all His work on it, which God had created to make
Whitelaw[8] (1958)
   he had rested from all his work which God created to make
YLT (1862)
   He hath ceased from all His work which God had prepared for making
Whitefield[9] (2009)
   He had ceased from all the work which God had created for making
Mine (see Appendix A)
   He ceased from all His work which God created to do

I know that is a lot to follow but it is important because I believe this verse is telling us God created work for Himself to do after the 7 Days. Notice that of the 14 major translations (not including mine), 7 of them say essentially the same thing. God created work for Himself to do, to make, or for making. That matches well with Genesis 2:2 with God doing a seven-day work of proclaiming what He was going to fulfill over time.

Consider also the order of the Hebrew text of the last part of 2:3 (Remember that Hebrew reads right to left):

בָּרָא אֱלֹהִים לַעֲשׂוֹת
la'asówth   Elohim   bara'
for doing[10]   God   created

Also, keep in mind that the Hebrew word translated "made" is most often translated as a form of the verb "to do" and designates causal responsibility.[11] A survey of the translations of Gen 2:3 reveals three primary interpretations here.

First, the KJV, NKJV, and NASB (ignoring the footnotes) insert "and" between "created" and "made", even though it is not in the Hebrew. By connecting "created" and "made" with an "and" it might give the impression "all the work" was what God "created and made" within the 7 Days. However, even if we accept this as a legitimate translation, the text does not say "all the work" was done in seven days. All it says is that God ceased from all His work on the 7th Day. It says nothing about how long the creating and making took. Regardless, in Hebrew the word "God" (*Elohim*) is between "created" (*bara*) and "made" (*asah*) without an "and" thus making those translations the least supported of the three.

Second, the ESV, NRSV, NIV, and JPS are all similar in that they have "made" modifying "create", meaning the work of creating is something God did. In this case, "all the work" refers to creating alone. Though this translation may be correct it makes the last part of the clause somewhat redundant, simply saying God worked by creating and He created by doing. It also does not capture the sense of causal responsibility inherent in the Hebrew word *asah* (to do).

Third, the last five, and footnotes of the first two, say the most literal translation of the last part is "created to make", which could then also be "created for making", "created for doing", or "created to cause".[11] Though the majority is not always right (7 out of 14 here), it at least shows the translation is a legitimate option. If correct, the verse is telling us "all the work" *extended beyond the 7 Days*, which supports the Prophetic Days View. However, even in this case the causal responsibility of "to do" may not be fully captured.

An interestingly nuanced fourth interpretation of this verse comes from the Complete Jewish Bible, "…God rested from all his work which he had created, so that it itself could produce." This translation seems to be attempting to capture a fuller meaning involving causality. They have interpreted the verse to mean God created this world to begin producing (causing) on its own. In other words, God set everything in motion (the Prime Mover), and secondary causes began. If this interpretation is correct, it captures the causal responsibility of the Hebrew word *asah* and shows the account is speaking of mediated creation through instigated means which requires longer periods of time than seven days.

No matter which of those four is correct, none of them cause a problem for the PDV by saying all was completed in seven days. In fact, the opposite is true. The textual evidence shows what God said could not be completed in seven days because of how He said it. Instead, by proclamation God both worked by creating and created work to do.

Genesis 1 is not the only example of God proclaiming "work" to be done that was carried out over an extended time.[12] Exodus 35:29 says, "The Israelites, all the men and women, whose heart moved them to bring material for all the work, which the LORD had commanded through Moses to be done ["to be made" – KJV], brought a freewill offering to the LORD." This example shows God has proclaimed work to be done that takes a while to accomplish.

The bottom line is Genesis 2:1-3 is not a problem for the PDV. God completed a work in six days wherein He proclaimed what He was going to do to the Earth. In that first work, by proclamation, He created more work (fulfillments) for Him to do, but He ceased activity for a day as a pattern for humanity to follow, and then He proceeded to fulfill the proclamations, i.e. doing "all" the work He created for Himself *to cause to happen* (*asah*).

The Second Objection to Point 4: Exodus 20:8-11

The most often cited verses in objection to any Old-Earth View come from the text of Exodus 20:8-11.

> [8]Remember the sabbath day, to keep it holy. [9]Six days you shall labor and do all your work, [10]but the seventh day is a sabbath of the LORD your God; in it you shall not do any work, you or your son or your daughter, your male or your female servant or your cattle or your sojourner who stays with you. [11]For in six days the LORD made the heavens and the earth, the sea and all that is in them, and rested on the seventh day; therefore the LORD blessed the sabbath day and made it holy.

God set the pattern He expected humanity to follow: work 6 days and rest on the 7th and obviously Exodus is referring back to Genesis 1. YEC take these verses as settling any controversy over any attempt to interpret an old Earth into Genesis. "**Exodus 20:9-11 blocks all attempts to fit millions of years into Genesis 1.** [bold in the original because it is the heading of a section]"[13] Also, "Thus the creation of the heavens and the earth (Genesis 1:1) and the sea and *all that is in them* (the rest of creation) was completed in six days. [emphasis his]"[14] (Ham) I cannot emphasize enough how often YEC use this argument. For that reason, it deserves a comprehensive response.

The Short Answer: Exodus 20:11 is taken literally by the PDV: in six days God completed a work of proclaiming what He was going to do on Earth thereby *causing* the heavens and the land, the sea, and all that is in them to become as *we perceive them today from the surface of the Earth*. The PDV does not deny a literal seven-day week occurred wherein God did a work that *caused our perspective* of the heavens and Earth. However, a huge difference exists between what the YEV believes the Bible says was done in that week and what the PDV says was done in that week.

64

Chapter 5 – Objections to the Prophetic Days View

The Deep: Does Exodus 20:11 (and 31:17) settle this question once and for all, and force us to conclude *everything*, "the heavens and the earth, the sea and all that is in them", were completed in 6 days? Even one OEC rejects the PDV saying, "I don't see how [the PDV] can be consistent with the Sabbath commandment, which locates God's work during the six days – and which relies on the analogy between God's work and rest and ours."[15] (Collins) Obviously he thinks the work God completed in six days was everything Genesis 1 lists, but I have just answered that objection. The work God completed in six days was to proclaim what He was going to do. Also, God completing His proclamation work over six literal Earth days and resting the seventh is *exactly* like our work week, not just analogous. But there are still three aspects of Exodus 20:11 which must be examined to show all was not completed in 6 days.

First, the YEV quote above, "Thus the creation of the heavens and the earth (Genesis 1:1) and the sea and *all that is in them* (the rest of creation) was completed in six days" is immediately incorrect. Exodus 20:11 does not use the word "completed" nor "created." (Referencing a verse should be done exactly) Exodus 20:11 uses the word "made" (Hebrew – *asah*) and "made" is not the best way to translate the Hebrew word here because of its English connotation.

The word *asah* is used very broadly in the Hebrew Bible and is translated into many words including: make, bearing (as it is used in Gen 1:11-12 to refer to bearing fruit), accomplish, deal with, commit, offer, execute, keep, show, prepare, work, perform, bring to pass, get, dress, maintain, care for, and trim. But it is most often translated as a form of the very common verb "to do" (do, does, did, done, etc.). A scan of those words including "to do" reveals that *asah* generally means *to cause something to happen*, whether good or bad, whether causing order or disorder. *It is a word that shows causal responsibility.* For that reason, it is used for both Divine actions *and* human actions. The first time it is used of human action is in Gen. 3:13 after Adam and Eve ate from the tree God forbade, "Then the LORD God said to the woman, 'What is this you have done [*asah*]?'" Responsibility and causality are clearly related to the Fall of mankind.

We should therefore be very careful what English word is used to translate *asah* in Ex. 20:11 and consider any connotations to its meaning. In English (and Hebrew), the verb "to do" has many applications, for example, "So where do you get your fingernails done?" (Even in Hebrew *asah* is used of trimming fingernails, Dt. 21:12) But unfortunately, the word "made" in English gives a connotation to any translation that may not be intended by *asah*. For example, try substituting "made" into the previous question, "So where do you get your fingernails made?" The two questions are completely different. In English "to make" something usually means to assemble, build, construct, or form it. But in Hebrew *asah* has a much broader meaning than that. So, to avoid any English connotations not intended by the Hebrew the best way to translate the word in Exodus 20:11 is "caused" because, like the Hebrew word "*asah*", it does not imply *how God did it*. Translating *asah* as "made" in English is too specific because it implies formation of parts or assemblage of pieces and that may not be how God did it, particularly since we are talking about things as diverse as stars, planets, life, and spirits. That being the case, the verse reads better as, "For in six days God caused the heavens and the earth, the sea and all that is in them..."

How does translating it as "caused" make any difference? "Caused" does not imply an immediate completion. God proclaiming what is going to happen automatically causes it to happen, if for no other reason than He will do what He says. But just because God said something will happen does not mean it had to happen immediately. The Bible never says God created everything in six days.

YEC object by saying that *asah* (made) is synonymous with *bara'* (create). For example, "the Hebrew words are synonyms."[16] (MacArthur) And, "For 'he made' (*'asah*) dare not be construed as involving a mode of operation radically different from creating (*bara'*), for a comparison of the use of the two verbs in [Gen 1:21 and 25] shows that they may be used interchangeably."[17] (Leupold) I disagree. Verse 21 is where God "creates" the water and flying creatures and verse 25 is where God "made" land animals. *Bara* means God *created* something completely new for the first time (animate life) and then in verse 25 God *did/caused* something else with the new thing He *created* in verse 21. The two operations are different, *creating* a new design for animate life that did not exist previously vs. *doing* something else using the same basic design.

Asah means *to cause something to happen* and applies to actions by both God and humanity, but *bara'* is different. In the OT *bara'* refers only to Divine actions. Only God can create something new so it is no surprise *bara'* is only used of God's actions, not human. *Bara* is used four times in Genesis 1:1-2:4a[18], and in each case something new is created that did not exist before. Three of the uses have long been understood as the three major stages of creation: (1) the initial creation of the universe (1:1), (2) the creation of animate life (1:21), and (3) the creation of humanity (1:27). The fourth use is in Gen. 2:3 which we just looked at and refers to God creating work for Him to do.

The fact that *asah* and *bara* are different Hebrew verbs, and *bara* refers exclusively to the actions of God, and *bara* has a very specific usage in Gen. 1, compels us to see that God did not use them synonymously or interchangeably. Just because both words may apply to the same thing (God *creating* the heavens and the Earth – Gen. 1:1, and God *causing* the heavens and the Earth – Ex. 31:17) is no reason to conclude the verbs are interchangeable. God both brought the substances and conditions of the universe into existence (creation) and caused (made/did) the various objects that fill the universe in those conditions and out of those substances.

Genesis 1:26-27 is also used to support that *asah* and *bara* are interchangeable. In verse 26 God proclaims, "Let Us make [*asah*] man in Our image..." and verse 27 says, "God created [*bara*] man in His own image..." However, even here there is a difference. For God to fulfill His proclamation to *make* humanity in His image, He first had to *create* something new that was different from the animals. With this newly *created* thing (a spiritual nature) He then *made* (caused) humanity.

Some other verses used to equate *asah* and *bara* are II Kings 19:15, "Thou [God] hast made [*asah*] heaven and earth" and Psalm 146:6, "Who [God] made heaven and earth, the sea and all that is in them..." Because *asah* is used there and in other places similarly (II Chron 2:12, Ps 121:2 and 134:3), and Gen 1:1 says God created (*bara*) the heavens and the earth, some consider the two terms synonymous. Also, because the Hebrew phrase "the heavens and the earth" is a figure of speech for "the all", and God both caused *and* created "the heavens and the earth", the two words are considered synonymous. But that conclusion does not necessarily follow. They are still emphasizing different parts of the events. When the Bible says God *created* "the heavens and the earth" it is referring to the initial creation of the universe in Gen. 1:1 (Is. 40:26 and 42:5), or creation *ex nihilo* (out of nothing – Ps. 148:5 and Is. 65:17). But, when the Bible says He *caused or did* "the heavens and the earth" it is referring to the work God finished in six days (II Kings 19:15, II Chr. 2:12, Ps. 121:2, 134:3, and 146:6).

One scholar says, "Perhaps the best way to describe their semantic relationship is to say that 'to make' is the broader term of the two: that is, 'to create' is 'to make,' but 'to make' might or might not be 'to create.'"[19] (Collins)

Second, as discussed in Point 3 of Chapter 2, we should remember that the Genesis 1 account, and the Bible in general, were *written from the human perspective of the surface of the Earth* so all people from all ages, times, and education levels could understand it. We can say God caused "the heavens and the earth, the sea and all that is in them" in six days *as we perceive them* because that perspective of the heavens and the earth came to be as a result of the 6 Days God proclaimed what He was going to do. Before the proclamations, our current perspective of the heavens and land did not exist, now it does.

YEC object by saying Exodus does not just refer to what was done *on* the Earth; it is also referring to all that was done in the whole universe, "all that is in them [including the heavens]". I agree, except that I would qualify it was *our perspective* of the Sun, Moon, and stars that was caused in 6 days, not that *they* were caused in 6 days. Genesis 1:14 says God proclaimed for lights to come to be in the expanding clear space of the heavens. From a human perspective, the lights did just that. The expanding clear space (expanse) from Day 2 expanded to include the lights that already existed. Genesis 1:16, which says God made (caused) the lights, is not to be understood as occurring *on* the 4th Day. As we have seen, it is out of sequence with verses 14 and 15 and is a parenthetical note. *Our view* of the Sun, Moon, and stars was *caused* by the proclamation on Day 4.

Picture what it was like for a moment and, if you can, try it as if you did not know modern astronomy. If we had been in a boat on the surface of Earth, as described in Genesis 1:2, we would not have been able to see anything because it was completely dark. We would have known the heavens had already been created (Gen. 1:1), because something was up there above us even though we could not see it. Then, as a result of Day 1's proclamation, we could see, but it was foggy. We still could not see the sky because there was no expanse. Later, as a result of Day 2, we could see clouds above like an overcast day, but we still could not see what was causing the light (the expanse was limited to being *between* the waters). Later still, as a result of Day 4, we could now see the lights. The logical conclusion we should make is that the lights we can now see were what caused the light from Day 1, which would also have to mean the lights were made either on or before Day 1. This new perspective of ours was caused by God in six days, but the lights were there before we could see them, and it took longer than six days to be completed.

Also keep in mind the evidence in the text of Genesis 1 is strongly in favor of "the heavens and the earth" being created in an unspecified block of time *before the 6 Days started.* The conclusion then is neither Exodus 20:11 or 31:17 teach God "made" absolutely everything within six days. Some creation was done before the 7 Days and the fulfillments were completed after. But our perspective of the heavens and the earth was caused by a six-day work wherein God proclaimed what He was going to do. Exodus 20:11 and 31:17 would not have contradicted what Genesis had already said and can be taken at face value. God *caused* the way we see the heavens and Earth in six days.

Third, the word "in" is not in the Hebrew of Ex. 20:11.

Putting all that together, I submit this translation of the verse, "For six days God caused *our perspective of* the heavens and the land, the sea, and all that is in them." With that understanding the verse causes no problem for the PDV because God literally did a six-day work that ultimately caused the universe as humanity experiences it, i.e. from the surface of our planet.

The Third Objection to Point 4: Jesus – a Young-Earth Creationist?

Young-Earth Creationists frequently claim Jesus was on their side by quoting Jesus' words in Mark 10:6.

> In Mark 10:6 we have the clearest (but not the only) statement showing Jesus was a young-earth creationist. He teaches that Adam and Eve were made at the *"beginning* of creation," not billions of years after the beginning, as would be the case if the universe were really billions of years old. So, if Jesus was a young-earth creationist, then how can His faithful followers have any different view?[20] [Mortenson]

Mark 10:2-9 reads:

> Some Pharisees came up to Jesus, testing Him, and began to question Him whether it was lawful for a man to divorce a wife. And He answered and said to them, "What did Moses command you?" They said, "Moses permitted a man TO WRITE A CERTIFICATE OF DIVORCE AND SEND her AWAY." But Jesus said to them, "Because of your hardness of heart he wrote you this commandment. But from the beginning of creation, God MADE THEM MALE AND FEMALE. FOR THIS REASON A MAN SHALL LEAVE HIS FATHER AND MOTHER, AND THE TWO SHALL BECOME ONE FLESH; so they are no longer two, but one flesh. What therefore God has joined together, let no man separate."

The next three paragraphs are the Short Answer: YEC use this argument so often it is worth everyone seeing a full response.

First, clarifying the meaning of Mark, the parallel account in Matthew 19:4 and 8 says, "And He answered and said, 'Have you not read that He who created them from the beginning MADE THEM MALE AND FEMALE'... He said to them, 'Because of your hardness of heart Moses permitted you to divorce your wives; but from the beginning it has not been this way.'" Notice Mark says "from the beginning of creation" which could be misconstrued to mean what YEC say. But the Matthew account is more specific to what Jesus meant, "He who created *them* [my emphasis] from the beginning" is referring only to the creation of humanity, not the whole of creation. The "beginning" is the beginning of the existence of humanity and marriage. Even in Mark it says from the beginning of creation "God MADE THEM", not everything.

But YEC still object and say:

> Some would wishfully claim that it simply means 'from the beginning of 'their' creation.' But this makes little sense – of course they were male and female from the beginning of their own creation. What else would they have been – hermaphrodites? No, the context is clear that Jesus is pointing out God's plan right from the beginning of creation.[21] [Sarfati]

Ignoring the irrelevant sarcasm for the moment, Jesus is *quoting* Genesis 1:27 and 2:24, verses referring to *the creation of humanity and marriage only*, which sets the context of Jesus' comments at *their* beginning, not the beginning of all creation. Unfortunately, this YEC is responding with the kind of roll-your-eyes smarter-than-thou sarcasm characteristic of too many YEC. Regardless, God telling us His image included *both* male and female from our beginning makes a lot of sense and is very important. Males are not exclusively in God's image.

Second, Hugh Ross points out another obvious flaw in this YEC thinking:

> However, even from a young-earth perspective on the creation week, this interpretation of Mark 10:6 cannot be correct. Adam and Eve were not created until the sixth creation day, *after* the creation of the universe and the earth. Therefore, Adam and Eve could not have been present at the beginning of the universe.[22]

The point is well taken. The 6th Day is not at the beginning of creation, it is at the end. But YEC respond, "...Adam and Eve were created on day 6, which, on the scale of 4000 years [from when Jesus said it], is almost indistinguishable from the beginning..."[23] (Sarfati) So, the YEC response is they were created *relatively* near the beginning. To that I say, make up your mind. You claim to be taking Jesus *literally* at His word, and then not so literally. Which is it? It is neither. The best and most literal way to take Mark 10:6 is that Jesus was referring to the beginning of humanity and marriage, not the whole of creation.

The Fourth Objection to Point 4: If Day 1 was fulfilled immediately all were

If one of the proclamations was fulfilled in a day then the others were too.[24] Because the proclamation on Day 1 for light to come to be on the surface of the Earth *had to be* fulfilled on that Day (otherwise each "morning" of the other

Days could not have been measured from the surface) someone could extrapolate that to say the rest of the proclamations were fulfilled immediately too. But that conclusion does not necessarily follow. The proclamations, fulfillments, and actions listed on each Day could have been worded in such a way as to show fulfillment in a day, but *that is not the way God chose to word it*. God proclaimed some of them so that they *could not* be fulfilled in a day. And some actions listed in the text cannot have been done in a day. Because God chose to say it that way we should accept the text the way it is. Day 1's proclamation was fulfilled immediately, but the text should determine whether that was true of any of the other Days, and the wording of the text on the other Days makes it clear they could not all have been accomplished on the Day they were proclaimed.

The Fifth Objection to Point 4: "And it was so" means immediate fulfillment

Many have long interpreted the fulfillments of each day's fiat to be instantaneous occurrences immediately after God spoke. For example, two YEC say, "...Psalm 33 affirms that God's completed creation is accomplished as quickly as words are spoken or commands are given. There is no hint of long intervening ages or of interposed agents: 'By the word of the Lord were the heavens made, their starry host by the breath of his mouth' (v. 6)."[25] And after quoting Ps 33:9, "For He spoke, and it was done; He commanded, and it stood fast" they say, "Nothing occurs between God's speaking (commanding) and the coming into existence of creation (its standing firm)."[25]

This belief is pervasive among YEC. Speaking of how close in the text the fiats are to their fulfillments one says, "This would seem to emphasize the immediate fulfillment of the fiat. As Currid has stated, 'The construction of the account is such that a command is given and then immediately accomplished. A clear sense of the spontaneous and instantaneous cloaks the account. No delay or lingering is sanctioned by the text.'"[26] And another, "God's creative work was instantaneous, accomplished by nothing more or less than His creative decree. He simply gave the command for things to appear – 'and it was so'... What He commanded was instantly made complete, fixed, and in place..."[27]

The Short Answer: While I will agree that *the brevity* of Genesis 1 could give the impression of immediate fulfillment, careful consideration should be given to what the text actually says was proclaimed by God, what the text says happened, what extra information the text gives, and the non-chronological order of the narrative. Just because *these YEC* see "and it was so" meaning instant fulfillment does not mean that is what it means. Others[28] see it differently. God speaks and it will happen (on that we all agree), but the timeframe for fulfillment is not specified even though the account is concise. Chapter 2 showed the evidence from the text is that the proclamations took longer than six days to complete, therefore, "and it was so" does not mean immediate fulfillment.

That "and it was so" does not mean "and it immediately occurred" is simple to show just by giving another place where the *exact* Hebrew wording is used in the Bible, but what occurred did not happen immediately. II Kings 15:12 (ESV) reads, "This was the promise of the LORD that he gave to Jehu, 'Your sons shall sit on the throne of Israel to the fourth generation.' And so it came to pass [exact Hebrew wording as in Genesis]." Obviously, "and it was so" does not have to mean immediate fulfillment.

Adding to this are the many times[29] the KJV translates this Hebrew verb as "and it came to pass". If Genesis had been translated as "And so it came to pass" (which is entirely possible for the phrase), then maybe some of the YEC above might not have been so dogmatic about instantaneous fulfillment.

The Deep: In Point 4 of Chapter 2 I listed seven Biblical evidences that show the proclamations could not have been fulfilled in a day. Most of these show slow natural processes at work, so substituting "and so it came to pass" for "and it was so" is quite appropriate. YEC will disagree with all seven so here is what they say, or are likely to say, about each.

One – My first point in Chapter 2 was that the text of Day 3 carries the connotation of a slow process for gathering waters and rising land because God's actions are completely missing from Day 3, except making the proclamation. How the fulfillment was done is not specified.

Far from seeing the action of the waters as slow moving however, one YEC commentator thinks the "and it was so" (1:10) phrase describes the complete opposite. "The verse concludes with the customary 'and it was (or became) so' to indicate that that which is bidden to come into being at once forms itself."[30] But this commentator is reading that into the text. The "and it was so" phrase itself does not indicate anything except that what God proclaimed came to pass. *It does not say when or how fast*. The *only reason* to conclude "and it was so" indicates "at once" action is an assumption all was completed in 6 days. And I have already covered above the only verses used by the YEV to attempt to prove that point. If the presupposition is removed then the text can mean what it says: the waters gathered to one place naturally flowing off the rising land. The waters were not rapidly transported by God off the millions of square miles of instantly uplifted continents.

Psalm 104:5-9 could be used against my argument.

> He established the earth upon its foundations,
> So that it will not totter forever and ever.
> Thou didst cover it with the deep as with a garment;
> The waters were standing above the mountains.
> At Thy rebuke they fled;
> At the sound of Thy thunder they hurried away.
> The mountains rose; the valleys sank down
> To the place which Thou didst establish for them.
> Thou didst set a boundary that they may not pass over;
> So that they will not return to cover the earth.

One point the psalmist makes is that the waters "fled" and "hurried away". Like Psalm 114:3-4 the Psalmist is poetically describing water moving like people with *reactions out of fear*. The emphasis is on the fact that what God says is obeyed and on God's sovereign control over nature, not speed. Notice in the Psalm that the waters are still doing the moving *on their own*. They are moving as fast as they can. God is not pushing them. As the mountains rose the waters naturally flowed away as God designed them. Psalms is poetic and does not require an interpretation of God moving the water instantly.

Two – The second proclamation on Day 3 describing the land sprouting and bringing forth plants shows those actions cannot be accomplished in a day. God proclaimed for *the land to do it* and if the land did it then it happened slowly.

Of this Day some YEC say, "Here we see that even mediate creation comes from the hand of God and depends upon Him entirely for its procreational powers."[31] These same authors then appear to contradict themselves (or change the meaning of the term "mediate creation"), "...we cannot legitimately interpret any of the Old Testament Scriptures to support mediated creation (i.e., creation that depends on normal providence and secondary agents). Instead, the consistent Old Testament view is that creation is *unmediated*, 'by the word of his power.'"[32] They just said Genesis 1:11-12 is "mediate creation" and then they say there are no OT verses that "support mediated creation". Huh?

What is mediated creation? Mediated creation is God using secondary means to bring about His desired result. Notice that God did not say, "Let the earth create plants." That would make no sense because the land can sprout and bring forth plants (from seeds as a secondary cause) like the verses say, as we see every year, but it cannot create anything. One thing is sure: when God uses secondary means He does not step in and speed up the process, because *that would not be mediated creation!*

Still another YEC says, "...the dry land just formed is at once to bring forth all forms of vegetation... In this instance the earth is the mediate agent, being bidden to produce whatever vegetation is necessary by a process of highly accelerated growth."[33] (Leupold) These authors are all *struggling* with what *they know* Genesis 1:12 says. The text says the *land* did it, not God. *So how could it possibly have been true that "the earth is the mediate agent" that accomplished "highly accelerated growth"*? That makes no sense at all. The land cannot do that. Only God could do that, but *God is not mentioned doing anything there* except making an initial proclamation.

However, the sprouting and producing of vegetation should be understood as only possible after the land is given seeds, and seeds do not evolve from dirt. So, God must have made the seeds to fulfill the proclamation (a statement oddly missing from the text – see Chap. 3 for a possible explanation) and then the land took over under natural circumstances like the verses say. *These verses are worded like this for a reason* and it is not just to make a YEC commentator's job more difficult. Genesis 1:11-12 says *the land* (not God) sprouted and brought forth plants. It is not that God cannot make a full-grown tree; of course He can. The important point is that *God tells us that is not the way He did it*. If He had done it that way He would not have said the land brought forth trees. He made the olive seed first, *planted* it (Gen. 2:8), then the land sprouted an olive tree, and then the land caused it to grow into a mature tree that produced more olives and more trees, and that takes years. *The text **literally and explicitly** says the land sprouted and produced vegetation, not God.*

YEC respond to this argument from Genesis 1:11-12 and 2:8-9 by saying, "This objection is not well-founded. We are not compelled to take the words in the sense of what we observe after creation. If the events described were supernatural, then obviously, the text does not refer to the natural process of growth."[34] The problem is, they *should* be compelled. Their presupposition is that the events described *in the proclamation* are supernatural. They should pay closer attention to what *God actually proclaimed.* For example, when God said, "Let the earth sprout vegetation..." (Gen. 1:11) and "Let the earth bring forth living creatures after their kind..." (Gen. 1:24) we should understand that *it does not say*, "Let Us make plants" and "Let Us make living creatures on the land." Let me say this carefully. *What God proclaimed to happen on Days 3 and 6 was for natural processes to begin to work in the plant and animal kingdoms.* So, the events described *in the proclamations* were *not supernatural.* The proclamation itself and origination of plants and animals were supernatural, but what was proclaimed to happen was not. A supernatural cause[35] was necessary for the Earth to do its part, but the fulfillment of the proclamation was not supernatural. Therefore, because of YEC presuppositions their conclusion is what is not "well-founded". We *are* "compelled to take the words in the sense of what we observe after creation" because that is what they describe.

Also, when trying to explain the difference between why God proclaimed for the land to "sprout" plants (v. 11) and verse 12 saying the land "brought forth"[36] plants, YEC resort to another explanation that fails miserably. "Verse 12 gives the particulars of... '*then* it was so,' and in so doing reiterates, with slight variation, what was indicated in the fiat of v. 11."[37] He is saying verse 12 reiterates verse 11 and calls the change of verb from "sprout" to "brought forth" only a "slight variation". That is no slight variation. The verbs and nouns have completely different meanings. That is why God wrote it that way. Plants sprouted (new growth) from the land, and the land brought forth (produced more) plants, meaning the plants grew and reproduced. The Genesis account is not being redundant or reiterating anything here. It has no need to do so because the account already told us the proclamation was fulfilled, "it was so" (occurring *between* the proclamation and verse 12). Verse 12 offers *new* information specifically telling us natural plant growth began working on land and, though God was the initial cause of it, He did not directly cause trees to spring up fully grown in a day.

Though the text says the land produced plants someone could still argue the proclamation could happen in a day. Plants could sprout in a day fulfilling the proclamation and then the land could take it from there, but that idea creates its own problems for the YEV. It leaves only three days growth for humanity and animals to eat on Day 6. Plants produce practically nothing useful for humanity in three days. Are we to believe Adam and Eve ate only bean sprouts? No, Genesis says full grown trees were in the garden (Gen. 2:9 and 16-17).

The conclusion about the second proclamation on Day 3 is that it presents a picture of natural growth. That is the way it was meant to be understood. That is the way God said it. The only reason to cram the growing of forests into one day comes from the presupposition that all was completed in six days, but if the presupposition is wrong then the conclusion is wrong too.

Three – Genesis 1:14 says, "Let there be lights in the expanse of the heavens… and let them be for signs and for seasons and for days and years." And then verse 15 adds, "…and it was so", *they were used for signs*. It could not have been "so" that the lights were signs until they were used for that purpose. Therefore, the proclamation on Day 4 could not have been fulfilled on Day 4 because the lights could not have been used for their purposes until humanity arrived on Earth so the fulfillment of the Day 4 proclamation occurred well *after Day 6*, after humanity had time to study the sky. Plants could not use the lights for signs, and animals were not around on Day 4 either. This proclamation could not be fulfilled in a day. I know of no objections to this argument, yet.

Four – On Day 5 the blessing for the sea and flying creatures to "be fruitful and multiply," fill the seas, and multiply on land cannot be accomplished in a day. My first inclination was to write, "I doubt that any YEC will disagree with that," but I was wrong. Jonathon Sarfati's newest book says this, "So now God fills the land with different kinds… a day after He filled the sea and air with them."[38] He is commenting on God making the land full of living creatures on Day 6 and he refers back to Day 5. His assertion just goes to show the assumption with which many YEC approach the text of Genesis. They assume it teaches God did it all in six days and gloss right past the plain literal meaning, i.e. *God blessed the sea creatures to fill the seas*. If God had created the seas full of sea creatures He would not have blessed the sea creatures to do it. Genesis clearly says the sea creatures filled the seas themselves. The point is: there are *definitely* some statements in Genesis 1 that cannot be accomplished in a day. That opens the possibility there are others.

Five – Genesis 1:24-25 says, "Then God said, 'Let the earth bring forth living creatures after their kind: cattle and creeping things and beasts of the earth after their kind'; and it was so. God made the beasts of the earth after their kind, and the cattle after their kind, and everything that creeps on the ground after its kind…" This first proclamation on Day 6 for the land to produce land animals is impossible to fulfill in a day. The land only produces animals by natural processes and we all know that takes longer than a day. But the land could not do its part until God made the land animals. *God making animals did not fulfill the proclamation; it only made it possible for the proclamation to be fulfilled.* That is one of the reasons why verse 25 is out of time sequence with the "and it was so" of verse 24.

Please do not misunderstand what I am saying. Old-Earth Creationists are *creationists*, not Theistic Evolutionists. Because of the proclamation on Day 6, God made land animals "after their kind" so the land could fulfill the proclamation. Take bears for example. Let us say God made four pair and put them in various locations around the Earth.[39] These bears begin to reproduce in their natural habitat based on their circumstances thus fulfilling the proclamation. Because God is wise He made bears with the ability to vary and adapt to changing environmental conditions so they would not quickly go extinct. Through small changes over a long period of time these original bears are now different bear species: Grizzly, Brown, Black, Polar, Kodiak, etc. Can we say God alone accomplished this? Yes and no. Yes, He was ultimately the originator and planner of all of it. And no, the bears were given the ability to reproduce, vary, and adapt *on their own*.

That is not progressive evolution the way secular biology sees it. In fact, I prefer the words de-evolution[40] or devolving to describe it. Even though these new species became better able to survive in their specific environment, overall, bears *devolved* away from their original created form, and various mutations crept in, and genetic information has been lost through extinction in some cases never to be regained. Bears did not evolve from something that was not a bear, but they have devolved into a variety of different bears. Currently, bears have less potential genetic variability and are not getting better with time; they are wearing out like everything else. Common sense tells us that extreme complexity is not self-originating. Intelligence is necessary to make that happen. Common sense also tells us complexity breaks down with time.

Concerning 1:24 one YEC says:

> We have a kind of mediate creation as on the third day (v. 11), for the earth is bidden to produce them or bring them forth... The situation is really very simple, as far as the text is concerned. God could have called forth these creatures by His mere word; instead He speaks the word that enables the earth to bring them forth.[41] [Leupold]

Then referring to verse 25 this same commentator describes God making the animals as "The report as to how God proceeded to carry out the thing He ordains in v. 24..."[42]

Does anyone see the inherent contradiction in those statements? At first, he is saying that God accomplished the proclamation through mediated creation. By definition, mediated creation is *not* directly caused by God, which would have to mean the land bringing forth animals was not done quickly. He says the earth is enabled to bring forth the animals. So how is that done in a day? YEC say God made all the land animals at once on Day 6, but the text says God proclaimed for the earth to bring forth animals. While the land can be visualized producing trees in a highly accelerated fashion I do not believe it is possible for the same to be said of animal production. Are we to imagine highly accelerated animal intercourse, gestation, and birth? That would look bizarre to say the least. On the other hand, if we picture God forming multitudes of animals from the dust of the ground (Gen. 2:19) there is no possible way to describe *that* as the land *producing* animals. Do we believe Gen. 2:19 contradicts Gen. 1:24? No.

This whole issue of YEC struggling to explain mediate creation completely misses the much simpler and straight forward meaning of the text. *Verses 24 and 25 are talking about different events!* God proclaimed for natural reproduction to begin to work on the land, but for that to happen He had to make the animals first. The reason YEC do not see this is because they start with the idea all was fulfilled inside six days so they must interpret the text to say that. But if the presupposition is removed so is any difficulty with the text. The text really is quite simple, but not what YEC do to it.

Six – The second proclamation on Day 6 for humanity to rule the Earth cannot be fulfilled in a day because it had to take humanity longer than that to do it. Notice the subtle way one YEC tries to get around the implications of this proclamation, "Man in reality became the controlling power. Yet there remains – even on the primeval state there remained – much to be achieved by way of a perfect mastery of his whole territory."[43] (Leupold) He is saying man became the ruler but from the start he had a lot to learn to do his job well. *He recognizes that the proclamation by God involved more than just putting man in charge*; it also involved humanity working toward *accomplishing the job*. Genesis 1:26 says, "...let them rule over the fish of the sea and over the birds of the sky and over the cattle and over all the earth [land], and over every creeping thing that creeps on the earth [land]." "Rule" is the *verb* in the sentence, but this YEC says man became the ruler (controlling power – noun). But the proclamation was not "Let man be (or become) the ruler". The text says "let man rule" so when it says "and it was so" (v. 30), it means it came to pass that man actually accomplished ruling, albeit poorly. If the verse only meant God put man in charge then it makes no sense He would tell humanity to subdue and rule in verse 28, because, if it was already true humanity ruled the land, then God would not have had to tell them to accomplish the task. He would have simply told them they were already the rulers.

Regardless of when it happened and to what extent, Genesis 1:30 says "and it was so" (and so it came to pass) concerning the second proclamation on Day 6. That means "it was so" that humanity *accomplished* ruling "the fish of the sea and over the birds of the sky and over the cattle and over all the earth [land], and over every creeping thing that creeps on the earth", at least before 1:30 was written. When and exactly how it was accomplished is not mentioned, but again, the proclamation could not have been accomplished in a day.

Seven – The blessing of the 7th Day was not done on that Day. On this, one YEC says, "Procksch remarks rightly and pointedly: 'for the present the Sabbath stays in heaven.'"[44] (Leupold) What he means is God did not tell humanity of the blessing of the Sabbath on the 7th Day even though he thinks God actually did it then, thus explaining why the wording of the blessing is not recorded as it is to sea and flying creatures, and humanity. But that misses the point that God blessing the Sabbath *on the Sabbath* would have been work, of which according to Genesis 2:1-3 God ceased doing. This remains as another example that all the events recorded on a Day were not done on that Day.

The textual evidence is clear, God did not completely fulfill everything in six days in the same way that He did not fulfill prophecies immediately. YEC still say, "There is no hint of long intervening ages..." And, "...when Genesis 1 declares the formula 'God said...and it was so,' the text does not indicate that it means 'God said...and it took a while.'"[45] As we have just seen, they are wrong.

Genesis speaks of natural processes and the passage of time, "And so it came to pass", and *the text makes it impossible* for everything to have been completed in six days. *The text literally tells us directly*, "God said...and it took a while."

The Sixth Objection to Point 4:

Another objection to Point 4 by YEC goes like this, "...direct creation in a short time magnifies the miraculous creative work of God..."[46] and "In reality, to deny the immediacy of creation's completion is to reduce or diminish the power of God..."[47]

The Short Answer: Timeframes of completion have nothing to do with magnifying God. If God wanted completion time to be an indicator of His power then He would have done it all instantaneously without bothering to take six days. The Young-Earth View does not hold the high ground on magnifying God. Limiting God to any timeframe minimizes God, and neither OEC nor YEC limit God to time regardless of how long they believe the fulfillments took.

The Deep: For YEC to say that OEC "reduce or diminish the power of God" is simply not true. Creationism, *old or young*, magnifies God. To say that God allowed His creations to run their course and mature over time while fulfilling His proclamations does not diminish God's capabilities in any way. YEC have created an either/or fallacy. Either you believe God completed it all immediately or you believe in some kind of naturalistic evolution, but those are not the only choices. The part that God did was miraculous, but the completion of the whole universe could have taken a long time if that is how God wanted it.

We should let the text speak for itself. For example, on Day 6 God proclaimed, "Let the earth bring forth living creatures after their kind". (1:24) But there were no land animals for the land to work with when God said it. OEC do not believe the land created or made the animals in some evolutionary way. God's proclamation could not be fulfilled until God did His part. He first made the animals (how is neither specified nor likely comprehendible except to say, "Out of the ground the LORD God formed every beast of the field and every bird of the sky" – Gen. 2:19), then the land could do what it was proclaimed to do, and once the land did its part, which had to take some time, the proclamation could be said to be fulfilled, "And so it came to pass".

In no way does time diminish God's power, especially when one considers *He inspired it this way*. Just because He did not specify how long it took for the fulfillments to be completed does not reduce His power. This debate is not some kind of contest to see whose view magnifies God more or is the most reliant on miracles. The debate should only be about truth and what the Bible says.

The Seventh Objection to Point 4:

The Young-Earth View has been the traditional view of respected theologians for centuries. The list includes the likes of Basil, Ambrose, Aquinas,

Luther, Calvin, Ussher, Babington, Lightfoot, Wesley, the Puritans, and many more. Surely those great theologians of the past cannot *all* be wrong. If the Bible actually taught the PDV one would think at least one of those great minds would have seen it.

Two YEC (Duncan and Hall) issue this challenge to OEC:

> To present a compelling case, advocates of long days will have to address two key hermeneutical questions by giving more persuasive answers than they have until now.
> - Why do the Old Testament and New Testament fail to allude to long days or slow, developmental creation? In other words, where in Scripture is the affirmative statement to prove that the days of creation refer to anything other than normal days?
> - Why didn't any interpreters discover long days or slow, developmental creation until after certain scientific revolutions? If these interpretations are contrary to the history of exegesis, how can Christians be so convinced that these interpretations are not additional illustrations of conforming Christ to culture?[48]

I love how their two key hermeneutical questions are actually four, but regardless, they are fair questions. It is also very common to see YEC say OEC interpretations of Genesis did not arise until the early 1800's when scientists became convinced the universe and Earth were at least millions of years old. Another YEC puts it this way:

> ...conservative commentators have tried to preserve biblical inerrancy by reinterpreting Genesis to fit with long-age 'science.' The fact that these views were unknown before the rise of uniformitarian 'science' is strong evidence that these views are not grounded in the biblical *text* itself but are a (misguided) *reaction* to this 'science.'[49] [Sarfati – emphasis his]

I cannot deny that OEC interpretations primarily came about because of modern science. And the fact that a long list of distinguished and highly qualified theologians believed the YEV needs a persuasive response. Still, I cannot help but wonder how many of those men would have thought differently if presented with the PDV or the weight of the scientific evidence available these days. Would any of them have changed their mind? We will never know. However, they were only human. They were battling the skeptics of their day with their limited knowledge just as we are now, and they were just as subject to biases and presuppositions as any of us. So, the possibility that the majority of the church has been wrong about a major doctrine for so long is not out of the realm of possibilities. But, strong Biblical and scientific evidence must be provided if the traditional view is to change, and that is what I am trying to do.

There is no short answer. My response is five-fold:

First, I agree with the YEV that the Days of Genesis 1 are normal Earth days so that is why the OT and NT do not allude to anything but normal days.

Chapter 5 – Objections to the Prophetic Days View

All those theologians got that part right. The fact "daylight" is the most natural way to understand "day" as defined in Genesis 1:5, the repeats of the evening and morning phrase, and the general use of numbered days in the OT strongly support that this was a normal week on Earth.[50]

Second, the OT does allude to slow developmental processes and shows everything could not have been fulfilled in six days. We have just seen Genesis gives abundant affirmative support for slow developmental processes.

Third, interpreters *have* known and commented on the texts that show slow processes, but they have (incorrectly) developed ways to explain these "problematic" verses away because they believe(d) all was accomplished in six days. If that presupposition is removed then the difficulties in the text they have had to explain (like the wording of Gen. 1:11-12, 24-25, 2:8-9, which Day God created the Earth, and the out-of-sequence phrases) will go away. Theologians and commentators have seen the difficulties for *thousands*[51] of years, but have insufficiently explained them with the YEV. The YEV thinks the text says all was fulfilled within six days, and then make the problematic texts fit that idea, but by doing so they have it backwards. The text says all was not done, nor fulfilled, in six days and this should make us take a closer look at verses that might *appear* to say otherwise, like Ex. 20:11, 31:17, and the text of Day 7. That thought apparently has come to few at this point in history, probably because no one had a reason to question it until certain scientific revolutions came along.

Fourth, as to why OEC interpretations were not discovered until certain scientific revolutions, the answer is because they did not need them until then. No one questioned the Bible with any good evidence the universe or Earth were very old until then. This is no different than Galileo and Copernicus causing some to question the interpretation of Biblical passages that seemed to say the Earth does not move and the Sun revolves around us (Josh. 10:12-13, Ps. 104:5, 113:3, etc.). These verses are written from our perspective on the surface of the Earth.[52] Also, let us not forget the passages that say the earth (land) has four corners (Is. 11:12, Rev. 7:1). These are common expressions of the day regarding the four primary directions or boundaries of the land, not cosmological statements of the shape of the planet. The point is, science *does* affect our interpretation of some Biblical verses despite oversimplified comments by YEC like, "Nothing is on par with Scripture. We are to interpret nature in light of Scripture, not vice versa."[53] Or, "Scripture, not science, is the ultimate test of all truth."[54] If we were to take those statements in a modern scientifically literal sense then we would have to conclude the Bible says the Earth does not move and the Sun rotates around us. The *only reason* the original Bible interpretation was reexamined is because scientists clearly proved beyond doubt Earth orbits the Sun.

One of the reasons we know Scripture *is* Scripture is because the books that claim to be from God are verifiable by history, archaeology, biology, astronomy, cosmology, theology, philosophy, fulfilled prophecy, etc. In short, the Bible is verifiable. If the Bible is inspired then true science will not contradict it. That is why this whole issue of the age of the Earth is controversial. It is possible a faulty interpretation has blinded the eyes of theologians for hundreds of years because no one saw any reason to question it and had no concept to interpret it any other way, except to take the opposite extreme like Augustine's argument an omnipotent God would not have taken six days to complete it, but did it all instantly. Without a challenge, doctrines do not change.

And *fifth*, my interpretation is "not additional illustrations of conforming Christ to culture" if it is what the Bible really says, which I believe I have demonstrated. I believe "the history of exegesis" of Genesis 1 has forced interpretations of immediate fulfillment on the text because it has missed an important point:

Point 4 – The fulfillments of the proclamations (prophecies) that God said on the 6 Days were not all meant to be understood as fulfilled or initiated *within* the Day they were given.

Objections to Point 3: The creation account is given by God to humanity from our perspective, as if we were watching what God was doing from the surface of the Earth.

This whole section on Point 3 is deep water: The idea that Genesis 1 is written from our perspective on the surface of the Earth is not new. Even some YEC agree, "…from this point [1:2] onward the point of approach may be said to be geocentric."[55] (Leupold) And, "From this point on [1:2], the entire creation account is told from the perspective of an observer on earth."[56] (MacArthur) So the controversial issues are not necessarily the perspective of Genesis, but the way the PDV and other OEC views apply this perspective to interpreting the events of Genesis 1:2 and Days 1, 2, and 4. Taking another look at each is our task then.

Genesis 1:2 – From the perspective of the surface of Earth, Genesis 1:2 says, "and darkness was over the surface of the deep." It was dark on the surface of the Earth only, not in the entire universe. YEC see it differently, "All of what had thus far come into being was wrapped in complete and absolute darkness."[57] (Leupold) And, the universe "was also engulfed in total, absolute darkness."[58] (MacArthur) These statements are made by their authors without any supporting evidence from the text. They are only assumed to be true because of a belief the light of Day 1 is the first light to ever exist anywhere, so the darkness in verse 2 must be "complete and absolute". But that is not what the text says. Verse 2 should lead the way to interpret verse 3, not vice versa. *Verse 2 specifically and explicitly tells us where it was dark,* "over the surface of the deep". To add to that statement is to go beyond the text.

Job 38:4-12 is *devastating* to the YEV on this. Not only does it explain why it was dark on the Earth (because of the swaddling of thick clouds), it also says the "morning stars" and "sons of God" (both references to angels) were present when Earth's foundations were laid and they sang and shouted for joy. Now, if all that was done in "complete and absolute darkness" how did the angels know what was happening? And why would *God* describe this to Job referring to angels as "morning stars" if light and stars were completely absent at the time?

Chapter 5 – Objections to the Prophetic Days View

The YEV has gone *far beyond* what the text of Genesis 1:2 says when they interpret it to mean no light whatsoever existed in the universe prior to Earth's creation. The Bible only says it was dark on Earth.

Day 1 – If the darkness from verse 2 is only on the Earth then the light that appeared on Day 1 is also *only on the Earth*. Just to make that clear God called it "day". God did not make it day in the entire universe. He made it day *in the only place that makes sense*, on Earth. *The light of Genesis 1:3 is only the day on Earth, not in the entire universe.*

Even some old-Earth commentators take the opposite view:

> …the least satisfactory explanation…is that which understands the sun to have been created a perfectly finished luminous body from the first, though hitherto its light had been intercepted by the earth's vapours, which were now dispersed by Divine command. But the language of Elohim is too exalted to be applied to so familiar a phenomenon as the dissipation of terrestrial mists, and, besides, expressly negatives the hypothesis in question by affirming that the light was summoned into *being*, and not simply into *appearance*.[59] [Whitelaw]

Three problems exist with his arguments. *First*, to say Day 1 refers to the original production of light in the universe because of "exalted" language is a poor argument. Even if the light is appearing only on Earth for the first time it still exalts God. The text tells us later (1:16) God made the Sun and stars, so the idea God is the Creator of all light is not lost. *Second*, the *initial* "dissipation of terrestrial mists" is not a familiar phenomenon. Job 38:4-12 specifically describes why it was dark on the Earth and it was because of terrestrial mists. Nothing like that has happened on the Earth since. And *third*, from the perspective of the surface of Earth light did come to be after being "summoned into *being*". It was not on the surface before Day 1 so it can be described as coming into being *on the surface of the Earth*.

Every clue from the text (listed in Chapter 2) says the light from Day 1 is only referring to light coming to be on the surface of Earth for the first time.

Day 2 – The separation of the "waters above" from the "waters below" is only occurring on Earth. I have already covered in Chapter 2 some of the more recent YEC ideas that these waters represent invisible waters in outer space, either at the edge of the solar system or universe, and how ironic it is YEC are trying to make the text fit *their science*, something to which they claim to be radically opposed when OEC try it. Sarfati picks up on the idea the "waters above" were something other than rain and attempts to use II Peter 3:5, *"the earth was formed out of water and by water,"* to prove his point. He says II Peter "…suggests that God first created an enormous ball of water"[60] and "One plausible understanding is that water was the raw material that God transformed into the other substances of the earth."[61] That is an "enormous" burden to put on II Peter 3:5, especially when it has such an easy better interpretation. Peter was not saying God made the universe out of water, he was simply saying God caused the land to form up out of the water (dry land appearing – Gen. 1:9) and

81

water *shaped* the surface of the land, as any observant person can tell. Even Sarfati sees it but then denies it because of a faulty interpretation of II Peter, "But were it not for that Peter passage, the phrase 'the dry land *appeared*' gives the impression of *pre-existing* land released by the gathering of water."[62]

On the other hand, many commentators see the waters above the expanse as nothing more than the clouds and rain, as I do. "The 'waters above' the sky is likely a reference to the clouds."[63] (Sailhamer) "The *upper* waters are... the waters floating about in the higher spaces of the air."[64] (Whitelaw) "These clouds constitute the upper waters."[65] (Leupold) The simplicity of the Genesis account to speak from the human perspective on the surface of Earth comes through loud and clear.

Day 4 – The lights are proclaimed to come to be "in the expanse of the heavens" and from the perspective of the surface of Earth that means the expanse (clear space) expanded out to include the lights that were already there. Genesis 1:2 and Job 38:9 describe Earth's surface in complete darkness because of thick clouds. There was no expanse (clear space). Then light comes to be on the surface for the first time as a result of the proclamation on Day 1, but there is still no clear space. God proclaims on Day 2 for an expanse to be "in the midst" (between) the waters, and though a clear space now exists, it is *limited* to the space between the surface waters and the clouds where God proclaimed it to be. Then on Day 4, God proclaimed for this expanding clear space to expand out to include the Sun, Moon, and stars. This interpretation of Day 4 is not entirely new though practically no thought is given by any commentators on why the phrase "in the expanse of the heavens" is repeated three times in the text of Day 4. God is emphasizing for us, though many are missing it, that it was the *location* of the lights from our perspective on Earth that He proclaimed, *not their origination*. The clear space below the clouds was now going to expand to include the lights that were above the clouds. I am not aware of anyone commenting on that interpretation of Day 4 because everyone I have read has ignored the repeat of the phrase and its significance.[66]

However, many from various views have commented on the idea Day 4 only represents the appearing of the lights rather than the making of the lights.

So consider their objections to this Day 4 interpretation:

First, one YEC says, "This does not, however, now mean that 'the atmosphere being completely purified – the sun, moon and stars were for the first time unveiled in all their glory in the cloudless sky' (Jamieson), for such a result would have been achieved automatically without divine fiat by the work of the second day."[67] (Leupold)

This objection assumes too much for the proclamation of Day 2. That proclamation was for an expanse to come to be "in the midst of the waters" (1:6). On Day 2 the waters above (clouds) cannot be assumed to have cleared enough to see outer space, especially considering that they were thick enough prior to Day 1 to make the surface of Earth completely dark. Also, if the source of the light was visible on Day 2 then the expanse would not have been "in the midst of the waters" the way the text specifically says. Based on the proclamation on Day 2, it took another proclamation by God to clear the atmosphere sufficiently to make outer space visible rather than it happening "automatically without divine fiat" on Day 2.

Second, Sarfati says, "If God had *meant* 'appeared,' then He presumably would have *used* the Hebrew word for appear (*ra'ah*), as He did when He said that the dry land 'appeared' as the waters gathered in one place on day 3 (Gen. 1:9)."[68] This objection is in reference to 1:16 saying God "made" (*asah*) the lights, not "made them appear".

Should God have used the Hebrew word for "appear" (*ra'ah*) if He was telling us the Sun, Moon, and stars only became visible because of the proclamation on Day 4 rather than being made as a result of the fiat? How God chose to tell us something is His business. I do not want to presume to say what God should or should not have said. I believe He used the word *hayah* ("Let there be") specifically because something new needed to happen for the lights to "come to be" (*hayah*) *in the expanse of the heavens*. It took God's actions for the clear space (expanse) to expand beyond the cloud layer to include the lights. The delicate balance necessary for Earth to have a transparent atmosphere should not be taken lightly. If it had said, "And God made the lights appear" in verse 16 then Genesis would not have specified the origin of the Sun, Moon, and stars. Instead, the word *hayah* is used to proclaim the expanse to include the lights and then we are parenthetically told (verse 16) God made the lights.

Third, some insist that the use of the verb "to be" (*hayah*) at the beginning of verse 14 *requires* the lights to come into existence. Meaning, by using *hayah* the text *has to mean* the Sun, Moon, and stars could not have preexisted Day 4. "If one admits that this fiat language describes divine origination when used on the other days, consistency demands that the same meaning be applied to Day 4."[69] (Irons and Kline) Does the use of the verb "to be" in the proclamations have to always mean God originated something? Yes, but *we must be very careful to understand what is proclaimed to be, because every word from God is used here purposefully*. For a long time I thought God had proclaimed for the Sun, Moon, and stars to come into existence on Day 4, but *that is not what is proclaimed*. God did not say, "Let there be lights" and stop there. He said, "Let there be lights in the expanse of the heavens…" *The location of the Sun, Moon, and stars is what is proclaimed.*

Maybe this will help clarify. If, as a result of God's proclamation on Day 4, the sky cleared enough for the Sun to become visible from the surface of the Earth, could it be said that the Sun came to be "in the expanse of the heavens"? Yes, God said, "Let there be lights *in the expanding-clear-space of the heavens*" and that is what happened, the clear space expanded to include the lights. What needs to be understood is that prior to the proclamation on Day 4, and *from the perspective of the surface of the Earth*, the lights *did not exist in the clear space* (expanse). After the proclamation, what did not exist before (the Sun, Moon, and stars *in* the expanding clear space) came to exist, but the Sun, Moon, and stars could have preexisted the expanse. It is not the lights themselves that are coming to be, it is the *location* of the lights *in the expanse* that is coming to be. Were the lights *in the expanse* prior to the proclamation of Day 4? No. Were the lights in existence prior to Day 4? The text does not say, so they could have been.

Something was causing the light. We should let God's word define what the expanse is and it did on Day 2. The expanse *was* the clear space *between* the seas and the clouds. Now as a result of the proclamation on Day 4, the clear space (expanse) includes the Sun, Moon, and stars.

Fourth, and related to the third objection, many say the use of the verb *hayah* (to be) "...signifies the producing of objects... Contextual evidence makes it unmistakably clear that the [and it was so] of fulfillment signifies an act of production."[70] (Irons and Kline) That would mean that not only must *hayah* mean a coming into existence, but it also means God would have to *produce* something associated with His proclamation, and because verse 16 says God made the lights, He would have to have made the lights *on Day 4*. I agree and disagree. I agree that the use of *hayah* signifies production of something. What God said must come to pass and something new would have to be produced, but I disagree that it is the lights themselves that need to be produced. Again, it is the location of the lights that was proclaimed, and to fulfill the proclamation does not take a production of the lights, but it does take a production of the expansion of the clear space.

Fifth, YEC simply believe Genesis 1:16 says the Sun, Moon, and stars were made *on Day 4*. "The straightforward meaning of the text... is that God made things in the sequence given, and on day 4 He made the heavenly bodies..."[71] (Williams and Hartnett) Chapter 2 showed that is clearly not true. The straightforward meaning of the text of Day 4 is that *it is non-sequential* and *the making of the heavenly bodies is not what was proclaimed*. There is no possible way to make it sequential because the proclamation is said to be fulfilled before the making of the lights is mentioned, and *the proclamation could not be fulfilled in a day* because it could not be fulfilled until humanity used the lights for their proclaimed purpose. Day 4 is plainly not as simple as he said.

However, one of the few who recognized that verse 16 is out of chronological order with verses 14 and 15 says this, "...the account of how the original order was carried out affords sufficient variety of form to serve as a commentary upon the first statement of v. 14, 15. Stereotyped repetition would be both mechanical and wearisome."[72] (Leupold) He is dismissing the out-of-sequence problem as a variety of form because to write each Day in the same order would be "mechanical and wearisome". Also, he says verses 16 and 17 "...give detail to the fulfillment..."[73] This view that verse 16 gives more detail of how the fulfillment was done still does not answer the original question, "*Why is verse 16 out of sequence?*" If the "and it was so" came after "And God made" (*like Day 2*) we would not be having this conversation because Day 4 could be understood as sequential. "Variety of form" is a poor reason for the textual sequence. Surely God had more in mind than mixing up the order just to not sound "mechanical and wearisome". God purposefully reversed the order for good reason, like He did in the latter proclamation of Day 3 and the first proclamation on Day 6, and *YEC do not have a good answer why*. Most of them just pass by the problem and assert verse 16 says God made the lights on Day 4.

In response, close attention should be paid to what is listed after the fulfillment phrases of each Day. If you look at each phrase after each fulfillment phrase on each Day you will see that *in every case the phrases after the fulfillment do not fulfill the proclamation.*[74] It makes perfect sense the text does not say more about how the fulfillment was done *after* the fulfillment phrase. The pattern of the Days is the fulfillment is mentioned and what follows is extra information, but it is not detail of how the fulfillment was accomplished. *God listed verse 16 out of sequence because it is not what fulfilled the proclamation.* If verse 16 does not refer to the fulfillment, and is out of chronological order, then the events it describes could have preceded the proclamation.

The conclusion then is that God *did not* proclaim for the Sun, Moon, and stars to come into existence on Day 4. He proclaimed for the Sun, Moon, and stars to come to be in the expanding-clear-space of the heavens, and that is what happened. The clear space expanded to include them so that, from our perspective on Earth, they are now in the expanse.

To conclude the objections to Point 3: *Genesis says* it was dark *only* over the surface of the deep, not in the entire universe. Light came to be on Day 1 on the surface of Earth *only*, not in the entire universe. The expanse of Day 2 was the transparent clear space limited to being between the seas and the clouds. As a result of the proclamation on Day 4 the transparent clear space expanded to include the Sun, Moon, and stars thus making it possible for us to see them from the surface. Based on the text, the YEV is deficient in offering good alternative explanations. Also, this perspective of the account has significant applications to interpreting other Scriptures, particularly Exodus 20:11 and 31:17. Point 3 and its applications remain intact:

Point 3 – The creation account is given by God to humanity from our perspective, as if we were watching what God was doing from the surface of the Earth.

Objections to Point 2: The "beginning" in Genesis 1:1 was an unspecified *block of time*, not a moment, in which God initially created "the heavens and the earth" before the 7 Days.

No deep water here: People think of the beginning of something as the very first moment of its existence or the specific place where it starts, but according to Hebrew scholar John Sailhamer[75] the Bible has something much broader in mind when using the word "beginning" (*reshith*). *Reshith* refers to the first part of the whole of something[76] and, in the case of Genesis 1:1, is referring to *a block of time*, not a specific moment. Within that block of time God created the heavens and Earth. Because this has implications on any Biblical age estimate of the universe and Earth this definition of "the beginning" naturally has its opponents. Though one YEC praised Sailhamer as "...among the first rank of Hebrew and Old Testament scholars"[77] YEC must disagree with his position. Those who disagree identify three issues:

First, "According to Sailhamer, *bereshit* [In the beginning] tells us that God created the universe over a period of time, rather than a single instant. But this is a very dubious conclusion indeed. *Qal* perfect verbs, which refer to actions (such as *bara*, 'created') rather than states of being, indicate an event not a process."[78] In response, I agree creation was an event and not a process, but the initial event(s) may have had long lasting multiple secondary effects. The "beginning" is the timeframe where possibly numerous events of creation, or the effects of the initial event, took place, like God creating time and space, energy and matter, the heavens and Earth; or where events occurred we are not told about, like God creating angels or distant galaxies; or where events occurred we are not given specific details about, like how and when God formed the Earth.

Second, "...the notion of a unique self-existent God bringing everything into being through creation *ex nihilo* (John 1:3) would be lost."[79] How would it be lost? God is still the one doing the creating out of nothing (*ex nihilo*). Just because He may have chosen to create numerous times over an extended period of time, and chose to let creation run its course for a while, makes no difference to creation out of nothing. God is still the one who set up the initial conditions of the universe which speaks powerfully for creation *ex nihilo*.

Third: YEC offer this counter argument:

> ...even if *bereshit* was understood as [suggested], there is no basis for claiming that it could refer to a *long* period of time. Rather, it would merely represent an unspecified period of time. Zedekiah [Jer. 28:1] reigned for 11 years so 'in the beginning of the reign of Zedekiah' most likely refers to the first few years of his reign. It should be clear that 'the beginning' refers to a much smaller amount of time compared with the total time in which the king reigned.[80]

In the verses I used to support Point 2 (Gen. 10:10, Job 8:7, 42:12, Jer. 28:1, Hos. 9:10) what he says above "should be clear" is not so clear. In Genesis 10 the timeframe is not specified so we cannot assume it was shorter. In Job the beginning could have been longer than the end, but again we are not told so one should not assume. For Zedekiah *the timeframe is specified* and the beginning amounts to 40% of the total (4 years 5 months/11 years) which is definitely not "much smaller" than the whole. In Hosea the beginning is measured in years.

Based on these examples, the best that can be concluded of the portion of time occupied by the "beginning" compared to the whole is that it is of *comparable length*. The YEC author above is mainly using this argument against Sailhamer's view of Genesis (the Limited-Creation View) where there is a *huge* difference between the time occupied by the "beginning" (billions of years) and the time since (thousands). However, I will agree the "beginning" is comparable to the time period after it thus alleviating any issue with this objection.[81]

None of these objections are substantive enough to overturn Point 2.

Point 2 – The "beginning" in Genesis 1:1 was an unspecified *block of time*, not a moment, in which God initially created "the heavens and the earth" before the 7 Days.

Chapter 5 – Objections to the Prophetic Days View

Objections to Point 1: **The Earth existed an unspecified amount of time *before* the 7 Days started.**

Not too deep at first: Point 1 was the first textual difficulty I encountered as a YEC. Textually the YEV is incapable of putting the creation of the heavens and Earth within the 6 Days. In addition it seemed odd to me that no recorded proclamation by God ever said, "Let there be a heavens and an earth." Each Day records a proclamation and its fulfillment, but there is no proclamation for the initial creation. Genesis 1:1 mentions the initial creation of the heavens and Earth, and after that their existence is assumed in the text. Genesis 1:2 then gives the condition of the Earth *before* the 7 Days began.

This interpretation of the text is contrary to the YEV which insists *the entire universe* was completed in six days. Rather than let Genesis interpret Exodus the YEV has reversed it and insisted on pressing *their interpretation* of Exodus 20:11 and 31:17 onto Genesis. If the YEV insists all was done in six days then what Day do they say "the heavens and the earth" were created? They really have only two choices because if they agree with me the heavens and Earth were created before the 7 Days, even if only for the tiniest fraction of a second, then *it cannot be true all was completed in six days*. Their two choices are Day's 1 and 3. The most common choice is Day 1, but Day 3 is gaining an audience.

Does Genesis say the heavens and land were created *on Day 1*? The evidence in Chapter 2 shows it does not and the YEV at this point has nothing in print[82] I could find responding to the six evidences I gave: **(1)** Nowhere on any of the 6 Days *between* the phrase "Then God said..." and the evening and morning phrase does the text say anything about the creation of Earth. **(2)** Genesis 1:2 says "The earth was..." and this is mentioned before Day 1 starts with "Then God said..." **(3)** Each Day has a fulfillment that matches each Day's proclamation and none of the Days has a proclamation for the creation of the Earth. **(4)** The light had to be there before the 7 Days could be measured, and the Earth was there in darkness before the light, therefore the Earth had to be there before the 7 Days. **(5)** The Hebrew verb structure places verses 1-2 outside the main narrative before Day 1. **(6)** Job 38:4-12 has the same order of events as Genesis (Earth's foundations laid, Earth covered in darkness, and then light dawns).

Still YEC insist the creation of the heavens and Earth must have occurred on Day 1. Explicit statements to that effect are not hard to find, "Verse one is the record of the first part of the work brought into being on the first day: first the heavens and the earth in a basic form as to their material, then light. These two things constitute what God created on the first day."[83] (Leupold) He offers no supporting evidence to this statement and likely assumes most readers will just take his word for it, and many do, but saying it is so does not make it so. The text is clear on the fivefold pattern followed by the 6 Days: proclamation, fulfillment, action (though sometimes actions are before the fulfillment), the evening and morning phrase, and a numbered day.[84] That being the case, *we cannot just assume something mentioned outside that pattern belongs in it.* Textual evidence would be needed, but there is none.

Two main YEC arguments attempt to put the creation of the heavens and Earth on Day 1, and the responses are not too deep:

First, many point out that the Jews measure their days from sundown to sundown so darkness is the first part of a day. Therefore, the heavens and Earth could have been created during Day 1's darkness and the light appears half-way through Day 1. The problem with that argument is the Jews began reckoning a day from sunset to sunset as a result of God's command later in history than Genesis (Ex. 12:18, Lev. 23:32). Genesis 1 defines for us that its Days begin with sunrise. *The fact God later commanded them to reverse it implies they were previously measuring it the other way.*

Each Day of Genesis (except the 7th) ends with "and there was evening and there was morning [the nth] day." What should not be missed is that *evening is mentioned first*. Why? Because, *evening is the first to occur after the daylight*. God worked (by proclamation) during the daylight hours, and then evening came, and then morning came, and the text says nothing of what God did at night, i.e. between evening and morning.[85] He was presumably setting the pattern for humanity by ceasing (resting) until sunrise the next day. That this has to be the meaning of the evening and morning phrase is evident simply by the order of the text, "And there was evening and there was morning, one day."[86] The evening *and* morning *follow* the "day" (light) and then that becomes the "one day". The text mentions morning before it numbers the Day. Even some YEC badly misunderstand the phrase, "…the evening and morning mark the *beginning* and end of a day respectively."[87] (Sarfati – emphasis his) However, the text cannot be understood to mean one day was from evening to morning because *that is only half a day*. In Genesis the nighttime of each Day is *between* evening and morning and follows its daylight. Therefore, the heavens and Earth were not created during the darkness of Day 1 because Day 1's darkness *followed* its daylight as the text literally reads.

Second, some want to interpret Genesis 1:1 as only a summary phrase for the whole creation account because the phrase "the heavens and the earth" is a Hebrew figure of speech for "the all" or "the universe". As a summary of the whole account Genesis 1:1 would thus not be part of the narrative sequence of the account, leaving open the possibility the Earth was created on Day 1.

Though I agree the phrase is a figure of speech and performs the function of an introduction and title, I do not agree that verse 1 is a summary. The heavens and Earth as used in verse 1 only refer to "the all" *up to that point in time*. It did not include all that was to be done as a result of the proclamations on the 6 Days. This is evident by Genesis 2:1, "Thus the heavens and the earth were completed, and all their hosts." The extra phrase "and all their hosts" is completely unnecessary if "the heavens and the earth" meant absolutely everything. The extra phrase is added to clarify that *2:1 refers to more than 1:1* because 2:1 now includes all that was done as a result of the 6 Days.

Genesis 1:1 makes more sense as part of the narrative sequence, and therefore not a summary. It tells us God first created the heavens and Earth during an unspecified block of time called "the beginning", and then He did His 6 Day work to prepare the Earth for our habitation because it was uninhabitable as described in 1:2. Then He fulfilled His proclamations over another unspecified amount of time leading up to placing Adam and Eve in the garden.

Day 1 does not work textually for the Earth's creation.

If the Earth was not made on Day 1, what about Day 3? Matthew Henry (1662-1714) shows the influence of Greek cosmology[88] on interpretations of Genesis when he writes concerning the use of "earth" in verse 1, "A chaos was the first matter. It is here called the earth (though the earth, properly taken, was not made till the third day *v*. 10), because it did most resemble that which afterwards was called earth..."[89] He interpreted the description of Earth in Genesis 1:2, "without form and void" (KJV), as meaning Earth was then only a "shapeless"[89] chaos of matter, not a planet. Then, because the word *erets* (earth/land) in verse 10 is the same word used in verse 1, he took the *appearing* of dry ground on Day 3 as the making of the *whole Earth* in its present form. By suggesting Day 3 Matthew Henry recognized the need for the YEV to insert the creation of Earth somewhere within the 6 Days to maintain their belief all was completed in that time.

More recently and dressed in modern scientific language this idea Earth was made on Day 3 has been revived. One author[90] advocates a Day 3 creation based on a Young-Earth scientific hypothesis the universe formed in a rapid expansion of something unknown from which God first formed matter/energy/light on Day 1, then separated the initial matter (waters?) into two parts on Day 2, then formed the Earth from the inner part on Day 3, and then formed the rest of the universe (galaxies, stars, and all) from the outer part on Day 4. He says,

> So, [Gen 1:2] informs us that the initial earth (a) had no form or structure, (b) had not inhabitants of components, (c) was a 'deep' or 'abyss', which was dark (at least on the surface, but no light yet means it was dark throughout), and (d) was a 'waters' or 'liquid'...[91]

Please note that he says the initial earth *was* "a 'deep'" and *was* "a 'waters'" or liquid, meaning it had no resemblance to a solid planet. He says,

> [The earth] was amorphous, empty, dark, deep and liquid (or possibly gaseous, all of it) and it had (an amorphous) surface. It was a 'lump of clay' (raw material), ready to be made into what God had in mind. Furthermore, as we see later in the text, a major portion of the initial earth was probably used to make things other than the planet.[92]

He says it was not until Day 3 that the Earth as a planet was formed. Prior to that the "earth" was "formless" in the manner he describes. This same author agrees Genesis 1:2 should be translated as "formless"[93], meaning not formed.

The Short Answer: Are we to think Genesis 1 is only now comprehendible in modern times after this YEC hypothesis has arrived? No, the Genesis account was written in simple terms that all people at all times could understand as I advocated in Chapter 1. Ancient peoples to whom this account was written understood it from the only perspective they could know: *Genesis tells us the origin of the land and sky from the perspective of the land.* It speaks from a human perspective without telling us we are standing on a planet orbiting a star. Therefore, the description of Earth in Genesis 1:2 is best understood as describing a time when the condition of the land (not planet) was uninhabitable, uninhabited, wet, and dark. *That is easy for anyone to understand regardless of when they lived.* Trying to make Genesis conform to a bad modern scientific hypothesis by contorting the meaning of simple words in Hebrew to represent complicated concepts in English is "gross eisegesis"[94] of the highest degree. Also, Genesis 1:2 is not telling us the land "was a 'deep'" and "was a 'waters'". *Obviously, land and deep water are physically different.* Genesis is telling us the land was there, but it was *wet*, and God caused dry-ground to "appear" (1:9), not be created. That is the best, easiest, and most natural way to interpret it.

The Deep: More specifically I have five responses to these arguments Earth was created on Day 3:

First, the phrase "formless and void" is better translated as "desolate and lifeless".[95] Genesis 1:2 is not describing the chaotic matter of an unformed planet floating in space. It is describing the condition of Earth as it would have been to a hypothetical observer (the hearer of the story) before God began His six-day work. That condition is best understood from the point of view of a fully formed planet with a dark "surface" wet with water from the "deep". If "formless and void" referred to a chaotic mass then Jeremiah 4:23 would be describing the land again becoming a chaotic formless mass because it uses *the exact same phrase* as Genesis 1:1, but Jeremiah was describing how Judah could become "desolate and lifeless", like a desert. He was not describing how Judah could become a formless cloud of floating space debris.

Second, the evening and morning phrase becomes meaningless on Day's 1 and 2 if planet Earth is not created until Day 3. How can you have evening and morning on a *formless* chaotic "amorphous" mass of matter? And how can you call it "day" and "night" without a dark and light side of a planet? The Hebrew is simple. Turning it into complicated modern cosmology is just wrong.

Third, when Genesis 1:9 says "...let dry land appear" it does not use the Hebrew word for land (*erets*). The words "dry land" are one word in Hebrew.[96] God did not proclaim for planet Earth to form, only dry ground to "appear" out of the deep waters of an existent submerged landscape. The use of the verb "appear" indicates the land was *already there* but underwater and unseen from the surface and *God bid it to be seen, not be created.* It became *visible* above the surface of the water; it did not form from water. Calling it "dry" also implies the land was there but wet. Psalm 104:5-9 clearly speaks of the initial land rising out of the water.

Fourth, when Genesis 1:10 says "God called the dry land earth" it means to narrow the focus of the account to the dry ground on which we live rather than all land (including what was underwater).[97] It is not equating causing dry ground to appear by creating planet Earth.

Fifth, by saying "a major portion of the initial earth was probably used to make things other than the planet" this author has redefined the initial "earth" as something completely foreign to the meaning of the Hebrew word (*erets*). His statement is also a severe understatement because he believes the separation of the waters mentioned on Day 2 separated the substances of what would become the Earth from what would become *the rest of the universe*. That would *not* mean a "major portion" of the initial Earth was used for something else, it would mean practically all of the substance was used for something else because the mass of Earth compared to the universe is so insignificant it makes his argument meaningless.

This same author also calls it erroneous to presuppose "the definition of 'heavens' and 'earth' rather than allowing the text to define those terms..."[98] However, the account was written in a language (Hebrew) wherein the words *already had definitions*. A certain level of definition *must* be presupposed to make sense of any narrative. No narrative defines every word it uses (which is impossible) and Genesis is no different. Genesis 1:1 says, "In the beginning God created the heavens and the earth" and the words "heavens" (*shamayim*) and "earth" (*erets*) have the respective meanings of *all that is above the land* and *the land upon which we stand.*[99]

The bottom line is the Earth was not created on Day 3 either.

Genesis does not say the Earth was created on any of the 6 Days. It says it was created in a time called "the beginning" which was before God's work week. Therefore, Genesis 1 plainly says *everything was not completed within six days*. Point 1 remains intact also.

Point 1 – The Earth existed an unspecified amount of time *before* the 7 Days started.

Conclusion of Chapter 5

In concluding this chapter some might think I forgot Point 5. The reason I did not start with Point 5 is because it is a valid conclusion based on the premises of Points 2 and 4. Because, as far as I can tell, Points 1-4 are true, and what Genesis actually says, and remain intact after all objections I could find, or think of, have been answered (except the big one answered in the next chapter), Point 5 is also a sound conclusion to the Prophetic Days View. Genesis does not commit itself to any particular age of the universe and Earth. Because Genesis leaves the question open, any age scientists assign to the universe and Earth does not contradict the Bible. Thus, the controversy over the age of the Earth becomes a non-issue.

I believe strongly the Prophetic Days View is the correct view of Genesis 1, what the author meant to say, and the view the original audience would have understood. It is the most faithful literal historical view of the text, and contains the least problems with science.

The Five Points of the Prophetic Days View of Genesis 1

Point 1 – The Earth existed an unspecified amount of time *before* the 7 Days started.

Point 2 – The "beginning" in Genesis 1:1 was an unspecified *block of time*, not a moment, in which God initially created "the heavens and the earth" before the 7 Days.

Point 3 – The creation account is given by God to humanity from our perspective, as if we were watching what God was doing from the surface of the Earth.

Point 4 – The fulfillments of the proclamations (prophecies) that God said on the 6 Days were not all meant to be understood as fulfilled or initiated *within* the Day they were given.

Point 5 – Because the "beginning" was an unspecified block of time before the 6 Days (Point 2), and the prophecies given on those Days were not all completely fulfilled on the Days given (Point 4), *Genesis does not tell us the age of the universe and Earth.*

6

Death *Before* the Fall
(The depths of this topic need to be fathomed by all.)

Technically this chapter does not address an objection aimed solely at the Prophetic Days View. It addresses the biggest objection repeatedly applied against almost every Old-Earth Creationist view. As one YEC puts it, "Probably the most serious problem with all compromise views of Genesis is the origin of death and suffering."[1] (Sarfati) The YEV is most zealously defended because many believe a god who would allow the death of animals before the Fall cannot be the good God of the Bible. Having to accept death before the Fall is a huge obstacle that prevents many YEC from becoming OEC. To some YEC this problem is so severe that if Earth really is billions of years old they have said it would destroy their faith.[2] Hopefully, they will soon see this objection is not as serious for Old-Earth Creationism as some think.

Let me be blunt: If geology, and OEC in general, are correct then the fossil record is a long history of death and disease *of animals* stretching back millions of years before Adam and Eve, and God would have to be responsible for it, and all of it would have to be considered "very good" by Biblical standards. Do those thoughts bother you? If so, I want to ask you "why?" Is your moral repulse to those ideas really a result of Biblical teaching or is it purely *a feeling* animal death cannot be very good?

Two things need emphasis before this objection is answered:

First, only God defines what is good and He does so in His word, the Bible. If we are going to call something evil or "not good" we must make sure the Bible calls it that. Often our feelings will lead us astray on determining right and wrong because they are affected by cultural influences that might not be Biblical. Though our conscience is a good tool created and used by God to guide moral behavior, we must not forget we are fallen sinful creatures with a heart that is "more deceitful than all else" (Jer. 17:9) and even in the regenerated state of being "born again" this depravity is a fight to overcome (Rms. 7:14-25). It is to the Bible we must turn to judge our thinking and feeling about what is good and evil.

Second, the only issue here is animal death. Most OEC[3] believe humans would not have died prior to the Fall, and death came upon *all men* because of Adam's sin. As for animals, because the fossil record shows animal death by predation, natural processes, and disaster, and shows animals that had diseases like cancer and gout, the issue here is whether this contradicts the Bible or not. Why would God have created nature that way? Are all predation and disease evil and a result of the Fall? Just because some may think a pride of lions tearing a live zebra apart is cruel and repulsive, does that mean it never happened prior to sin entering the world? Does the Bible teach there was absolutely no pain and disease of animals prior to the Fall? The Bible must be the one to tell us directly, not someone's overzealous interpretation of the Bible, or someone's feelings that animal death is bad.

Sometimes even Young-Earth Creationists like Ken Ham make surprisingly candid admissions like, "...there is no verse of Scripture that specifically teaches that there was no animal death before sin. However, there are passages of Scripture that, when taken together, lead to conclude this."[4] Their circumstantial case for no animal death before sin is succinctly summarized in the following quote which will serve as the outline for answering their claims. They make nine points:

> Genesis 1 says six times that God called the creation "good," and when He finished creation on Day 6, [1] He called everything "very good." Man and animals and birds [2] were originally vegetarian (Gen. 1:29-30, plants are not "living creatures," as people and animals are, according to Scripture). But Adam and Eve sinned, resulting in [3] the judgment of God on the whole creation. Instantly Adam and Eve [4] died spiritually, and after God's curse they began to die physically. The serpent and Eve were changed physically and the ground itself was [5] cursed (Genesis 3:14-19). The whole creation now groans in [6] bondage to corruption, waiting for the final redemption of Christians (Romans 8:19-25) when we will see the [7] restoration of all things (Acts 3:21; Colossians 1:20) to a state similar to the pre-Fall world, when there will be no more carnivorous behavior (Isaiah 11:6-9) and no disease, suffering, or death (Revelation 21:3-5) because there will be no more Curse (Revelation 22:3). To accept millions of years of animal death before the creation and Fall of man contradicts and destroys the Bible's teaching on death and [8] the full redemptive work of Christ. It also makes God into a bumbling, [9] cruel creator who uses (or can't prevent) disease, natural disasters, and extinctions to mar His creative work, without any moral cause, but still calls it all "very good."[5]

The nine points that need responses are as follows:

1. The use of the phrase "very good" in Genesis 1:31 to describe the finished creation means the original creation had no death or disease.
2. Genesis 1:29-30 means God created all creatures, including humanity, vegetarians.
3. God's judgment on the whole creation because of man's Fall included animal death and predation.
4. Adam and Eve immediately died spiritually and began to die physically after they sinned.
5. God caused most (if not all) pain, thorns, and sweat as a punishment on humanity for the Fall.

6. The whole creation was subjected to a bondage to corruption as a result of the Fall.
7. The Biblical promise that God will restore all things refers to remaking the heavens and Earth back into something like the original creation.
8. Teaching that death and bloodshed existed prior to the Fall destroys the meaning of the full redemptive work of Christ.
9. If God's original "very good" creation contained death and disease then God must be incompetent, impotent, or cruel.

This vision of Genesis has been taught to us for generations and is entrenched in Protestant Evangelical Christianity so deeply many do not even question it. But is it true? Is it what the Bible really says or just a traditional interpretation? Many become very agitated, even when conservative believers like me, question these things for Biblical authenticity because questioning their truthfulness is seen as an attack on the foundations of our faith. I can assure you I am not attacking the foundations of Christianity. I am attempting to bolster them and make them relevant again to generations of people who have rejected the Bible because of a fantasy type interpretation of Genesis.

Here is the problem: *eight of these nine points are wrong* (in the way YEC mean them). Eight of these arguments are *interpretative exaggerations* of what the text says, or they are just plain wrong. Francis Schaeffer used to say the authority of Scripture can be destroyed in two ways: liberals do it by taking away verses, and conservatives do it by adding to what is written. Many YEC are examples of conservatives adding exaggerated dogmatic interpretations to texts and then labeling other views as compromises. They fail to recognize the texts are not nearly as dogmatic as their interpretations of it.

My responses to each of these nine arguments are as follows:

1. The phrase "very good" in Genesis 1:31 to describe the finished creation means the original creation had no death and disease.

Genesis 1:31 says, "God saw all that He had made, and behold, it was very good." To many YEC the term "very good" is all that is needed to show that no death preceded the Fall. One YEC says, "This is enough to refute ideas of millions of years, because such views put the fossil record in this 'very good' world. This would entail that cancer and gout [because the fossil record shows evidence of these] are 'very good.'"[6] [Sarfati]

Does "very good" mean there was no animal death in God's original creation prior to the Fall? Take a close look at what Genesis 1:31 says again. Notice, it says that *all God made* (caused) was "very good". What God did, and does, is *always all very good* because *God is good*. So let me ask you this, did God do anything to His creation after the Fall that should be considered bad? No, some consequences of the Fall may be uncomfortable and harmful *to us*, but if God did them then they are not evil or bad. God uses the unfulfilling nature of the world and our discontent and discomfort as tools to drive us to Himself. The creation was never meant to be a substitute for a relationship with God, even before the Fall, so for God to have designed some level of discontent in the original pre-Fall creation is understandable. The creation itself would never have completely satisfied humanity no matter how good it was. Too much of a good thing is possible with God's creation, but not with a relationship with God Himself. Therefore, a level of discontent with the original creation could have included animal death, and yet still be very good for God's purposes.

So, is the creation still very good? OEC point out that aspects of the creation like Rebekah's beauty (Gen. 24:16), the Promised Land (Num. 14:7), the land of Laish (Judges 18:9), Bathsheba's beauty (II Sam. 11:2), Adonijah's handsomeness (I Kings 1:6), and figs (Jer. 24:2-3) are still called "very good" even after the Fall. From that we can at least see that *everything* is not now "very bad". The Curse did not completely change everything from "very good" to "not good at all". But YEC are quick to point out:

> Certainly, the phrase *can* be used of people and things in a fallen world. But the specific context of Genesis 1 shows what God meant by [very good]. The 'very good' was the culmination of creation week, where God had already pronounced things 'good' six times. This is a clear indication of no principle of actual evil in what God had made.[7] [Sarfati]

Notice the assumption in his argument. What he says is "clear" is that "very good" must contain "no principle of actual evil" (so far so good), but by that he means no animal death (whoa horsey!). *That* is a big leap and is not as clear as he says. The Bible must tell us that animal death is evil for it to be evil, but the phrase "very good" does not do that. While it can definitely be said that Adam and Eve had done nothing evil and no human had died when God saw that it was very good, that is not the same thing as an absence of animal death.

In fact, that animal death *is* "very good" can be seen by two simple arguments. *First*, is an overpopulation of animals bad for humanity? Another way I like to ask that is, "Is rat and roach death very good for humans?" Yes, because animals would consume all resources and make rest difficult! Then God making animal death to avoid overpopulation is good. And *second*, animal death must be good because God caused it and everything God does is good.

Just because humanity may find some things objectionable about God's creation does not mean those uncomfortable things are evil and a result of the Fall/Curse. The Bible is silent on the origin of things like viruses, disease, pain, itching, muscle soreness, and the like. Just because humanity does not find everything about God's creation to be beautiful does not mean ugly things are a result of the Fall/Curse (especially because ugliness is somewhat subjective). It may just mean we need to adjust our vision to see the beauty in it. After all, God, not Satan, must be responsible for the creation of unappealing things like warthogs, vultures, insects, snakes, rats, maggots, feces, and mold. Are we to believe God did not make poison ivy, mosquitoes, ticks, fleas, lice, leeches, jellyfish, and hornets, and the various irritations they may cause humans, until after the Fall? Or, is it more reasonable God made these things for a purpose and could have warned Adam and Eve how to avoid them, and possibly use and enjoy them? The inaccessibility of knowledge from losing fellowship with God had plenty of negative consequences and was its own curse.

The meaning of "very good" is too vague to make dogmatic statements like no animal death existed before the Fall. Besides, as we shall see below, even some YEC do not believe *absolutely all death* was caused by God *after* the Fall. Some believe the death of certain categories of animals preceded the Fall. An argument that says "very good" clearly means "no principle of actual evil", and "no principle of actual evil" means no animal death (even if only certain categories of animals are meant), is leaping to conclusions by gigantic bounds. Only humans commit evil acts. One animal killing another animal is never described as morally evil in the Bible because *animals can do no evil*. They have no choice in how they behave. The use of "very good" as an argument to support no animal death prior to the Fall only works on those who have judged by their own *feelings*, not Biblically, that one animal killing another cannot be good.

What does "very good" mean then? It means that what God did was good overall and that *the creation was perfectly suited for God's purposes for humanity*. Genesis 1-3 says *nothing* about when animal death began, so let no one exaggerate an interpretation of "very good" into scripturally unfounded realms. That God made animals to kill one another is the only option, therefore it must be good.

But, YEC are emphatically dogmatic on this issue, "The world (and indeed the universe) was originally perfect."[8] Even though the Bible *never says* the original creation was perfect, they then quote Genesis 1:31 as a proof-text, then say, "A perfect God would make nothing less... The original creation was perfect, but we can see by looking at the world around us that there has been a drastic change. The change was a result of the Fall of man – an event which fundamentally altered the world."[9] Many YEC apparently believe they are qualified to define perfection as the absence of animal death simply by observing the world around us, but that is not the way to define it. If animal death is the result of the Fall, let the Bible define it as such, but it does not.

This idea that "very good" means a perfect world and a perfect world means no animal death can create an impasse. YEC think "very good" is a rock solid argument and as clear as glass. OEC see that "very good" is vague and subjective and cannot be used as a proof-text for something as specific as animal death. Even some YEC admit the Bible is silent on the origin of carnivorous activity, "the Bible doesn't specifically say..."[10] and "The Bible doesn't specifically explain how carnivory originated, but because creation was finished after day 6 (Gen. 2:1-3), there is no possibility that God later created new carnivorous animals."[11] If the Bible does not say, then how can YEC be so dogmatic that they know it must have begun after the Fall? They attempt to use the arguments below for support of their conclusion, but, as we will see, their Biblical evidence is extremely weak.

As for cancer and gout in animals (disease in general) being considered "very good", if animal death existed prior to the Fall, that would have to be true. That may sound like a radical statement, but consider four points before you make the judgment it cannot be true:

First, what is animal death to God? Though we know that not even a sparrow can die without God's knowledge (Lk 10:6), *the Earth was not created for their ultimate survival.* God *only blessed humanity* to "fill" the land (1:28). The sea creatures were blessed to "fill" *the seas* (1:22), but flying creatures were only blessed to *multiply* on the land. Neither birds nor land creatures were blessed to fill the land. In fact no blessing is recorded to land creatures, most likely for two reasons: (1) the first proclamation on Day 6 was for the earth to produce land creatures, so by fiat alone land creatures would have increased on the land, and (2) *the land creatures were never meant to fill the land.* That was reserved for humanity. God would not have blessed both to fill the land because that would have been contradictory. Most importantly, understand that *with God's blessing,* if humanity had *filled the land,* even *before* the Fall, it would obviously mean some land animals would get displaced. In other words, some of them would have died. Therefore, it was *always* God's plan for animal's to die.

Second, making animal death available before the Fall benefits the whole Earth. If *absolutely no death* occurred prior to the Fall then bacteria, locusts, roaches, and rodents (just to name a few) would have quickly become serious nuisances just by eating everything, if for no other reason. Therefore, creating a world where predation and disease eliminate the weak, potential pests, and overpopulation actually benefits the whole. Is rat and roach death very good for humanity? Yes!

Third, the origin of animal death is missing in the Bible. The Bible says nothing about it. (Rms. 5:12 and I Cor. 15:21, which refer to human death only, will be covered in point 3 below.) God tells us He created our world, and unless the Bible tells us otherwise, that means *God made it the way we see it today.*

And *fourth,* death and disease were originally intended for animals, but they were not originally meant to affect humans. Someone could turn one of my arguments against me and say we must conclude human death is good because God caused that too, and I would agree with one caveat. Human death is good only as a punishment for sin, and that condition was part of the original "very good" creation. That cannot be said of animals.

Exaggerating the text by defining "very good" to mean an absence of animal death should be avoided. The term is too vague and subjective.

2. Genesis 1:29-30 means God created all creatures, including humanity, as vegetarians.

"Probably the best support for the position that no animals died before the Fall comes from the original diets in Genesis 1:29-30... This teaches that vegetarianism was a worldwide phenomenon, not just restricted to Eden."[12] (Sarfati) If that is their best support they are in trouble. Genesis 1:29-30 does not teach strict vegetarianism for humanity or anything else. Look closely at what it says:

> Then God said, "Behold, I have given you every plant yielding seed that is on the surface of all the earth, and every tree which has fruit yielding seed;

it shall be food for you; and to every beast of the earth and to every bird of the sky and to every thing that moves on the earth which has life, I have given every green plant for food."

Did God intend for humans and animals to be vegetarians? Some commentators think so and some do not. As one commentator writes:

> Whether man was a vegetarian prior to the fall is debated. On the one hand it is contended that the original grant does not formally exclude the animals (Macdonald); that we cannot positively affirm that man's dominion over the animals did not involve the use of them for food (Murphy); and that as men offered sacrifices from their flocks, it is probable they ate the flesh of the victims (Calvin). On the other hand it is argued that the Divine language cannot be held as importing more than it really says, and that [Gen. 9:3] distinctly teaches that man's right to the animal creation dates from the time of Noah (Kalisch, Knobel, Alford, &c.). Almost all nations have traditions of a golden age of innocence, when men abstained from killing animals...[13]

Genesis 9:1-4 reads:

> And God blessed Noah and his sons and said to them, "Be fruitful and multiply and fill the earth. And the fear of you and the terror of you shall be on every beast of the earth and on every bird of the sky; with everything that creeps on the ground, and all the fish of the sea, into your hand they are given. Every moving thing that is alive shall be food for you; I give all to you, as *I gave* the green plant. Only you shall not eat flesh with its life, *that is*, its blood."

A main component of both Genesis 1:29-30 and 9:3 is that they are *permissions only*, not prohibitions (except for the part about eating blood). Because it is likely Adam and Eve were told about their food shortly after their creation, it should be no wonder they were told about plants first, especially because eating meat would have taken far more instruction by God.

Genesis 9 gave humanity permission to eat "every moving thing that is alive", but does that mean no meat could be eaten before then? YEC think so, "Otherwise, God's statement to Noah after the flood in Genesis 9:3 makes no sense."[14] According to them it makes no sense God would tell Noah he could eat meat after the Flood if they were already eating meat with His permission before the Flood. I disagree; sense *can* be made of the statement to Noah even if they had been eating meat previously. How? Genesis 7:2 and 8 make it clear that Noah understood the difference between "clean" and "not clean" animals. Clean for what? Eating is the major reason, which means Noah and family were already eating animals, but were *limiting themselves* to the clean ones. Genesis 9 then specifically gives them permission to eat *every* moving thing, not just the clean ones. YEC are incorrect, sense can be made of Genesis 9 apart from relating it to the first permissible vegetarianism departure.

Some might object and say God had already told Noah and his antecedents the differences between clean and unclean sacrifice animals (though that revelation is not listed). However, as my son astutely observed, the sacrifice of an animal is not really a sacrifice for humans unless there is a cost. The same animals that are clean for sacrifice are also clean for eating, and vice versa. The reason that sacrificing an animal is a sacrifice is more than the fact it costs the animal its life. It costs the human something also, namely the effort it took to raise the animal and several good meals. Therefore, the clean and unclean distinction to Noah was not purely for sacrificial reasons; it also meant they were eating the animals with God's permission.

That vegetarianism is *not* the meaning of Genesis 1:29-30 is evidenced by the following:

First, the verses *do not forbid eating meat*. Because eating meat was not forbidden, no definitive statement can really be made about it. God gave very few recorded commandments prior to the Law. To explain to Adam and Eve immediately after their creation about eating meat would have taken more instruction than what is recorded in Genesis 1. God could have given it later, after He killed an animal and made clothes for example, though we are not given that revelation. If God had meant for humanity to not eat meat it would have been a simple statement to make. He clearly forbade Adam and Eve from eating of the tree of the knowledge of good and evil. Giving them permission on their first day of existence to eat fruits and grains when they got hungry and telling them what to feed their animals makes sense. Vegetarianism was not commanded and eating meat was not forbidden. They were simply initially told *some* of what they could eat.

Second, Genesis 4:4 has a telling detail, "And Abel, on his part also brought of the firstlings of his flock and of their fat portions..." The last phrase, "of their fat portions", clearly indicates the flocks were at least being butchered for their fat (from which comes oil for a host of uses). The fact animals were being killed regularly, which God demonstrated first (Gen. 3:21), and being used for more than just their skin, gives strong evidence they were eating the meat portions. It would have been wasteful to not use the entire animal for something.

Third, following Calvin, it is likely humans partook of their sacrifices. As soon as one was sacrificed on a fire the smell would have been hard to resist. Since God did not say to not eat it, it only makes sense they would have.

Fourth, somehow humanity got the idea there were clean and unclean animals by Noah's time (Gen. 7:2, 8). That implies men were eating animals with God's permission prior to the command in Genesis 9 because *God is the one who called them* "clean" and "not clean" in Genesis 7. Clean and unclean make the most sense referring to what is permissible to eat because sacrificing an animal that is not edible means nothing to a human.

Fifth, notice that sea creatures are left out of the animal list in Genesis 1:30. Why? Because, nearly every sea creature eats other sea creatures which includes sea mammals too. A strict vegetarian diet for all sea creatures is impossible.

Sixth, Psalm 104 provides extra support that God made some animals to eat meat. Verse 21 says, "The young lions roar after their prey, and seek their food from God." This verse indicates God gave some animals to be prey for lions and it is obvious that lions are designed to kill. YEC object on several grounds. *First*, they say you should not "interpret scripture against scripture."[15] I agree and I believe Scripture does not contradict itself so if two verses seem to be contradictory then one is likely being interpreted incorrectly and, in this case, *it is Genesis that is being incorrectly interpreted by YEC*. Psalms is interpreted correctly as meaning God gives lions their prey and designed them to be predators. *Second*, YEC say the verb in Ps. 104:21 is in the present tense whereas the earlier part of the Psalm is in the past tense, so therefore this latter part is referring to the present, but not the way God originally designed it.[16] To that I say that the present tense in the Psalm is being used to speak of things that are still happening, whereas the past tense describes things God completed in the past. Also, because the Psalm is a parallel account with Genesis 1 (David's take on Genesis), it is not unreasonable to conclude David is speaking of God giving predators their prey as the condition in which they were originally created.

The conclusion is that Genesis 1:29-30 does not teach vegetarianism for humans or animals. It is only a permissive statement made to the newly created human couple that it was okay for them to eat two categories of the plants in His garden and the animals were allowed to eat all of them. I am sure the Master Chef intended on latter occasions to show Adam and Eve many parts of His creation that were good to eat and delectable ways to prepare them.

3. God's judgment on the whole creation because of man's Fall included animal death and predation.

This issue is not as simple as that opening statement makes it sound because YEC disagree about whether absolutely ALL death was caused by Adam's sin. Some YEC from the distant past were much more narrow and simple in their belief all death was caused by Adam, whereas some recent YEC accept levels of death in the original finished creation. Take the words of John Wesley versus the words of a more recent popular YEC for example:

> Wesley – The paradisiacal earth afforded a sufficiency of food for all its inhabitants; so that none of them had any need or temptation to prey upon the other. The spider was then as harmless as the fly, and did not then lie in wait for blood. The weakest of them crept securely over the earth... without any to make them afraid. Meantime, the reptiles of every kind were equally harmless...[17]

> Recent YEC (Sarfati) – Creationists have often pointed out that the creatures affected [by the Fall] were those the Bible calls... (*nephesh chayah*). When it refers to man, it is often translated "living soul," but, of other creatures, including fish, it is often translated "living creature." However, it is never applied to plants and invertebrates [animals without an internal skeletal structure like insects]. ...the pre-Fall diet of animals did not necessarily exclude invertebrates.[18]

Dear reader, please understand what some of *the most influential Young-Earth Creationists* are saying these days. *They agree with OEC that some death existed prior to the Fall!* Some YEC believe it only affected invertebrates. OEC believe it affected all animals, but not humans.

Where do the recent YEC get this idea that only invertebrates died before the Fall? Obviously they recognize a belief that absolutely no death before the Fall is *indefensible*. Insects would have been in danger of death almost instantly after their creation because a much bigger animal, while eating leaves or grass, might have accidentally stepped on or eaten one. Or a gnat might have accidentally flown in another animal's mouth or eye. Also, the fact that many animals are *designed* to seek, capture, and consume insects is undeniable. Just consider spiders, praying mantises, shrews, anteaters, chameleons, frogs, and woodpeckers to name very few. Are we really to believe chameleons and frogs used their tongues to eat plants before the Fall?[19] If so, why do they not still do this, at least sometimes? Obviously, they do not need their tongue to eat plants because all they have to do for that is climb out to the food and eat it directly. Leaves, fruits, and seeds do not try to evade anything, but insects do, hence the reason *God designed* a long quick sticky tongue.

With that being true YEC are left trying to draw a line somewhere between what God designed to die and what was not. But where? The line between invertebrates and vertebrates seems logical, especially because most humans do not care much for bugs anyway. (As far as my wife is concerned the only good bug is a dead bug.) Being a logical choice it is then up to YEC to show the Bible confirms it. Some YEC believe they have found it in the Hebrew term "*nephesh chayah*" which is most often translated "living creature" in most modern translations (*nephesh* meaning creature or soul, and *chayah* meaning living).

According to the YEC above, *nephesh chayah* is "never applied to plants and invertebrates" in the Bible, and I agree. Genesis does not consider plants to be living because they do not move[20] (have a form of locomotion). As for invertebrates, YEC are just plain wrong evidenced by two strong reasons:

First, in the Old Testament the term *nephesh chayah* applies to *all* animals, including invertebrates. Simply look at its first three uses in Genesis to clearly see that is the case. Genesis 1:20-21:

> Then God said, 'Let the waters teem with swarms of living creatures [*nephesh chayah*], and let birds fly above the earth in the open expanse of the heavens.' God created the great sea monsters and every living creature [*nephesh chayah*] that moves, with which the waters swarmed after their kind, and every winged bird after its kind...

Here Genesis twice applies *nephesh chayah* to *ALL* creatures of the sea and sky, "every living creature that moves, with which the waters swarmed... [which includes many invertebrates] and every winged bird [flier]." The word translated "bird" in Genesis 1:20-21 is a generic term referring to all flying creatures which includes all flying insects (invertebrates).[21]

The third use of the term is in Genesis 1:24-25:

> Then God said, 'Let the earth bring forth living creatures [*nephesh chayah*] after their kind cattle and creeping things and beasts of the earth after their kind'; and it was so. God made the beasts of the earth after their kind, and the cattle after their kind, and everything that creeps on the ground after its kind...

Here the term applies to "everything that creeps on the ground." Can these references be any clearer? "Every living creature that moves" and "everything that creeps on the ground" are *impossible* to restrict to vertebrates. *Nephesh chayah* clearly applies to all animals (vertebrate, invertebrate, or otherwise) which is also abundantly clear from its use in Leviticus 11. After naming all the clean and unclean animals which humanity could eat and not eat, including all types of winged insects, locusts, grasshoppers, crickets, and all the teeming life of the sea *without* fins and scales, and all the swarming creatures on land with *many feet* (including spiders and millipedes), verses 46-47 sum up the whole list, "This is the law regarding the animal, and the bird, and every living thing [*nephesh chayah*] that moves in the waters, and everything that swarms on the earth, to make a distinction between the unclean and the clean, and between the edible creature and the creature which is not to be eaten." The YEC argument is bogus. The Bible does not restrict *nephesh chayah* to vertebrates.

Second, an argument that no vertebrates died prior to the Fall is as indefensible as no invertebrates dying. For example, if we allow small hatchling crocodiles to eat water bugs, what did the adult versions eat? Did they switch over to plants after they attained a certain size when even big insects were not enough to satisfy them? Or what about the extinct 40 foot crocodilian *Sarcosuchus*? What kind of plants does a 40 ft. croc eat? Or what is the difference between a baby anaconda eating a grasshopper and its 15 ft. mother eating a tapir? Or what about monitor lizards eating the eggs of sea turtles and crocodiles? And let us not forget that *nearly every sea creature eats other sea creatures*. Plants cannot grow without light and anglerfishes live at depths where the only choice of food is other sea creatures. Did sharks not eat fish before the Fall? Based simply upon a shark's design is it not ridiculous to suggest sharks ate kelp and seaweed only? How impossible would it be for the basking shark to not eat some fish when it swims with its gigantic mouth wide open to swallow anything in its path? Would it not also have been impossible for baleen whales eating krill before the Fall to avoid swallowing some fish in the process? And would it not have been just as impossible for an elephant or brachiosaur to not accidentally kill a mole, lizard, salamander, or fish as it would be to not accidentally kill an insect? And are we to really believe that a heron wading in the shallows would restrict itself to grabbing insects and leave small fish, snakes, and frogs alone? And what about all the animals that are obviously *designed* to hunt and kill other large animals: big cats, sharks, killer whales, snakes, alligators, birds of prey, tyrannosaurs, velociraptors, bears, and wolves? And is it not just as obvious that some animals appear to be *designed* to be eaten: fish, chicken, and cattle for example? And let us not forget a whole host of creatures *designed* to scavenge, clean, and rid the Earth of carcasses (maggots, carrion beetles, and vultures to name a few). For what purpose is a vulture's bald head except to prevent bacteria from getting in its feathers while eating, or its keen sense of smell except to find rotting meat from great distances? And why would animals like porcupines, skunks, poisonous frogs, and stingrays need defense mechanisms if they did not have predators after them? YEC exceed all possible limits of credibility with this "no animal death before the Fall" nonsense.

Design is intuitively obvious to me in the world, but YEC do not seem to want to come to terms with the implications of the obvious design features among animals. If all animals were herbivores then it would not be long before all food sources would run out so God designed some animals to prey upon other animals (Ps. 104:21). This is not cruel (a subject taken up in more detail in point 9 below), it is amazing! Nature brings itself to a balance when left alone for enough time. Humans are the ones who often upset the balance by killing off something important or introducing non-indigenous species where they do not belong, usually accompanied by unexpected harmful results.

YEC have two responses to these problems:

First, they say design features like poisons, sharp teeth, and claws were used for other purposes. "Before the Fall, many attack/defense structures could have been used in a vegetarian lifestyle,"[22] but they do see "this perspective has shortcomings."[23] Shortcomings indeed! How about impossibilities for the reasons listed above? Saying attack and defense mechanisms were originally used in a vegetarian lifestyle leaves the YEC in the unenviable position of having to explain how they specifically helped a vegetarian lifestyle. For example, what did a snake do with its venom before it used it to paralyze and kill prey? Why did it need fangs at all? That all animal features had a vegetarian purpose surely cannot be correct because structures like fangs (being hollow and able to fold into place) and poison (being available in the right place, i.e. in the fangs, and able to incapacitate its victim rather than just make it mad) are design features for which only God could have been responsible. The Bible never says Satan or demons have powers to make or refashion living creatures, and blind chance cannot do it, so God must have done it.

Second, YEC say God foreknew humanity would not go long without sinning so overpopulation or lack of resources would not have become a problem and attack/defense mechanisms were designed into animals, but came out after the Fall. "God foreknew the Fall, so He programmed creatures with the information for attack and defense features, which they would need in a cursed world. This information was 'switched on' at the Fall."[24] Aside from the speculative *ad hoc* nature of this argument, the other problem with playing the foreknowledge card is that it cuts both ways. One could just as easily argue God designed the world outside the Garden of Eden as we see it today knowing it would not be long before Adam and Eve sinned. Also, most attack and defense features do not appear to have any purpose in a "switched off" position, like stingers, quills, and armor. And some attack features cannot be switched off, like talons, claws, and sharp teeth. And why did God really have to change it as a result of Adam's sin? Why punish animals for what humanity did? All these questions become moot if we just accept that God designed animals as we see them: self-sustaining and self-regulating predators and prey.

Still YEC always fall back on their claim the Bible teaches vertebrate death began with the Fall, but the burden of proof is on them to support their claim and besides their interpretation of the Fall (covered here in Point 5), they attempt to use two other Biblical passages as proof, Romans 5 and I Corinthians 15, in which I challenge anyone to find *anything* about animal death.

Romans 5:12 says, "Therefore, just as through one man sin entered into the world, and death through sin, and so death spread to all men, because all sinned..." and 5:17-19 says,

> For if by the transgression of the one, death reigned through the one, much more those who receive the abundance of grace and of the gift of righteousness will reign in life through the One, Jesus Christ. So then as through one transgression there resulted condemnation to all men, even so through one act of righteousness there resulted justification of life to all men. For as through the one man's disobedience the many were made sinners, even so through the obedience of the One the many will be made righteous.

I Corinthians 15:21-22 reads, "For since by a man came death, by a man also came the resurrection of the dead. For as in Adam all die, so also in Christ all will be made alive."

The response to these verses is easy. Is it not obvious *they refer to human death only*? "Death spread to all men, because all sinned..." Animals do not sin, only humans. "Through one transgression there resulted condemnation to all men..." "For as in Adam all die, so also in Christ all will be made alive." If all animals die in Adam (which is not true, only humans are "in Adam"), then would that mean *all* animals will be made alive in Christ? Will Christ resurrect every rat and rabbit, fish and fowl, dinosaur and Dodo bird? Obviously not, the verses only refer to humans and some YEC know it. "Verses such as Genesis 2:17, Genesis 3:17-19, Romans 5:12, 1 Corinthians 15:21-22 are very clear on the sin-death connection. While these verses refer exclusively to human death, Genesis 3 is clear that Adam's sin had further unpleasant effects because Adam was the federal head of creation."[25] (Sarfati) He knows *these verses refer exclusively to human death*, so why do he and other YEC still attempt to use them to support animal death by Adam's sin? *Because, they have no others.* That is how weak their case is.

In conclusion then, by calling *all animals* "living creatures" (*nephesh chayah*) the Bible leaves us with an either/or scenario. Either absolutely no death of any kind existed prior to the Fall (an impossible scenario even to YEC and a position the Bible never takes), or any and all animals died and were designed to do so from the beginning. There is no Biblical middle ground. Therefore: (1) because Genesis tells us God created and made all living creatures; (2) we see animal death all around us; (3) the Bible is mostly silent on the origin of animal death except for Ps. 104:21 which tells us God made both prey and predator; (4) God only blessed humanity to fill the land which would result in a reduction of the number of animals in any location (i.e. death); (5) an overpopulation of animals is bad for humanity and thus animal death is good for humanity; and (6) attack and defense structures have a design for which only God could be responsible; we can conclude *God originally designed animals as we see them today*: dying, scavenging, preying, and being preyed upon.

Once the death of any kind of animal (even invertebrates) is accepted as Biblical prior to the Fall, it becomes very difficult, if not impossible, to draw a line between what died before the Fall and what died afterward unless you follow what the Bible actually teaches. The Bible draws the line between animals and humanity, "in the day that you eat from it you [*not everything*] will surely die" (Gen. 2:17). Before the Fall death affected all animals. Afterward it affected humanity too. Also, once the pre-Fall death of animals is accepted as Biblical, we lose any problems with a fossil record showing death before humanity.

4. Adam and Eve immediately died spiritually and began to die physically after they sinned.

Of the nine points the YEC make this is one I agree with and many OEC do too. The Bible tells us all humanity currently begins spiritually dead, separated from the life of God (Eph. 2:1-5), but Jesus came to give us new life (Jn. 10:10), and if we trust Him we have that life (I Jn. 5:12). And the verses I just discussed in the previous point (Rms. 5:12, 17-19 and I Cor. 15:21-22) definitely show Adam's sin ushered spiritual death into the world (and likely physical death also, though spiritual death is more important). Humanity in its originally created state must have had the ability to live forever somehow otherwise God's curse of returning to dust makes no sense (Gen. 3:19). This is why the Bible can call death "the last enemy" (I Cor. 15:26) because we were originally not meant to die. Now, for Christians, we have the promise death will be subjected to Christ and we will live forever with Him (I Th. 4:17), but for those who do not want to be with the Lord and reject His plan in place of their own, a second death awaits (Rev. 2:11, 20:14, and 21:8). Thus, death remains their enemy.

Yet, even though YEC and OEC agree for the most part on this point, ridiculous inflammatory quotes like this by YEC can still be found, "All (mis-)interpretations of Genesis which deny its plain meaning, and so involve death before sin, must assert that the 'last enemy' was part of God's 'very good' creation."[26] (Sarfati) *OEC believe no such thing* and any YEC who misrepresents the OEC position as bad as that should be ashamed, repent, and apologize. Because OEC believe that death as the "last enemy" only applies to humanity, and humanity would not have died in God's original "very good" creation, it can be emphatically stated that *OEC believe the last enemy was not part of God's very good creation.*

5. God caused most (if not all) pain, thorns, and sweat as a punishment on humanity for the Fall.

Many have tried to determine the extent of the effects of the Fall as recorded in Genesis 3 and many have speculated various effects based on the science of their day. Exactly what did God do to the universe, Earth, Satan, animals, and humanity as a result of the Fall? That is the question we consider here, but I ask the reader to try to let go of any preconceived ideas you may have and look at Genesis 3 with an open mind.

Genesis 3:14-19 reads:

> [14]The LORD God said to the serpent, "Because you have done this [tempted Adam and Eve], Cursed are you more than all cattle, And more than every beast of the field; On your belly you will go, And dust you will eat All the days of your life; [15]And I will put enmity Between you and the woman, And between your seed and her seed; He shall bruise you on the head, And you shall bruise him on the heel." [16]To the woman He said, "I will greatly multiply your pain in childbirth, In pain you will bring forth children; Yet your desire will be for your husband, And he will rule over you." [17]Then to Adam He said, "Because you have listened to the voice of your wife, and have eaten from the tree about which I commanded you, saying, 'You shall not eat from it'; Cursed is the ground because of you; In toil you will eat of it All the days of your life. [18]Both thorns and thistles it shall grow for you; And you will eat the plants of the field; [19]By the sweat of your face You will eat bread, Till you return to the ground, Because from it you were taken; For you are dust, And to dust you shall return."

The Curse had the following relevant[27] effects to our discussion:

First, *some* animals were cursed. The text says the serpent was cursed "more than all cattle, And more than every beast of the field." Notice that not every category of animals mentioned in Genesis 1 is cursed. All sea and flying creatures, some beasts *of the earth* (as opposed to beasts of the field), and creeping things are left out. Why? YEC interpret this part of Genesis 3:14 to mean predation began and vertebrate animals began to die as a result of the Curse, "...the whole creation was cursed... which included death to animals, with the end of the exclusively vegetarian diet originally mandated for both humans and animals..."[28] If that is true then why are some animal categories left out of the animals cursed in 3:14? Why does 3:14 only mention cattle and beasts *of the field*? The answer is because what God pronounced in the Curse had to do with what *only* affected humanity directly, *and what humanity would directly affect*, rather than any supposed affect on the "whole creation". YEC have exaggerated the text, as usual. If God had meant the entire creation was under a curse as a result of Satan, Adam, and Eve's sin then Genesis would have said so instead of specifying only parts relevant to humanity and Satan.

The narrowing of the focus of creation to parts most relevant to humanity is evident throughout Genesis 1, 2 and 3. Genesis 1:1 begins with the initial creation. Then 1:2 narrows the focus to the surface of the waters and 1:9-10 emphasizes dividing the whole wet earth into dry land and seas. Genesis 1:11

refers to *all* "vegetation" then narrows to those relevant for humanity, "plants yielding seed, and fruit trees on the earth bearing fruit after their kind with seed in them", which is the same two categories of plants in Gen. 1:29 which God told Adam and Eve they could eat. Genesis 2 and 3 are part of the same overall context of Genesis 2:4b-5:1 which is one of the twelve sections of Genesis.[29] Genesis 2:5, "no shrub of the field was yet in the earth, and no plant of the field had yet sprouted", is contrasted with "every plant yielding seed that is on the surface of all the earth (1:29)" specifying *of the field* (humanity's location) against *all the earth*. The story then moves specifically to "a garden toward the east, in Eden; and there He placed the man whom He had formed" (2:8). This garden God planted remains the location of the story until humanity is expelled from it (3:23). Genesis has thus moved from the whole universe, to the surface of the Earth with no dry land, to dry ground, and finally to a specific location where God placed the first humans. Therefore, Genesis 3:14 only refers to animals in the vicinity of humanity; that is, animals that were in the cultivated garden (fields) of Eden and surrounding areas.

Also, Genesis 2:20 specifies, "The man gave names to all the cattle, and to the birds of the sky, and to every beast of the field." Notice here again Adam does not name any sea creatures, or every beast of the whole earth, or any of the creeping things, only those animals *of the field* (in the garden) and flying in it. In 3:1 snakes are included as one of the beasts *of the field*. Then 3:14 specifies which animals were involved in the Curse. The Curse is *only* in the context and location of the Garden of Eden, *not the whole of creation or even the whole land* and only specifies *some* animals were cursed, not all. Therefore, the idea *all* animal death and predation began as a result of the Curse is expanding the meaning of the text far beyond its specific context. The Curse had nothing to do with the origin of animal death, disease, and predation.

In what way were the cattle and beasts of the field cursed then? Simply this: seen from the perspective of *what humanity would do to the animals*, the animals were cursed because they would be mistreated, abused, and wasted by the ignorant and premeditated actions of fallen sinful humanity. Humanity would truly be a curse on the animals, but it would also backfire. For example, if humanity had wiped out all snakes in a given area it may have given rise to the animals the snakes preyed upon, like rats. One cannot upset the equilibrium of an ecosystem or mistreat animals and not expect it to have consequences.

It appears to me wholly unlike the character of a perfectly just God to *directly* punish *all* animals for something in which they were innocent. However, for God to set up a creation where disobedience has negative consequences for which responsibility rests solely on the volitional party is completely in character for God. This part of the Curse recognized that sinful humanity would now have a detrimental effect on creation and it would be bad (a curse) for humanity, animals, and the land. In other words, the animals and ground would no longer be "very good" *because of what humanity would do to them*, not because of what God would do to them. *The text gives no indication God caused predation and animal death as a result of the Fall.* YEC are reading that into the text.

As for the serpent, its curse appears to have a double meaning. Part of it refers to how God punished Satan and part of it is symbolic to that fact. Snakes were cursed more than all the other animals in humanity's vicinity, and to this day it would be difficult to name an animal more despised and abused than snakes. Even harmless snakes are frequently killed for no reason other than the fact they are snakes. I once read of a study that showed people hated snakes so much some would risk damage to their vehicle and deliberately drive off the road to run over a rubber snake placed on the shoulder. The Curse thus proves to remain active.

Second, Eve's pain in childbirth would "greatly multiply" (3:16). OEC point out that the verse says the pain will be *multiplied*, not instituted for the first time, meaning she would have experienced some measure of pain in the original creation and *that pain* would be increased. It would follow then that humans could have experienced pain as we do today if they had burned themselves or stubbed a toe. Some YEC say Eve would not have experienced any pain (or discomfort) in childbirth if not for the Fall and this can be extrapolated to teach no pain would have occurred at all in the original creation. Other YEC are not as dogmatic on this point and concede "below some threshold, it [pain] might even have had a pleasurable component."[30] However, this same author says the OEC argument above is invalid because "zero pain to some pain is an increase!"[31] arguing the text does not have to mean Eve would have experienced a moderate tolerable amount of pain in childbirth, even before the Fall. Even some OEC do not see a necessity of the text teaching moderate pain existed previous to the Fall, "the Hebrew verb simply means 'to cause to be numerous' and makes no comment about whether there were any [pain] to begin with."[32] (Collins)

In response, I believe they are missing a crucial point. The text says Eve's pain would "multiply" which is the same word used in Genesis 1:22 and 28 to describe animals and humanity multiplying their numbers on the land. For animals and humans to multiply *they had to exist already*. The Hebrew word does not seem to allow multiplying from zero pain to some pain because for something to multiply it has to exist already. Even if the Hebrew word is defined as "to cause to be numerous" the implication is to ask, "cause what?" and the answer is to cause that which already exists to become numerous, namely "pain" in 3:16. Therefore, some measure of pain must have existed in the original creation, and once some level of pain is accepted it becomes impossible to limit the amount of potential pain a human may have been able to experience. And it would follow that animals likely felt pain originally also.

Third, the ground was cursed and God placed the blame solely on Adam, "Because you have listened to the voice of your wife, and have eaten..." (3:17) Therefore God said, "Both thorns and thistles it shall grow for you." (3:18) Does this mean there were no thorns or thistles prior to the Curse? According to YEC it does. "Genesis 3 also reveals that the ground was cursed. Thorns and thistles were now part of the world."[33] The problem again is this text does not demand as strict an interpretation as YEC give it. God's statement can just as easily mean that Adam was clueless what he was about to have to deal with outside the garden without the knowledge God would have taught him.

God planted the garden in Eden and it must have been spectacular. It was designed for the comfort of humanity. And, "the LORD God took the man and put him into the garden of Eden to cultivate it and keep it." (Gen. 2:15) God likely designed it so that only minimal maintenance was required. Natural barriers and deterrents, like flowers animals do not like to eat, and trained animals to keep rabbits and deer away, may have been involved. It may have even had a natural fence of hedges or possibly unnatural barriers like a stone wall or wooden fence to keep undesirable animals out. God may have even built a shelter for the first couple.

Regardless of those speculations, the text says God put Adam in the garden to cultivate and keep it and this has to mean the garden was not in a wild condition as often depicted in movies or books. Wild forests do not need to be cultivated and kept. Therefore, for Adam to be banned from the garden and have to make his own attempt at duplicating what he had seen would now be much more difficult than he imagined because there were thorns and thistles outside the garden. It is entirely possible Adam had no idea what it was like out there, especially given our lack of knowledge of the garden's size. Genesis gives us very little detail about how much time transpired between Adam's creation and his Fall, meaning he may not have had time to explore anywhere but the garden.

If thorns were already in existence prior to the Fall, YEC say God telling Adam the ground would produce thorns makes no sense, which they illustrate by a cartoon depicting God telling Adam the earth would bring forth thorns and thistles and Adam responding, "So what? Thorns have been around for millions of years!"[34] However, even if Adam knew what it was like outside the garden, it only means he would have had a better understanding of what the consequences of his disobedience were going to be. Either way, the text does not have to mean thorns appeared for the first time. It could just as easily mean Adam was now going to have to deal with them in a much more serious way than just pulling a few up from where he did not want them. Again, the YEC view has taken too dogmatic a stand on a verse that has several plausible interpretations.

In the same way the Curse on the animals would come from the hands of man, so the curse on the land would also come from humanity's ignorant abuse of it, not by something God would do to it. Laws that would come later through Moses were meant to optimize the use of land, like allowing it a Sabbath rest (Lev. 25:1-12). Among the many purposes of the Law was to reverse and limit some of the effects of the Curse *caused by humanity*.

Fourth, Adam would now find providing for himself and his family to be toilsome labor (painful drudgery). "In toil you will eat of it all the days of your life… And you will eat the plants of the field; by the sweat of your face you will eat bread." (3:17-19) The Hebrew word translated "toil" is the same word translated "pain" when referring to Eve in 3:16, "pain in childbirth". The word has more in mind than physical pain, it also includes emotional pain. Satisfaction from labor appears to be built into the original creation as evidenced by the fact God "put [Adam] into the garden of Eden to cultivate it and keep it." (2:15) However, Adam's labor would become increasingly painful, physically and emotionally, because of the curse on the ground he was going to cause.

Did God institute sweat as a punishment for sin? Was Adam's body changed drastically from having no sweat glands to suddenly being covered with them? The text says, "By the sweat of your face you will eat bread." Does that mean Adam did not sweat *at all* before the Fall, even in exerting play or sexual intercourse for example? Again, that interpretation is not demanded by the text. Genesis intentionally gives us details of life for Adam and Eve that shows the original creation was not drastically different than today. For example, Adam and Eve are said to hear God walking in the garden "in the cool of the day" (3:8). That indicates there were temperature changes in the original creation, and our bodies naturally use sweat to cool down in the *heat* of the day, so sweat was likely present prior to the Curse. Also, the fact that Adam could fall into a deep sleep (2:21), would need food (1:29 and 2:9), and was given nighttime (1:4) [35] and a Sabbath to rest (2:3 – if he knew about it), indicates his body was not tireless and would need to be reenergized and rested just like we do.

That most effects of the Curse *were not felt immediately* should not be missed. For example, Eve's pain in childbirth would not have been felt until she had a child. Returning to the dust (3:19 – physical death) would not occur for Adam for 930 years (5:5). The slow effects of feeling the Curse would also contribute to humanity indulging in sin because when no immediate consequence is experienced it deceives us into thinking none exists (Eccl. 8:11). The ground outside the garden may have been good ground (God chose that spot to plant a garden after all), but it would not stay that way after humanity used it poorly. Adam's painful toil may have taken years to take effect.

In concluding point number five, we have seen the Curse's effects on humanity and the Earth are not what many of us were taught. The animals involved were only those in man's vicinity and the Curse had nothing to do with animal death, except maybe by abusive humans. The text *says nothing* of God causing animal predation as a result of sin. The Curse was not the cause of *all* pain. The Curse on the ground was also going to be caused by humanity's abuse of it; it did not have to mean absolutely no thorns existed previously. And finally, man's painful labor and death took some time to unfold so the Curse did not entirely consist of effects God instituted immediately.

What is really important to understand about the Curse is that the worst effects of it were going to be caused by humanity, not God. That idea should cause a radical change from our traditional view of the original creation. It was not a magical fantasy-like utopia on a garden planet with food everywhere, no thorns or animal death, and no pain, where kids played on Tyrannosaurs and swam with crocodiles.[36] Instead it was Earth not very different from the best we see it today. Animals behaved as we observe which means they were dangerous if not handled properly. The same plants grew. Temperature changes and minor discomforts were experienced. Adam and Eve had some labor to do to eat and maintain a garden God planted. In this garden the Lord walked with them and would have taught them wonders we may never know, but disobedience led to spiritual death, estrangement from God, a loss of education, prohibition from the garden's protections and pleasures, and the need for a sacrifice for sin.

6. The whole creation was subjected to a bondage to corruption as a result of the Fall.

Some YEC believe Romans 8:18-23 teaches the Curse had tremendous effects on the Earth, indeed *the entire universe*. It reads:

> [18]For I consider that the sufferings of this present time are not worthy to be compared with the glory that is to be revealed to us. [19]For the anxious longing of the creation waits eagerly for the revealing of the sons of God. [20]For the creation was subjected to futility, not willingly, but because of Him who subjected it, in hope [21]that the creation itself also will be set free from its slavery to corruption into the freedom of the glory of the children of God. [22]For we know that the whole creation groans and suffers the pains of childbirth together until now. [23]And not only this, but also we ourselves, having the first fruits of the Spirit, even we ourselves groan within ourselves, waiting eagerly for our adoption as sons, the redemption of our body.

According to YEC this passage teaches God cursed the whole creation as a result of humanity's sin and the curse brought in *all* death, including animals, and *all* natural disasters, like earthquakes and hurricanes.

> In the beginning, God sustained His creation in its perfect state... When Adam sinned, however, the Lord cursed the universe. In essence there was a change, and along with that change God began to uphold the creation in a cursed state. Suffering and death entered into His creation. The whole universe now suffers from the effects of sin (Romans 8:22).
>
> The sad things... [like death, tsunamis, and hurricanes] are reminders that sin has consequences...[37]

Did God curse the *whole universe* because Adam sinned? The short answer is YEC have again seriously exaggerated the meaning of this text. Two questions must be answered to understand what Romans says: Should "whole creation" be taken literally? And, what do the words "futility" and "corruption" mean?

Should "whole creation" be taken literally? Even though universal language is sometimes used in a relative sense in the Bible (Lk. 2:1, Acts 19:27) and is used as such in the near immediate context of Romans 8 (Rms. 1:8), one should not immediately jump to the conclusion that is the case here. Sometimes when universal language is used it is meant to be universal. I believe that is true here because the word "creation" is used three times in verses 19-21 before Paul adds "whole" to it. That seems to indicate Paul intended to emphasize "whole" and thus refer literally to the whole creation.

In opposition to that conclusion, Romans 1:8 says the Roman Christians' "faith is being proclaimed throughout the whole world." I do not think Paul meant to include southern Africa, India, China, Australia, and the Americas although all were populated at the time. It is possible Paul *literally* meant the

Chapter 6 – Death *Before* the Fall

whole *Roman* world however. Either way, Romans 8 still appears to literally mean the whole creation.

What do the words "futility" and "corruption" mean? This is not the first time both words are used together in Romans. Romans 1:20-23 says:

> For since the creation of the world His invisible attributes, His eternal power and divine nature, have been clearly seen, being understood through what has been made, so that they are without excuse. For even though they knew God, they did not honor Him as God or give thanks, but they became **futile** [vain – KJV] in their speculations, and their foolish heart was darkened. Professing to be wise, they became fools, and exchanged the glory of the **incorruptible** God for an image in the form of **corruptible** man and of birds and four-footed animals and crawling creatures. [emphases mine]

The first word is used in this context for people's hearts and minds becoming *futile*, meaning their thinking is useless and in vain when they do not recognize God as their God. And the *corruptibility* of the creation is contrasted with the *incorruptibility* (same Greek word with a negating participle) of the Creator. The creation is corruptible, meaning it does not last; it decays and perishes, or can be destroyed. In contrast, God is incorruptibly eternal.

Romans 8:20 says the "creation was subjected to futility", thus the creation itself became futile, or useless, or more properly, used for profitless useless vanity rather than that for which it was created. And God was the one who subjected it to that. *But the question is when*? If it was subjected to being used improperly, then it could only have been done after someone was present to abuse it, i.e. after humanity was created, and so the most proper time for the subjection to futility is when God pronounced the Curse on humanity.

That interpretation fits well with the phrase "suffers the pains of childbirth together" in verse 22. That phrase is actually the translation of one compound word in Greek, a combination of "labor pains" "together". The whole creation suffers together. The reference to birth pangs appears to refer back to the Curse on Eve that her "pain in childbirth" would be greatly multiplied (Gen. 3:16). Collins points out the Greek word for "pain" used in the Septuagint to translate the Hebrew word for "pain" in Genesis is *not* used in Romans and by that he concludes Paul is not referencing the Curse.[38] But, the reference to child birth travail in Romans surely is not a coincidental metaphor Paul used, even if the Greek equivalent of the Hebrew in Genesis is not used.

YEC are probably thinking, "Well, if the passage is referring to the whole creation and the Fall caused the subjection to futility, what's the problem?" The question is: Does that mean the "slavery to corruption" of 8:21 also occurred at the Curse? The overall context of these verses is to comfort those who suffer by reminding them better things are coming (v. 18). The creation anxiously longs for the "revealing of the sons of God" (v. 19), that is, the time when we, and it, are changed from corruptible to incorruptible (I Cor. 15:50-54) and we suffer no longer, but before we can be changed God had to subject the creation to futility

113

(v. 20). He had to make it so we suffer here for a little while in hope of liberating the creation from its slavery to corruption, its bondage to decay (v. 21). The whole of creation is literally burning out and becoming more random, and as a result, decaying and perishing. When was it enslaved to corruption? Logically, according to these verses, it must have occurred *before* the subjection to futility because the subjection was done to solve the corruption problem.[39] Was it done immediately before, or long before? Verse 21 does not tell us when it began, so we must not be dogmatic and insist on a particular time.

To continue the context then, the next verse says the "whole creation" groans and suffers (v. 22) because it must endure its subjection to futility at the Curse, and because of its continued bondage to corruption, but that conclusion presents no issue for OEC. Why? Because the timeframe for when the bondage to corruption began is not listed, except to say it was before the subjection to futility (i.e. before the Curse). Therefore, *the Curse was not the cause of the bondage to decay.*

The "slavery to corruption" or "bondage to decay" (NIV) is often equated with the Second Law of Thermodynamics which "forbids heat to flow spontaneously from cold to hot bodies while allowing it to flow from hot to cold."[40] This unidirectional heat flow results in the decrease of useable energy in the universe and also results in the impossibility of getting more energy out of something than is put into it. Because the net effect of the Second Law is decay it has been asserted by some YEC (because of Romans 8) that it was instituted at the Curse. However, many YEC see the serious problems with that conclusion. "Some older creationist literature claims that the second law of thermodynamics began at the Fall. However, the second law is responsible for a number of good things... solar heating of the earth... walking... breathing... digestion... [and] baking a cake..."[41] (Sarfati) This YEC correctly sees that without the Second Law reality as we know it would be more than just a little different. The universe, the laws of physics, and all living creatures would have to have had a completely different design, but there is no indication in Genesis, or anywhere else, that God instituted that radical of a design change at the Curse. The Second Law is fundamental to the way we experience this universe and appears to be designed that way by God from the beginning.

The real problem in Romans is YEC jump to the conclusion the bondage to decay caused all animal death and natural disasters at the Curse. The Bible does not say that. Romans says the bondage to decay occurred *before* the Fall, and says nothing about when animal death and natural disasters began. It seems as though YEC already have in mind the doctrines they want to prove, and then they set about to take whatever Scriptures come the closest to saying that and interpret them that way. *This exaggeration of the Scriptures should stop.*

7. The Biblical promise that God will restore all things refers to making a new heavens and new Earth back into something like the original creation.

The dispute here is over what it means for God to restore all things. YEC equate the description of the future (?) in Isaiah 11:1-10 and 65:17-25 to what

Chapter 6 – Death *Before* the Fall

they think it will be like during "the period of the restoration of all things" as mentioned in Acts 3:18-21:

> [18]"But the things which God announced beforehand by the mouth of all the prophets, that His Christ would suffer, He has thus fulfilled. [19]"Therefore repent and return, so that your sins may be wiped away, in order that times of refreshing may come from the presence of the Lord; [20]and that He may send Jesus, the Christ appointed for you, [21]whom heaven must receive **until the period of restoration of all things** about which God spoke by the mouth of His holy prophets from ancient time. [emphasis mine]

Now look at portions of Isaiah 11 and 65 [emphases and comments mine]:

> 11:[1]Then **a shoot will spring from the stem of Jesse [a messianic prophecy fulfilled when Jesus came]**, And a branch from his roots will bear fruit. [2]The Spirit of the LORD will rest on Him... [4b]And He will strike the earth with the rod of His mouth, And with the breath of His lips He will slay the wicked **[when?]**... [6]And the wolf will dwell with the lamb, And the leopard will lie down with the young goat, And the calf and the young lion and the fatling together; And a little boy will lead them. [7]Also the cow and the bear will graze, Their young will lie down together, And the lion will eat straw like the ox. [8]The nursing child will play by the hole of the cobra, And the weaned child will put his hand on the viper's den. [9]They will not hurt or destroy in all My holy mountain **[only there?]**, For the earth will be full of the knowledge of the LORD As the waters cover the sea. [10]Then **in that day The nations** will resort to the root of Jesse... **[*Nations* in the restoration? And Rms. 15:12 quotes 11:10 as if it was being fulfilled in Paul's time.]**

> 65:[17]"For behold, **I create new heavens and a new earth [same as Rev. 21:1?]**; And the former things will not be remembered or come to mind... [19]"I will also rejoice in Jerusalem and be glad in My people; And there will no longer be heard in her The voice of weeping and the sound of crying. [20]"No longer will there be in it an infant who lives but a few days, Or an old man who does not live out his days; **For the youth will die at the age of one hundred And the one who does not reach the age of one hundred** Will be thought accursed... **[There will be death after the restoration and new heavens and earth?]** [23]"They will not **labor in vain, Or bear children** for calamity... **[We will still be working and having babies then too?]** [25]"The wolf and the lamb will graze together, and the lion will eat straw like the ox; and dust will be the serpent's food **[literally? Snakes will eat dust?]**. They will do no evil or harm in all My holy mountain **[again, only there?]**," says the LORD.

I point out the difficulties of these texts not because I have all the answers (I don't) or wish to engage in an eschatological debate (definitely not my strength),

115

but only to show how cautious one must be taking them literally. YEC want to take the parts about animals not eating each other and not being dangerous very literally as a restoration of Eden, but it would leave them with nations and human death in the restoration. It seems like one could interpret much of this as already having happened or currently happening, especially if some of it is taken figuratively.[42] I certainly would not want to defend the doctrine of "no animal death before the Curse" using these verses. It opens up far too many peripheral questions. I have read nothing in the Bible that says our future will be exactly like Eden so taking these verses as a future state similar to a previous state is an interpretational leap similar to many other YEC Olympic long-jumps.

8. Teaching that death and bloodshed existed prior to the Fall destroys the meaning of the full redemptive work of Christ.

YEC think that a belief in death before the Fall destroys a crucial doctrine of Christianity: the Atonement. Please do not take me wrong, undermining the meaning of the atoning sacrifice of Jesus would be a serious offense. He died for you and me and all humanity.[43] I just believe animal death before the Fall has *nothing* to do with Jesus' death. Jesus did not die for Garfield and Odie. But YEC say:

> I agree that the whole philosophy of the Atonement is undermined by teaching that there were millions of years of bloodshed before sin.[44] [Sarfati]
> The god of an old earth is one who uses death as part of creating. Death therefore can't be the penalty for sin and can't be described as the last enemy (I Corinthians 15:26).[45] [Ham]
> There's no doubt – the god of an old earth destroys the gospel.[46] [Ham]

I have four responses:

First, the *whole* philosophy of the atonement is undermined by animal predation? Sarfati needs to be more specific than that. While I agree that animal bloodshed can be symbolic of the Atonement (after all one animal dies that another could live), it should not be a surprise that a symbolism for the Atonement could have been built into the creation from the beginning before sin. The creation has many symbolisms of God, like the Sun as a powerful life-giving energy source (Ps. 84:11), or the way a hen gathers its chicks (Mt. 23:37), or the way an eagle broods over its nest (Dt. 32:11). These were all in place before humanity so the fact animal predation can symbolize the Atonement in no way detracts from the real thing any more than the Sun detracts from God's glory. That is especially true in light of the fact we were chosen *from the foundation of the world* to be adopted as sons of God through Jesus (Eph. 1:3-5, Acts 2:23, Rev. 13:8). *A sacrifice was planned from the beginning.* YEC make a mistake by connecting the bloodshed of animal predation with animal sacrifice.[47] They are not the same. One animal killing another may be symbolic of atonement, but it does not atone for sin because animals do not sin. And humans sacrificing animals may be a temporary atonement, but even they were only symbolic of what Jesus would do (Heb. 9:23).

Second, I know of no Old-Earth *Creationist* who believes God used death to create anything. Maybe some Theistic Evolutionists believe that, but no OEC. YEC frequently equate the idea of an old Earth with evolution and they have done such a good job of it that the common church-goer has now mistakenly made the connection. The problem is, beliefs in an old Earth and universe are not the same as belief in naturalistic evolution. The universe could be a trillion years old and still OEC would believe naturalistic evolution is impossible.

Third, Ken Ham is just plain wrong when he says death could not be a penalty for sin if animal death preexisted sin. It can still be a penalty for sin *for humanity* if humanity was not going to die unless they sinned. He states this like an open and shut case when the response against it is so simple and obvious. I do not blame him for not answering every argument against him in simple bad-answer books, but I do blame him for using bad arguments when he should know better, especially since some people only hear his side and trust him.

Fourth, the implication behind using "god" rather than "God" in the quote above is very serious. Some YEC are in essence accusing OEC of worshipping a different god. If true that would have serious consequences. To be fair, most YEC do not do that. These horrendous accusations are most noticeably coming from one organization: Answers in Genesis headed by Ken Ham.

To conclude, predation before the Fall does not destroy the Gospel nor the Atonement. It has nothing to do with them except as a symbol. "Christ Jesus came into the world to save sinners" (I Tim. 1:15). *Animals are not sinners.*

9. If God's original "very good" creation contained death and disease God must be non-existent, incompetent, impotent, or cruel.

This argument is unique in that both skeptics and YEC use it, albeit in different ways. Skeptics use it as an argument against the existence of God. For example, it is well known that the early death of Charles Darwin's daughter caused him to reject God. Skeptics see disease and death and say an omnipotent omniscient God could have done better.

YEC and OEC use different approaches to answer the skeptics on this. YEC agree with the skeptics a good God would not have caused death and disease except as punishment for sin, and argue all was different before the Fall. The OEC answer is more complicated because the skeptic's argument must be divided into parts and the parts have different answers. I will cover that below.

Before we get too deep on this ninth point let us do a quick survey of what we can conclude concerning death and disease thus far: An omnipotent eternal God can make His own rules and it follows that whatever He does and approves must be good. God determines what is good.[49] When we observe the way the world is (containing death, disease, and natural disasters), several questions come to mind. Is this the way God originally made it and if not, why did it change? From the standpoint of those of us who believe the Bible is God's word, we would expect it to provide some answers on this.

What then have we seen that the Bible says? It says God saw everything He had made and it was "very good" (Gen. 1:31), but it does not define "very good" as an absence of animal death. The Bible is silent for the most part (except Ps. 104:21) on the origin of death *for animals*. It is not silent however on the origin of death for humans. God told Adam and Eve if they ate the fruit they would die (Gen. 2:17). Then, after they ate it, He pronounced that Adam would return to the dust from whence he came (Gen. 3:17-19) and humans have died ever since with few exceptions.[48] God did not prohibit humans from eating meat in Genesis 1:29-30, He simply gave them permission to eat from His garden. Later, He apparently gave someone eating instructions on clean and unclean animals because Noah knew (Gen. 7:2, 8). The Curse (Gen. 3:14-19) had much more to do with *what humanity would do* to the animals and the ground than what God did to either. Some level of pain was experienced by humanity in the original design, and sweat and thorns could have existed originally also. The bondage to decay (Rms. 8:21) of the universe existed before the Fall too. YEC interpretations of these things have gone far beyond what the text demands.

We also saw that God's original plan was for humanity to "Be fruitful and multiply, and fill the earth, and subdue it; and rule..." (Gen. 1:28) Part of subduing and ruling the Earth would have involved taming the wild outside the garden to duplicate the conditions in the garden. We know the garden was not in a wild state because it needed to be maintained. God blessed humanity to fill the land. If humanity had fulfilled that blessing before the Fall, then animals would have been replaced by humans, and would have died, and *thus it was God's plan all along for animals to die*. We also saw that animal death is good for the Earth and humanity because of overpopulation and limited resources.

In addition, consider why predators fascinate us. Why is it that we like to watch a Bald Eagle catch fish, or cheetahs run down a gazelle, or crocodiles spring up to snatch a wildebeest, or Great White Sharks consume a carcass, or spiders ensnare a fly, or Killer Whales surfing a beach for seals? Is our interest in these things really part of our fallen nature? Is it not obvious *God designed us to be the greatest predators* on Earth (responsibly of course)? Are these things interesting (and sometimes beautiful) because they can be seen as symbolic of the authority to fulfill our *God-given purpose* to responsibly rule and subdue the Earth? I think so.

With all that being true we must conclude that *God originally designed animals to die* which is also evidenced by many of their obvious *design* features like claws, sharp teeth, hunting instincts, poisons, defense mechanisms, and specialized features like long tongues, sonar, and stingers. God designed these things, not Satan or evolution.

The Bible thus describes *the original creation* as having animal death and predation, some discomfort with creation, some level of pain, some sweaty work maintaining a garden and temperature differences. The Bible is a very real book and presents a very real picture of the original creation as not much different than today. Within that original creation God designed an ideal place for Adam and Eve to live, a place for their comfort that met all of their God-given needs. God could have showed them multitudes of wonders regarding the purpose for

Chapter 6 – Death *Before* the Fall

every animal and plant, but they chose to listen to Satan and believe him instead of God so God allowed *the built-in* consequences of sin to run their course. And now we are reaping the results of the Curse we ourselves have caused by our ignorant and premeditated abusive actions, and it is getting worse.

Skeptics then complain about our condition and claim if God exists He would not allow suffering and He could have done a better job of creating than that. How quickly it seems some people believe they are qualified to judge God as if they could envision a better way. Their arrogance is staggering. Then, here come YEC quoting skeptics and agreeing that if the Earth is very old and animal death was here before sin the skeptics have a valid case, i.e. God would be cruel.

Regardless of the death of animals prior to the Fall, OEC are emphatic the skeptic's case holds no water. So, let us hear the skeptics' arguments some YECs quote as if they were valid:

Charles Templeton – The grim and inescapable reality is that *all life is predicated on death*. Every carnivorous creature *must* kill and devour another creature. It has no option. How could a loving and omnipotent God create such horrors?... Surely it would not be beyond the competence of an omniscient deity to create an animal world that could be sustained and perpetuated without suffering and death.[50] [emphases his]

Sir David Attenborough – When creationists talk about God creating every individual species as a separate act, they always instance hummingbirds, or orchids, sunflowers and beautiful things. But I tend to think instead of a parasitic worm that is boring through the eye of a boy sitting on the bank of a river in West Africa, [a worm] that's going to make him blind.

And [I ask them], "Are you telling me that the God you believe in, who you also say is an all-merciful God, who cares for each one of us individually, are you saying that God created this worm that can live in no other way than in an innocent child's eyeball? Because that doesn't seem to me to coincide with a God who's full of mercy."[51]

Carl Sagan – If God is omnipotent and omniscient, why didn't he start the universe out in the first place so it would come out the way he wants? Why is he constantly repairing and complaining? No, there's one thing the Bible makes clear: The biblical God is a sloppy manufacturer. He's not good at design, he's not good at execution. He'd be out of business if there was any competition.[52]

The skeptics' arguments can be broken down into three parts: **1.** God could have done better than creating horrible animal death as a means of sustaining His creation. **2.** God allowing human suffering and death is not loving or merciful. **3.** God is a poor designer if extinction was part of His plan.

Before I respond to each, one over-all response involves a lesson learned by C. S. Lewis which contributed to his rejection of atheism:

> My argument against God was that the universe seemed so cruel and unjust. But how had I got this idea of *just* and *unjust*? A man does not call a line crooked unless he has some idea of a straight line. What was I comparing this universe with when I called it unjust? If the whole show was bad and senseless from A to Z, so to speak, why did I, who was supposed to be part of the show, find myself in such violent reaction against it?... Of course I could have given up my idea of justice by saying it was nothing but a private idea of my own. But if I did that, then my argument against God collapsed too – for the argument depended on saying that the world was really unjust, not simply that it did not happen to please my fancies. Thus in the very act of trying to prove that God did not exist – in other words, that the whole of reality was senseless – I found I was forced to assume that one part of reality – namely my idea of justice – was full of sense. Consequently atheism turns out to be too simple.[53]

All of the skeptics' arguments amount to an objection against what God did, not against the fact that God is. To argue against God's existence they have attempted to use *an objective standard that only God could provide*. Without an objective standard, their argument collapses to their fancy. At best, this argument is against God being good *from a human perspective*, not against His existence. The skeptics do not like what God did, but who are we to define what is good? God is the standard by which goodness, love, mercy, and justice are defined. If He then reveals to us what He did, i.e. created animal death, then it is good, despite how some *feel* about it.

Please remember this book is not about the problem of evil though. My concentration in this chapter is to defend Old-Earth Creationism against those who think the Bible says animal death came after the Fall. From an old-Earth interpretation, animal death originating after the Fall is impossible[54], the death of animals must have preceded the Fall as evidenced by the fossil record. However, my responses to the skeptic's arguments are as follows:

Response to 1 – God could have done better than creating horrible animal death as a means of sustaining His creation.

For Templeton to make such an assertion we must ask by what standard is it horrible, by his arbitrary standard or by an objective standard from God? His standard is arbitrary, which means he may not personally like the idea of sustaining a creation with animal death but God, and others, may not see anything wrong with it. God must not have a problem with animal death, and neither do I for that matter. I believe this creation is sustained in such a way as to allow choice (love) to exist and apparently that must involve animal death. *No one knows* whether there is another way to do it, and to *ignorantly* accuse God of choosing a horrible method is to make a poor judgment.

Animal death is good for humanity because if no death existed all resources would have been used up very quickly. But the skeptic may argue that God did not have to make it that way. He could have done it so that every animal lived forever and resources were never used up. And reproduction would shut down at some point. And small animals would not die when big animals stepped on them or accidentally ate them. And Frosty the Snowman would never melt. Enough is enough! Do we not see the folly of trying to imagine such a place? God is all-wise and acts in ways that best accomplishes His purposes and we can either agree with Him or not. *Animal* death before the Fall causes me no faith-shaking trauma. Like it or not, it must be the best way to accomplish the purposes of God even if no one *fully* comprehends how.

Response to 2 – God allowing human suffering and death is not loving or merciful.

Human suffering and death, on the other hand, are an entirely different story. People have questioned the existence of God for ages because of suffering and the existence of evil. Why would God allow it? Why, if He can, does He not stop evil? How can He just sit idly by while evil of the worst kind imaginable happens before His eyes?

Though a full answer to the problem of evil is beyond the scope of this book I have eight brief responses.

First, I think the best explanation for why evil exists is because evil is a necessary consequence of free will. God cannot grant true freedom without allowing the tragedies that result from wrong choices (sin). Suffering and death for humans is the result of the freedom to sin, and they are the price to pay for the greater good of allowing freedom, pleasure, and love.

Second, before we blame God for all the suffering in the world we should consider the fact He would have protected Adam and Eve from all of it had they not sinned.

Third, humanity is the cause of the worst suffering in the world, not God. One could complain that God has allowed it, but we are the ones who have caused genocide, starvation, torture, murder, rape, disease, plagues, wars, sexual abuse, addiction, and are even responsible in many ways for massive deaths from natural disasters by living too close to volcanoes and shorelines, or building unsafe structures in earthquake prone areas. God could have shown Adam and Eve what was dangerous and how to avoid it. And let us not forget the damage humans have caused the planet and the undesirable effects that result.[55]

Fourth, only God can make sense out of suffering. If God does not exist there is no hope for ultimate justice; there is no life after death; all suffering is random and meaningless; and there is no ultimate purpose for life at all. Those consequences of atheism deserve far greater complaint than not fully understanding why God allows suffering.

Fifth, we cannot fully see the purposes for why God allows suffering. However, just because we do not understand does not mean there are no good reasons. "God causes all things to work together for good of those who love God, to those who are called according to *His* purpose." (Rms. 8:28) God always has reasons.

Sixth, suffering could be a lot worse were it not for God's constraint. (See I Cor. 10:13 and II Th. 2:6-7 for example)

Seventh, justice will be served one day for all those who have caused suffering. But before we get too excited about someone else's judgment, remember it is coming for all of us. "For we must all appear before the judgment seat of Christ, that each one may be recompensed for his deeds in the body, according to what he has done, whether good or bad." (II Cor. 5:10)

Eighth, death and suffering are *temporary*. There will come a time when God "shall wipe away every tear from their eyes; and there shall no longer be *any* death; there shall no longer be *any* mourning, or crying, or pain; the first things have passed away." (Rev. 21:4)

The Bible is about the human condition which includes suffering. It does not ignore suffering or deny it. It tells us its origins. It tells us some of its purposes. It does not downplay it. It expresses the emotions associated with it. It was written to comfort those who suffer. It assures us those who cause it will pay. It gives many examples of how people dealt with it. It corrects misconceptions about it. It tells of how Jesus suffered for us. And it ultimately tells us suffering will end.

Of all religious books the Bible meets suffering head-on and *offers the only meaningful answers one can find on the subject*. Atheism can only say, "that's just the way it is." Hinduism says you must accept your karma from previous lives and therefore offers no incentive to relieve others' suffering. Buddhism only promises an escape to nirvana where emotions are absorbed into the *impersonal* void of the one. Only Christianity tells of God who came to Earth, suffered in our place, overcame death, and promises eternal life with Him. Not only does that plan sound much better to me, here is the best part: it is true!

Response to 3 – God is a poor designer if extinction was part of His plan.

So Sagan says God is a "sloppy manufacturer". And I am sure he probably thought he could have done a better job if he was God. He uses the extinction of animals over the geologic ages as support for his disbelief. I guess the thought never occurred to him that the extinct animals may have fulfilled their purpose and were not needed any longer.

The universe is an incredibly hostile environment for life, and Earth is an exceptionally rare place in the universe,[56] and its conditions are just right to allow advanced life to exist for only a brief time,[57] and it would appear life was introduced at just the right times when the early conditions of the Earth could support it.[58] And God indicates in Genesis that humanity is special and was one of the purposes for Earth (Gen. 1:26-27). Earth was designed for us to live and have a worshipful relationship with Him. The methods God used for designing Earth are only partially specified in Genesis, and life and animals were part of that design, and many beneficial qualities for humanity resulted from the effects life had on our planet over its long history. The purpose for some animals, like dinosaurs, was apparently temporary to prepare the planet for our arrival. It was probably not a good idea to have non-domesticable giant reptilian predators like tyrannosaurs running around with humanity anyway, so God sent an asteroid to take care of the issue for the most part after their purpose on Earth was complete.[59]

I do not see that version of history in conflict with anything the Bible says. Animal death before sin is not a major (or minor) topic of the Bible and does no harm to the character of God or any doctrine. The issue is the reliability of Genesis as a revelation from God and we must not make Genesis say something it does not say and it says nothing about when animal death began or how long ago the universe and Earth were created.

Consider these four points before calling God a sloppy designer:

First, there are good reasons for God to not make everything last forever. He can certainly keep things in existence as long as He likes, but He chose to make this universe in such a way that it perishes and decays. One obvious reason for that is if humanity knew they would live forever, no matter what they did, there would be no incentive to behave. Limitations are there because some things need to be limited, like sin.

Second, it is impossible for an omnipotent God to waste anything because an infinite supply of energy cannot be wasted. Also, an infinite God cannot waste time. An infinite supply of anything cannot be exhausted, so to accuse an infinite Being of sloppy design because of the amount of energy or vast space He used, or the amount of time that elapsed before humanity was created is ridiculous. An immense powerful universe existing billions of years shows the magnificence of God compared to us puny mortals.

Third, limitations are unavoidable for finite creatures *by definition*. Humans have a limited lifespan, limited strength, limited eyesight, limited smell, etc. God cannot duplicate Himself so *He had to draw the line somewhere* (and skeptics would probably complain wherever the line was drawn). God never intended for humans to be completely self sufficient. He designed us with desires for interaction with Himself and other humans and animals. He created animals for our benefit. For example, an elephant's strength, a donkey's warning, and a dog's sense of smell can all serve humans, to name a very few. God declared, "It is not good for the man to be alone." (Gen. 2:18) God intended each of us to learn to rely on more than ourselves, particularly Him.

Fourth, we cannot do better. Calling God a poor designer is pure ignorance. We cannot possibly know all the reasons for the intricacies of what God did. We are just *barely* beginning to understand how it works, much less why.

The skeptics' arguments amount to nothing more than displeasure with God's designs. In effect they are calling what God did bad when God called it good, but God does not think that is a good idea, "Woe to those who call evil good, and good evil... Woe to those who are wise in their own eyes..." (Is. 5:20-21)

Response to YEC accusations that OEC make God cruel

Young-Earth Creationists pose a different problem than skeptics when they use animal death before the Fall to accuse OEC of tarnishing God's character.

Skeptics have only an arbitrary moral basis to claim God is cruel, but YEC claim to use the same standard OEC use (the Bible). However, the YEC case for animal death beginning at the Fall is essentially non-existent. The Bible teaches God designed and planned animals to die from the beginning. The following YEC quote from Jonathon Sarfati shows how they sympathize with the skeptics. (The bold comments are my comments and *corrections*.)

> The origin of death and suffering is vitally important in defending Christianity **[agreed, but only as it relates to humans]**. Many people use the present suffering and death as an excuse not to believe… **[But they still have no excuse because of all the evidence *for* God's existence.]**
>
> The big picture is that Adam's sin is the reason for all the death in the world… **[This statement is misleading and self-contradictory because just 13 pages prior, this same author argued some animals, namely invertebrates, died before sin. (See Point 3 in this chapter)]**
>
> But if a Christian teaches that suffering existed before there was any sin to warrant it, how then can he give a good apologetic answer to questions such as "Why would God allow mass murderers such as the terrorist attack on New York?" **[Easy, the same way *he* does, human suffering and death began at the Fall and so did sinful acts of violence like terrorism. But animal death is not the same as human suffering.]** A consistent biblical answer points out that death is an intruder **[for humans, the Bible has no problem with animal death]**, so it is not part of God's original creation **[for humans]**, but is ultimately due to man's sin. However, according to long-age theology, death has always been with us… **[Not so, OEC believe human death began at the Fall. He is being inconsistent because even he believes invertebrate death preceded sin.]**
>
> However, a consistent biblical view, that death is an intruder **[for humans]**, provides a coherent solution. But this is impossible unless the fossil record was formed after Adam's sin, which rules out billions of years. **[Not so, animal death *is* part of a consistent *Biblical* view so the fossil record is no problem.]**
>
> It's sad to see [Hugh] Ross promoting the same view as Darwin's clerical contemporaries. He claims that this long-age view is *more* acceptable to unbelievers than the literal Genesis view **[The YEV is *not* the best literal view, it is an exaggerated view]**, failing to realize that this approach had already been tried and failed miserably in Darwin's day.[60]

It is highly debatable which approach has failed considering "long-age" views are still around, are successful converting unbelievers, and are the direction Christian scholarship is moving. The decline of belief in the inerrancy and authority of the Bible could possibly be a direct result of the Young-Earth View successfully convincing several generations of Christians the Bible advocates a young universe and Earth when the Bible says no such thing. The age of the Earth controversy is created by the YEC interpretation colliding head-on with modern science. At least one of them is wrong.

Do YEC and OEC believe in the same God?

The idea a loving God made the original creation to include animal death is so unacceptable to *some* YEC that they accuse OEC of redefining the nature of God. Consider these incitive words by Ken Ham:

> Christians who believe in an old earth (billions of years) need to come to grips with the real nature of the god of an old earth – it is *not* the loving God of the Bible... How could a God of love allow such horrible processes as disease, suffering, and death for millions of years as part of His 'very good" creation?... The god of an old earth cannot therefore be the God of the Bible who is able to save us from sin and death. Thus, when Christians compromise with the millions of years attributed by many scientists to the fossil record, they are, in that sense, seemingly worshipping a different god – the cruel god of an old earth.[61]

I have four responses and I am done with this long chapter:

First, while it is true that various religious groups can accept the authority of the Bible and define God differently (Jehovah's Witnesses and Mormons for example), and thus worship different gods, that does not apply to the differences between YEC and OEC. Christians believe the one God became a man in Jesus Christ. Jehovah's Witnesses believe their god never became a man and Jesus was a lesser god (demigod). Mormons believe in multiple gods, two of which were the Father, who was once a man and became a god, and Jesus, who was the human and spiritual offspring of the Father, who also became a god. Only one of those three can be correct and the Bible commands us to worship the one true God and warns us against those who would worship another Jesus (II Cor. 11:4). It is thus very important to define God properly, but OEC do not disagree with YEC on the *nature or attributes* of God. Both agree Jesus is the one true God and God is love for example. At worst there is only a difference of opinion on defining what love or good means.

Second, the Bible does not call animal death horrible (as Ham did) so he should not either.

Third, God can still save us from sin and death despite designing animal death from the beginning. Ham's conclusion does not follow from his premises.

Fourth, accepting the truth nature reveals is not compromise. Denying strong scientific evidence, a small portion of which is presented in Chapter 8, is much worse and shows similar pharisaical characteristics displayed by Jesus' adversaries. They denied the truth *evidenced* right before their eyes.

OEC and YEC believe in the same God of the Bible and are most often on the same side against the skeptics, atheists, and relativists. Though I believe strongly the YEV is wrong, I will gladly serve and worship alongside them as long as they allow my position to be heard. God's purposes are not served when an opposing side is silenced. A humble open forum where God's guidance is sought, and all points of view are presented, and the evidence weighed, and righteous judgment is executed, cannot help but find the truth.

This has been a long chapter but the issue of animal death before the Fall is *the* major stumbling block for many YEC and thus needed a comprehensive response. The final conclusion is the Bible has no problem with animal death before the Fall and neither should anyone else. God designed it as the limited "very good" system that it is: a self-regulating, self-sustaining system of making human life possible on our planet. The oceans, the sediments, the volcanic and plate tectonic activity, the plant life, and the animal life all play major roles in keeping our environment and atmosphere conducive to our survival.[62] That is still "very good" as God said it was.

A comment from Bruce Waltke, a respected Bible scholar, is an appropriate ending:

> The precreated state of the earth with darkness and chaos suggests that everything hostile to life is not a result of sin. This is Job's discovery (Job 38-41). Job is mystified by his whole experience of suffering. God's response is to make clear that everything negative in the creation from the human perspective is not a result of human sin.[63]

7

The Top Ten Views of Genesis 1
(One destination but many boats)

Many Christians think they have a boat that will get us to the place where science and a literal interpretation of Genesis are in harmony on the age of the universe and Earth. Current evangelical attempts to reconcile Genesis with astronomy and geology have left us on three heavily divided islands. All three are attempting to defend Christianity against pirates and are generally conservative in nature, meaning they adhere to a literal resurrection of Jesus, the Deity of Christ, and some sense of the Bible being God's authoritative inerrant word (though theological definitions of inerrancy vary). But, the three islands are not three simple divisions. Young-Earth vs. old-Earth is one huge division, and then the old-Earth island is divided into those who believe the destination exists and those who believe it does not. I used to be on the young-Earth island until my boat sank and I am now on the old-Earth island trying to convince people the destination exists and I know which boat gets us there. The three islands look something like this:

1. **Those who believe the universe and Earth are young (thousands of years old):** Young-Earth Creationists believe the only legitimate interpretation of Genesis 1 is that God *completed* the whole universe in 6 literal Earth days which forces them to reinterpret modern astronomy and geology to fit the age of the universe and Earth into something like 6000-10,000 years because *they believe* the Bible teaches they cannot be older than that. YEC also believe Noah's Flood was global and dramatically altered Earth's appearance and formed most geologic formations we see today. For YEC this amounts to a near wholesale rejection of modern astronomy and geology. With only minor variations, *all YEC are unified around their one interpretation of Genesis.*

On the other hand, evangelicals who believe the universe and Earth are billions of years old are currently *a conglomerated exegetical mess*! It is easy to give up attempting to choose a good boat. There are at least nine views of Genesis 1 old-Earth believers advocate. And, to make it more complicated, there are some Christians who believe the Bible contains scientific inaccuracies (thinking our destination is a mirage).

2. **Those who believe the universe and Earth are old (billions of years) *but* believe the Bible is scientifically incorrect (naïve):** This group was difficult to name. At one time I called them Theistic Evolutionists and many still do, but because many in this group believe God *created* using evolutionary processes it is possible to loosely include this group under the title of Old-Earth Creationists (see Chapter 10 for more). I also came to realize that people in this group, and the next, advocate some of the same interpretations of Genesis 1, but disagree over whether scientific errors exist in the Bible. So, I suggest naming this group **Accommodationists** because they all believe in what is known theologically as *divine accommodation*. Divine accommodation is the idea that God inspired humans to write Scripture, but did not prevent them from including their ancient misunderstandings of the natural world. The Bible could then be seen as theologically inerrant, but not necessarily scientifically inerrant. Thus, perceived scientific errors of any sort can be dismissed as irrelevant while weakly (in my opinion) holding to some kind of authority structure to Scripture. By this thinking, making any attempt to reconcile the Bible to modern science is impossible because according to them it was written by people with a faulty ancient scientific understanding and was not written to affirm their ancient science. A fuller analysis of the idea will wait until Chapter 10. For now, it seems to me advocating error in the original Biblical texts opens the door to places we do not want to go. Divine accommodation is not a slippery slope to Biblical errancy; it is a monstrous precipice of no return because it already admits scientific error in the text.

And that leaves us with the third evangelical position:

3. **Those who believe the universe and Earth are old (billions of years) *and* believe the Bible is scientifically inerrant:** This group is called by a variety of names including Old-Earth Creationists, Progressive Creationists, and **Concordists**. Concordists believe the Bible and good science do not contradict (are in accord). This group accepts the modern scientific age of the universe and Earth, but rejects the evolution of all life from a common ancestor in favor of special creation. Concordists believe God progressively created distinct life-forms on the planet over a long period of time to prepare Earth for the habitation and special creation of humanity. From their originally created state, life-forms have *devolved* into what we see today through variation, adaption, speciation, and many have become extinct. Concordists agree the Bible is inerrant both theologically and scientifically, and that is our destination, but every OEC view cannot be correct.

Amongst Old-Earth Creationists, both Accommodationists and Concordists, all agree God is the Creator of all created things and the Bible does not specify the age of the universe or Earth. However, *OEC currently have no consensus on interpreting Genesis 1 and advocate at least nine different major views of the 7 Days*. Overall, that leaves us with 10 views of Genesis 1. Yep, that's 10 boats we are divided into, and they aren't all safe. At least nine of them are headed for the bottom of the ocean, like my former Young-Earth Creationist boat.

Ten Views of Genesis

Ten major interpretations of Genesis 1, and many slight variations of these ten, are all trying to solve the science problem, i.e. making sense of modern science in relation to what Genesis says. This list is most certainly not exhaustive, but it does cover all the major options. Some may find it amazing there are that many. When I was searching for which view of Genesis I believed I researched books and articles that taught every view of Genesis I could find comparing points and counterpoints of each. I did not plan for there to be ten views, I just wanted to give every view I could find a fair shot at convincing me of its position and there happened to be ten.

The following is a summary of 10 major views of the 7 Days of Genesis 1:

1. The Young-Earth View (YEV): This is the one view around which all YEC are unified. Proponents of this view believe everything listed in Genesis 1 was completed within six normal Earth days and they also believe the date for the origin of humanity can be determined by the genealogies[1] in Genesis 5 and 11 to be approximately 6000 years ago. Because the universe and Earth were created only five days before humanity that would make the universe and Earth only 6000 years old also. Belief in a young Earth is also closely associated with Flood Geology (the idea a global flood caused nearly *all* fossil bearing geological formations on Earth). According to YEC, there was no death, not even animals, until after the Fall of man, thus any record of an animal dying (like a fossil) had to have occurred after the Fall, and the Flood is the only Biblical event to potentially explain all those fossils. In reality YEC are not trying to harmonize Genesis with modern science; they are trying to change science into their view of Genesis. The only way to get the two to match, as far as the YEV is concerned, is to *reinterpret science in their favor*.

The YEV is also known as the Calendar Day View and the Traditional, Historical, Literal, 24-hour Day View or any number of combinations of those words. Although this view is a traditional view of our day, I object to calling it "historical" and "literal" because that implies it is the only historical and literal view. However, my view claims it is just as historical, and even more literal to the text than the YEV. Also, the YEV is not the only one to advocate the 7 Days are normal 24-hour days. However, it is the *only* view that *pushes* for a young age for the universe and Earth. Some YEC object however:

> I want to make it VERY clear that we don't want to be known *primarily* as "young-Earth creationists"... Believing in a relatively "young earth" is a *consequence* of accepting the authority of the Word of God as an infallible revelation from our omniscient Creator.[2] [Ken Ham – emphasis his]

Regardless of whether that is true or not, the best way to distinguish this view from others is to call it the Young-Earth View, because their interpretation dictates they *must* believe that.

Young-Earth Creationists see all Old-Earth Views as compromises put forth because of a modern belief the universe and Earth are billions of years old. To them, if it were not for efforts to make the Bible fit science none of the other views would have been needed, or even imagined in many cases.

The YEV is also one of only two views (the Gap View being the other one) that asserts no death (of certain "higher" animals at least) occurred before the Fall of man. The Gap View would differ slightly however, because it postulates the destruction, and thus death, of a previous creation, but no death after the new re-creation of the Earth until after the Fall.

Some people are amazed and scoff that there are a large number of people who believe the universe and Earth are only thousands of years old, but this View should not be taken lightly, especially since the highly publicized debate between Ken Ham and Bill Nye the Science Guy. Some of the most vocal defenders of Christianity are YEC and the YEV is still strongly present in Bible colleges and seminaries. However, the place where it has its strongest influence is in the home-school movement.

The idea that Genesis says everything was completed in six literal days only a few thousand years ago is also a position many atheists, skeptics, non-Christians, and liberal scholars hold. The big difference between those groups and YEC is that YEC believe the Earth really is young, whereas skeptics and liberal scholars think Genesis is at worst nonsense, and at best a myth. While holding that Genesis is untrue, atheists and skeptics are more than happy to tell everyone the Bible teaches the universe and Earth are young because it only strengthens their case against the reliability of the Bible.

Though I was once a YEC I no longer believe it is true, *neither Biblically* nor scientifically. Yes, you read me correctly. Some Old-Earth Creationists see the YEV as a viable option for interpreting Genesis, even though they disagree with it. I do not believe the YEV is even Biblically valid.

The 9 Old-Earth Creationists' Views

Within the Old-Earth Creationists camp there are at least nine major views of Genesis 1. Some are more popular than others and some are on the decline. Some are recent additions and some have been around for hundreds of years. Some are obscure and have never attracted a large following, but all have been advocated by their supporters as legitimate alternatives to the YEV.

2. The Day-Age View (DAV): This view is perhaps the most popular and oldest of the OEC views. It interprets the 7 Days as seven long periods of time, *not* normal 24-hour days. According to the DAV the six *ages* of creation correspond closely to the modern scientific interpretation of the history of Earth, making it a Concordist view. The seventh age is currently ongoing, but will end with the creation of a new heaven and new Earth in the future.

The DAV has its greatest modern proponent in Hugh Ross[3] from Reasons To Believe, an OEC organization that deals with science and the Bible that I highly respect and recommend. (Despite disagreeing with the DAV, I recommend all materials from RTB.[4])

Other possible titles for this view are the Divine Days View, or Heavenly Days View because some versions of it emphasize the 6 Days are not Earth days but God's days. Though almost no one would attempt to limit God to a particular timeframe, some still refer to the Days as being on Heaven's or God's timescale (figuratively speaking), not ours.

Every view of Genesis other than the DAV sees the Days referring to normal 24-hour days, though in two cases not referring to *actual* Earth days (the Framework View and Analogical Days View). Many people are not aware there are six views that allow for old age *and* advocate real historical Earth days.

As for the DAV, I believe the textual evidence is much stronger the Days were normal 24-hour days, not ages (as I touched on in Chapter 1). Also, day-ages do not solve the scientific order problem. (See Chapter 9 for more on both)

3. The Gap View (GV) or **Ruin-Reconstruction View:** The main premise of this view is that a gap of time exists *between* Genesis 1:1 and 1:2, and the conditions of the Earth as formless, void, wet, and dark in verse 2 were a result of a previous judgment by God whereby He flooded the Earth and destroyed all living things (hence Ruin). He then re-created the Earth in six days a relatively short time ago (hence Reconstruction). This re-creation was without death of both humans and animals until Adam and Eve sinned in the Garden of Eden, which makes this view similar in many ways to the YEV. The previous judgment of the Earth was either for the rebellion of a pre-Adamic race, or because of the fall of Satan and his demons, or for some unrevealed reason.

This view is not as popular as it once was, but it is still advanced by some recent commentators.[5] The GV was perhaps advocated most strongly by the late Arthur C. Custance[6] (1910-1985). It survives mainly amongst pastors and lay-people of the church who have usually not stayed current with science/faith issues and debates. Nearly every major commentary and commentator on Genesis I have read takes the time to spell out the GV's Biblical problems. Also, the scientific contradictions with the view are as insurmountable as the YEV. Like most other old-Earth views of Genesis, the Gap View ends up not solving the problem it intended to solve.

I believe the textual evidence does not permit a gap *between* Genesis 1:1 and 1:2 (See Chapters 2 and 9), nor a previous destruction before Noah, and the science problems for the GV are as bad as the YEV.

4. The Framework View (FV): This view might be the most difficult to quickly grasp by anyone who hears it for the first time. Here is a simple overview by supporters of the view, "The Holy Spirit has given us an inerrant historical account of the creation of the world, but that account has been shaped, not by a concern to satisfy our curiosity regarding sequence or chronology, but by predominantly theological and literary concerns."[7] The Framework View takes a non-chronological view of Genesis; that is, the events that are described on the 7 Days were historical events occurring some time ago, but they were not necessarily listed chronologically or sequentially. The 7 Days are only a literary framework (metaphor or figurative description) and thus not *actual* days or real periods of time. The FV asserts God used the real days of a human work week as a metaphor to tell us what He actually did over an unspecified period of time.

Meredith Kline[8] (1922-2007) was perhaps the Framework View's greatest advocate though many have picked up his mantle. The FV is most likely to be found amongst professional theologians rather than the average church attendee and it is likely to stay that way. This view, along with the last six of the OEC views, has not yet made any serious impressions on the general public the way the Day-Age View and Gap View have.

The topical and non-sequential nature of Genesis 1 has already been shown in Chapter 1 and the FV would agree, but advocates of the FV draw unwarranted conclusions from those observations by saying the 7 Days are figurative and not an actual week on Earth. I believe the figurative and metaphorical leanings of the FV are a result of FV advocates being predominantly Accommodationists, believing the Bible teaches a faulty ancient cosmology.

As for the FV, I find it very difficult to accept the author of Genesis intentionally planned the first part of human history around a metaphor, so I do not believe the FV is correct. I believe the chronological parts of the narrative were meant by the author to be understood as accurate history (see Chapter 9), and the non-chronological parts of the text play the major role in understanding how science and Genesis are reconciled (see Chapter 2).

5. The Analogical Days View (ADV): This is another view that is not easily grasped at first, so again, here is a brief summary of the view by C. John Collins, its originator, "...the days are God's workdays, their length is neither specified nor important, and not everything in the account needs to be taken as historically sequential... Their length makes little difference to the account, which is based on analogy rather than identity between God's work and man's."[9] In the ADV the 7 Days are not a metaphor, they are an analogy. Similar to the Framework View, the ADV believes the author gave us the account *like* God was working during a human work week, but unlike the FV the days were *His* "workdays" (real periods of time). Thus, the 7 Days *were not actual Earth days*, but they were real periods of time of unspecified length.

I almost did not classify the ADV and DAV as different views because both believe the Days were long periods of time. Describing the Days as God's work days "analogous" to our work week is not much different than Day-ages and essentially says the Days of Genesis are longer than ours and long Days are the defining point of the DAV. Proponents of the ADV even use many of the same arguments the DAV uses to prove the Days must have been longer than 24 hours.[10] Despite all that, I ultimately classified them separately because organizations like the Presbyterian Church of America classify them as separate views[11], and the DAV, unlike the ADV, would not call the 7 Days an analogy, but consider the Days themselves to be actual long periods of time on Earth. Nor would they say Genesis is actually describing a human week of normal days. Also, the DAV is more concerned with chronology.

The ADV is increasing in acceptance, and it looks like that will continue, but like the FV it is only well known within Christian academia, not by the average church member. Also, the main supporter of the ADV (Collins), says his "sympathies are with the harmonizers"[12], meaning he leans toward being a Concordist, which does not describe many FV supporters. At the same time, some Accommodationists like Davis Young have "sympathy"[13] for elements of the ADV. Lines between some views get really blurry sometimes.

Like the FV, my problems with the ADV start with having to accept that the author did not intend to describe a real human week within which God worked, but again, more on that in Chapter 9.

6. The Intermittent Days View (IDV) or **Age-Separated Days View**: This view sees each of the 7 Days as being *separated* by long periods of time. The days themselves are normal Earth days, but millions or billions of years pass between them. Although this view is a fairly obvious option to fit long ages of time in Genesis, it also is not that popular, but it has recently been advocated by Robert Newman[14] and John Lennox[15] (who will likely give it a boost because of his popularity).

The questions arising from this interpretation are whether Genesis allows gaps of time *between* the Days, and whether the time it takes to fulfill the proclamations overlaps the Days. Chapter 9 will discuss that further.

Some of these views may be starting to sound alike, but the next four views will not.

7. The Limited-Creation View (LCV): I have renamed this view for the reader to have a better idea of what it proposes. John Sailhamer, the originator and main supporter of the view calls it Historical Creationism and Textual Creationism[16] but I do not like those titles because they imply this view is the only historically or textually correct view. Advocates of the other views would make those same claims. This view is most often called the **Focus-on-Palestine View**[17].

The LCV sees the 7 Days being *limited* to the creation of the *land* God promised to the Israelites, *not the whole Earth*. The Hebrew word *'erets* is frequently translated as both "earth" (as in Gen. 1:1) and "land" (as in Promised Land), and it is likely the original audience did not understand they lived on a large spherical object floating in space. *To them*, the word *'erets* did not produce mental pictures of a blue and white swirled planet orbiting the Sun like the word "Earth" does for us today. *To them*, *'erets* most often referred to the dry ground we are standing on (as God called it – Gen. 1:10). Because the gift of the Promised Land to the Jews is one of the themes of the whole Pentateuch (the first five books of the Bible), Sailhamer suggests the 7 Days only refer to the limited creation of the Promised Land a relatively short time ago.

The LCV uses a slightly similar interpretation of Genesis 1:1-2 as the Gap View to reconcile science and Genesis. It sees the long ages of an old Earth *completely occurring within verse 1*, including the formation of stars and planets and *nearly all the animals in the fossil record, including the fossil record itself*. Unlike the Gap View, the LCV sees no gap of time *between* verses 1 and 2, but instead sees the term "beginning" referring to the whole time from the first moment of creation to the time when the "land" was in the condition described in verse 2. Therefore, the verses have no gap of time *between* them, but verses 1 and 2 are part of an undetermined block of time *before* the 7 Days begin. These may sound like only semantic technicalities but it amounts to a big difference. This idea "the beginning" refers to a block of time before the 6 Days is not unique to the LCV, but the idea the Days refer only to the Promised Land is.

While it is clear the focus of Genesis narrows from the whole Earth to a particular "land" (i.e. the Garden of Eden), the biggest problem with this view is that the work proclaimed on the Days appears to have a much grander scale in mind than just God making a particular "land" for humanity. The Days appear to most commentators to refer to God originating the earthly creation in its entirety, not a limited portion.

8. The Revelatory Days View (RDV) or **Days of Revelation View**: This view suggests that the 6 Days are not the actual days God did His work. Instead they refer to the days that God revealed to humanity what He had done long ago, either through Moses, Enoch, Adam, or someone anonymous. In other words, God revealed what He created and made to a man over a period of six 24-hour days, but we are not to take the events revealed on each day as the order in which the work was actually done, or to think that the actual creating or making was done *on* those days. Meaning, when the text says, "And God said..." it means God was telling the story to a man *after* He had already finished everything. Certainly there were prophets to whom God chose to give revelations of the past that humanity could not have witnessed (John in Rev. 12 for example). This view sees Genesis as one of those after-the-fact revelations.

The RDV had its two biggest supporters in the late father and son team of P.J. Wiseman (1888-1948) and Donald J. Wiseman (1918-2010).[18] Many commentators list this view among Genesis interpretation options, but it does not appear to be gaining any supporters. Though it is admitted Genesis 1 must have been revealed (spoken?) to someone, because no human could have witnessed it, the biggest issue with the RDV is that Genesis does not read like an account of God telling the story to someone. It reads more like someone telling a story of the actual historical events.

9. The Cosmic Temple View (CTV): This is the rookie view on the field, born out of ancient cosmology and Accommodationist thinking. The CTV agrees with the basic structure of the Framework View which says Genesis used a human week framework to reveal theological truths[19], but the CTV says the Days also represent a *real week* wherein God inaugurated the *functional purposes* of His creation. According to the CTV, the 7 Days did *not* involve the *material* origins of creation, only its *functional* origins. Let's hear it from John Walton, the view's originator:

> In summary, we have suggested that the seven days are not given as the period of time over which the material cosmos came into existence, but the period of time devoted to the inauguration of the functions of the cosmic temple, and perhaps also its annual reenactment.[20]

And he says:

> [Genesis 1] …was never intended to be an account of material origins. Rather it was intended as an account of functional origins in relation to people in the image of God viewing the cosmos as a temple.[21]

Walton gives an excellent illustration of what he is talking about by using the institution of a college.[22] For example, let's say God said, "Let there be a college over there." Walton says we would be mistaken to say the college existed immediately after the buildings were made (the *material* construction phase). The college would only exist after it was *functioning* as such, meaning with a campus, buildings, students, and faculty doing what a college does.

The point is well taken and it makes sense the original audience could have thought that way (as Walton argues). God's creation was not complete until it was functioning for the purposes God created it and Genesis 1 is the account of how the creation came to function. I doubt anyone will disagree with that part of the CTV. Walton's point of including functional origins in the creation account was needed because too many views emphasize the material origin only. Walton also asserts the ancients saw the cosmos as a temple in which God (or gods) had taken residence and ruling authority. Those are reasonable conclusions, but the conclusion with which many disagree is that Genesis is *only* concerned about functional origins. The question is whether *both* material *and* functional origins are intended by the creation account and Walton knows this (see Chapter 9).

In the book on his view, Walton names it the **Cosmic Temple Inauguration View**[23] but many have shortened it and it could go by several names including the Functional View, the Functional Framework View, or the Inauguration Days View. One could also see the CTV as very similar to the RDV if the week occurred after humanity was created and God was speaking directly to them. Walton does not address that idea and does not specify *when* he thinks the week occurred.

And that leaves only one more view, the one I have advocated in this book.

10. The Prophetic Days View (PDV) or **Proclamation Days View**: I also renamed this view. It is usually called the **Days of Divine Fiat View**[24], but I do not like that title because it does not speak the language of the average Bible reader. Rarely do you ever hear the word "fiat" used outside formal theological settings, except in reference to a car. The PDV was the view advocated by Alan Hayward[25] (1923-2008). I do not believe it has been given proper respect among the more popular OEC views. I have argued in Chapter 2 the Prophetic Days View is the simplest interpretation of Genesis containing the fewest potential problems and is *the original intended meaning of the text by the author*.

The PDV essentially argues that at the time Genesis 1:2 describes the Spirit of God brooding over the dark waters of an already existent "desolate and lifeless"[26] Earth, God completed a one week work of prophesying (proclaiming) *in a topical order* what He was *going to do* to change the Earth's condition. The actions that the text says God did to fulfill the proclamations He did afterward over an unspecified period of time leading up to the creation of Adam and Eve in the Garden. The fulfillments of the proclamations *were not fulfilled on the 6 Days He spoke*. Like other prophecies God gave us, the fulfillment was some time after the prophecy (fiat) was given. According to the PDV, Genesis 1 is primarily a record of what God *said* on the 6 Days and His actions and fulfillments were carried out over an unspecified period of time, in an unspecified order, following the historical week in which He said the proclamations.

Summary

Perhaps a summary of the 10 Views will help to understand the ocean of options into which we must plunge. The 10 views of the 7 Days of Genesis 1 as related to the scientific age of the Earth fall into six options:

1. Seven literal days *before* billions of years of Earth history. This is the position of the Prophetic Days View and the view this book advocates.

2. Seven literal days *after* billions of years passed. The Gap View, Limited-Creation View, Revelatory Days View, and Cosmic Temple View[27] are all in this category, but they all differ on what occurred *within* the 7 Days. The GV says the days refer to a near complete recent re-creation of a destroyed previous creation. The LCV says the days refer to the creation of only the Promised Land after a previous creation of the whole Earth. The RDV believes the days are the days God revealed to humanity what He had been doing for billions of years. And the CTV believes the 7 Days are the days God established the final functional purposes for His creation and inaugurated His sovereignty over it.

3. Seven literal days *separated* by billions of years. This is the position of the Intermittent Days View.

4. Seven *day-ages* or *God's days* that add up to billions of years. These are the Day-Age View and Analogical Days View respectively. The difference between the two is that the DAV says the Days themselves were actual long periods of time, but the ADV says the Days of the text refer to normal Earth days as an analogy to God's actual "days" of longer time within which the work was done.

5. Seven *metaphorical* days describing God's real actions sometime in the past. This is the Framework View. The difference between the FV's metaphorical or figurative days and the ADV's analogical days is that the FV does not see the Days as seven actual periods of time whereas the ADV does.

6. Seven literal days with *no* billions of years involved. This is the Young-Earth View.

Technically, the Old-Earth Creationist views above do not specify "billions" of years. All of them say the Bible does not give an age for the universe or Earth, but most agree science has established it as billions of years. However, even though I believe the scientific evidence is overwhelmingly in favor of the universe and Earth being billions of years old[28], *I do not want to force Genesis to conform to that*. I do not want to import any ideas into it, in the way some conservative good-intentioned authors do. For example, "In many faithful Christian's minds, we have reached a point of knowledge today regarding age of the universe allowing us to evaluate the word 'day' in Genesis 1 using general revelation."[29] What he means is, God given human observation of the world (general revelation) has discovered the universe and Earth to be billions of years old, and therefore we should interpret the Days of Genesis 1 to be long periods of time.

If Genesis was ambiguous about the definition of "day" then I would agree general revelation can help. We could use outside information to settle the issue, in the same way we use our modern knowledge of Earth's orbit around the Sun to interpret Bible passages referring to sunrise and sunset as phenomenological language (describing it as it appears to us on Earth). However, since Genesis defines "day" as the lighted portion of a 24-hour period, using science to define it as a long period of time is the wrong approach. We should not take science and force it upon Genesis just because we want them to match, especially if careful analysis of the text reveals a plain meaning.

So my question is: Which one of these 10 views is correct? I am aiming for *the* correct interpretation of Genesis 1, *the one the author originally meant*, if we can find it. One would think with 10 views of Genesis 1 that have developed over thousands of years at least one of them would be what the author meant. Determining what the text says is the human act of interpretation and it is no wonder such a diversity of opinions exist. For example, leaders of the Presbyterian Church in America (PCA) deliberated for two years in the late 1990s to attempt some consensus. Though they determined agreement on many important issues, "The Committee has been unable to come to unanimity over the nature and duration of the creation days."[30] They ultimately could only list "the four most prominent views of the creation days in the PCA"[31]: the Young Earth View, the Day-Age View, the Framework View, and the Analogical Days View (though they did list six others[32] including mine).

Many Christians do not like to argue over doctrines. In many ways the church has succumbed to the post-modern relativistic influences of saying, "Hey, whatever you believe is true for you and that is fine with me" (I do not in any way mean to accuse the PCA of believing that. They do not.). The truth, however, is much more rigid than what someone believes. Truth is truth whether someone believes it or not. Beliefs do not determine truth; beliefs either line up with truth or they do not. Finding the truth is the difficult part.

Surely the author of Genesis knew what he was trying to tell us about the origin of the universe. Can it really be so difficult to discover it? Despite the many nuances and difficulties of the text, I think it is possible for the church to come to a general consensus on its meaning and interpretation. (Call me naïve if you like.) For the sake of truth, Christians should not avoid controversy by dancing around the issue of advocating a view of Genesis because it is complicated. The world will need reasonable answers if they are ever to believe. This book is written to help Christians who accept the idea that the universe and Earth are very old, yet are not sure which view of Genesis they believe. Hopefully this book will help them make up their mind.

I believe my view of Genesis, presented back in Chapter 2, has the answers and is easily understood. The five points I gave can be understood even by a child (and I have tried it on some to be sure). After years of in-depth study I have come to believe Genesis 1 is very simple, *though it requires seeing the story through the eyes of the ancients.* As we have already seen, reconciling it with an old universe and Earth is simple also.

However, the other nine views of Genesis are different than mine and the chapters that follow explain why I rejected them.

8

Why I Repented of the Young-Earth View
(The YEV has big holes. We need a boat that floats.)

Dinosaurs were my passion as a child. I loved drawing them, coloring them, playing with them (toys that is – I am not that old), looking at any pictures I could find, and memorizing their names. My first plastic models were dinosaurs. I was envious of my son's *Jurassic Park* toys and had the movie been released when I was a child I would have begged and pleaded to see it. Instead, Ray Harryhausen's stop-motion animation was the best we had and still holds a nostalgic place in my heart. It was at least much better than the movies that dressed up iguanas, monitor lizards, and alligators as prehistoric beasts, or the movies that had goofy looking man-in-a-suit monsters. Dinosaurs are very powerful images that eventually cause worldview questions and God calls us all to the truth through a variety of means. One of mine was Tyrannosaurus Rex.

I grew up in a Southern Baptist church in the 70's and dinosaurs were *never* mentioned that I can recall. Then I was out of church for about six years until I graduated high school in New Jersey, moved back to Georgia, and began to attend Georgia Tech in 1983. A year and a half into college in January 1985, after becoming very unhappy with my life of drunken frat parties, trying to afford life, and difficult classes, I devoted my life to following Jesus Christ. Not long after that a speaker at a youth meeting told me about creationist literature which I promptly purchased at a Christian bookstore and I went from being a directionless new Christian to a zealot with a purpose to tell anyone who would listen about the "truth" I had learned, and how many scientists were blind to it, and how I suddenly knew better than all those doctorates. I quickly became an arrogant ignorant over-zealous Young-Earth Creationist. Thankfully with Jesus there was hope.

Part of my problem was for some ten years I was one-sided. As a new believer I trusted the YEC books I was reading to present the opposing view's *best* arguments and reasonable responses to them. Though they dealt with surface level material I was not expecting to be confronted with arguments I had never heard because I believed those books equipped me properly; *but I had never read an Old-Earth Creationist book.* To this day I often ask YEC if they have ever read the opposing view and the vast majority tell me they have not. Of course, the reverse is true also, many OEC have never read YEC books. People on both sides have told me they could not "stomach" to read all the way through a book by the other side, which is problematic by itself.

All that changed for me somewhere around 1995-96. I found a book by Hugh Ross in a Christian bookstore, recognized his name because of all the negatives YEC had said about him, purchased the book, and began reading it fully expecting to be able to refute everything this "compromiser" had to say. *I was wrong.* Let me say that again so even my wife can hear it: **I was wrong!**

I was also disappointed because the YEC books I had been reading had not fully answered all the scientific facts involved in the debate. Currently, I generally find YEC science arguments to be short on explaining detail and long on speculation and *ad hoc* responses. Rarely, if ever, will the YEC be able to present their evidence as the last word on a subject. Traditional astronomers and geologists have been much more successful at explaining YEC challenges than YEC are at adequately responding to mainstream scientific challenges. The sad part is that most Christians who even bother to investigate any of this give up when it gets too complicated, which for many is not too far into it. Truly the process can get technical and goes over many Christian's heads. Let's face it, modern science is extremely complicated and specialized. If you do not think so you have not looked at it deep enough. The problem is, instead of humbly admitting ignorance, and being open to other options and expert opinions, some Christians retreat into suppressing and/or ignoring the opposition, a dangerous Pharisaical position.

Here are three examples, out of *many* that could be given, that convince me of serious scientific problems with the Young-Earth View, and I simply ask the reader to apply *common sense* to the facts.

Lake Varves

Scientists believe sedimentary layers (varves) at the bottom of some deep lakes are formed *annually* (like tree rings) and, in fact, the layers are *observed* forming today. Counting the layers determines the deposits in those lakes are far older than a young Earth of 6-15,000 years can explain. For example, Lake Suigetsu in Japan has over 100,000 varve couplets, implying it is at least 100,000 years old.[1]

YEC see the problem this data causes to the age of the Earth demanded by their interpretation of Genesis. Jonathon Sarfati devotes four pages to the problem.[2] He asserts scientific studies have determined fine layering can be formed quickly saying, "The evolutionary journal *Nature* published a cover story about the fact that multiple laminæ can form rapidly"[3]. He offers four processes that can cause quick fine layering: rapid sorting of a mixture of different sized grains, pyroclastic flows of mud and ash observed after the eruption of Mount St. Helens, and underwater landslides and turbidity currents. At the end of his arguments many are left with the *feeling* he has answered the issue in detail and that the layers could have formed quickly rather than over 100,000 years. YEC conclude the layers need not be interpreted as annual layers and are only interpreted that way because scientists make the *assumption* slow processes have always operated the same in the past, and because scientists want

Chapter 8 – Why I Repented of the Young Earth View

to prove long ages of time necessary for evolution, and because of a scientific bias against the Bible.

Enter the scientists again who respond that the deposition methods YEC describe *have nothing to do with these lake formations*, and I would add that it can be proven with a little common sense observation of the facts. Consider some simple details observed. In Lake Suigetsu the lake varves are alternating dark and light layers with one layer formed in the warmer months and the other layer formed in the cold months. One layer consists of *organic material* like diatoms, leaves, twigs, and insect parts formed in the warm months. The other layer is made of mostly inorganic fine grained silt transported into the lake in the colder months. The problem is YEC do not initially mention the part about organic material found in the layers. Is that not a detail one would expect to be included? Is it also not *extremely obvious* that processes like volcanic eruptions and underwater landslides cannot explain 100,000 fine-grained alternating layers of organic material and inorganic silt?

Another simple fact is left out also. The very small size of the grains of silt and diatoms in the lake *will not settle out of moving water* and are so small they take days to settle even in still water. No quick process can account for *these types* of deposits. In this case, *scientists are clearly only following the path the evidence leads*. They do not care whether the bottom of the lake is 6000 years old or 100,000, and those amounts of time are nearly insignificant to evolution. But YEC are seriously in error if the lake is 100,000 years old, *leading to bias being grievously expressed by the YEC*, not the scientists.

Add to this the not so simple factor of carbon dating. The count of the layers corresponds to the decay of radiocarbon down to about 45,000 years.[4] Meaning, if you count down to the 20,000th layer, that layer shows 20,000 years of ^{14}C decay, and the same is true for *every* layer down to about 45,000 layers (because that is the approximate limit of ^{14}C dating). That indicates ^{14}C has actually been decaying that long. Regardless of your opinion of the overall accuracy of carbon dating, *why would the layers show a decay of Carbon-14 from top to bottom that corresponds to the layer counts if they all formed quickly at the same time?* Are these evidences coincidental? A worse idea, as some really ignorant people have suggested to me, is that these facts are something God did to deliberately keep unbelievers deceived. What a horrible thought! And some of them accuse *us* of tarnishing God's character!

Enter the YEC again where recent evaluation of the Lake Suigetsu varves in a more scholarly sounding publication gives us this response. They agree there are more than 100,000 diatom (organic) and clay (inorganic) varve couplets at the bottom of the lake, and realize volcanic eruptions, turbidity currents, and mudslides did not cause them, but they have to deny they represent 100,000 years. According to YEC, for scientists to interpret the layers as slow annual deposits is only "…using their bias"[5] to interpret the data as long ages.

> For example, they assume that the lake remained unchanged for thousands of years, ever since the first varve formed… But couplets can be created rapidly, and this would have been especially true during the Ice Age.

141

Diatom blooms can occur several times a year in a lake for example, during the spring and fall turnovers. ...dozens of diatom/clay couplets could have occurred each year [in the Ice Age].[6]

Dear YEC reader, please understand, according to this YEC Ice Age model, *all 100,000 plus blooming diatom layers have to have formed since the Flood.* YEC now say the Flood formed the geologic layers below the varves and then the varves formed in the lake since the Flood, specifically during the 700 years of the Ice Age after the Flood.[7] If we are generous and say that fifty diatom/clay couplets formed every year (which is impossible) during the Ice Age, 50x700=35,000 still leaving 65,000 layers which have to be accounted for in the last 3700 years since the YEC say the Ice Age ended (which again, is impossible). And let us not forget that each layer has corresponding ^{14}C decay with the lowest 50,000+ layers having no appreciable ^{14}C, which means it had to have all decayed away (which again is impossible in 4400 years).

Reasonable YEC explanations of the lake varves and corresponding ^{14}C decay are completely non-existent. Is it any wonder I became *very* disillusioned with the people I once trusted? However, I did not lose my faith in the Bible; I lost my faith in the YEC interpretation of the Bible.

Dinosaur Footprints

Dinosaur fossils are exposed in many locations across the western United States and some include footprints and nests. Scientists interpret these fossils as forming in various environmental conditions occurring over long passages of time long ago. Some fossils show rapid burial and some do not, but even the rapid burials are often explainable by flooding rivers and streams, or volcanic eruptions. Multiple such events in multiple environments suggest significant passage of time.

Naturally YEC object and *have to* interpret the majority of the fossil formations to have been deposited by the Flood in less than one year because the Flood is the only Biblical event since the creation week that can account for that many fossils. They claim the fossils require rapid formation because footprints and dinosaur eggs are delicate features only preservable by rapid burial of sediment.

Aside from the vast amount of details that could be discussed related to these deposits, one major generality seems to have escaped many YEC. Geologists point out that dinosaur footprints and nests are fossilized sandwiched *between* very thick geologic layers. All of these fossil dinosaur formations lie *on top of thousands of feet* of sedimentary rock and are also buried *under thousands of feet* of sediment[8] now removed by erosion in many places. According to YEC, all of this sediment is supposed to have been deposited by the Flood, because *it all contains fossils.* So, will some YEC please explain to me how dinosaurs were casually walking around leaving tracks in the mud, hunting one another, building nests, and otherwise going about their *daily lives* in an area that just had thousands of feet of sediment deposited on it, and is awaiting thousands of feet more coming any moment? And all this must be accomplished within the first *150 days* of the Flood![9]

The more details are added to this preposterous *interpretation* of the Bible, the worse it gets. For example, fossilized dinosaur nests in a relatively small area in Montana have been found on at least nine different levels.[10] On a different layer nearby lies the fossils of a herd of some 10,000 dinosaurs that are mixed with a layer of volcanic ash.[11] That means that dinosaurs built nests over at least nine seasons that were preserved by small stream floods and in the midst of that suffered a catastrophic mass destruction by a volcano, but kept coming back and building more nests. In the area of some of these nests are found mud cracks, which means the nest building was also interspersed with dry periods where the freshwater lake they were near dried up.[12] All that is supposed to happen within 150 days between catastrophic depositions of thousands of feet of sediment. Some of the footprints in Dinosaur National Monument show imprints of crushed clams and flattened plants the dinosaurs were stepping on in the marsh.[13] How are plants growing on mud that has just been deposited by a monstrous flood?

The fossil evidence of animals being buried *while doing normal daily activities throughout VERTICAL MILES of strata in the geologic column* is very strong evidence the fossils were formed at different times widely separated from each other. Once my knowledge of geology grew beyond the superficial to the detailed, it became very obvious Flood Geology could not account for the geologic column.

YEC have made some recent attempts to explain the dinosaur trace fossils, "According to the Bible [their interpretation], all terrestrial, air-breathing animals died by day 150 (Genesis 7:19-24) [of the Flood]. Since tracks and eggs are activities of live dinosaurs, they must have been made early in the Flood..."[14] They also realize that evidence from around the globe shows massive tectonic shifts, vast deposits of fossil-bearing sediment (very much of which is marine), and extensive erosion[15], all of which only fit into their Bible story at the Flood. The best they have is to suggest in the midst of all that, "The stress of flight would have caused egg-bearing females to discharge any eggs."[16]

Problems with their attempts at explaining the fossils are numerous though. For example, stressed out females would not likely have laid their eggs in spiral and circular patterns in dug out indentations in the soil (nests), as the fossils are found. Also, the eggs are all the same size, indicating they were not discharged early.[17] Some of the eggs have fossilized baby dinosaurs *in them* showing the eggs had been in the nest for a while,[18] not freshly laid. Other nests have baby dinosaur bones in them showing the babies had hatched and stayed in the nests.[19] Nor would all the females, if they were seriously stressed, have bothered to lay their eggs all in the same location, at just the right distances apart to make room for adult dinosaurs to maneuver between, again, as the *nesting grounds* are found.[20] And to top it off, dinosaur fossils were not the only ones discovered. Small mammals, lizards, and insects were also present indicating the sites were fossilized as small normal environments[21], not panicking animals running from a flood. Ecological communities need time to form and the first 150 days of a worldwide cataclysm is not a conducive environment for anything normal. Flood Geology plainly does not fit the common sense evidence.

Notice also the YEC spin on the nests being on multiple layers, "Some clutches show eggs at different bedding levels, implying ongoing sedimentation while the eggs were being laid. This is consistent with rapid sedimentation during the Flood, but not with uniformitarian scenarios."[22] YEC throw these types of assertions around like they are indisputable. They are suggesting normal geological processes (uniformitarian – an abused word by YEC[23]) are incapable of explaining the deposits. But, geologists and paleontologists have no problems with these fossils and it is their interpretation of the data (and anyone using a little common sense) that causes the YEC to respond in the first place.

The fossils represent multiple nesting periods of live, normal dinosaur activity interspersed with periodic *local* flooding and volcanic eruptions. That is the best way to explain them *based on all the evidence*, not on a preconceived bias toward forcing long ages of time on the data, but because *the data suggests the passage of time*. The idea a catastrophic flood first deposited *thousands of feet* of sediment, and then slowed down enough to allow mud cracks to form in a *dry* lake bed, and then dinosaurs by the thousands, that had *survived* (who knows how?!) the first mega waves of the Flood, left tracks, nests, and eggs, all within 150 days, makes no sense at all. The evidence is clearly not on the YEC side. One must choose then to believe the common sense evidence or a poor interpretation of the Bible. YEC choose the latter.

Supernova Remnants – SNR's

Stars explode in glorious and very dangerous fashion and those explosions are called supernovae. When a star runs down on fuel to the point where the outward forces of fusion are overcome by the gravitational force of its mass, the star collapses quickly, which then causes it to violently explode. What remains of what was once a star is an expanding cloud of debris and gas called a supernova remnant (SNR). These can be seen through telescopes today and *their rate of expansion can be measured and observed*. YEC agree with all this up to this point.

However, mainstream astronomers also believe the expansion rate of the expanding gas cloud (SNR) can give a reasonable measurement of the time elapsed since the star exploded. In fact, the idea can be tested. In 1054 the Chinese recorded the occurrence of a supernova and when we look today where they said it was we see the Crab Nebula, an expanding SNR. *Calculations of its age based upon its expansion rate agree with its historically recorded age.* Scientists are not being unreasonable then in their inference because their conclusions follow from the data they *observe and measure*, and their predictions have been verified.

The next obvious question then is: Are there any SNRs that show ages greater than 10,000 years? If there are, then how do YEC explain them? The answer is, *there are many*. One example is centered on the constellation Antlia Pnuematica with an age of at least 1.1 million years[24]. As for the YEC, they are left with two possibilities. First, they could say the SNR is really not the remnant of an exploded star, it only looks like one. This leaves them in the unenviable position of saying God created an expanding gas cloud that looks like a 1.1 million year old SNR. Is God a deceiver? Most YEC say no. Their main alternative thus far is an idea called White Hole Cosmology using time dilation[25], which proposes that time has moved faster for the vast majority of the universe than it has for us here on Earth. That proposal effectively *agrees that the universe really is as old as mainstream astronomers think it is*, but the Earth is not. Some prominent YEC disagree with the hypothesis[26] and mainstream science sees no merit to the idea either.[27] YEC are stuck between a rock and a hard place on this one. Either God created something that gives all the appearance of being 1.1 million years old or they can defend a hypothesis that does not work.

When presenting this evidence to pastors and laypeople, the most common response I get is that any creation by God requires some appearance of age. While that is true to an extent, SNR data is different. If God created the remnants of an exploded star, it is *an appearance of history* not an appearance of age. If God did that it would be deceptive. YEC who understand the issues agree, "...it would make God into a deceiver, by *showing 'evidence' of events that have not happened.*"[28] (Sarfati – emphasis his) By all observational evidence a star burned out over time, exploded, and its remnants expanded over a long time. Considering that God hates falsehood (Ps. 119:128) and says false witnesses speak deceit (Pr. 12:17), God would not create something that gives false witness of great age, therefore *it must really be very old.*

The most reasonable conclusion is that the SNR centered on Antlia Pnuematica really is 1.1 million years old, and the others are as old as their observations show them to be, and thus the universe is far older than 10,000 years. SNR evidence was one of the first serious challenges to my young-Earth beliefs for which I had no answer. This argument is so rock-solid it now amazes me how anyone can deny its conclusions.

Gut Wrenching Doubt

I distinctly remember the deep gut-feelings I had that I might be badly wrong about some very important doctrines. Some of my readers may be feeling the same way right now if they have made it this far. That feeling is not easy to ignore. It was humbling because I realized I did not know as much as I thought, and it was scary because my faith was being shaken. God does that sometimes (Heb. 12:25-29). If I accepted that Earth was billions of years old, how was that going to affect my belief in the inerrancy of Scripture? I realized it could upset my entire worldview. Ultimately, it led to an intense study even deeper than before, both Biblically and scientifically and this book is the fruit.

I do not want to give the impression I just woke up one day and changed my mind. These were not easy decisions for me and the process took years during which I wavered back and forth several times (depending on which book I was reading), but somewhere around 2005 I finally declared myself an Old-Earth

Creationist. There was just too much evidence against a young universe and Earth. Still, three to four years would pass before I worked out the details of the Prophetic-Days View even though I had first heard it back in 1995-96.

And now here we are. The debate rages on and in fact is more complicated than it was 20 years ago because not only has scientific knowledge multiplied exponentially, Theistic Evolution's influence has grown and interpretations of Genesis have increased too. The task of finding the truth has become more difficult, at least as far as reconciling Genesis and science on the age of the Earth is concerned, and the worst part is many are convinced reconciliation is impossible. My goal is to know the truth, which brings me back to the main subject of this chapter.

Why did I change my mind about Young-Earth Creationism?

The simple answer is because it is not true. What I once thought was true turned out to be false, scientifically *and Biblically*. And I pray others will see the light and make the switch too. In conversations with YEC God has used me with success in converting "young-Earthers" to seeing the Bible does not say what they think it says and that it is possible to believe in an old Earth and not compromise belief in the inerrancy of Scripture. My Biblical arguments in Chapter 2, *when in the right Spirit*, often have the effect of stopping YEC in their tracks because it seems almost no one attempts to challenge their interpretation of Genesis. The YEV is treated like a legitimate option, even by many people who oppose it, but I do not think it is.

Many times when an OEC and YEC meet the conversation revolves around science, concepts like radiometric dating, starlight travel time, and the formation of Grand Canyon. I have found this approach to YEC mostly unproductive *at first* because it raises defense walls too quickly, though I admit it worked on me (but from a book, not in person, and over a long time). YEC often do not trust scientists and in many cases will not even contemplate scientific arguments because they believe the YEV is the only legitimate interpretation of Genesis. However, when I tell YEC's their interpretation of Genesis is wrong, or even better, when I ask them simple Biblical questions they cannot answer, I find them to be much more open to discussion. And when I give them a few simple opposing Biblical interpretations it is very interesting to see their reaction when they realize the verses can easily mean exactly what I said. That is not the time for anything remotely similar to gloating or celebration. It is the time for *gentle* correction.

To successfully convince YEC their interpretation is wrong it is necessary to know what the Bible says and be able to explain it because *YEC often know the Bible better than OEC*. That is why I tried to make Chapter 2 a simple five point approach. It presents an easy affirmative interpretation of Genesis that even a child can understand. From there it may be possible to broach the scientific issues.

Comparing the Young-Earth View with the Prophetic-Days View

All of the following was covered thoroughly in Chapters 2, 5, and 6, but there it was presented advocating or defending the PDV. Here, and in Chapter 9, the similarities and differences between the views are summarized for comparison.

Three major *agreements* between the YEV and the PDV:

1. The Bible is the inerrant and authoritative Word of God.

Advocates of the YEV and PDV believe the Bible is a revelation from God. As such, YEC and OEC should agree on the major Biblical doctrines that define Christianity.[29] God cannot make mistakes so it follows that the original documents inspired by God cannot have errors, despite having been written by men. Human errors have crept into our *copies* over the years, mostly in the form of copying errors or spelling variations, but if the originals came from God they must have been without error. A God capable of creating the universe is certainly capable of communicating errorlessly with humans and whatever He said, *regardless of the subject*, must be true. That conclusion allows us to test many of the claims of the Bible to see if they really did come from God, as opposed to being just various authors' opinions. Though the account contains metaphors (because God's actions are near impossible to describe without using anthropomorphisms), and the account is not written like a modern science textbook, the author means for us to believe God really did what it says He did. But all agree the details of *how* God did it are limited or not given.

2. The Days of Genesis 1 are normal Earth days and a real week on Earth.

The PDV and some YEC agree the easiest most natural way to understand the Days of Genesis 1 is to see them as they are defined in the account – as the lighted portion of a normal Earth day, not a long period of time, "And God called the light day." (Gen. 1:5) Both views also agree the evenings and the mornings of the 6 Days were normal evenings and mornings on Earth. Neither view sees the Days of Genesis 1 as a myth, framework, metaphor, or analogy of a normal Earth week. Though some YEC believe "day" refers to the whole 24-hour period, not just the daylight, both the PDV and YEV at least agree the account describes a real week on Earth.

3. The various kinds of living creatures were created, not evolved.

The YEV and PDV are creationist views. Neither view believes all life can be traced back to a universal common ancestor from which evolved all the various species of life ever to have lived on planet Earth (even if with God's help). Both views agree God acted in history and formed man and animals from the dust of the ground, not through the process of macro-evolution.[30]

Ten major *differences* between the YEV and the PDV: Please note that some of these differences do not apply to every YEC. They are listed in the order they appear in Genesis.

1. The heavens and Earth were created before the 6 Days.

YEC believe all was finished within 6 Days which would have to have included the initial creation of the heavens and Earth, but that is not what the text says. The narrative of the 6 Days *begins in verse 3* with, "Then God said…" which is the way each of the 6 Days begins. But the creation of the heavens and Earth are mentioned only in verse 1 *before* Day 1 begins, within a timeframe called the "beginning" which is a time of unspecified length before the 6 Days. Therefore, the Earth already existed uninhabitable, empty of life, dark, and wet when God began His six day work. (See Points 1 and 2 in Chapter 2 and the objections to those points in Chapter 5 for details.)

2. Genesis 1:1 is not a summary of the whole account.

Some YEC believe Genesis 1:1 is only a summary of the whole account, but if that were true then the account does not tell us when God created the heavens and Earth. Nowhere in the account will you find a proclamation like, "Let there be a heavens and earth." Nor will you find a statement like, "And God made the earth." Therefore, the creation of the heavens and Earth are part of the sequential narrative of the account. First, God created them (1:1), and then He told us the condition they were in (1:2), and then He began a 6 day work to change them (1:3). (See the introduction to the Five Points in Chapter 2.)

3. "Formless and void" are better translated "desolate and lifeless".

In most translations of Genesis 1:2 the Earth is described as "formless and void" or "without form and void" and some YEC think that means the Earth was not formed yet, i.e. it had no form. However, that connotation is incorrect. It makes no sense to think God created the land (earth) in 1:1 and then the land (earth) was shapeless in 1:2. One could not rightly call it "earth", "land", or "created" in 1:1 if it was unformed in 1:2. Interpreting the first word as "formless" comes from Greek influences on the text. The Hebrew word describes places that are humanly uninhabitable and desolate. The second word *can* mean "void" but the question is "void of what?" The answer is "void of life", because Earth was uninhabitable. Therefore, I prefer to translate it "lifeless" rather than "void". (See Appendix A under "formless" and "void".)

4. Genesis 1:2 says it was dark *on Earth*, not in the whole universe.

YEC believe it was dark in the entire universe when God began His 6 Day work, but Genesis 1:2 specifies that "darkness was upon the surface of the deep". The text specifically says it was dark on the surface of the Earth, not in the whole universe. The YEV has exaggerated the literal reading of the text. The text tells us nothing of the condition of the universe at that time only that it was already created. (See Point 3 in Chapter 2 and the objections to Point 3 in Chapter 5.)

5. The light God commanded to appear on Day 1 was on Earth only.

A very common misconception of Genesis is that when God said, "Let there be light," He was commanding light to come to be in the whole universe. However, the account was written from the perspective of the surface of the Earth, and the darkness in 1:2 was only on the surface, so it makes the most sense to say the light God proclaimed on Day 1 was only on the surface too. Just so we would not misinterpret it, God called the light "day", and it is never day and night in space. It is only day and night on the surface of a planet (or moon). Therefore, the proclamation, "Let there be light," only applies to light on Earth. *The light God proclaimed on Day 1 was daylight on Earth.* (See Point 3 in Chapter 2 and the objections to Point 3 in Chapter 5.)

6. The "waters which were above the expanse" (Gen. 1:7) are rain.

Some YEC believe the waters above the expanse were a vapor canopy that eventually came down as the floodwaters of the Flood (Morris).[31] Some believe they could be waters that eventually *became* the entire solar system or universe (a whole lot of water!).[32] Both are wrong. The waters above the expanse are nothing more than rain that falls from the sky. Genesis 1 is written to an ancient and general audience, and describes aspects of creation with which almost every human is familiar. (See the third structural element in Chapter 1, Point 3 in Chapter 2, the objections to Point 3 in Chapter 5, and Appendix B.)

7. The proclamations God made on the 6 Days were not fulfilled in six days.

Many people believe that when God proclaimed something in Genesis 1 it happened immediately. Thus, the eight proclamations given over six days are believed to have been fulfilled within those six days and finished by the 7th Day. But that is not what Genesis 1 says.

First, "and it was so" does not mean instantaneous fulfillment. The verb is translated as "and it came to pass" elsewhere in the Bible and does not imply anything about the time it took for the proclamations to come to pass, only that they did indeed come to be so.

Second, the text is written in such a way that we should understand the two proclamations on Day 3, the proclamation on Day 4, the blessing on Day 5, and the two proclamations on Day 6, *could not be fulfilled* on the days they were proclaimed, and the blessing of the 7th Day *did not occur* on the 7th Day either. From the text, we can conclude: **(1)** The land did not rise nor did the waters run off *in a day*; the text does not say God was the one doing the actions, pushing the waters off or raising the land. **(2)** Plants did not sprout nor produce more plants in a day, because *the land* is doing the sprouting and producing and the land works slowly like it does today. **(3)** The Sun, Moon, and stars were not made on Day 4, because 1:16 is listed out of time sequence with 1:14-15 and the making of the lights is not what fulfilled the 4th Day proclamation. It was also not "so" that the lights were used for their purposes on Day 4. That part of the proclamation could not have been fulfilled until after mankind was created. **(4)** The sea creatures did not fill the seas, nor did birds multiply on the land, in a day, because God blessed them to do it themselves. **(5)** Land animals did not reproduce in a day, again, because it does not work that way. The land producing animals (1:24) is not the same as God making the animals (1:25). Verse 25 is out of time sequence and does not describe the fulfillment of the proclamation; it only makes it possible for the fulfillment to occur. **(6)** Mankind was not successful at ruling and subduing the land in a day, because they had a lot to learn before they could do that. **(7)** God did not bless the 7th Day on the 7th Day because He ceased from activity on that day and mankind was not there yet anyway. These seven points show the proclamations were not all meant to be understood as fulfilled on the day they were proclaimed.

Third, the work God completed in seven days was to proclaim what He was going to do to a desolate, lifeless, dark, and deluged planet. He carried out the fulfillments *after* He finished working (proclaiming) for seven days. God created a work for Him to do, and He did it, culminating in the creation of mankind and placing them in the Garden of Eden.

The proclamations were said in such a way that they could not be fulfilled in six days, and just so we would not take them that way, the account is written with out-of-sequence phrases. *The account did not have to be written non-chronologically* but it was, and it was done that way for a reason, i.e. so we would understand the information given after the fulfillment phrases is extra information God wanted us to know, and *was not what fulfilled the proclamations.* For example, God making the Sun, Moon, and stars (1:16) is not what fulfilled the proclamation for the location of the lights to come to be in the expanding clear space of the heavens (1:14). And *God making* the land animals (1:26) is not what fulfilled the proclamation for *the land* to produce land animals (1:25). (See Point 4 in Chapter 2, the fourth main point under Point 3 in Chapter 2, and their respective objections in Chapter 5.)

Also, we will soon see in Chapter 9 that further evidence exists in the text that all could not have been fulfilled in six days because: (1) The Earth was operating the way we naturally see it operating today, so much of the account describes natural processes at work, not super-miraculous instantaneous miracles. (2) God planted a garden and it grew, which takes longer than a week. And (3) too many events were said to have happened in Genesis 2 than could have happened in the daytime of Day 6.

8. Death and disease *of animals* existed before the Fall.

Chapter 6 covered in detail the differences between YEC and OEC concerning the origin of death for animals. It is worth repeating, however, that

YEC and OEC agree that *human death* began at the Fall. As for animal death, that is a world of difference. YEC believe animal death began at the Fall, but the Bible does not say that. The Bible shows an original creation with animal death and predation, some discomfort in creation, some level of pain, some sweaty work maintaining a garden, temperature differences, and possibly thorns. Also, that God's original plan included animal death is obvious from five arguments: **(1)** Animal death is good for humanity because resources are limited. **(2)** God blessed humanity to fill the land, not land animals or birds, which had to mean animals would die. **(3)** God gave man a purpose to rule the animals and subdue the land which would inevitably lead to some animal death. **(4)** At some time *before* the Flood God gave instruction on what was clean and unclean to eat. **(5)** Some animals are obviously designed to kill, some are designed with elaborate defense mechanisms, and some are designed to be eaten. We also saw that the Bible does not teach an original vegetarian diet, nor define "very good" so as to exclude animal death. Finally, we saw that animal death before the Fall does no harm to the doctrine of the Atonement or God's character. Biblically, many YEC's have this one all wrong. (See Chapter 6)

9. The Bible does not give us a method to estimate the age of the Earth.

YEC believe the universe and Earth must be young (compared to billions of years) because they believe the genealogies of Genesis 5 and 11 show humanity was created approximately 6000 years ago. If all was created just a few days before humanity, the heavens and Earth could not be billions of years old. However, while the genealogies (even if not complete) may give some reasonable estimate for the age of humanity, the Bible does not tell us how long "the beginning" was before the 7 Days began, nor does it tell us how long God took to fulfill His proclamations after the 7 Days ended. With the 7 Days sandwiched between two unspecified blocks of time, the Bible leaves the age of the universe and Earth wide open for us to discover on our own. (See Point 5 in Chapter 2.)

10. The Flood did not cause most of the geologic formations of Earth.

Because YEC believe the universe and Earth are young, and they believe animal death did not precede the Fall, their *only option* for explaining the majority of fossils (remains of dead animals) is to say they died in the Flood and the Flood caused nearly all of those formations. I have already covered some of the scientific reasons I ultimately abandoned the YEC Flood model, and I have already stated this book is not focused on what Genesis says about the Flood (though I do not think YEC have that right either), but more on the Flood will have to wait for another book. For now, obviously, OEC and YEC are in major disagreement over the effects, extent, and cause(s) of Noah's Flood.

My final conclusion about the YEV is that it is Biblically and scientifically wrong and that is why I repented of it. As Christians we should seek and love the truth because Jesus is the truth. Humility is a must because we are fallible. As fallible we should judge the evidence (all of it – as much as possible) and be willing to change our view if evidence does not support it, and be willing to admit ignorance when necessary. It is important to be on the side of truth because all error eventually has consequences, somewhere, somehow.

For those who are in authoritative positions of influence, like pastors, teachers, professors, and home school association leaders, please let me encourage you to not be deceived by what look like good simple Young-Earth Creationist answers to very complex scientific questions. Issues surrounding Genesis 1 and science are really not simple, and humility and knowledge are a must. Offering simplistic dogmatic answers to really complex science issues makes Christians look obtuse. Therefore, please hear out all sides and do not exclude or silence the voice of the opposition. Jesus never shut the mouths of His human adversaries *with His authority*. He gave people *answers* and it was His answers that silenced the critics because they had no response. Young-Earth scientific arguments are not silencing the critics; they are providing the fuel for the ridicule. It is the YEC that are silenced by the most specific of the scientific arguments.

I have one thing to repeatedly say to Young-Earth Creationists, "Your boat has big holes and is sinking! Abandon ship!"

9

Evaluating other Old-Earth Creationist Views
(Only one boat gets us to our destination.)

In today's theological environment I do not envy the predicament of the person who believes the universe and Earth are old, but has not decided which view of Genesis is the most faithful to the text and best assimilates the scientific data. Nine major views of Genesis 1 are currently vying to replace the traditional Young-Earth View. Chapter 2 advocated the Prophetic Days View as the correct view, but it is not one of the best known of the nine (though I hope this book propels it there). After my world was temporarily turned upside down by the evidence for an old universe and Earth I had to replace the YEV with a theologically sound interpretation of Genesis, especially when I realized the YEV interpretation was wrong. To make that decision I sifted through all nine views comparing them with one another point for point, counterpoint for counterpoint, and this chapter summarizes the agreements and disagreements between my view and the others and hopefully helps those in search of a view to solidify their choice.

The nine major Old-Earth Views briefly summarized in Chapter 7 are:

1. **The Prophetic Days View (PDV)** – the view I proposed in Chapter 2
2. **The Gap View (GV)** – one of the oldest OEV's which is now virtually absent from Christian academia but somewhat popular among the laity
3. **The Day-Age View (DAV)** – one of the oldest and the most popular OEV advocated by Hugh Ross of Reasons To Believe
4. **The Analogical-Days View (ADV)** – one of the newest and fastest growing views originated by John C. Collins
5. **The Intermittent-Days View (IDV)** – view most recently advocated by John Lennox
6. **The Framework View (FV)** – popular academic view
7. **The Revelatory-Days View (RDV)** – older view that never caught on
8. **The Limited-Creation View (LCV)** – very recent view originated by John Sailhamer but not very popular
9. **The Cosmic Temple View (CTV)** – newest view originated by John Walton

That is quite an array of choices that have arisen over the last 200 years[1] and unfortunately choosing one over another is a detailed process. Some in fact may not even see a need to choose one and are quite satisfied with simply believing

God created it all and they do not need the specifics. That may be fine for some, but not me. *I really want to know what the original author meant to say*, and I am inclined to believe it has to be one of those nine, particularly mine, because it is even more difficult for me to believe we have all missed it and another interpretation awaits.

Evidence for an age of Earth greater than thousands of years began to accumulate in the 1700s. From that time it has grown from tens of thousands, to hundreds of thousands, to millions, and now to billions. The age currently stands at approximately 4.5 billion and is not likely to change again other than further refinements to that number. Theologians were not slow with interpretations designed to account for the new numbers and the first ones on the scene were the Gap View and Day-Age View. Both views are still around as the most well known of the old Earth views, but many recognize the textual problems surrounding them. That they have proved unsatisfactory to many is evident from the fact more views have arisen since their appearance. If either view was overwhelmingly compelling it is likely the others would never have been sought.

Now here we are with nine views from which to choose, so allow me to show you why I rejected eight of them. My reasons are illustrated by revisiting (a little deeper) parts of the six structural elements listed in Chapter 1, but condensed to three questions:

I. Did God *really* say those words?
II. Were the 7 Days a normal Earth week?
III. How do we deal with the scientific order-of-appearance problem?

I. Did God *really* say those words?

Genesis 1 says God made eight proclamations (fiats – Gen. 1:3, 6, 9, 11, 14, 20, 24, and 26) that caused our perspective of the heavens and Earth. It also states God spoke a blessing *to humanity* (Gen. 1:28-30). Interpreting God speaking to humanity as metaphorical or figurative would be difficult, so Genesis means to tell us God really did speak that blessing (at least those ideas, even if it was not those exact words), and if God really did speak to humanity, then it is most likely the fiats were historical also. Therefore, Genesis tells us God really did speak those proclamations. Verses like Psalm 33:6 and 9, John 1:1-3, and Hebrews 11:3 corroborate the testimony God creates by speaking.

That brings to my mind four questions. **1.** To whom was God speaking the proclamations? **2.** Are those eight proclamations exactly what God said, or all God said, on the 6 Days? **3.** Because God is spirit and does not have a mouth, how does God say anything? And **4.** If God really did say those proclamations, then when and where did that happen from our perspective?

I.1 – To whom was God speaking the proclamations?

Job 38:4 and 7 say, "Where were you when I laid the foundations of the earth?... When the morning stars sang together, And all the sons of God shouted for joy?" The "sons of God" and "morning stars" are references to angels (Job 1:6, 2:1, Is. 14:12-13). Apparently the angels were present when God laid the foundations of the Earth so it is possible God was speaking to them. However, Genesis 1:26 says, "...Let Us make man in Our image, according to Our likeness..." This must be a reference to God speaking within the Godhead because it makes no sense this was spoken to the angels because: (1) The angels are never said to have participated in making anything. (2) Nowhere does the Bible say we are created in the image of angels. And (3) verse 27 says we are created "in the image of God" so the "Us" and "Our" of verse 26 refer to God. Therefore, God definitely spoke some of this (maybe all) within Himself (that is, the three persons of the Trinity communicated), and maybe the angels heard it.

Another possibility is God was speaking to the person receiving the revelation of Genesis (the Revelatory-Days View). For example, He may have been speaking to Adam after his creation. Or He could have been speaking to Moses when He was with him on Mount Sinai (Ex. 24:18). The problem with this idea is if God was speaking to a man, support for it is lacking from the Bible. If God had been speaking to a human one would think the text would say something about it. For example, it might have started by identifying the author and the circumstances where the revelation was occurring, or the revelation story would be told elsewhere. Because those are missing, the idea that God was speaking to a human here is speculation. However, if Moses was the compiler of Genesis (and I believe he was), he had to get this account from somewhere. Genesis *was* revealed to Moses either directly, or through God "guiding" his hand at compiling old records where the story (or stories) had been revealed to others. The question is whether Genesis 1 is a record of that revealing process, or whether Genesis 1 is the story revealed. The text does not look like God is speaking to a man nor does it directly say He was. Because to think otherwise is only speculating, my conclusion then is that Genesis 1 is the story revealed, not a record of the revealing process. It is not a story of the revealing; it is a revealing of the story.

I.2 – Are those eight proclamations exactly what God said, or all God said, on the 6 Days?

We cannot be sure our wording of the proclamations is exactly what God said or all God said on the 6 Days, but we know He at least said that much, whether in those exact words or not (God was likely not speaking Hebrew, the language in which we have Genesis recorded). We also know some things God said are not recorded. For example, the specific words of the blessing of the 7th Day (2:3) are not recorded like they are for the other two blessings (1:22 and 28). I believe that is because God did not work on the 7th Day and saying a blessing could be misconstrued as work, and humanity was not there on that Day anyway. The proclamation to make man was not fulfilled yet, so there was no need to bless it at that time because it was meant for humanity's benefit (Mark 2:27). It is more likely God blessed it after He revealed to Adam and Eve what He had done or when the Law was given – Ex. 16:22-29, 20:8-11.

Also, Genesis 5:2 says, "...He [God] blessed them and named them Man in the day when they were created."[2] In Genesis 1 God only names five things (day, night, heavens, earth, and sea), but in Genesis 5 we find He also named "Man". However, the fact that everything God said is not recorded does not require God to have spoken more than the eight fiats on the 6 Days, but He could have. If God had spoken *everything* that was going to happen very specifically there is no way that could be recorded, or understood for that matter, considering how complicated we already know it is. The proclamations were more for our benefit as a revelation than they were actually necessary for God to create anything.

I.3 – Because God is a spirit and does not have a mouth, how does God say anything?

All that can be dogmatically stated about this is that *God is capable of communication*. Phrases such as "God said", "God saw", and "God called" are best understood as anthropomorphisms (spoken from a human perspective). In other words God was telling us what He did in concepts we can understand without specifying exactly how He did it. We know God is capable of speaking audibly if He desires.

I.4 – If God really did say those proclamations, then when and where did that happen?

Thus far we have: God really spoke those proclamations, and audibly to angels or within Himself are irrelevant to the fact it is said to have taken place in a real-time[3] human historical setting sometime after the initial creation of the heavens and Earth. If that is true, the questions move to "When?" and "Where?"

As to where, Genesis 1:2 specifically tells us God's Spirit was "moving over the surface of the waters". This detail seems to be completely useless unless it is telling us a true location where God was "at" and about to work. Considering the account is written from a human perspective, this detail of 1:2 makes the most sense as a particular spot on Earth, though the exact location is not specified.

As to when, the text seems to plainly say the proclamations were spoken some time after the Earth's initial creation when it was in the condition described in verse 2. Is it then not obvious Genesis 1 claims God said the proclamations over a period of six days? But what does that mean?

II. Were the 7 Days a normal Earth week?

Three questions must be addressed to determine if the 7 Days were a normal week. **1.** How long were the Days? **2.** Were the Days contiguous (occurring immediately after one another with no gaps between)? And **3.** Were they a *real* week on Earth, as opposed to a figurative or metaphorical device? The answers narrow the choices for which view of Genesis 1 best fits the text.

II.1 – How long were the Days?

My case for normal days centers on two arguments: the word "day" is defined in the account, and the meaning of the "evening and morning" phrase.

The word "day" is defined in Genesis 1: Some of what I said in Chapter 1 bears repeating. In reference to Day 1 Genesis 1:3-5 says:

> Then God said, "Let there be light"; and there was light. God saw that the light was good; and God separated the light from the darkness. God called the light day, and the darkness He called night. And there was evening and there was morning, one day.

Please notice one very simple point, *Genesis is defining "day" for us here.* Therefore, *we* do not have to struggle to define "day". "God called the light day..." and everyone who is not literally completely blind understands what daylight is. Thus, *in the Bible's first use of the word*, Genesis defines "day" as the *lighted portion* of a normal day on Earth (*not* as a full 24 hour day I might add). Simplicity and clarity are preferred interpretations in my mind. If the Bible is going to make it clear then why complicate it?

But we have complicated it, so what about that second use of the word, "one day"? My simple questions are twofold. Is there any *contextual* reason to believe *within two sentences* that the author of Genesis has used "day" to mean something else?[4] No, *every other use* of "day" in Genesis 1 refers to daylight, so why should its uses at the end of the Days be any different? Also, no other words used in Genesis 1 have multiple definitions *in the account*. So why should "day" be an exception? Answers to long-day arguments are below.

The importance of the "evening and morning" phrase: Each of the 6 Days ends with the phrase "and there was evening and there was morning, the [n[th]] day." The word "evening" is *'ereb* in Hebrew and simply means "evening or dusk."[5] It does *not* include the "night" which is *layil* though it is unfortunately sometimes translated that way. In verse 5 the darkness is called "night" and evening is that period of light *after* sunset *before* night. The word "morning" is *boqer* and simply means "morning or dawn"[6] but is sometimes translated as "early". It does *not* include the "day". Morning (*boqer*) refers to the lighted time just *before* sunrise *after* night, and then sunrise begins a new day. "Evening" and "morning" should be taken as the *boundaries* of the nighttime as they are in Ex. 27:21 and Lev. 24:3. (Also note Ex. 18:13 where "morning" and "evening" are used as boundaries for daytime.) Literally, morning and evening are *transitions* between day and night.

At first glance it appears the textual order of evening and morning should have been reversed. Why is evening listed first when we normally think of morning coming before evening? Some want to say it is because the Jews reckon a day beginning at sunset, but that started as a result of God's command *later in history after Genesis* (Ex. 12:18 and Lev. 23:32 – see Ch. 5 objections to

Point 1). However, there is a simpler and better answer. The text means, "And there was evening [the end of the daylight], and there was morning [the end of that night]" or paraphrased as, "And evening came after the daylight and morning came just before the next daylight began". The first day began with daylight and it ended with sunset followed by evening, night, and morning. As one YEC commentator succinctly put it, "For 'evening' marks the conclusion of the day, and 'morning' marks the conclusion of the night."[7] (Leopold) This means God's activities were during the daylight hours and it also means *Genesis is delineating day-evening-night-morning* thus defining a full 24-hour period from *sunrise to sunrise.*

This straightforward *simple* interpretation of the evening and morning phrase has the following implications to any overall view of Genesis:

First, the phrase is in the order one would expect when reading the Days as normal *daylight,* not as long periods of time or 24 hours.

Second, the phrase becomes a bridge linking each Day consecutively and *contiguously* to the next one. The phrase seems to prevent time gaps between the Days (like in the Intermittent-Days View). In Genesis 1:5 the "morning" marks the first 24-hour day's *end* right before daylight on Day 2 and thus connects Day 1 with Day 2. From the Genesis 1 perspective, God acted in the daylight of Day 1, then evening came and it became night, then morning came just before the next Day began, and *that was one numbered day.* Then Day 2 began, and then God proclaimed something else, and so on...

Third, the consecutive and contiguous nature of the phrase prevents an interpretation allowing the Days to overlap because Day 1 ends where Day 2 begins and so on...

Fourth, this interpretation helps us understand why the verb "was" is used twice in the phrase. The rendering of the KJV as, "And the evening and the morning were the first day" is incorrect and the NASB, NIV, and ESV have all corrected it. The verb "was" appears twice in the Hebrew text, not once. The KJV could give the impression that from evening to morning is a whole day, but it is not. Literally, evening to morning is only half a day. Also, if the text had said, "And there was morning and there was evening" we would have a logically incoherent statement and the same problem, only half a day. The text makes the best sense the way it is, evening and morning sandwiching the night.

Therefore: *The simplest most natural way*[8] *to understand the Days of Genesis is to see them as the lighted portions of normal Earth 24-hour periods.*

Objections to my interpretation of the "evening and morning" phrase: Day-Age View advocates disagree with my interpretation and say that "evening" and "morning" can mean the ending and beginning of an unspecified finite time period and therefore are not required to be interpreted literally as the "evening" and "morning" of a normal day. Hugh Ross explains:

> In other words, 'evening' and 'morning' refer to the beginning and ending of a day, whatever definition of 'day' applies. For example, 'in my grandfather's day' refers to the time period surrounding his lifetime. The

morning and evening of his lifetime would be my grandfather's youth and old age.[9]

The problem with his interpretation becomes obvious by noticing that he cannot speak of the beginning and ending of his grandfather's day *without listing morning first*, unlike the text.

Assuming for the sake of argument he is correct and the Days are ages of time, why doesn't Genesis list "morning" first? If the answer given is that the first evening refers to the end of Day 1 and then morning refers to the beginning of Day 2 then there is another problem with his interpretation. The text reads "And there was evening and there was morning, one day" meaning the evening *and* morning *both preceded the enumeration of Day 1*. If evening referred to the ending of Day 1 and morning referred to the beginning of Day 2 then the text should read something more like, "And there was evening, one day. And there was morning, and God said…" Because of *the order of the text*, interpreting the evening and morning phrase as an ending and beginning of an age does not work and cannot be legitimately considered an option.

Answering arguments for long days: Some Day-Age View advocates admit that the Days can be interpreted as normal days, but primarily use three arguments to support the idea the Days were actually long periods of time: **1.** The word *yôm* (day) sometimes means a longer period of time than the lighted portion of a day. **2.** The 7th Day is longer than a normal day so the others were too. And **3.** too much activity for Day 6 is listed in Genesis 2 to have occurred in a normal day.

Two other arguments are also used by other views to argue the Days, or the creation timeframe, were longer than six 24-hour periods: **4.** The Framework View uses what is known as the "because it had not rained" argument which is a particular interpretation of Gen. 2:5-6. And **5.** the Analogical Days View uses a different interpretation of Gen. 2:5-6 to reach a similar conclusion.

1. The word "day" sometimes means a time longer than 24 hours: The word *yôm* (day) can sometimes literally mean a longer period of time than the lighted portion of a day. That is true, but the problem is that almost every time the Bible uses *yôm* to mean an indefinite amount of time it is either in the form *b^{e}yôm* (in the day[10] – as in Gen. 2:4, Is. 23:15, and many more), or "day" is qualified by a phrase like "day of the LORD" (Ezek. 30:3) or "day of vengeance" (Is. 34:8), etc. The uses of "day" at the end of the 6 Days are singular without a prefix and it would be helpful for the DAV if there were multiple similar uses of "day" in the OT that mean long periods of time, but there are not.[11]

Young-Earth Creationists like to point out that every time the word "day" is used with a number outside of Genesis 1 it refers to a normal day, not a long period of time. DAV defenders respond by saying no rule in Hebrew requires "day" to mean daylight when accompanied with a number (which is true). However, I still lean with the YEV on this one. If "day" with a number could mean a longer period of time it would be helpful if there were multiple examples of it in the Bible, especially considering it is associated with a number *hundreds* of times. Some DAV advocates add that the Hebrew structure of the numbered days in Genesis 1 is unique in the Bible (which again is true). However, I would point out that the unique structure does not require it to mean long periods of time either. I am sure DAV advocates would agree, but add that the Hebrew thus *allows* for "day" to mean a long period of time. I agree that *the Hebrew structure of the numbered days in Genesis 1 is inconclusive by itself*. However, reading the Days as normal days is strongly supported by the fact numbered days are combined with the evening and morning phrase, and Genesis 1:5 defines "day" as the daylight portion of a 24-hour period, and no contextual reason exists for changing the definition in the refrain. Just from the way it is written, it appears the author is trying to emphasize normal days.

2. Is the 7th Day longer than 24 hours? The Day-Age View, Framework View, and Analogical Days View all see the 7th Day as having begun after the 6th Day ended and continuing to this day. Where do they get that idea? It comes from the fact the 7th Day does not contain a concluding phrase like "and there was evening and there was morning the seventh day" as the other 6 Days do. This fact is used as the primary piece of evidence to say the 7th Day is still continuing and thus supports the Days not being 24 hours long. "Given the parallel structure in the narration of the creation days, such a distinct omission from the description of the seventh day strongly suggests that this day has (or had) not yet ended."[12] (Ross) And, "It follows that this day lacks the refrain because it has no end – it is not an ordinary day by any stretch of the imagination, and this makes us question whether the other days are supposed to be ordinary in their length."[13] (Collins)

Does the absence of the evening and morning phrase mean the 7th Day has not yet ended? I do not believe so for the following reasons:

First, the parallel structure of the Days only applies to Days 1-6 (See Figure 1.1 in Chapter 1). *Day 7 is missing all of the structural elements of the 6 Days*, not just the refrain. The 7th Day *is the ending* of the account and already has a formal colophon[14] (ending – Gen. 2:4a), so it does not need the refrain.

Second, there is a more reasonable explanation why the refrain is missing; it is unnecessary. The refrain connects the 7 Days in sequence; therefore, because there is no 8th Day of importance, there is no need for a phrase that would connect it to the next day. *The purpose of the 7th Day text is not to move on to another day.* It is to point out God ceased from work on the 7th Day and hallowed it as a pattern for humanity.

Third, God is finished with the heavens and Earth and He ceased activity on the 7th Day, but just because He is finished does not have to mean He is still resting. If I finished my yard work on Saturday and rest Sunday, when Monday comes I can still say I am finished with the yard work, but I cannot say it is still Sunday. That means there is no necessary logical reason to conclude the 7th Day is continuing just because God is finished. The 7th Day can only be assumed to be long *if we presuppose God is still resting*.[15] If He is not still resting then the 7th Day could have been a normal day. One should also note the text says "God rested [past tense] on the seventh day…" not "God is resting".

Because the Day-Age View, Analogical Days View, and Framework View all make much of three other passages of Scripture they believe support God's rest continuing, I must include here what I believe these other verses mean.

1. John 5:16-17 says, "For this reason [healing a lame man and telling him to carry his mat] the Jews were persecuting Jesus, because He was doing these things on the Sabbath. But He answered them, 'My Father is working until now, and I Myself am working.'" The argument from the Day-Age View says, "Jesus' appeal is that He is honoring the Sabbath the same way His Father does. That is, His Father works 'to this very day' [NIV] even though 'this very day' is part of the Sabbath rest."[16] The Framework View says, "The argument presupposes that the Father's work occurs on His Sabbath. Thus, if the Father is working on the Sabbath 'until now,' then His Sabbath rest must also continue 'until now.'"[17] Both of these arguments emphasize the phrase "until now" or "to this very day" saying Jesus' argument presupposes God is working on His Sabbath rest. That is a heavy burden to attach to such a small statement. Jesus' point is that *His Father works on Sabbath days* and has done so even after His 7th Day rest, but it does not have to mean God's Sabbath is continuing.

To me the verse looks just the opposite of what they are saying. God is not resting, *He is working*. Genesis 2:2 says God ceased from His "work" on the 7th Day, but God is currently working, which means it is no longer the 7th Day. Jesus was clarifying both that He and His Father work on the Sabbath, and that God approved and was present with Him doing these mighty works. These verses do not presuppose the Father works on His Sabbath. They only tell us plainly that God was working *on that Sabbath* and He continued working even after the 7th Day. How is it a ceasing of activity for Him if He is still working?

But the Framework View objects, "If [the 7th Day] was not an eternal day, are we to imagine that on the eighth day God returned to work? Obviously not."[18] I say it is not so "obviously not". Yes, we are to understand God resumed work on the eighth day, but not on the work-project He finished the week before. Jesus' words, "My Father is working until now" can be understood in just that way. On the eighth day until now God is working, but we are not to understand that God takes a break every Sabbath. "Jesus said to them, 'The Sabbath was made for man, and not man for the Sabbath. So the Son of Man is Lord even of the Sabbath.'" (Mark 2:27-28) Neither God nor Jesus have to observe the Sabbath, They are Lord of it.

2. Psalm 95:10-11 says, "For forty years I loathed that generation, And said they are a people who err in their heart, And they do not know My ways. Therefore I swore in My anger, Truly they shall not enter into My rest." The question here is whether "My rest" refers to the rest God took on the 7th Day, or whether it means a "rest" *that belongs to God*, prepared for His people, namely the Promised Land, His rest (possessive). As the book of Hebrews is about to show us below, the Promised Land is a typology of salvation. The people still enslaved in Egypt in their heart are like us when we were lost. When we get saved we enter into a rest He prepared for us, one that belongs to Him, and one that is *analogous* to the rest He took *in the past*.

3. Hebrews 3:18-19, 4:3-6, and 9-10 say,

And to whom did He swear that they would not enter His rest, but to those who were disobedient? So we see that they were not able to enter because of unbelief... we who have believed enter that rest... For He has said somewhere concerning the seventh day: "AND GOD RESTED ON THE SEVENTH DAY FROM ALL HIS WORKS"; and again in this passage, "THEY SHALL NOT ENTER MY REST." Therefore, since it remains for some to enter it, and those who formerly had good news preached to them failed to enter because of disobedience... there remains a Sabbath rest for the people of God. For the one who has entered His rest has himself also rested from his works, as God did from His.

The Day-Age View speaks a lot about verse 9, "there remains a Sabbath rest", as if that means *God's* 7th Day rest remains, but that is not what Hebrews means. The Sabbath rest that remains is "for the people of God", *not for God Himself.*

The Framework View speaks of this rest as "...an eschatological, heavenly rest to which the people of God are called to enter by faith in Christ. ...the seventh day itself is equated with the Sabbath rest that awaits the people of God."[19] That would make the "rest" a future rest, but according to Hebrews, the people of God *already enter it now*, not in the future. For "we who have believed enter that rest" refers to someone who *has already entered* a rest that belongs to God, one He gave us *in this life*. What is the rest we enter? It is a rest from *dead works* that cannot earn salvation (Heb. 6:1). He who enters, rests "from his works" (4:10). Which works? *It cannot be a rest in heaven and ceasing from Earthly works if we already have it.* Nor can it mean an absolute rest from all work when we get to heaven; the Bible never promises a lack of productive activity in the afterlife. So, it must be a rest from works *in this life*, which can only be a rest from a futile attempt to work our way into God's favor through the Law. It cannot be a rest from good works produced as fruit of salvation because we should still be doing that.

None of these scriptures are conclusive enough to say the 7th Day is continuing. The missing refrain from the 7th Day does not necessitate such a conclusion either. The argument the 7th Day is still ongoing because the refrain is missing is an argument from silence. Nowhere does the Bible explicitly say God is still resting.

3. Too much activity for Day 6 is listed in Genesis 2 to have occurred in a normal day. Genesis 2 records that God made the land animals, formed man from dust, planted and grew a garden, placed Adam in the garden to tend it, gave Adam time to name the animals in the garden to find a companion for him, gave him time to realize his loneliness, put him to sleep, formed woman from his side, and then presented Eve to him. There are no shortages of OEC who use that as a compelling argument to prove the Days had to be longer than 24 hours because all that could not have happened in a day.

Two parts of this argument from Genesis 2 stand out in my mind as the most convincing: the fact God *planted* and *grew* a garden, and the time it would have taken for Adam to feel lonely without a suitable companion. Even though I am convinced the events of Genesis 2 cannot happen in a day, a major flaw exists with this argument, or any other which uses anything from Genesis 2 to prove the Days of Genesis 1 were longer than normal. The major flaw is the conclusion does not follow from the premise. The only conclusion that can be drawn from too much activity in Genesis 2 is that it cannot happen in day, not that the Days were longer. The reason people make the connection has to do with an attempt to rescue the stories in Genesis 1 and 2 from contradicting one another. However, the possibility exists that they do contradict one another (they do not, but of all possible scenarios between the two, one is that they were written by separate authors and tell different stories).

Skeptics have long emphasized the differences between Genesis 1 and 2 to say they are contradictory accounts. For example, according to skeptics and liberal theologians, Genesis 1 lists the chronologic order of creation as plants first (1:11-12), then birds (1:21), then land animals (1:25), then humanity (male and female at the same time – 1:27), and uses the word *elohim* for God. In contrast, Genesis 2 uses the compound name LORD God (*Yahweh elohim*) which many say suggests a different author. Also, the chronologic order of Genesis 2 is man (male) formed first (2:7), then plants (2:9), then land animals (2:19), then birds (2:19), and finally Eve (female – 2:22).

Responses by conservative scholars point out that the accounts have two different emphases and are written from two perspectives and then sometimes translate the problematic verbs in Genesis 2 into a pluperfect tense, rather than a simple past tense. For example, Genesis 2:19 is translated as "the LORD God *had formed* out of the ground all of the beasts" (NIV – my emphasis) rather than "the LORD God formed every beast" (NASB), even though in Hebrew the verb structure is *exactly the same* as 2:7, "the LORD God formed the man from the dust of the ground" (NIV). "Had formed" shifts the timeline of animal formation (in English) to a prior time before the formation of man. But, is that what the Hebrew writer intended? The same is sometimes suggested for Genesis 1:16 and 1:25 in order to alleviate the out-of-sequence problem I have mentioned many times now.

I disagree with changing the verb structure in English when the Hebrew verb structure is consistently the same, and I believe the solution to the order "differences" in Genesis 1 and 2 is much much simpler. Hebrew thinking is not like ours. *A series of past tense completed action verbs strung together in Hebrew narrative does not always represent a chronologic sequence.*[20] Subjects are sometimes mentioned *as they come up*, like parenthetical notes, or subjects are listed *topically*, like Genesis 1. Therefore, other means must be used to determine time sequence, like logic and time reference.

Simply translating the past tense verbs as such, with the understanding the sentences may not be in chronologic order, alleviates any problem between the two accounts and answers the skeptic's challenge to inerrancy, even *if* Genesis 1 and 2 were written by different authors. From Genesis 1 logic shows 1:16 and 1:25 are clearly out of sequence. Genesis 2 (which is part of the larger context of 2:4b – 5:1) concentrates on a more detailed story about the early history of humanity, and as details are needed they are provided (like God planting a garden – 2:8, and God forming animals – 2:19) without necessarily being in chronologic order. Therefore, the order of Genesis 1 does not contradict Genesis 2 because neither is in chronologic order.

If the two accounts were written by two authors (possibly), and the structures of the accounts have different purposes and focuses, and the Prophetic Days View is correct, two conclusions follow. *First*, everything listed in Genesis 2 *was not done on the 6th Day* because the 6th Day passed long before the fulfillments occurred. And *second*, the amount of activity in Genesis 2 cannot be used as an argument to say the 6th Day was long, but it can be used to show too much activity is listed for one day (thus providing further evidence against the YEV, but not positive evidence for the Day-Age View or the Analogical Days View). Too many activities in Genesis 2 for a day does not equate to the Days being long, it only proves the events listed in Genesis 2 did not occur in a day.

Still, the two parts most convincing to me of significant time passage can be used to show the YEV is incompatible with Genesis 2.

First, Genesis 2:8-9 says, "The LORD God planted a garden toward the east, in Eden; and there He placed the man whom He had formed. Out of the ground the LORD God caused to grow every tree..." If this is referring to super-miraculous instantaneous appearances of fully grown trees it is a strange way to say it. *Planting* and *growing* a garden are terms that describe normal plant growth from seeds. If words mean anything this *cannot* be taken as highly accelerated miraculous growth. The words "caused to grow" in verse 9 are one word in Hebrew and mean "to grow". A noun derived from that Hebrew verb means a branch or bud (Is. 55:10), thus the plants God planted *grew* and *budded*. This is no different than saying, "Farmer Brown grew a garden." God grew a garden He planted and He even *walked* among it (Gen. 3:8), so He may have actually plowed the ground (with the help of animals I suspect) rather than twitching His nose or waving a wand. Hyperactive growth is not indicated in these words any more than in Ps. 147:8, "... [God] makes grass to grow on the mountains" (same verb). Clearly, if the garden was planted and grew naturally it took longer than a day.

Second, Genesis 2:18-20 says:

> Then the LORD God said, 'It is not good for the man to be alone; I will make him a helper suitable for him.' Out of the ground the LORD God formed every beast of the field and every bird of the sky, and brought them to the man to see what he would call them... but for Adam there was not found a helper suitable for him.

The general meaning of these verses is that God designed man to have companionship, but *He wanted man to discover that for himself* before God solved the problem because the man would appreciate it more. Of course man's dominion over the animals is included in these verses, but that alone does not explain why Adam naming the animals is sandwiched between the statement, "it is not good for the man to be alone", and the animals not providing a suitable helper for him. So my point is, for Adam to discover loneliness in a significant way, he would need to be alone for a while. As a man, I can say a man in a new environment of discovery can easily keep himself occupied for days, maybe weeks, before a true sense of loneliness sets in. *These verses do not paint a picture of God hurrying at all.* Adam is given time to work, explore, examine, and observe (maybe even animal reproduction). God is not standing by saying, "Hurry up with the names already! I got a schedule to keep." Instead, significant passage of time is implied. One can imagine Adam excitedly explaining to Eve all he had discovered once she arrived, and Eve probably enjoyed it because she was *with him*, not because of how much he knew. And *'adam* still doesn't often get it. (men, meditate on that last line for a bit)

4 and 5. More contributions of Genesis 2 to the debate: Both the Framework View and the Analogical Days View use Genesis 2:5-6 to show that ordinary providence (God sustaining the normal operating procedures of the universe) is present in this creation story, not just extraordinary providence (miraculous intervention). Ordinary providence operates at what we perceive as normal speed, i.e. slow. Genesis 2:4-7 describes a situation where the reasons for the lack of plants are listed as twofold:

> ⁴This is the account of the heavens and the earth when they were created, in the day that the LORD God made earth and heaven. ⁵Now no shrub of the field was yet in the earth, and no plant of the field had yet sprouted, for the LORD God had not yet caused it to rain upon the earth (and there was no man to cultivate the ground). ⁶So a rain-cloud began to arise from the earth and watered the whole surface of the ground. ⁷Then the LORD God formed man of dust from the ground... [Translation of 5-6 from Irons and Kline[21]]

Many commentators agree these verses give two reasons *why* there were no plants: (1) God had not sent rain, and (2) there was no man to cultivate the ground. Then the text offers two solutions: (1) A rain-cloud began to arise to cause it to rain, and (2) God formed man to cultivate the land.

An important point to notice is that neither solution involves God creating plants (extraordinary providence). Instead two processes (rain and cultivation) are given to solve the problems respectively[22] and these are slow and facilitate normal plant growth (the same we normally associate with growing a garden). This conclusion is then used by both the FV and ADV (with detailed differences[23]) to show everything in Genesis 2 could not happen in a day. On that I agree, but again, it should be noticed it does not mean Day 6 was longer than 24 hours (as the ADV and DAV believe). It only means everything in Genesis 2 could not happen in a day and the YEV cannot be correct.

The conclusion then of the question "How long were the Days?" is that the Days are as the text defines them: *daylight hours on Earth* as opposed to nighttime. The arguments above only prove the activity listed in Genesis 2 cannot have happened in a day because they were slow processes like plant growth, lonely feelings, and the operations of ordinary providence. From that we can conclude the YEV is wrong because it says everything was finished in six days when, in fact, the text says it took longer, but we cannot conclude the Days were eons long. The Day-Age View is actually *alone* in interpreting the Days as long periods of time. *Every other view* sees that the best evidence from the text is that the Days were normal Earth days, or represent them in some fashion, either as a metaphor or analogy. The fact the DAV stands alone on this casts serious doubt upon its exegetical value. Arguments for long days have been rejected by many knowledgeable theologians.

II.2 Were the Days contiguous (no gaps between them)?

The Intermittent-Days View (IDV) is the only view of Genesis 1 that believes gaps were *between* the Days. We already concluded the Days read better as normal daylight hours on Earth, but did any time exist between them?

The answer is found in the "evening and morning" phrase. In the section above on the importance of the refrain I said the phrase is a bridge linking each Day consecutively and *contiguously* to the next one. Thus, it seems to prevent time gaps between the Days. Technically, the verb usage in the refrain does not prevent a time gap, but the use of the terms "evening" and "morning" suggest the only things between them are day and night, as is in Ex. 18:13, 27:21 and Lev. 24:3.

If the IDV is correct, the evening and morning refrain appears meaningless or out of sequence. Like in the case of the DAV, if the first evening is taken as the ending of Day 1 and the morning is taken as the beginning of Day 2 then it seems like the numbering of the Day ("one day", etc.) should have been listed before the morning, something like: and there was evening, one day, and there was morning and God said... In fact, if the IDV was what the author meant, I would be at a complete loss to understand why the refrain is there at all.

If we take the text the way it is, there does not appear to be any room for gaps between the Days other than nighttime. Ironic then (and personally gratifying I must say) that a primary advocate for the IDV, Robert C. Newman, made this comment:

> Some of the objections to my model could be avoided by adopting Hugh Capron's version of the intermittent-day view, in which the six days refer solely to God's commands in creation, rather than to their fulfillment, so that there is no need to correlate order of command with order of fulfillment. I prefer my scheme here as it produces a much higher correlation between Genesis and scientific models of origins.[24]

Newman here calls my view a version of the "intermittent-day view". This could be because he was writing before the name Days of Divine Fiat View distinguished it from the IDV. I still prefer to call it the Prophetic Days View.

As for the reason Newman adopted the IDV over the PDV, we will soon see the order of correlation of Genesis 1 and paleontology becomes an even worse problem for those who wish to reconcile Genesis and science with some kind of sequential view (like the DAV, ADV, and IDV). We must ask what the text and author meant. Did God intend to reveal the events in modern scientific

Chapter 9 – Evaluating Other Old-Earth Creationist Views

chronologic order? I do not believe so because the proclamations are in topical order. Does the text support gaps between the Days other than nighttime? No. That is the end of the story for the IDV as far as I am concerned regardless of scientific correlation. Not only do I disagree with his hermeneutic, I disagree with his conclusion. At least he recognizes some of the objections against him are answered by the PDV. Personally I think they all are.

The importance of the evening and morning phrase cannot be underestimated in determining the overall interpretation of the 7 Days. The Days read best as 6 normal Earth daylight periods followed by 6 evenings, 6 nights, and 6 mornings with a 7th Day at the end. That would mean they describe one normal week on Earth. But, was it a *real* historical week or just some figurative device used to describe real historical events?

II.3 Were the 7 Days a *real* historical week on Earth?

The Framework View (FV) is the only Old-Earth view that does not see the 7 Days as a real series of 7 time periods on Earth. Even its close kin brother, the Cosmic Temple View (CTV), admits it was a real week.[25] The FV advocates *the original intent of the author* was to present to us what God did in history in the form of a *metaphorical* human work week, being inspired to put the historical details into the figurative framework of work week. My question is, "Was that really what the author intended?" I do not believe so.

We have already seen the author intended for us to believe God *really* did speak the fiats, the blessings to humanity, and the blessings to the sea and flying creatures. Advocates of the FV agree the account records *real* historical events, "The Holy Spirit has given us an inerrant historical account of the creation of the world…"[26] With all that being real, I find it impossible to believe the author did not believe the week was real also. It is not as though God *had* to work during a real Earth week. Instead, He chose to do it as a pattern for humanity to follow. The best way to set a pattern for others to follow is to follow the actual pattern yourself, as all good managers would agree.

However, Framework View advocates give at least nine reasons to support the 7 Days as a figurative device and thus not meant to be taken literally:

1. The text of Genesis 1 is not completely chronological. Yes, we have seen that to be true in Chapters 1, 2, and 5, but, does that mean the week was not real? No, it only means the text of Genesis 1 is not completely chronological; it does not mean the Days themselves are dischronologized. Some FV advocates suggest, "It seems reasonable to assume that the narrator has offered a dischronologized presentation of the events in order to emphasize a theological point. God is not dependant on the luminaries."[27] Waltke says Day 4 is recapping the events of Day 1 for theological reasons, thus equating the events of the two Days and causing the 7 Days themselves to be out of sequence.

I have said several times now that Hebrew is not always written chronologically and sequence must be determined by logic and time markers. Logic dictates there are dischronologies in the account and very few deny this. However, time markers *cannot be ignored* and there are two *really BIG* ones in

167

Genesis 1. *First*, the Days are numbered, and numbering something is a clear way of determining sequence (i.e. actual chronology). And second, the evening and morning refrain gives us a literal evening (dusk) and a literal morning (dawn) *in sequence* on each of the 6 Days. These two time markers cannot be passed over as if they mean nothing. If the FV is correct then the numbered Days and evenings and mornings are not real. The numbers could make sense as seven days in a metaphorical week, but the evening and morning refrain makes no sense as a metaphorical device.

Unfortunately I believe many FV advocates take the route of advocating a non-literal view of Genesis 1 because they believe Genesis has scientific order problems and they see their route as the only alternative to maintaining some sense of Scriptural inerrancy, a subject also covered in Chapter 10. For now, let it be understood the time markers in the account lend strong credibility to the idea the author intended us to believe this was a real week on Earth.

2. Days 1-3 and 4-6 parallel one another. Yes, that is true (See Chapter 1 and Figure 1.1). That argues *strongly* in favor of the account being *deliberately arranged topically*, not chronologically. Agreed, but does that mean the week was not real? No, again, that would be ignoring the time markers in the account. Because of the time markers, it makes more sense to say God said the fiats chronologically over six real days in a topical order and then carried out the fulfillments in a non-sequential order, than it does to say the topical order is supreme and implies the week is not literal. The evidence from paleontology shows it would have been impossible to list the fulfillments of the proclamations chronologically because they overlapped one another. Once Point 4 of the PDV is accepted, that the fulfillments did not occur on the Day they were proclaimed, it frees us to see both the 7 Days as a real chronological week, and makes sense of the topical structure of the account. The Prophetic Days View is a beautifully simple view.

3. The 7th Day is missing the evening and morning refrain indicating it is an unending Day. I have already discussed this at length above. The missing refrain on the 7th Day only infers the account did not intend to connect the 7 Days to an 8th day. It does not have to mean the 7th Day is still continuing, and if the 7th Day has ended, any attempt to use the 7th Day to make the week metaphorical fails.

4. The use of the number 7 as a symbol in the Bible and other Near-Eastern accounts argues against a literal week. Many Bible commentators agree the number 7 represents a symbol of completion, but this creates a chicken and egg problem. The obvious question is whether the use of the number 7 as a symbol originated because of God's work week, or whether the work week is a metaphor based on some other origin of the idea. We do not know. Therefore, to use this argument to make a metaphor out of the week is weak indeed.

5. The 7 Days are preceded by different articles. Yes, it is true there is a peculiar arrangement of the articles associated with the numbered Days. The NASB has the Hebrew correct when it translates each as: "one day", "a second day", "a third day", "a fourth day", "a fifth day", "the sixth day", and "the seventh day." Notice that Genesis 1:5 says "one day", not the first day. And the

6th and 7th Days are preceded by "the" rather than "a" meaning the author intended to call particular attention to those two. The question is, "Why?"

As for why Day 1 is listed as "one day" one commentator says it may be because Day 1 was not the very first day on Earth, because the Earth had been there for some time before the 7 Days began, so Day 1 was just "one day", not the first day ever to exist.[28] However, it *was* the very first measurable day from the perspective of the surface because light first appeared that Day to separate light from darkness and thus begin the day/night cycle.

As for the significance of using the article "the" on the 6th and 7th Days, consider the significance of those Days. Day 6 was the Day God proclaimed the existence of humanity, for whom the whole Earth was designed, and contains the crescendo of the Genesis 1 account, verse 27, "God created man in His own image, in the image of God He created him; male and female He created them." The repeat of the selectively used word "create" three times in this verse surely has strong significance. As one commentator puts it:

> ...in the rest of the ancient world creation was set up to serve the gods, a theocentric view, in Genesis, creation is not set up for the benefit of God but for the benefit of humanity, an anthropocentric view. Thus we can say that humanity is the climax of the creation account.[29] [Walton]

Because particular attention is drawn to 1:27, it is obvious why the 6th Day uses the article "the" to emphasize its importance.

Considering the major Sabbath rest theme throughout the Law and prophets, the same can be said of "the" 7th Day. The specific articles and unique use of "one day" in Genesis 1 do not imply a metaphorical week, they are used for emphasis on aspects of the account to which the author wished to draw attention.

6. Light appears before the Sun. I find it unusual the FV would use this to say the account is not literal. The argument begs the question. It assumes you cannot have light without the Sun and everyone knows that, therefore Day 4 must be recapping Day 1, and thus the week is not literal. But their premise is questionable. Yes, everyone (even the ancients) can see the Sun now causes light on Earth, but was it obvious to the ancients the Sun had always been the only light source?[30] Apparently not, two FV advocates point out that Egyptian and Mesopotamian cosmogonies both have light before the Sun.[31] If the ancients believed light before the Sun was possible, using this to argue for a metaphorical week does not work.

Their argument also assumes Genesis says the Sun was made on Day 4, but we have already seen that is not true in Chapter 2 in the fourth point under Point 3, and in Chapter 5 under Objections to Point 3.

7. Exodus 31:17 speaks of God needing to catch His breath. This verse is difficult for anyone to explain. It says, "...for in six days the LORD made heaven and earth, but on the seventh day He ceased from labor, and was refreshed." The last word "refreshed" is the problem. It is a Hebrew root word meaning "to breathe"[32] and is only used two other times in the Bible (Ex. 23:12 and II Sam. 16:14) and there it refers to humans resting. We know an

omnipotent God does not need a breather, rest, or refreshment (Is. 40:28-29). The word "rest" is translated in the NASB as "ceased" which allows it to be taken literally. God can cease activity. If the week in Ex. 31:17 is literal, and the ceasing is literal, then what do we do with "refreshed"? The FV explains this verse like most others by saying "refreshed" is figurative, but then argues if "refreshed" is figurative then the week is also figurative, which is not unreasonable, albeit based upon one difficult verse.

But what if "refreshed" is literal? Is that possible? The following argument is speculative, but it seems to fit other Scriptures. What if God not only literally spoke during a literal week but was also literally there in some physical form? God "brought" the animals to Adam (Gen. 2:19). Adam and Eve "heard the sound of the LORD God walking in the garden" (Gen. 3:8), and God made clothes for them (3:21) which only makes sense to me as a physical form of God actually present. Also, references to the angel of the LORD are frequent in the OT and many see these as Theophanies. Perhaps God created while in human form or some other physical form related to angels. Job 1:6 describes the angels presenting themselves before the LORD and Revelation 4 and 5 describe One who is on the throne. These suggest the angels can see to whom they relate. Because no one can see God in His glory and live (Ex. 33:20), God must accommodate Himself when relating to humanity (and all created beings), but I admit this does not require Him to get tired. Also, Genesis 1:2 could be used against this argument because it says "the Spirit of God was moving over the waters", not a body. I will not be too dogmatic on this point but it seems to me a literal interpretation of Ex. 31:17 is not out of the realm of possibilities. However, I also do not have a problem with "refreshed" being symbolic of a human breather, without causing the whole account to be figurative.

8. The account uses anthropomorphic language to describe God's actions. For example, God is said to see and speak and these terms are probably not literal in the sense of God having eyes or a mouth (unless He was in a physical form). So Waltke says, "If the narrator's descriptions of God are anthropomorphic, might not the days and other aspects also be anthropomorphic?"[33] It is true we do not know *how* God experiences *anything* therefore we describe God's actions using language familiar with *our* experience even though the comparison is actually analogous, not identical. God perceives and communicates and we also perceive and communicate. We do it by seeing and speaking, therefore, we describe God as seeing and speaking though our meaning is analogous. The problem with applying this to the Days is that anthropomorphic language is used when we are describing something of which we have *no direct experience*, but that is not true of Earth days. We know what days are so figurative language is not needed. By Waltke's reasoning, anything in the account could be figurative including God being the Creator, but I do not think any evangelical wants to go down that path.

9. The account is structured as a polemic against Egyptian, Mesopotamian, and/or Canaanite cosmogonies. Even if that is true it still does not negate the fiats being spoken literally over a literal week any more than a topical structure does (#5 above).

To conclude the question of whether the week was real or not, the most natural and best way to interpret Genesis 1 is to say yes, the week was real. God working in a real Earth week *exactly* matches a human work week (not just symbolically or analogously), allows for a real timeframe wherein God could literally speak His fiats, and fits the description of the time markers in the account. I do not see any good evidence the intent of the author was to present anything but a real week.

Also, to conclude the question, "Were the 7 Days a normal Earth week?" the answer is also yes. The evidence shows Genesis 1 literally, not figuratively, describes a normal Earth week with normal Earth days with no gaps between the Days. If Genesis 1 refers to a real week on Earth of real Earth days, it eliminates the Day-Age View, the Analogical Days View, the Intermittent Days View, and the Framework View as legitimate interpretations.

III. How do we deal with the scientific order-of-appearance problem?

Young-Earth Creationists, Accommodationists[34], and skeptics agree on one thing if nothing else, *the Genesis 1 account is not in modern scientific chronological order*. However, from that they all derive different conclusions. YEC conclude scientists are wrong and look for ways to reinterpret the data to fit their faulty interpretation of Genesis. Accommodationists say the Bible is not written as a science book and accept the science, concluding God accommodated the naïve views of the ancients to reveal theological truths only. Skeptics agree with YEC interpretations of the Bible and Accommodationists' acceptance of science and reject the Bible as errant. Then the old-Earth Concordists step in and try to find ways to interpret the Bible to not contradict science. Now we have 10 major interpretations of Genesis 1 all trying to accomplish the same thing – solve the science problem.[35]

Here is the problem: *The order of events on Earth as indicated by geology and paleontology does not match the order of what God caused in Genesis 1.* Various authors list different quantities of "contradictions" in the order. The longest list I have seen is 20, but it is not necessary to list or answer them all, or see who has the longest list, because all it takes is one indisputable example to show it is a Biblical problem that must be answered. In Chapter 1 I listed three, but I am going to reduce that to two here to show the various ways the different views deal with the problem.

First, in Genesis 1:11 God proclaims the existence of "fruit trees on the earth bearing fruit after their kind with seed in them" and this proclamation precedes 1:21, "every living creature that moves, with which the waters swarmed... and every winged bird". That seems to put fruit trees on the land before any sea creatures or flying creatures like insects. (The Hebrew word translated "bird" is broader in definition and includes all flying creatures including insects.[36]) Paleontology would see that scenario as nonsense. Life began on a single-celled level and various creatures swam the seas long before fruit trees grew on land.

171

Second, in Genesis 1:21 God proclaims "every winged bird" to come into existence before 1:25 says God made "everything that creeps on the ground". That seems to put the existence of birds before all land animals, including reptiles and flightless bugs. And again, paleontology would say reptiles, spiders, and scorpions preceded birds.

Among evangelicals who think this issue *can be solved* four methods are used:

1. Reinterpret science to solve the problem: Young-Earth Creationists claim God actually caused creation in the order Genesis lists it and insist paleontology is wrong. I cannot answer that here except to say that after years of reading YEC Flood geology explanations of fossils and geologic formations I can regretfully say they are badly wrong. Flood geology cannot account for the geologic column and all its various fossil bearing formations (as I touched on briefly with just two examples in Chapter 8). I believe scientists generally have the geologic history of the Earth correct.

Also, if geology is generally correct then two other OEC views fit into this category of reinterpreting science with the YEV. Both the traditional Gap View and the Limited Creation View (John Sailhamer), relegate the fossil record to the distant past described in Genesis as the "beginning" (Gen. 1:1). Both believe most of the geologic column (particularly the fossil bearing part) was formed in the block of time before the 7 Days. That part would work scientifically, but after that the traditional GV believes Earth was destroyed and re-created a relatively short time ago (thousands of years), and that is just as scientifically unsupported as the YEV. The LCV does not believe Earth was destroyed. It believes the 7 Days refer to the creation of the Promised Land only, not the whole Earth. Again, that is as scientifically unsupported as the YEV, so neither the GV nor the LCV will work to solve the science problems.

2. A closer examination of the Hebrew word definitions solves the problem: This is the route taken by Hugh Ross[37] at Reasons To Believe. Ross is an advocate of the Day-Age View, where the ages match the paleontological record. Consider the answers he gives to the two problems above.

In regards to fruit trees on Day 3 he says:

> The *'es* [the Hebrew word for tree] certainly includes all large plants containing cellulose and could possibly refer to all larger-than-microscopic plants whose fibers provide a measure of stiffness. Thus these terms do include the relatively primitive plant species scientists have identified as the first land vegetation.[38]

What he is doing is defining the Hebrew word for "tree" so broadly that it could include plants identified by paleobotanists as the first land plants. My question is whether the ancients to whom this account was written would have understood it that way. To them it simply referred to what humans identify as fruit trees (i.e. fig, olive, etc.). The Hebrew word for "tree" does have a broad definition, but not as broad as Ross takes it. It refers to any plant we might normally call a tree or that contains wood[39], including some bushes probably, but it is doubtful the word refers to tiny or small plants with relatively stiff fibers, like grass and flowers. The ancients would not have seen those as trees, nor would most people today. Nor could those plants rightly be described as bearing fruit with seeds. Genesis is written to an audience who would have understood its definitions. Fruit trees are listed on Day 3 foreshadowing the trees in the garden (2:9) from which Adam and Eve could eat (1:29), and not eat (3:2-6).

Ross is trying to reconcile science to Genesis by *broadening* the definition of the Hebrew word for "tree" so big it encompasses nearly all plants. But Genesis 1:11 already did that with the word "vegetation", "Let the earth sprout vegetation, plants yielding seed, *and* fruit trees on the earth bearing fruit after their kind with seed in them." That verse uses three words for the plants: "vegetation", "plants", and "trees". The word "vegetation" is the most generic and refers to all plants.[40] *Notice its use is not qualified like the other two*. The second word "plants" is qualified with "yielding seed", and "trees" is qualified using "fruit" and "fruit... with seed". These qualifications narrow the last two to plants associated with humanity, i.e. grains and fruit trees.[40] If "fruit trees" refers to what we normally think of when we say the words then the scientific order-of-appearance problem is not solved. Ross broadening definitions of the Hebrew to make it fit science is not the right approach.

To Ross's credit, another of his suggestions gets him closer to solving the plant problem. He says, "As to whether the creation days might overlap, the syntax suggests they do not. On each creation day God initiates a specific transformative event."[41] He goes on to suggest the fulfillments of the proclamations *were not completed on the Day initiated*, which is close to the PDV except that the PDV does not even have to have the fulfillments initiated on the Days proclaimed. From the DAV, God could have initiated plant production on Day-Age 3, but not fulfilled the "fruit tree" part until a later Age. In this case, Ross is actually agreeing with me that the fulfillments were not completed on the Days they were proclaimed.

While that may solve the plant problem for the DAV, it does not work for the animals. God proclaimed for flying creatures to come into being on Day 5, which means they would have to be initiated on Day 5, which means they would have preceded the land creatures. Paleontology tells it differently.

In regards to birds and reptiles, Ross says:

> Genesis 1:20-21 goes on to introduce some animal species radically different from any previously mentioned. These creatures are identified by the Hebrew noun *nephesh*... The word *nephesh* appears many times in the Bible. Occasionally, as in Leviticus 11:46, the context connotes the broad definition, land creature with the breath of life, meant to include nearly all "living" animals – reptiles, amphibians, insects, birds, and mammals. Most of the time, the narrower definition, soulish creature or creature capable of expressing yearnings, emotions, passions, and will, is implied.[42]

> The sixth day begins with God making (*'asa*) three specific kinds of land mammals... This list does not purport to include all the land mammals God

173

made. Rather, it focuses on three varieties of land mammals that would cohabit with and provide support for the human beings to come later.

The three Hebrew nouns used for these creatures are *behema*, *remes*, and *chayya*, respectively. Though *remes* refers occasionally in Hebrew literature to reptiles, the opening phrase of Genesis 1:25 makes clear that these are mammals.[43]

Here, instead of broadening definitions, Ross is *narrowing* definitions to solve the science problem. He says the words for the land animals refer only to mammals, and thus attempts to solve the birds-before-reptile problem by not including reptiles or flightless bugs on Day 6. It even forces him to say of dinosaurs, "Their creation and duration on Earth most likely occurred on the fifth creation day."[44] The problem is, the text says nothing like that. Day 5 is about God proclaiming *life in the waters* ("with which the waters swarmed") *and sky*, not on land. All this gives the impression of forcing the text to fit the science data by inconsistently choosing definitions. Ross's interpretation also would mean Genesis 1 does not tell us the origin of all insects and reptiles.

I have already discussed the way some YEC misuse the term *nephesh chayah* ("living creature" – see the third main point in Chapter 6). Here we find an OEC misusing it also. Ross is correct to reference Lev. 11:46 where the terms refer to a broad spectrum of animals, but where he gets the idea a narrower definition is used "most of the time" (including Genesis) I do not know. The two terms (*nephesh* – soul or creature, and *chayah* – living) are used *together* only eleven times[45] in the OT, nine of which are in Genesis and two in Leviticus, and *in every case* (except the one referring exclusively to humanity – Gen. 2:7) the context *demands* broad categories of animals. Nor do I see where Genesis 1:25 "makes clear" *remes* (creeping things) refers to mammals only. It seems the only thing that would make someone think "everything that creeps [*remes*] on the ground" (1:25) refers to mammals only is because if it refers to reptiles and bugs it causes a scientific order-of-appearance problem. But we are not supposed to assume the text means what we want it to mean. "Everything that creeps on the ground" means any creature Adam would have seen scurrying on the ground, including reptiles and spiders, and thus the scientific order problem remains.

Even if we granted Ross his argument Day 6 animals were only mammals related to humanity because, as he says, "The theme of the account... is the preparation of Earth for Adam and Eve and their progeny"[46], he still has a problem with consistency. His argument for solving the fruit tree problem was to broaden the definition, but if the account was written about things related to humanity only, then so were the plants on Day 3, and that leaves the fruit tree problem intact. He is stuck either way, and I have only mentioned two examples. There are more, and hence, defining terms in Genesis to solve the order-of-appearance problem fails and became one of the two main reasons I rejected the Day-Age View (the other one being defining the Days as ages).

3. Overlapping the fulfillments of the proclamations solves the problem. This is the solution chosen by the Intermittent Days View of Robert Newman[47] and the Analogical Days View of which C. John Collins writes:

The days are broadly sequential, which means they are successive periods of unspecified length; but since this sequence is part of the analogy, it is possible that parts of the days overlap and that events on a particular day may be grouped for logical rather than chronological reasons.[48]

How do parts of the Days overlap? *The Days themselves cannot overlap.* Each Day 1-6 ends with the evening and morning refrain which *concludes* that Day and proceeds on to the next in the same way a numbered sequence ends the number before and moves to the next number. Numbers do not overlap. What he must mean, similar to Hugh Ross, is that some fulfillments of the proclamations on some Days extended into the following Day(s). That also *has to be* what the IDV advocates because in that view the Days are normal Earth days separated by long periods of time, so by definition the Days themselves do not overlap.

Do overlapping fulfillments solve the order-of-appearance problem? At first glance it seems like it might, but upon closer inspection I do not believe it does for the following reason. Think for a minute on what it means to have overlapping fulfillments and specifically when the fulfillments *began to occur*. If the IDV, ADV, and DAV say the fulfillments *began on the Day* they were proclaimed, meaning something happened on that Day, or at least before the next Day, to initiate the fulfillment, then there is a problem. In our two examples, on Day 3 God proclaimed the existence of *land* plants (not sea plants), "And God said, 'Let the *earth* sprout vegetation, plants yielding seed, *and* fruit trees... *on the earth*'" (1:11 – emphasis mine) and on Day 5 God proclaimed the existence of all flying creatures, "And God said, '...let birds fly above the earth... [literally – "let flyers fly"[49]]' And God created... every winged bird [flyer] after its kind" (1:20-21). Land plants and all flying creatures are proclaimed to come into existence *before all land animals*, and plants were proclaimed a full 3 Days before. If the fulfillment of these proclamations initiated before the Day 6 proclamation that would have to mean some form of flying creature was the first land animal, and fruit trees grew on land *long* before animals crawled on land, neither of which is scientifically feasible.

Paleontologically speaking, current thought says land plants preceded land animals (though the question is not easily answered), which might seem to validate Genesis. However, that could switch and Genesis is not talking about just any land plants, it refers specifically to plants *useful for humanity*, i.e. grains and fruit trees. And those plants *did not* precede land animals. If the fulfillment for fruit trees had to initiate before land animals were proclaimed, even if the fulfillment was not completed until after the proclamation on Day 6, it still contradicts current paleontology and overlapping the fulfillments does not help.

The same is true for flying creatures. Fossils show crawling creatures preceded flying creatures, but if the proclamation for flying creatures had to at least be initiated on God-Day 5 (ADV and DAV) or between Days 5 and 6 (IDV) then again we have a scientific contradiction overlapping fulfillments cannot solve.

Alternately, if the ADV or IDV attempt to say that the fulfillments of the Day 3 or 5 proclamations did not begin before Day 6, *they are agreeing with me the fulfillments were not initiated on the Day proclaimed* and the IDV might as well slide all 7 Days together to form a chronological week and the ADV might as well give up the Days being God's days and accept them as real Earth days.

However, I really think the scientific order of appearance problem is not an issue, because...

4. The account was never intended to be in modern scientific order. This is where I stand with the PDV. Genesis 1 never meant to list what God caused in chronologic scientific order because *they were proclaimed topically.* God proclaimed the fiats in topical order so we should not expect the list of plants and animals in Genesis to be in scientific order. As I have already said, we now know the scientific order of appearance is extremely complex with various plants and animals appearing on Earth throughout a long history. God knew He was going to do it that way so He proclaimed their existence topically for an easy revelation to humanity. Over a six day period God completed a work of speaking eight proclamations (prophecies) of what was going to happen, and they all happened, but not necessarily in the order He said them. The order that they actually happened could not have been specified without being encyclopedic and incomprehensible to many generations of people.

Genesis 1 is a topical list. It is difficult to deny the topical arrangement of the account, but it is this structure, and the fact the proclamations were not fulfilled on the Days proclaimed, that provides the reconciliation with science many think does not exist.

Day 1 – Light	Day 4 – Source and purpose of the lights
Day 2 – Waters and sky	Day 5 – Creatures in the water and sky
Day 3 – Dry land and plants	Day 6 – Land creatures and humanity that eat plants

Days 1-3 and 4-6 parallel each other. Days 1-3 are about changing the uninhabitable condition of the Earth to inhabitable. Then Days 4-6 are about changing the empty-of-life condition of the Earth to a full-of-life condition.

In similar fashion, John Walton points out that Days 1-3 involve setting up the primary functions of the cosmos for humanity (time, weather, and food)[50], and Days 4-6 involve setting up the functionaries in that environment. He also points out that separating and naming are primarily on Days 1-3.[51] To that I would add that God separated and named those portions of His creation which means He reserved them to remain under His direct rule whereas God setup other governors and rulers on Days 4-6. The Sun and Moon are to govern the day and night by proclamation on Day 4, and Day 6 establishes humanity to rule and subdue the land, and Genesis 2:19-20 says God gave Adam the responsibility of naming the animals, the portion he was to rule.

If Genesis 1 is a non-chronological list of what was going to happen, and the fulfillments were never meant to be understood as occurring or initiating on the Day they were proclaimed[52], and all that was proclaimed was not completed

Chapter 9 – Evaluating Other Old-Earth Creationist Views

in a week[53], then *the topical order of events in Genesis causes no scientific problems.* The beauty and wisdom of God revealing creation the way Genesis 1 is written is that throughout all of human history (past, present, and future), and regardless of education level, it does not matter what order humanity believed (or will believe) plants and animals appeared on Earth because *it will never contradict Genesis*, because Genesis 1 is not a chronological list. The Prophetic Days View is a beautifully simple view.

Comparing other Old-Earth Views with the Prophetic-Days View

This chapter has thus far discussed in detail how some of the structural elements of Genesis 1 affect any overall view of the account. What follows is a summarized comparison of the PDV to the eight other old-Earth views.

Three major *agreements* between all OEC views:

1. The age of the universe and Earth cannot be determined from the Bible.

While the various OEV's of Genesis do not agree on how to reconcile the account to astronomy and geology, or in some cases whether it can even be done, they all agree the Bible does not teach the universe and Earth are young. They all say the Bible leaves the question open and allows for an old universe and Earth. They all reject the dogmatism of some YEC who insist a correct interpretation of Genesis 1 requires belief in a young Earth.

2. All nine old-Earth views are attempting to defend Christianity.

They are all evangelical in their approach to Scripture, meaning they take a high authoritative view of it. Even though they may have differing definitions of inerrancy, all of them defend the Bible as the inspired word of God.

3. All nine old-Earth views agree God did not finish the entire creation in seven normal Earth days.

Though all old-Earth views disagree on what happened on the Days of Genesis 1, they all agree God did not finish the entire creation within seven normal days. All agree it took longer than a week to create the universe and fulfill all the proclamations.

The *one major disagreement* between the PDV and *ALL* the others

One aspect of the Prophetic Days View sets it apart from all the other old-Earth views and therefore, all the others disagree with it. It is defended as Point 4 in Chapter 2 and is the defining point of the PDV: The fulfillments of the proclamations (prophecies) that God said on the 6 Days were not all meant to be understood as fulfilled or initiated *within* the Day they were given. The corollary to Point 4 is that all God proclaimed was not completed within the 6 Days (as defended in Chapter 5 under objections to Point 4), and God worked *after* His 7th Day rest to fulfill His proclamations. Please refer to those chapters to reinforce the truth of Point 4 if necessary. This disagreement is listed here to avoid listing it under each view.

The Prophetic Days View says that God completed a literal historical six day work wherein He proclaimed (prophesied) what was going to happen to a desolate, lifeless, dark, and deluged land. Then He fulfilled those proclamations over an unspecified period of time *after* ceasing from work on the 7th Day.

Disagreements between the PDV and the <u>Day-Age View</u>

1. The Days were not long ages of time. They were normal Earth days as defended above.
2. The DAV does not solve the scientific order-of-appearance problem as described above.

Disagreements between the PDV and the <u>Analogical Days View</u>

1. The Days were not God-days of unspecified length analogous to a human work week. It appears to me the author of Genesis 1 intended for the Days to be understood as a normal week on Earth. (See above) I have a difficult time believing the author intentionally wrote only an analogy and did not think of the Days as an actual ordinary week. What is the purpose of the evening and morning refrain in an analogy? Why say evenings and mornings came to pass if real evenings and mornings did not come to pass?

C. John Collins, the main advocate of the ADV, says the refrain best describes "the end points of the nighttime."[54] He references Numbers 9:15-16 where the cloud covered the tabernacle from evening to morning, meaning *all night,* to prove his point. I agree, and it indicates to me the evening and morning of each Day were *real*. However, Collins says, "The days are God's workdays, which are understood by analogy to human work" and they are "of unspecified length."[57] He also says, "The ESV rendering of the refrain allows us to see what it is doing: marking the end points of each of the workdays."[58] But how are the evening *and* the morning marking the end points of an "unspecified length" of time when they normally describe "the end points of the nighttime"? How can a long God-Day have a nighttime? Did God work for a long time and then take a long "nighttime" break? These questions become irrelevant if we simply take the Days as a real week of daytimes and nighttimes.

2. I also think the ADV ends up with a similar problem as the FV. How can the Days be only an analogy when the creation of the heavens and Earth are real, the condition of the Earth as unproductive, dark, and wet was real, the proclamations were real, what God did to fulfill them was real, and God's other actions were real? If almost the entire account describes real events without analogy or figurative language, why must the Days be an analogy? Again, all this goes away if the Days were a normal week.

3. The ADV does not solve the scientific order problem by advocating overlapping fulfillments because in some cases a fulfillment that begins on the Day it was proclaimed is already out of scientific chronology with a subsequent Day. If it is conceded the fulfillments did not even begin on the God-Day they were proclaimed, then why suggest the Days were of unspecified length? One might as well accept the Days as a real week rather than an analogy. It would be great if Collins adopted the Prophetic Days View.

Disagreements between the PDV and the Framework View

1. The Days were not a figurative device to describe what God did. Though I agree with the FV the Days are arranged topically, that does not mean the proclamations could not have been said over a real week in Earth history. I have a very difficult time believing the author did not intend to describe a real week on Earth. The problem with introducing figurative elements to the story is that it opens the door to the whole account being figurative. If the account is historical about what God did, why aren't the Days historical too? I think some FV thinkers would say if the Days are taken literally it forces us into the YEV, but I have already shown that to not be true in Chapters 2 and 5.

2. The FV has problems with what God said and when. Did God really say those proclamations? If the answer is yes, then *when* did He say them if not on consecutive real Earth days? It appears the account tells us God said them on Earth sometime. Genesis 1:2 says, "the Spirit of God was moving over the surface of the waters." Is that literally true? Was the Spirit there on Earth? And if He was, then it would appear God really said those proclamations *on Earth* too and then we are back to, "when?" If God was really there on Earth, and He really said those fiats sometime in real Earth time, and He really fulfilled those proclamations, and He really saw that everything was good, and He really said those blessings, how can we then say those evenings and mornings were figurative? On the other hand, if an advocate of the FV thinks God really did not say those fiats in Earth history, then we would see a further slide toward the account becoming completely figurative.

3. Many who hold the FV are Accommodationists which means they believe there are scientific errors in the Bible and God accommodated the ignorance of the writers to reveal theological truths which are the real message of the story. I think that weakens the foundation of Christianity. The Bible does not separate categories of truth into theology and science; it simply claims to speak the truth. However, as I explain in the next chapter (and in Appendix B), the Bible does not have scientific errors so an Accommodationist position is unnecessary.

Disagreements between the PDV and the Intermittent Days View

1. The text gives no reason to support gaps of time between the Days. It reads like each Day is followed immediately by the next Day. If there were gaps of time then the evening and morning phrase loses all meaning. Also, it is

difficult to compare a human work week with the idea of having Day 1, then a long period of time, then Day 2, then a long period of time, then Day 3, etc.

2. The IDV also has no reason to separate the 7 Days when, by its own definition, no fulfillment occurred on any of the Days anyway. If the fulfillments were not done on any of the Days, and they were not listed chronologically, and they were not completely fulfilled between the Days, why separate the Days?

Disagreements between the PDV and the Gap View

1. The traditional Gap View has been around a long time and asserts a major gap of time between the beginning in Genesis 1:1 and the condition of the Earth as described in Genesis 1:2. At first this may look like Point 2 of the PDV (see Chapter 2), but it is far from it. The GV says that the formless and void conditions of the Earth were a result of God judging a previous creation and destroying it. The 7 Days then refer to a re-creation of Earth by God. However, Point 2 of the PDV says the "beginning" was a *block of time* before the 7 Days began and disagrees Genesis 1:2 refers to a previous judgment.

2. Arguments the GV uses to support its position are exegetically unsound. Three unsound arguments that are still used by laypeople and uninformed pastors to support the GV are:

One, Gen 1:2 can be translated as "and the earth *became* formless and void" (as footnoted in the NIV). Collins[57], Leupold[58], Whitelaw[59], and many others emphatically insist that is not so. The verb cannot be translated as "became".

Two, the phrase "formless and void" implies the Earth was judged into that condition in the same way Jeremiah saw a vision of the land becoming judged that way again (Jer. 4:23). However, "formless and void" are better translated "desolate (or unproductive) and lifeless" and do not necessarily imply a judged condition.[60] Interpreting them as the initial conditions that God needed to change for humanity does no harm to God's intentions for the Earth. God changed it from being uninhabitable to very good for humanity.

Three, Isaiah 45:18 is used to say the formless (desolate – *tohu* in Hebrew[60]) condition of the earth in Genesis 1:2 was not the way God originally created it, "For thus says the LORD who created the heavens (He is the God who formed the earth and made it, He established it and did not create it a waste place [*tohu*], *But* formed it to be inhabited)." Isaiah uses the same word as Genesis but says God "did not create it a waste place" whereas Genesis says the earth was in that condition after its creation. From that, the GV suggests that the condition of the Earth in 1:2 is not the way God originally created it and that it must have become that way by judgment. The problem is, as above, Genesis does not say the earth "became" that way but was simply in that condition. And it should be noted Isaiah contrasts the desolate condition to a habitable condition and Genesis does not leave the Earth in a desolate condition. Isaiah can be understood to be saying that God did not create the earth desolate *with the intent on leaving it that way*, but instead intended for it to be habitable.

Fourth, the KJV translation of Genesis 1:28 as "and God said... replenish the earth" implies in today's English that Adam and Eve were to repopulate the

Earth, but the word "replenish" is better translated as "fill" (as in the NKJV, NASB, NIV, and ESV) and has *nothing to do with repopulating*, only populating.

3. The GV creates more science problems than it solves. The idea the Earth was destroyed, dark, and *covered with water* 6-10,000 years ago (or even 100k) and then completely re-created, mountain ranges and all, since that time, and then destroyed again in the Flood, is as scientifically unsupportable as the YEV.

Disagreements between the PDV and the Limited Creation View

Point 2 of the PDV (see Chapter 2) comes directly from John Sailhamer, advocator of the LCV (or Focus-on-Palestine View as it is most commonly called), but his interpretation of what was initially created as the heavens and Earth differs greatly from the PDV. Sailhamer believes the "beginning" block of time refers to the creation of Earth mostly as we see it today, including all fossilized creatures of the past, and that *only the Promised Land* was desolate and empty as described in 1:2, not the whole Earth. Whereas, the PDV, DAV, ADV, and IDV believe that 1:1 refers only to the creation of the primeval heavens and Earth ending with the *entire Earth* (all land) being desolate and lifeless. The difference is significant.

That Genesis begins to narrow the focus of "land" (earth) is clear from the text. It starts with all land (1:1 – thus, the whole Earth including what was underwater), then it moves to dry ground (1:9-10), and then it moves to a specific garden in a specific place (2:8-15). But narrowing the focus of the land does not have to mean the creation account is only referring to a specific land. The account starts with *no dry land at all*, and even though the Promised Land is a huge theme in the Pentateuch, I think Israel understood the "land" (earth) in 1:1 referred to more than the parcel promised to them.

Another difference between the LCV and PDV is Sailhamer attempts to solve the age of the Earth problem by relegating the entire creation to the unspecified distant past. But, that causes a host of bizarre interpretations of Gen. 1:3-31 which have no reasonable explanation, neither Biblically or scientifically. For example:

1. How was only the Promised Land covered with water (Gen. 1:2) without destroying the rest of the Earth? Other creation passages like Psalm 104:5-9 and Job 38:4-11, discuss laying the foundations of the Earth and water covering it, including the mountains, and then the sea retreated to its place and the mountains rose to theirs. These other creation accounts clearly have the entire Earth in mind, and in the case of Psalm 104, are a poetic commentary on Genesis 1. If David understood Genesis to refer to all land then we should too.

2. Sailhamer says, "There is darkness over the face of the waters in Genesis 1:2 because it is nighttime when God first begins to speak."[61] His explanation of why it was dark is it was night. However, was not the darkness permanent at that time as Job 38:8-9 describes? With the darkness as only nighttime it leads Sailhamer to say the "light" on Day 1 "...is merely a description of the sunrise on the first day of the week."[62] Really? God commanded something to happen

181

that was *going to happen anyway*? I think that interpretation runs into trouble with reconciling God "commanding the morning" in Job 38:12-13. It also destroys the analogy Paul makes in II Cor. 4:6, "For God who said, 'Light shall shine out of darkness,' is the One who has shown in our hearts to give the light of the knowledge of the glory of God in the face of Christ." Our darkness is a permanent bad condition without God giving us light, in the same way the darkness of the initial Earth was.

3. The expanse of Day 2 becomes a very bizarre question in the LCV. Were there no heavens, clouds, or rain over the Promised Land after the initial creation of the Earth? If so, why did God have to not only speak the expanse into existence (1:6), but also make it (1:7)?

4. The situation would be just as bizarre for living creatures. Why did God have to create and make animals in the Promised Land when all they had to do was walk, fly, or swim over? Genesis appears to describe the *origin* of all living creatures, not just their entrance into the Promised Land.

The LCV causes more scientific problems than it solves and does not make sense to me Biblically either. Despite the many good contributions by Sailhamer[63] to the body of Christ, the LCV is not one of them.

Disagreements between the PDV and the Revelatory Days View

I have already discussed this view above by saying the Genesis account does not appear to be God speaking a revelation to a man over six days. God's speaking parts in the story are directed at either the habitation deficiencies of the Earth, the angels, within Himself, or giving blessings to the sea creatures, flying creatures, and humans. The account is not told like one would expect if it was the story of God revealing to humanity over six days what He had done in the distant past. Even though God had to reveal Genesis 1 to humanity in some way, the 7 Days read like a narrative, part of the revealed story, not the days God did the revealing. The proclamations look like God is speaking things into existence, not telling us about it afterward.

Disagreements between the PDV and the Cosmic Temple View

The CTV's originator, John Walton, says of the 7 Days, "These are seven twenty-four-hour days. This has always been the best reading of the Hebrew text."[64] On that we agree, therefore it is likely very little that I have said in this chapter about the interpretation of the length of the Days would be disputed by him. However, there is a huge difference between the PDV and CTV on what happened on those Days. Also, Walton is someone who exemplifies the conflict between Accommodationists and Concordists. At its heart the CTV is not about an accord between modern science and the Bible. Accommodationists (like Walton) see the methodology of the Concordists (like me) as deeply flawed because they say it is reading an ancient text through a modern mindset. (See the next chapter for more on that) The type of reconciliation Accommodationists provide attempting to salvage their version of "inerrancy" comes at the expense of denying the scientific accuracy of the Bible.

The CTV claims, against all other views, that Genesis 1 is not about the *material* origins of the universe and its features. Walton claims the account is about *functional* origins only. Everyone should agree with Walton that God's creation was not complete until it was *functioning* for the purposes God created it and Genesis 1 is the account of how the creation came to function. But, did the author of Genesis also have in mind that God created, caused, shaped, and/or formed the *material* part also? If he did then many of Walton's 18 propositions[65] would need revising and that is where I will focus here.

I believe Genesis 1 is the *whole story* of our origins, including material origins, functional origins, purposes, theology, and work-week pattern. Excluding material origins from the account, or emphasizing any one part, apparently trying to relieve the account of scientific errors Accommodationists claim exist in it, does not make me feel better about the implications of scientific error. A God capable of creating the universe and raising the dead is certainly capable of speaking through humans and preventing them from expressing erroneous scientific views rather than accommodating them.

As a side note, saying that Genesis involves material creation does not negate that God had more in mind than just matter and energy with His creation. The proposition that God created the functions of the creation and took a "seat" upon the throne of His "cosmic temple" as its sovereign Ruler can still be true. It would just mean the proclamations were much wider in scope than many people have seen, a fact I am willing to incorporate into the PDV. My studies of the various views of Genesis 1 have expanded my scope of the structure of the account. It amazes me so much can be gleaned from only 35 short verses of Genesis 1:1-2:4a and it increases my faith in our Creator.

As for whether Genesis teaches *both* material and functional origins, Walton anticipates the challenge to his view:

> It is easy to see the functional orientation of the account, but does the material aspect have to be eliminated altogether? In answer to this question, if we say that the text includes a material element alongside the functional, this view has to be demonstrated, not just retained because it is the perspective most familiar to us... We must be led by the text. A material aspect cannot be assumed by default, it must be demonstrated...[66]

What I then find interesting scattered through his book are statements like these:

> Of course something must have physical properties before it can be given its function, but the critical question is, what stage is defined as "creation"? (p. 25)

> Would [Ancient Near Easterners] have believed that their gods also manufactured the material? Absolutely, for nothing can be thought to stand apart from the gods. (p. 34)

> Even if the account in Genesis 1 is taken as an account of functional origins, it would not therefore imply that God is not responsible for material origins. The biblical view is that whatever exists from any perspective is the work of God. (p. 141)

But then notice how he turns this on its head.

> To that audience [of Genesis], however, it would likewise have been unthinkable that God was somehow uninvolved in the material origins of creation. Hence there wouldn't have been any need to stress a material creation account with God depicted as centrally involved in material aspects of creation. (p. 95)

He is saying they assumed God created the material so they did not need an account stating He did. So why did they need an account stating functional origins? They probably assumed that too. Also, if the "biblical view is that whatever exists from any perspective is the work of God", *where does it say that in the Bible*, particularly in the OT, if not in Genesis?

Regardless of my questions, I think it can be demonstrated material origins were also involved in Genesis. Walton does a good job of showing the Hebrew word for "create" (*bara'*) does not always mean creation out of nothing (*ex nihilo*). Sometimes the word is used of creating using existing material (the wind – Amos 4:13) or spiritually (a pure heart – Ps. 51:10). Also, all agree, including Walton, "create" is only used of God's actions, not man's. Many also agree a working definition of the word is *to make a new thing, i.e. something that did not exist before*, even if out of existing materials. I agree that the proclamations God said do not necessarily involve Him creating new material, but *they do involve Him doing something with existing material*, or creating a function and/or forming something more complicated, like plants or animals. At the very least, in many cases, one must admit that *the functional origin had to involve the rearrangement of existing materials*. Is that not a material origin also?

For the CTV to say the proclamations God said did not involve material creation, Walton must believe that the various features and creatures proclaimed on the 6 Days *preexisted materially* before the 6 Days, meaning they were already there. God then proclaimed their final function. What should not be missed however, is that if the features and creatures *did not exist* prior to the functional proclamations, then the proclamations *had to involve material origins* because they were proclaiming for the features and creatures to come *to be*, not just come to function for an intended purpose. The question is then: does the account give any indication the features and creatures proclaimed did not exist before the proclamations?

Day 1: Walton's own really good argument is that "We are compelled by the demands of verses 4 and 5 to translate verse 3 as 'God said, "Let there be a period of light."' If we had previously been inclined to treat this as an act of material creation, we can no longer sustain that opinion."[67] As stated in Chapter 2, I agree with the light being a period of time, but think a little deeper about

Chapter 9 – Evaluating Other Old-Earth Creationist Views

what had to happen to fulfill this proclamation. For a period of daylight to *begin functioning* on Earth one must assume daylight was *not functioning at the time of the proclamation* which means light was not reaching the surface of Earth. God had to clear something out of the way to make that happen or create the light source, both of which involve doing something with material. Also, the Day 1 proclamation involved the phrase "Let there be" which indicates that the period of light proclaimed did not "be" before the proclamation. Therefore, material origins were involved.

Also, consider that if no period of light was functioning prior to Day 1, then Day 1 must have been before the creatures in the account existed because they would have needed a day/night cycle in order to live. That indicates the proclamations occurred before the material origins of the creatures and thus involved material origins.

Day 2: Walton believes Genesis 1 shares common ancient cosmological ideas that were not entirely scientifically accurate, primarily the idea the sky had a solid dome holding back a heavenly ocean of waters above the dome. I believe Genesis 1 says nothing about a solid sky and the waters above the expanse refer to rain clouds. The "expanse" is an expanding clear space (see Appendix B). Though I agree Day 2 has a strong functional element and much less on the material side, setting up the expanse still involved working with material. And, Day 2 also contains the phrase "Let there be" which indicates the expanse did not exist prior to the proclamation.

Day 3: Walton says Day 3 has "no statement of creation of any material component."[68] Really? God said, "Let the waters below the heavens be gathered to one place and let dry land appear." (1:9) Technically yes, the verse does not say God created the water and land from nothing, as if they were not already there. Obviously they were there because they are mentioned in verses 1, 2, and 7. But again, fulfilling this proclamation had to involve the rearrangement of existing material, water moving and land appearing. As for the second proclamation on Day 3, "Let the earth sprout vegetation…" (1:11): *How can that not involve material origins*? True, it does not say "God made the plants" like it does for the expanse and land animals, but *this must be referencing the origin of land plants*, not just their purpose. The verses imply the Earth was not sprouting plants prior to the proclamation, and afterward it was, which then had to involve material origin. It seems clear here God set up the function by working the material.

Day 4: Walton says Day 4 has "material components, but the text explicitly deals with them only on the functional level."[69] *Only* on the functional level? That conclusion is far too narrow to me. It is true verses 14-15 proclaim the purposes (functions) for the lights, but verse 16 says God *made* (caused) the lights. One could argue that God did not make the lights on Day 4 (which I argued in Chapters 2 and 5), therefore material origins are not mentioned on this day. However, as with Days 1 and 2, Day 4 also has the phrase "Let there be". We saw in Chapter 2 that what God proclaimed to come to be was for the lights to come to be in a new location from the perspective of the surface of Earth. That involved clearing the expanse to see the lights, which involves material.

Days 5 and 6: I do not wish to belabor the point but it is clear the proclamations on these Days were to originate sea creatures, flying creatures, land animals, and humans, *none of which existed before the proclamations*. Even if Walton argued that the Hebrew words *"bara"* (create) and *"asah"* (make) do not mean material origin was involved, the fact a daylight period was not operating until Day 1, as we saw above, indicates the creatures here did not exist prior to the proclamations because they could not have lived without light. Therefore, material origins must have been involved.

In all these cases the original audience would have understood God was proclaiming the existence of things that did not exist previously. While it is true the proclamations were not fully complete until all was functioning as God intended, the fulfillments must have involved material origin also, even if it was only a rearrangement of existing materials.

Walton also leaves some major questions unanswered regarding His view. When did the week occur? Did God proclaim the functions of His creation before it actually existed? Or did God proclaim the functions after He had already done the material construction phase, even after creating humans?

If Walton believes the functional proclamations were made before the material construction phase, which would appear to have to be the case based on the Day 1 proclamation, then his view is not much different than mine, except for excluding the material origin in the proclamations and his Accommodationism, which we must consider in the next chapter.

Conclusion

A host of information is here to ponder regarding the nine old-Earth views of Genesis 1. I know because I have been pondering them for quite some time. This has been a summary of differences between the PDV and the others, and the reasons why I rejected the other eight. The positive reasons for choosing the PDV were set forth back in Chapter 2.

In conclusion of the options and textual evidence, the Prophetic Days View best assimilates all six of the structural elements listed in Chapter 1: a unique easy to memorize pattern, a five-fold repetition on each Day, the broad generic near-exhaustive nature of the account, a topical arrangement of the fiats, anachronistic fulfillment statements, and the simplest and most natural way to read the text – an actual normal historical week on Earth. Unlike the others, it gets us to our destination of making sense of astronomy and geology in relation to Genesis 1. In my opinion, the Prophetic Days View is the only one that can do all that and remain faithful to a literal interpretation of the text.

10

Biblical Scientific Inerrancy?
(Can our destination be reached?)

From the start this book has advocated that a proper view of modern science and a correct interpretation of Genesis are not incompatible. That proposition labels me a **Concordist**, one who believes modern science and the Bible are *in accord*, meaning that if the Bible says something that could potentially be verified by a scientific discipline the Bible will not be in error. However, many otherwise conservative[1] Christians who love Jesus have given up on finding accord between modern science and Genesis, and have taken it to the next level by saying it is wrong to even attempt it because to advocate scientific inerrancy for the Bible is to ignore the Bible's historical setting. They believe some Biblical writers had a faulty understanding of the cosmos, but rather than correct that, God accommodated Himself to their errors to convey a theological message (hence my label of **Accommodationists**). According to them, the ancients' faulty understanding of the cosmos is expressed in the Bible and thus the inspired Scriptures contain undeniable scientific inaccuracies. If that is true, what does it do to the doctrine of Biblical inerrancy? How can someone say the Bible contains scientific errors and remain authoritative about theological matters? How can I trust what I cannot verify (revealed theology) if I cannot trust what I can potentially verify (historical and scientific truth claims)?

The evangelical doctrine of Biblical inerrancy initially follows a simple path as Norman Geisler explains:

> The logic is simple and irrefutable:
> (1) God cannot err.
> (2) The Bible is the Word of God
> (3) Hence, the Bible cannot err.[2]

Of course that path can quickly become very complicated when it comes to specifically defining "Word of God" or "inspiration", topics I am going to avoid. However, hopefully we can all at least agree that God loves truth. Jesus said He is the truth (John 14:6). The Bible claims to be true, "Thy law is truth" (Ps. 119:142) and "Thy word is truth" (John 17:17). Psalm 119:128 is instructive, "Therefore I esteem right all *Thy* precepts concerning everything, I hate every false way." Falsehood is despised, "I hate and despise falsehood, But I love Thy law" (Ps. 119:163). As a general principle, God wants us to know the truth because it will set us free (John 8:32).

Rather than get into a lengthy discussion of inerrancy, let's take a simpler approach, or at least come at it from a different direction, and ask, "Does the Bible contain scientific errors?" If it does not, then the idea God accommodated Himself to an ancient faulty understanding of the cosmos becomes an unnecessary proposition. If we arrive at our destination of Biblical and scientific reconciliation the case is closed. We do not have to worry about whether the destination exists if we are there, but, that is the problem. Many have not arrived at that destination, some after decades of studying, and have given up on the search, if they were ever even looking for it. And worse, they are now discouraging others from even trying by saying it cannot be done.

The belief in Biblical scientific errors has left some Christians in the unenviable position of attempting to salvage an authoritative Bible from those "errors", and thus Accommodationism was born. Now it is growing, maturing, and *reproducing* and I do not see that as good. I see it as a malignant tumor which needs to be surgically removed, but, one does not just grab a knife and start cutting. That does more damage than good. Surgery is a delicate process, done, in this case, by recognizing the issues and answering them.

Accommodationists against the Concordists

Let's hear the problems from the Accommodationists:

Young Earth Creationists are one kind of concordist... they believe that all science will eventually be seen to agree with what they believe the Scriptures teach.[3]

Old Earth Creationists who try to find evidence for their position in Genesis 1 are another kind of concordist. They read the account through a different set of scientific lenses, starting with science and reading it into the Bible.[4]

Both views take Scripture seriously, and both believe in supernatural intervention in creation. Both, however, read the biblical text through the worldview of a modern person, not through the worldview of an ancient Israelite. In the end, one or the other may end up being correct [about the age of the Earth], but that is not the point. To understand the original intent and meaning of a biblical passage, we need to place ourselves in the position of the original readers as much as possible.[5]

The concordist position may sometimes be illustrated in a biblical text, or, by coincidence, discovered in the biblical text, but in our opinion it is always being read into the text... We do not believe that the primary purpose of Genesis is to give scientific answers to twenty-first-century questions.[6]

Have I been reading the text through the eyes of a modern person? I hope not because I said from the beginning I was going to try to read it as the original audience would see it (though it is quite possible I am blind to my own bias). I really believe the Prophetic Days View of Genesis was the way the original audience understood it. Have I read science into the Bible? Again, I hope not. Very little science has been discussed at this point. My attempt has been to discover what the text says and compare that to science, not take a theory or hypothesis of science and find it in the Bible. If a modern scientific position is found in the Bible, is it "always being read into the text"? I do not think so. I think it just shows the supernatural origin of the Scriptures, that God did what it says He did and gave us ways to verify it so that our faith is based upon solid convincing evidence and not blind dogma. It is a form of prophecy.

According to the Accommodationists, if we read the text through the eyes of the ancient Israelites we would see that they had an inaccurate view of the cosmos. A simple statement from an Accommodationist like, "Genesis 1 is ancient cosmology"[7] can easily be misunderstood (and misquoted) if the author's meaning is not understood. John Walton *did not* only mean that Genesis 1 is a very old story, something with which we all agree. What he means is that Genesis 1 reflects an ancient misunderstanding of the cosmos that is *scientifically incorrect*, i.e. describing a solid dome sky for example. Then he adds, "And God did not think it important to revise their thinking."[8] There lies the issue. Did God give us a revelation with scientific errors, speaking their language and accommodating their errors, only for the purpose of teaching us theology? Walton and others think so, but do not see the scientific errors as the problem. Instead, according to Walton:

> The problem is, we cannot translate their cosmology to our cosmology, nor should we. If we accept Genesis 1 as ancient cosmology [i.e. a scientifically inaccurate understanding of the cosmos], then we need to interpret it as ancient cosmology, rather than translate it into modern cosmology. If we try to turn it into modern cosmology, we are making the text say something it never said… Since we view the text as authoritative, it is a dangerous thing to change the meaning of the text into something it never intended to say.[9]

If I agreed with him that the Bible taught a scientifically flawed ancient cosmology I might be inclined to accept where that premise has led him. But, if the Bible is not scientifically flawed then there is no need to follow his path which I think ultimately leads to a sinking quagmire of potential Biblical inaccuracies dragging down anyone trying to stay on the solid ground of an authoritatively reliable revelation. The quicksand can be avoided if the Bible is scientifically accurate.

However, to show that the Bible is scientifically accurate we must test Scriptural claims by science and that leads to another issue. Accommodationists say Scripture does not "need evidence from science to prove it true."[10] Well, how else are we supposed to know Scripture is true then? Do we just accept it *blindly*? Do we search deeply for *a good feeling* about it like the Mormons, that mysterious inner witness? How are we different than the cults? Do we presuppose our good faith-filled-feelings are just instinctive knowledge from

God? That would leave us in a circular position of accepting the Bible as God's Word simply because it says it is God's Word. Some people (me if no one else) need reasons to believe Christianity is true and do not want to hear I need to believe it just because it says so. If we search for *historical* and *archaeological* reasons to corroborate Biblical historical claims, how is that any different than searching for scientific reasons to believe Biblical cosmological claims? By making truth claims the Bible opens itself up to verification by *whatever reliable means necessary*. The Biblical writers invite and encourage it and a broad spectrum of evidence is presented by the Bible as evidence for its claims. (See Ps. 19:1-6, Lk. 1:1-4, 24:27, Acts 1:3, 2:32, 17:11, 17, 31, 26:24-29, Rms. 1:18-23, I Cor. 15:3-8, I Th. 5:21, I Pet. 3:15, and II Pet. 1:16 to name *very few*.)

Is the Bible true? For many it simply comes down to this: if *any error* is found in the *original* writings, scientific or otherwise, then it is not inspired by God and becomes just someone's opinion of what they thought was true. What we need is a reliable objective revelation from God Himself about what He desires, wants, and expects from us. How we recognize which writings come from God is another story, one which I cannot cover in depth here, but it includes accuracy. However, inerrancy is not a conclusive test *by itself* because many things can be found to contain no errors (like math books) and not necessarily be inspired by God. Other factors must be considered, like: Does it claim to be from God? Was it written by someone with prophetic or apostolic authority? Was it generally accepted by the people of God? Does it facilitate the life-changing power of God? And does it demonstrate the power of God by prophetic utterance or other miraculous means?

One form of prophetic utterance is for the Bible to make a claim that could not have been verified by the original audience, but could be verified later. *That would include modern scientifically verifiable claims.* Therefore, if the Bible offers us information testable by modern science that ancient people had no way of verifying, and the Bible is found to be scientifically accurate, then I think that lends support to the miraculous revelation and inspiration of the Scriptures.

Is God capable of communicating scientifically accurate information to His prophets? God knows what He did and how He did it (and He also put us in a position to figure some of it out). He could have inspired authors in a way to keep them scientifically error free. Many of the misunderstandings about the cosmos by the ancients probably came from speculations on their part about the revelations they received from God. They assimilated their observations with what God had said and speculated *how* God did what He did, and we can make the same error. We have now reached a place where our methods of verification are better than theirs, but plenty is still beyond our means of inspection.

We must be very careful when we start to explain *how* God did something. The "how" is often what scientists are trying to discover and we may be able to make better and better observations of how things operate *without ever getting close to discovering how they originated*. Was God specific on *how* He did what He said He did? No, He was often very vague. However, some of it was specific enough to offer scientifically verifiable evidence of its inspiration. And, some methods of explaining origins can be eliminated as un-Biblical.

One problem involves defining science. Before we can delve into whether the Bible contains any science errors, it would be good to take a brief look at what science is.

Defining Science

Science is often defined to operate under the assumption of *methodological naturalism*, that is, it looks for natural explanations for phenomena. The worldview known as *philosophical naturalism* (or *materialism*) proposes that natural processes are *all* that exist and by that definition eliminates the existence of God from the start. Obviously philosophical naturalism is incompatible with a Christian worldview where nature (this space/time continuum we exist in) is not all that exists. If all phenomena are *assumed* to have a natural explanation then there is no place for the miraculous, i.e. creationism.

When it comes to what the Bible says about the origin of the heavens and Earth, at the very least we can say that Genesis plainly says God was involved in the process, even if few details are given as to how He did it. The point is: if God did *anything* apart from which the natural world would not exist, then *methodological naturalism will not be able to explain everything*. By its very definition methodological naturalism will only be able to explain natural phenomena, but one should not assume that everything has a natural explanation. If at any point in time God caused something to happen, *there will be no natural explanation for it*. From the start then, Genesis and science (defined as methodological naturalism) seem to be irreconcilable. Must we leave it there?

If by "explanation" one means a natural explanation, then to say "God did it" is not a natural explanation. However, if we define "explanation" as offering reasons for how something happened, then "God did it" *could be* an explanation, and indeed would be the only explanation for an event *if He did it*.

Should we define science as methodological naturalism? If we do, creationism is not science, and that might be okay as long as two things are understood: everything may not have a natural explanation, and natural explanations are not the only legitimate method of explaining phenomena. On the other hand, if science is a search for a true explanation, then the miraculous is not excluded and in some sense creationism can be considered science.

If processes for determining the necessity of an intelligent designer can be quantified, then creationism (some forms of it at least) can certainly be considered science. I believe it can and would suggest consulting at least two works by Intelligent Design advocate William Dembski[11] for more on that subject. Everyone should let the evidence guide them, and atheists should not reject the supernatural from the start, and theists should not give up the search for natural explanations.

Turning our attention back to Genesis then, clearly Genesis says God did a variety of actions to cause the heavens and Earth to be what they are today. Also, in a broader sense, the Bible says God causes phenomena we normally consider to be natural. This warrants a deeper look at mediated creation, secondary causes, and ordinary providence.

Mediated Creation, Secondary Causes, and Ordinary Providence

Mediated creation and secondary causes are terms to describe God using *indirect* means to accomplish His will rather than direct action. Ordinary providence is seen as God *sustaining the existence and operation* of the universe. Extraordinary providence is God doing something directly in His creation. The problem is, extraordinary providence can look like ordinary providence. An example is described in Acts 16:25-26 where Paul and Silas are singing in jail when a violent earthquake suddenly opens all the prison doors. Earthquakes are natural, but the timing of that one makes it miraculous, or extremely coincidental. The former is clearly indicated in Acts. For the earthquake to occur at just the right time to free Paul and Silas, and not harm anyone, looks like direct intervention on God's part (or angels), not merely an ordinary earthquake.

An example of secondary causes is Matthew 5:45, "...for He causes His sun to rise on the evil and the good, and sends rain on the righteous and the unrighteous." Jesus is speaking here. Consider what this verse means and how His audience would have understood it. Jesus' main point is that God blesses both the righteous and the unrighteous so we also should bless and love our enemies. The examples that Jesus gives for God's blessings are sunshine and rain. By saying that God causes them He is making a cosmological claim. If Jesus' statement about God causing them is in error, then the moral message lacks authority. If Jesus was wrong about the cosmological claim, how can we trust Him on the theological claim? Was Jesus wrong about God causing sunshine and rain? Consider how his audience understood it. Let's say some of His listeners believed that God literally caused the Sun to rise every day by angels pulling it around the Earth on a chariot. Was Jesus wrong? His listeners would be wrong about *how* God causes it, but they may not be wrong about the fact God does it. Jesus simply said God causes it, but He did not say how, and it is even possible Jesus (the man) did not know how. Is the Scripture in error then? No, because it does not explain how God does it.

Today we understand Jesus' words to mean God set things in motion (originated them, though we are still not sure exactly how) and then let them run on their own (naturally) and He sustains their existence and operation (Col. 1:16-17). He can certainly intervene anytime He wishes and cause it to rain or not rain where and when He desires (I Kings 17:1 and 18:1), but generally we think where and when it rains is somewhat random and natural and predictable. We also know the Earth orbits the Sun by gravity and that the Earth spins on its axis. By sustaining the existence and operation of His creation (which He could dissolve in an instant) God is indirectly causing the natural processes he began. In that way we can say God causes the Sun to rise and the clouds to rain, but He uses secondary causes to make it happen.

Consider another verse, Psalm 104:14 says, "He causes the grass to grow for the cattle." Did David or his audience know how grass grows? Certainly he was not aware of cellular life or photosynthesis, but David declares God causes it. Today we may understand a lot more about how it happens, but we can still say that God causes the grass to grow through secondary means. A naturalist might claim that science has disproved the Bible here because biology has determined grass grows by a series of natural processes that have nothing to do with supernatural activity. But, has biology explained the origin of plants? Even a biologist would have to say there are still many unanswered questions, but a naturalist may add that all of the answers known so far involve natural explanations so he may see no reason to add a supernatural element to fill in gaps in our knowledge, the so-called *God of the gaps* mentality.

This God of the gaps problem is accused of demotivating progress in science and one can see how that could be true. However, Christians should not fear the process of looking for a natural explanation for phenomena because the process may uncover something unexpected. It may reach a point where answers seem to be getting farther away rather than closer (like in the case of the origin of life). With every new discovery of the intricacies of how cellular life works, the origin of life by natural means (abiogenesis) has become all the more indefensible. Remember that if God did something there will be no natural explanation for it and so a deeper investigation into it will only go further to show a natural explanation does not exist.

A naturalist could complain that the theist always has an out with God as the sustainer of creation. On the claim of God causing grass growth (and similar claims) that is true, but it may not be true of every Biblical claim. In reverse though, the theist is not the only one with a built in get-out-of-jail-free card. The naturalist can always claim a natural explanation exists, but they do not know it yet. In that case they could be accused of a *nature of the gaps* fallacy. Neither theism nor naturalism should be assumed to be true. Let the evidence show whether nature's laws or intelligent design has the better explanation.

Does the Bible support secondary causes?

Did the ancients understand secondary causes? I think they did. Consider the Day 3 text. Two proclamations are made on Day 3 and the first one involves two parts. Genesis 1:9 says, "Then God said, 'Let the waters below the heavens be gathered into one place, and let the dry land appear'; and it was so." Notice these verses do not say something like, "Let Us gather the waters" or "Let Us make dry land". The implication of the verse is the waters move and land appears by some underlying cause by God, but the water and land are the ones doing the action.

The second proclamation is clearer, 1:11-12 says, "Then God said, 'Let the earth sprout vegetation…' and it was so. The earth brought forth vegetation…" In this case the land is sprouting and producing plants, not God. The text could easily have read, "Let us create plants and God made the plants", but it does not. The same is true for 1:24. (Note that God making the animals (1:25) or God forming the animals (2:19) is not the same as the land producing animals (1:24) as we saw back in Chapters 2 and 5.) God proclaimed them to happen which means they would not have happened unless God did something, and yet they are described operating indirectly, and we are not told specifically how God did it. The implication is that God did His part first and then let them run on their own after that. From the first chapter in the Bible we have multiple instances of mediated fulfillment and secondary causes.

A few other examples of ordinary providence are: Psalm 104:22 says, "the sun rises", not God raises the Sun. Ecclesiastes 11:3 says, "If the clouds are full, they pour out rain…" meaning the clouds cause rain. II Samuel 23:3-4 says, "He who rules over men righteously, Who rules in the fear of God, Is as the light of the morning when the sun rises, A morning without clouds, When the tender grass springs out of the earth, Through sunshine after rain." This is obvious the ancients understood water and sunlight were necessary for plants to grow. II Kings 19:29 says, "Then this shall be the sign for you: you will eat this year what grows of itself, in the second year what springs from the same, and in the third year sow, reap, plant vineyards, and eat their fruit." The straight forward understanding of "grows of itself" seems clear.

One more is instructive. Ecclesiastes 11:4-6 says:

> He who watches the wind will not sow and he who looks at the clouds will not reap. Just as you do not know the path of the wind and how bones are formed in the womb of the pregnant woman, so you do not know the activity of God who makes all things. Sow your seed in the morning and do not be idle in the evening, for you do not know whether morning or evening sowing will succeed, or whether both of them alike will be good.

Solomon obviously realized neither he nor his hearers knew *how* God "makes [causes[12]] all things". Since he was wisely claiming ignorance on the subject one should not presume the ancients had a method in mind when they wrote of God's activities, nor that they believed God directly causes all things.

What scientific errors?

Thus far we can say that science should not be read into the text, but scientifically verifiable statements may be made in the Bible. The author's intent should be considered in determining the meaning of a text, but it is possible even the author did not understand everything God inspired him to write. God's actions can be an explanation for an event, but details of how God acts are often not specified. Investigation into His methodology is not a problem and is invited by God. After all, God is the one who created us with a curious mind. And, the ancients understood, to some degree at least, secondary causes and mediated creation. With all that in mind let us proceed to an investigation into verses used to say the Bible contains science errors.

Accommodationists and skeptics claim scientific errors exist in the Bible. If demonstration is given the Biblical authors did not communicate any of their scientifically inferior cosmology into the text, if they had any, then the Accommodationist position is unnecessary.

A host of Biblical scientific errors have been suggested over the past two centuries and I cannot cover them all, but I am going to attempt to cover many of them. My primary concentration here will be scientific issues used by Accommodationists to make their case the ancients had a faulty cosmology. Biological evolution is also used to make their case but it is too broad a topic to cover in this book. Reconciling the Bible with biology, anthropology, and evolution will have to wait for another book, which is in the works.

Here are the most common Biblical issues Accommodationists use to make their point that the ancients had a bad understanding of the nature of the world.

Jesus the Botanist

Mark 4:30-32 (paralleled in Mt. 13:31-32) says of Jesus, "And He said, 'How shall we picture the kingdom of God, or by what parable shall we present it? *It is* like a mustard seed, which, when sown upon the soil, though it is smaller than all the seeds that are upon the soil, yet when it is sown, it grows up and becomes larger than all the garden plants ...'" This mustard seed issue seems to constantly recur among skeptics of the Bible, and it frequents Accommodationist literature also. Truth is, the mustard seed is not absolutely the smallest seed in the world. Orchids and a few others have smaller seeds. Was Jesus wrong then? Was Jesus merely accommodating the ignorance of His listeners? Neither, He was correct. The mustard seed *is* the smallest seed an Israelite farmer would sow "upon the soil". Jesus was not asserting that the mustard seed was the absolute smallest seed in the world, only that it was the smallest seed they sowed in their fields. These verses are an extremely poor example of supposed accommodation to scientific error.

A more difficult example is found in John 12:23-25 which says,

> And Jesus answered them, saying, "The hour has come for the Son of Man to be glorified. Truly, truly, I say to you, unless a grain of wheat falls into the earth and dies, it remains alone; but if it dies, it bears much fruit. He who loves his life loses it, and he who hates his life in this world will keep it to life eternal."

The problems here are whether seeds die, and whether Jesus was right or wrong about it, and the problems are complicated by whether ancient definitions of "die" were the same as ours. We have already seen that Genesis does not consider plants to be alive (see Point 3 of Chapter 6). The New Testament seems to take a different approach to defining life, an approach more in line with our present thinking. Here in John a seed is considered to be alive as part of a plant before it falls to the ground, and this is used as a metaphor for Jesus' death and resurrection and the fruit those events would produce. Even though the seed is used as a metaphor, the idea of a seed dying cannot be dismissed as figurative.

Jesus' metaphor is relying on the *reality* of a grain of wheat being sown, dying, and then producing fruit.

Here are the possibilities in dealing with the issue:

First, Jesus was wrong and *He knew it* supernaturally, but He was accommodating His divine knowledge to His audience's ignorance about seeds because the important point of the analogy is theological, not biological. If that was true then it lends credibility to interpreting other passages of Scripture the same way, and since I am opposing that position, I disagree that was what Jesus was doing. Jesus is the Truth which makes it totally out of His character to knowingly speak an error.

Second, He was wrong and *He did not know it,* meaning, *as a man* Jesus was wrong about seeds, like everyone else back then (at least on seeds dying). As a human, did Jesus ever make a mistake? Not a sin, a mistake, like getting a splinter or hitting His thumb or mismeasuring something He was building? We are told explicitly He never sinned (II Cor. 5:21, Heb. 4:15, 7:26-27, I John 3:5). And we are told explicitly that as a human there were things He did not know and *learned* (Mt. 24:36, Luke 2:52, 8:45, Heb. 5:8). Jesus knew supernaturally only what the Father revealed to Him (John 8:26-29). This seed dying issue could then be a time when Jesus made a mistake as a human. This option may not satisfy many, and could potentially cause stronger reactions, but it is a logically possible option. Statements exist in the Bible that simply report what was said without endorsing them (Gen. 3:4-5, 12:9, II Kings 5:22, Ps. 14:1, John 11:16, etc.). So maybe Jesus was wrong and John only recorded what He said. The problem is, even though a mistake is not a sin and is normal for human limitations (even Jesus), the wisest course is to not say something of which you are not reasonably certain, and Jesus was wise. Therefore, I do not think Jesus was speaking from ignorance of the truth about seeds here.

Third, Jesus was right. For the analogy of a seed to truly represent Jesus' resurrection, it would have to give its life for another. Is that what a seed does? One could argue yes. Seeds contain an embryo of a plant along with nutrients meant to support the embryo once it begins to grow. When planted or sown, the moisture and soil cause the seed to sprout and the seed becomes a plant. The seed ceases to exist *as a seed* (dies) and "gives its life" to the plant.

The real issue here though is defining life and death, which is not easy even today. Note a college level microbiology textbook definition, "Life can be defined as a complex set of processes resulting from the actions of proteins specified by nucleic acids."[13] Obviously that is a very modern definition and would have even been meaningless only 70 years ago prior to 1944 when "DNA was established as the hereditary material."[14] As more is learned about how life works the definition may change again and definitions are different among scientists even now. The Bible was clearly not written to provide that level of scientific detail. So, the question is: According to the ancients' definition of life and death, did a seed die? Apparently so, especially if Jesus' words are used as the definition. The point is: because the ancients defined life differently than we do today Jesus was not in error. That is not an accommodation on Jesus' part to ignorant humans; it was just the way they defined life at that time and could even be seen as a definition today (for everyday people, not microbiology). To accuse the Bible of error here is to equivocate on the definition of life.

The Accommodationist will complain that I am making way too much of this. Jesus was not trying to teach us the nature of seeds they will say; He was telling them about His resurrection and its subsequent fruit and the example it was for self-sacrificial living. Those are the important parts. I agree those parts are important, but I disagree whether the accuracy of Jesus' words about seeds is important to the main point. Again, if He was wrong about what we can verify, what does that say about what we cannot verify?

Another complaint of the Accommodationist could be that I am agreeing with them by saying Jesus and the people of His day defined life differently than we do, for that is what they are saying about other subjects in the Bible. However, saying the ancients defined a seed as dead is different than saying the ancients defined the sky as a solid dome (as will be claimed below). In the first case, "dead" can legitimately be defined as "not growing", which would include seeds, and not cause an error in the Bible. In the latter case, the sky cannot be defined as a solid dome and not cause an error.

The conclusion is simple: Jesus was right by His definition, He did not make a scientific error, nor did He accommodate ignorance.

Bovine Bunnies

Another Bible verse frequently used as an example of scientific error is Leviticus 11:6 which speaks of animals Jews were not allowed to eat, and says, "the rabbit also, for though it chews cud, it does not divide the hoof, it is unclean to you." Do rabbits (hares) chew cud? Again, it depends. If one insists "chews cud" must refer to our more restrictive English scientific definition of bovine rumination, then no. But, if it has a looser definition like re-chewing previously eaten food or finely chewing one's food, then yes. The Bible is almost certainly taking the broader meaning to insure hares were not eaten by the Israelites, because some of them, as many of us do, may have looked for every loophole to push the limits of the Law. Anyone casually observing rabbits can see them finely chewing their food and it looks similar to a cow eating. And people who raise rabbits can observe they will eat their pellets to get whatever nutritional value they may still contain. Just in case someone thought either of those activities is chewing cud, the Law clarified hares are not to be eaten because they do not have hooves.

The Matter of the Heart

The Jewish Shema is, "Hear, O Israel! The LORD is our God, the LORD is one! And you shall love the LORD your God with all your heart and with all your soul and with all your might." (Dt. 6:4-5) Does anyone see the scientific "error"? Maybe the first use of the Hebrew word in the Bible will reveal the problem a little clearer. Genesis 6:5 says, "Then the LORD saw that the wickedness of man was great on the earth, and that every intent of the thoughts

197

of his heart was only evil continually." See it now? Here is the problem: the bodily organ we call the heart does not think or love, it pumps blood.

John Walton speaks of this as a Concordist problem this way:

> For example, in the ancient world people believed the seat of intelligence, emotion and personhood was in the internal organs, particularly the heart... In modern language we still refer to the heart metaphorically as the seat of emotions. In the ancient world this was not metaphor, but physiology.[15]

Were the ancients being literal in their vast use of the word "heart"?[16] Did they really believe thinking or loving occurred in the organ beating in their chest? Was that really their physiological beliefs? We typically think of mental activity occurring inside our head, but is that a Western cultural phenomena because we know thinking is partially a function of the neural activity in the brain? Or is the idea the mind is in the head a normal experience for all humanity at all times because two prominent sensory devices (eyes and ears) are located in our head? I am inclined to think it is the normal experience for all people because thinking does not *feel* like it is happening in the hands or chest for example. Limbs have been shown to retain memory, and internal organs give us feelings, but thinking does not *feel* like it comes from there. We all know of gut feelings, but I have never heard someone say they have a gut thought.

What did the Bible writers think? Were they being literal or metaphorical? Clearly, in this case, they were being metaphorical, which is evident from the word's *second* use in the next verse after the first use. Genesis 6:6 says, "And the LORD was sorry that He had made man on the earth, and He was grieved in His heart." Did the ancients think a heart was literally part of God's physiology? I think not. Both God and people are said to speak from their heart (Gen. 8:21, 17:17). People are said to intend in their heart (Gen. 6:5, 8:21), fear (Gen. 42:28, 45:26), be glad (Ex. 4:14), harden (Ex. 8:32), be moved to give (Ex. 25:2), and to teach from the heart (Ex. 35:34) to give just a few examples.

From its initial uses in the Bible, and throughout, the heart appears to be a very general word for the internal workings of humanity – mind, will, emotions, and motives. The writers knew the heart was in the center of the chest and a beating heart was necessary for life, and this idea of centrality and central importance is good motivation to use the word metaphorically for everything associated with the spirit or soul, the center of our being. Undeniable metaphorical uses of "heart" are in the Bible: the heart of the sea (Ex. 15:8) and circumcision of the heart (Dt. 10:16, 30:6) are a couple of examples. Oddly enough, I could only find one definite *literal* use of "heart" (the organ) in the entire Bible (II Sam. 18:14 – though I Sam.4:13 may be another). Two other words are primarily used for literal internal organs and parts of the body.[17]

Considering "heart" is definitely used symbolically in the Bible, internal organs are mostly referenced by two other words, and clear physiological use of "heart" is nearly absent, it makes the most sense to say the primary use of the word "heart" is symbolic and thus, no scientific error exists. The many references to thinking and feeling in the heart are not physiological claims.

Ancient Cosmology

Cosmology is the study of the origin of the world (cosmos/universe) and leads to beliefs about its nature. The ancients were curious about the nature of their world just as we are today, but their means of examining it were more limited than ours, so it should be no surprise some of them made exaggerated speculations and serious mistakes, which we may also be prone to do. According to many popular writers[18] on Genesis, the Bible reflects an ancient misunderstanding of the nature of the cosmos. They claim the ancients thought the land (earth) was a flat round disk with edges, and mountains were usually found at the edges, and these mountains (or some other form of pillar) supported a solid dome forming the sky. This dome also had windows and was holding back a heavenly ocean from flooding the earth which was floating on another deep ocean of waters that rose to the surface in places (springs). The land was stabilized by pillars, though none seemed to speculate what those pillars were on, and lastly, there was a literal underworld.

That picture of the cosmos is obviously false. The question is whether the Bible describes the cosmos that way. There are six issues here: 1. a flat disk earth with edges, 2. a solid sky held up by pillars, 3. a heavenly ocean held back by the dome with windows, 4. land floating on lower deep waters, 5. the land having a foundation and pillars also, and 6. a literal underworld.

1. Does the Bible describe Earth as a flat disk with edges?

One author, after considerably documenting the historical evidence that pre-scientific cultures around the world believed the Earth was a flat disc, concludes, "Unless then we remove Gen 1 from its historical context, we must say that the historical meaning of 'earth' in Gen 1:10 is very probably a single continent in the shape of a flat circular disc."[19] I will not dispute the historical claim that some nations and cultures surrounding Israel believed the land was a flat disc with edges, or even that some Israelites did also, though it is possible not everyone agreed. The important question here is whether the Bible commits us to a flat disc interpretation. Here are the verses the Accommodationists use to support that it does.

Isaiah 40:22 says God "…sits above the circle of the earth…" Job 22:14 (Eliphaz speaking) says of God, "Clouds are a hiding place for Him, so that He cannot see; And He walks on the vault of heaven." Job 26:10 (Job speaking) says of God, "He has inscribed a circle on the face of the waters, At the boundary of light and darkness." Echoing this idea Proverbs 8:27 says God "…inscribed a circle on the face of the deep."

Those four passages are the only places this word "circle" is used in the Hebrew Bible, and notice it is used of three different things. Isaiah refers to the land. Job and Proverbs refer to the surface of the deep. And Eliphaz refers to the heavens, though the NASB, NIV, and ESV have translated "circle" as "vault". The NKJV has it as "circle of heaven". Accommodationists are quick to use Job 22:14 to say the sky is a solid dome/vault (I will get to the idea of solidity in a minute), but it should be clear that Eliphaz's use of "circle" *must refer to something spherical* (or at least semi-spherical like an upside down bowl). Therefore, though someone *might* get the impression from Isaiah or Proverbs that the land and surface of the deep were parts of a flat circular disk, it is obvious from Job that "spherical" is at least in the semantic range of possible interpretations.

Isaiah's description of God sitting above the circle of the earth is comparable to an earthly king sitting on a throne ruling over his kingdom. But does it mean God is *literally* sitting in a chair above the land somewhere? I do not think that is what the writer meant. Isaiah definitely uses figurative language in the same context. God is described as measuring the waters with the hollow of His hand and the heavens with its span (40:12). Solomon had said in I Kings 8:27 that "…the highest heaven cannot contain Thee" and Isaiah says God *can* contain (measure – same Hebrew word) the waters with His hand. It seems very obvious God is not literally sitting on a throne above the Earth unless we want to also say He has really big hands. Isaiah's main point is that God rules over the whole Earth.

What about the part where Isaiah described the land as a circle? Considering the word "circle" refers to a shape, it is likely all the writers above use it literally, because symbolic uses of shapes mean something completely different than their shape definition, otherwise they would not be metaphors. Consider the statement, "He is a square" meaning "he is boring or plain", for example. However, since spherical is in the semantic range of the word "circle", Isaiah's metaphorical description of God enthroned above the literal circle of the earth is not a problem.

In opposition, the suggestion is made that if Isaiah had meant the land was a sphere he would have used a different Hebrew word translated "ball" like he did in Isaiah 22:18.[20] However, that word is only used two other times in the OT and refers to "encircling" a camp (Is. 29:3) and a "pile" (circle) of wood under a pot (Ezek. 24:5). The word's use in 22:18 refers metaphorically to God rolling up a man like a ball and throwing him away. However, from the other uses of the word it is not clear it would have been a better word choice for "sphere".

As for Job 22:14 describing the heavens (sky) as spherical, two things should be noted. First, Eliphaz (one of Job's friends) is the one speaking and God later tells Job that the advice he had been getting, and Job's own understanding, were erroneous (Job 38:2, 42:7-8). Thus, the book of Job could be recording the actual words Job and his friends wrote or said, but *not endorsing their understanding of the facts*, in the same way Satan's words are recorded but recognized as deceitful (Gen. 3:4-5). Second, Job is poetic and often figurative, so the possibility also exists Eliphaz's words can be understood metaphorically (with difficulty though). These two options are *mutually exclusive*. I heavily lean toward the first, primarily because there are other verses in Job that are even more difficult to interpret figuratively.

So, what about the surface of the deep in Proverbs? Wisdom (God) is speaking so it cannot be wrong without doing serious damage to inerrancy. Notice "circle" is describing the *surface*, not the whole of the deep. In what way did God inscribe (set, appoint, decree[21]) a circle on the surface of the deep? Or, in what way could the ancients know the *surface* of the ocean as circular? A spherical understanding is not out of the realm of possibilities. An observant person can see that ships disappear over the horizon the farther out they sail and from a very high vantage point overlooking the ocean, one can see a slight curvature. Instead of being a scientific blunder, Proverbs is likely a scientific accuracy of the spherical shape of the surface of the globe, even if misunderstood. Does this mean Job (the man) was wrong to say God inscribed a circle on the surface of the waters? Though I have argued that Job and friends were wrong about some parts of the nature of the world that does not mean they were wrong about everything they said. It does seem clear that whichever way one interprets inscribing a circle on the surface of the waters it should be interpreted the same way in both Proverbs and Job.

If the word "circle" does not have to mean a flat Earth, maybe the idea is found in the Bible's description of the earth (land) having "edges", as several Hebrew words[22] are often translated. A few examples are Dt. 33:17, Job 28:24, 37:3, 38:13, Ps. 59:13, and Is. 40:28. There are many more. In what literal way can land be described as having ends or edges? There are several ways in fact. First, dry land ends at the sea. Usable land ends at mountain ranges and deserts. And a person's or kingdom's land ends at whatever borders are determined, like a river. Most uses of the phrase "ends of the earth" are a means to describe "everything" *in a particular area*, not absolutely everything. In some cases it could mean absolutely everything, but most times it means relatively everything, like everything in my possession, or everything within our boundaries.

Job 38:12-13 is about as difficult as this problem gets. "Have you ever in your life commanded the morning, And caused the dawn to know its place, That it might take hold of the ends of the earth, And the wicked be shaken out of it?" God is speaking here to Job which means there can be no error in His words. Some have compared this verse to taking the ends (edges) of a rug and shaking the dirt out of it. If that were the case it could make it sound like God is saying the Earth is flat. A couple of things should be taken into account about these two verses. First, the Hebrew word "ends" here is the word also used for a bird's wing.[22] It has the nuance of our English word "wingspan" which means it is describing the whole width of something, from one side (end) to the other. Therefore, it can be describing holding and shaking *anything of various shapes* without implying the item is flat. Second, obvious metaphorical language is going on here. The earth is not literally being shaken by the dawn. The light of the dawn is exposing the wicked in a similar way an object is shaken to expose its contents (shaking something out of the bottom of a clay pot comes to mind). The point is that even a globe has ends (sides – like a pot) and even if Job did not understand it that way he still could have recorded God's words correctly without necessarily knowing what the land's overall shape was.

Another argument used to say the land was flat involves Daniel 4:10-11 which is Nebuchadnezzar describing a dream he had where a huge tree grew from the "midst of the earth" and its "height reached to the sky" and it was "visible to the end of the whole earth." Here it is argued[23] that if the speaker knew the earth was a globe, a tree, no matter how high, could not be seen by the whole earth, but it could if the earth was flat. This argument is a serious stretch for at least three reasons: First, these are the words of a Babylonian king and as such may contain errors, like mentioning his own "god" (4:8). Second, this was a dream and, as we all know, dreams do not reflect reality. And third, the "whole earth" is likely relative and not absolute, meaning it only referred to Nebuchadnezzar's kingdom.

One last Biblical argument used to suggest a flat earth comes from Job 37:3, "Under the whole heaven He lets it [thunder] loose, And His lightening to the ends of the earth." Here it is argued[24] lightening could not be seen to the ends of the earth unless the earth was flat. This reasoning is flawed for at least two reasons: First, Job's statement is true. Lightening occurs over the whole Earth and has nothing to do with what Job could see because he could infer it occurs everywhere even if he could not see everywhere. Second, even if Job thought the earth was flat God said Job was without knowledge in some cases (38:2) and this may be one of them.

A potential science error is also suggested about "dry land". "For according to modern science the dry land on the globe preceded the formation of the sea by millions of years; but, according to Genesis 1:1-10, the sea... preceded the formation of the dry land."[25] This author is poorly interpreting what Genesis 1:1-10 actually says. All 1:2 asserts is that there was a time when Earth was desolate and lifeless, and it was dark over the deep, and the Spirit of God was hovering over the waters. *It does not say there had not been dry land prior to this* and *it did not say there was no land at all at that time*. What it suggests is that whatever land existed *at that time* (if any) was not dry.

Do we now know why any land that may have protruded out above the deep was wet? Yes we do, for two reasons, one Biblical and one scientific: First, the waters "above" came all the way down to the surface of the waters "below" because there was no separation between them (God had not yet spoken His proclamation on Day 2 to separate the waters), therefore any land would have been perpetually wet. Second, the story scientists currently give of Earth's origin speaks of a time approximately 3.9 billion years ago, after the collision of a Mars sized planet that formed the Moon, and Earth's oceans had condensed from a cooling atmosphere, when large life-destroying ocean-vaporizing impacts had ceased or slowed significantly.[26] During this time Earth's speed of rotation was faster creating enormous winds, and the moon was much closer causing catastrophic tides possibly a kilometer high (over 3200 feet).[27] The tides, winds, and atmosphere insured nothing was dry. Then out of that desolate and lifeless situation God transformed Earth into an inhabitable place with dry land. There is no scientific error here. Earth was once dark and wet and then it became light and dry just like Genesis accurately says.

The conclusion: Rather than the Bible being scientifically inaccurate teaching a flat disc earth with edges, it turns out to be scientifically accurate. Though it must be admitted Genesis 1 does not give any indication of the shape of the land, the Bible can legitimately be interpreted to teach a spherical Earth, and "edges" has many plausible literal interpretations apart from referring to the edges of a flat disk. This first accusation of Biblical cosmological error is the one in error.

2 and 3. Does the Bible teach a solid sky held up by pillars, and a heavenly ocean held back by the dome with windows to let water in on occasion?

Answering the questions of a solid sky and a heavenly ocean were so involved that it was necessary to write Appendix B. Here, I am going to give the conclusions of the appendix and let you fathom the depths of the topics there.

Many believe that the "firmament" (KJV and NKJV – "expanse" in NASB, NIV, and ESV) that God proclaimed into existence on Day 2 is the same as the hard domed sky of ancient cosmology. These same people believe the "waters which were above the expanse" (1:7) are a heavenly ocean held back by the dome. My conclusion in Appendix B is that the "expanse" of Day 2 is an *expanding clear space* that *is* the heavens. The expanse refers to *the whole heavens*, all that can be seen above the Earth from the surface, not a solid dome. The meaning of the Hebrew word for "expanse" (*raqîa'*), as discovered by its uses in the Old Testament, is not a solid dome. With the meaning of "expanse" being an expanding clear space, *there is no scientific error in Genesis*, and the same is true if the "waters which were above the expanse" are defined as rain. They are not a heavenly ocean; they are the fresh water that falls from the sky. Thus, the second and third points are scientific accuracies also, the second one being impressively so.

4. Is the land floating on the great deep?

Accommodationists believe the Bible agrees with ancient cosmology that the land is floating on the great deep from which the springs flow. However, for anyone to claim that God "'founded,' that is, firmly placed the earth upon the seas, the seas being a foundational base"[28] spreading out the land over the waters, misses a major flaw with the idea obvious to anyone at anytime. *Dirt does not float*. It makes no sense to say water is a foundation for the land, but to say land has a foundation that raises it above the water makes perfect sense, even to an ancient mind. If the land is floating on the sea how can it be said the land is immovable (I Chr. 16:30, Ps. 93:1, 96:10, 104:5, etc.) except when God chooses to move it (Ps. 99:1, Is. 24:19)? Anyone who has been on a boat knows one does not feel firmly founded on anything.

Some might accuse the Bible of teaching a geocentric universe because of these verses about immovability. It specifies no such thing. The Bible is written from a geocentric *perspective* and is an example of phenomenological language, describing the way it looks from the surface. But, even the ancients, per the Psalmist and Isaiah above, understood the land moved on occasion.

A prime example of a verse used as a proof text for land founded on water is Psalm 136:6, "To Him who spread out the earth above the waters…" But, this verse, and Ps. 24:2, mean the land is *higher than* (above) the water, not floating over it, on it, or in it. The same is true for Ex. 20:4 and Dt. 4:18 which mention "water below the earth". The verses are referring to water being *lower* than the land, not holding it up, especially considering Dt. 4:18 also refers to fish living in those waters. Isaiah 42:5 and 44:24 also refer to God spreading out the land, but say nothing of water. The Accommodationist's case is extremely weak here.

The word "deep" presents no scientific problems of land floating on water either. For examples, consider the following verses: Psalm 104:5-9 clearly indicates that when the foundations of the land were laid the "deep" *covered* the land, *which means the land is below the water*. Then further evidence of land below the waters is provided when it says the waters *receded as the valleys sank and the mountains rose*. Land is rising from beneath the deep, not floating on it. Proverbs 8:24-29 presents a similar picture. Isaiah 51:10 and 63:13 clearly indicate land is beneath the deep, not the other way around. *All these verses teach quite the opposite of land floating on the deep*. The deep was given boundaries which they cannot cross (Job 38:8-11, Ps. 104:8-9, and Pr. 8:29), meaning they will never again come up on land and cover the mountains as they once did. Land forms the *boundaries* of the deep, meaning the waters are contained by the land and the ancients knew it.

On the other hand, some verses indicate water is below the land. Genesis 49:25 and Dt. 33:13 speak of the blessings of the deep on inherited land, meaning fresh water springs and wells. And Ezekiel 31:4 shows that the ancients knew water flowed underground, but these verses say nothing of the land *floating* on the great deep, only that water existed deep below ground. A suggestion is made that Genesis 2:5, 6, 7:11, 8:2, and Proverbs 3:20 "…all make reference to earthly fresh-water springs having their water supplied by a sea (*tĕhôm*) beneath the earth."[29] The problem with that interpretation is *tehôm* (the Hebrew word for deep, not sea) is not a sea beneath the land. Proverbs 3:20 says the deep was "broken up"; meaning the original deep *is no longer in one place*. What is clear is that the ancients were observant and knew there was land beneath the sea and also knew water came from underground. Some of them probably speculated spring water came from great reservoirs beneath the land, which is true depending on how big one considers the reservoirs to be. But *the Bible gives no indication the land was floating on the deep*. In fact, God indicated that Job had no clue what was in the deep, "Have you entered into the springs of the sea? Or walked in the recesses of the deep?" (Job 38:16) By the way, "walking" in the recesses of the deep suggests *something solid to walk on*.

Potentially the most difficult verses about the deep come from Genesis 7:11 and 8:2 which speak of the fountains of the great deep. The word translated "fountain" is also sometimes translated "spring" or "well" (Prov. 8:28). These waters are said to be one of the main sources for the waters of the Flood and indicate that a large quantity of water *from the great deep* (sea) came up on land. (Ezek. 26:19 speaks of a similar judgment.) My opinion is this refers to tsunamis. Various natural disasters are certainly capable of causing large waves (even hundreds of feet high) with catastrophic results, but that is enough about the Flood for this book. The bottom line here is the "fountains" of the deep are not a scientific problem for the Bible. This fourth point also fails to produce a scientific error and leaves us with a host of scientific accuracies instead.

5. What are the foundations and pillars of the Earth?

In Hebrew "foundation" means an established thing, something set in place.[30] It reminds me of Jesus' words in Matthew 7:24, "Therefore everyone who hears these words of Mine, and acts upon them, may be compared to a wise man, who built his house upon the rock [not water]." Foundations connote stability and security. Some Biblical writers seem to have been very concerned about earthquakes. The Jordan valley and surrounding mountains are not in any of the most active earthquake zones on Earth but they are in a fault zone with frequent tremors.[31] The Bible is replete with references to God establishing the Earth for the purpose of assuring humanity they need not worry about a major disaster taking the land out from under their feet permanently. God is both said to establish the land (Job 38:4, Ps. 93:1, Prov. 8:29 to name a few) and cause those foundations to shake (Ps. 18:7, Is. 24:18-20), meaning that He is in control of it. We are given few details on how God laid the foundations of the Earth (Job 38:4-7).

"Pillars" is a common word used in many places in the Bible, but in almost every case it refers to pillars associated with buildings. However, four references are used for the Accommodationists' case.

I Samuel 2:8, Hannah's song, says "He raises the poor from the dust, He lifts the needy from the ash heap To make them sit with nobles, And inherit a seat of honor; For the pillars of the earth are the LORD'S, And He set the world on them." The word "pillars" here is not the same Hebrew word usually translated pillars in the Bible.[32] This word is only used one other time in the OT, the other one being I Samuel 14:5 where it describes a cliff (crag) that "rose" on either side of a pass. Considering this other usage, Hannah's words are better understood as saying the land (earth) is a "rising" upon which God set the inhabited "world".[33] Hence, there is no scientific error in her words, only obvious observation that the land rises (sits higher) out of the sea for the purpose of people to inhabit.

The other three references to pillars are:

Job 9:5-6 (Job speaking) says, "It is God who removes the mountains, they know not how, When He overturns them in His anger; Who shakes the earth out of its place, And its pillars tremble."

Job 26:10-11 (also Job speaking) says, "He has inscribed a circle on the surface of the waters At the boundary of light and darkness. The pillars of heaven tremble And are amazed at His rebuke."

And Psalm 75:3 says, "The earth and all who dwell in it melt; It is I who have firmly set its pillars. Selah." The NASB footnotes "totter" as a possible replacement for "melt" also.

Let me start by saying that all three are Hebrew poetry. That does not make them automatically figurative, but it would not make a figurative interpretation unusual. The question here really becomes: How literally do we interpret these verses that describe the pillars? Did the writers literally believe the land *and sky* had columns of some kind? Concerning these verses C. John Collins believes "...there is no reason to suppose that physical description is what these authors

205

were seeking."[34] As much as I would like to dismiss these verses as non-literal statements with only a theological purpose, as Collins does, it does not solve the whole problem. If they did not literally mean some kind of pillar what did they mean?

The way to deal with the Job verses is to say Job (the man) was mistaken, as I did above with Eliphaz concerning Job 22:14 about the vault of heaven. Job and his friends spoke of the cosmos like they were certain of its nature. Job said both the land and the heavens had pillars and God said Job spoke "words without knowledge" (Job 38:2). God corrected him on the pillars of the earth by showing him he really did not know what the land is founded upon (38:4-6), nor the heavens (38:33).

Psalm 75:3 is a little different. The author of the Psalm, Asaph, is claiming *God spoke these words*. God is the one saying He has "firmly set its pillars". Two explanations are available for interpreting this verse. First, this is a clear case of poetic meaning never meant to teach geology which is possibly better expressed by the NIV, "When the earth and all its people quake, it is I who hold its pillars firm." God is using a shaking building with pillars and fearful occupants as a metaphor for the Earth with dwellers fearful of God's judgment (the context of the whole Psalm). His purpose was to assure us He is the Earth's stabilizer because He holds its "pillars" firm, even if He is the one causing the people to quake for fear of judgment. Obviously, the intent of the author was not to say God was literally shaking pillars holding up the land any more than God was literally holding a cup of wine pouring it on people (75:8).

The second explanation is that the verse is literal and the land really does have pillars, i.e. columns of something that stand vertical.[35] Truth is, Earth has many geologic formations that look like columns[36], including mountains. Also, beneath the Earth there are formations, like batholiths, that can sometimes take columnar shapes, albeit really big ones. I am sure some will see that interpretation as a stretch, and I am inclined to agree and prefer what, in this case, is a clear figurative reference, but the literal option was worth mentioning.

6. Does the Bible say there is a *literal* underworld?

Another argument used to say the ancients misunderstood the cosmos involves Philippians 2:9-11. According to one Accommodationist,

> ...a more accurate translation of verse 10 is 'at the name of Jesus every knee should bow, [1] in heaven and [2] on earth and [3] in the underworld.' In other words, Paul is referring to an ancient understanding of the structure of the cosmos known as the '3-tier universe'...[37] [bracketed numbers in the original]

I agree "underworld" is an accurate translation, and that is the problem. Also, Revelation 5:3 and 13 are similar when they refer to spirit beings "under the earth". Were Paul and John saying there were people underground in a literal underworld? Is that scientifically accurate? Three possibilities present themselves here. First, Paul and John were using figurative common language of the day to mean "absolutely everybody", like the southern colloquialism my son suggested, "Everybody and his brother will bow to Jesus." (If Paul had said that I can hear someone accusing the Bible of error because everyone does not have a brother.) Second, they were being poetically figurative. Third, they literally believed there were souls in an underworld.

The first option appeals to some theologians, but I do not like it because, even though *ALL* agree the main point of the verse is to say absolutely everyone will kneel before Jesus, the universal language appears to literally appeal to real places, and we would have to prove their use of the phrase was actually a common figure of speech.

The second option is also supported by some theologians, but I do not like it because, as the Accommodationist above says, "Poetry is not limited to figurative language..."[38] Just because something is poetic does not mean parts of it cannot be literal, and besides, the Revelation verses are not poetic (though they are apocalyptic).

Do not scoff at the third option by passing it off as naïve too easily. Without going into great depth about what exactly happens after death, consider seven things: (1) Disembodied spirits really exist (II Cor. 5:8, Jms. 2:26) and are not omnipresent, meaning they are *limited* to some place. (2) Spirits are immaterial but they are something, which also likely means they exist in time and space, which means they are *somewhere*. (3) Paradise is a real place (Lk. 23:43, II Cor. 12:3-4) so *she'ōl* and *hādes* (Hebrew and Greek for "grave") are too. (4) The "grave" in the OT and NT is more than just a literal hole in the ground where the body goes (Gen. 37:35, Prov. 9:18). (5) The story of Lazarus and the rich man suggests departed spirits are conscious in a real place (Lk. 16:19-31). (6) Jesus may have literally *descended* somewhere under the earth (Eph. 4:8-10, I Pet. 3:18-20). (7) The place called *hādes* will be destroyed one day (Rev. 20:14) which means it exists somewhere.

By all indications the Bible says there really is a place of departed spirits and nothing prevents it from literally being under the ground, i.e in the Earth. A literal underworld interpretation also eliminates any scientific issues with the passages because an underworld is neither scientifically verifiable nor unverifiable. Even if it really is underground, that does not mean it is literally a large cavern or vacant space we can detect. Nor does it mean people are literally on fire there, especially considering the people there do not have bodies. We do not get new bodies until after the resurrection.

Conclusion

After surveying a range of Bible verses accused of containing scientific errors it should be clear the Bible is not as scientifically inept or inaccurate as its accusers believe. Despite a few difficult verses, scientific inerrancy remains intact and supports the authority of the Bible. I have yet to see anyone list a legitimate scientific error committed by the Bible. Someone might complain I have left out a major category of science where the Bible is horribly wrong, namely evolutionary biology. It is true... I have left it out, but not because I believe the Bible is horribly wrong. I left it out because it is too big a subject to adequately cover in one chapter. The evolutionary material will be covered in a future book.

The conclusion is: Concordism is supported and Accommodationism is unnecessary. Biblical writers used the language available to them to attempt to describe the cosmos and God's role in it. There is little detail about how God operates, but that does not mean the verses are full of scientific errors. In fact, as we have just seen, *there are no ancient cosmological errors here*, because questionable verses have better legitimate interpretations that maintain scientific accuracy, or they are vague enough about specifics to not commit the Bible to scientifically inaccurate positions. It looks to me like God inspired the Scriptures and preserved them from misunderstandings about the nature of the cosmos. He did not overlook the ignorance of the authors, but prevented them from expressing it, if they had it, and *corrected* them in some cases like Job, and even went so far as to give them accurate information they could not have known. The language of the Bible is perfectly compatible with modern cosmology, and its scientific accuracy testifies to its inspiration and authority.

Conclusion of Part II

Accusing the Bible of scientific error to attempt to resolve tensions between science and Genesis appears to me as surrender to the enemy. To do so also appears to undermine the authority of the Bible. As I have asked before, if I cannot trust the Bible to tell me the truth about matters that can be verified, how can I trust it on matters that cannot be verified, like theology? Considering Christians believe God inspired the writers to convey important revelations to humanity, could God have accomplished the job without allowing the authors to include their errant cosmological beliefs? I believe He could have and would not want His revelations tainted by untruths. Beyond that, I think I have demonstrated that the Bible has not committed any scientific errors, but actually got the facts correct.

In addition, after the dust settles from all the Old-Earth Creationist views of Genesis, I believe the Prophetic Days View best accounts for all the structural elements of Genesis and, unlike all the other views of Genesis 1, including the Young-Earth View, allows reconciliation between the Bible and the sciences of astronomy and geology on all the issues involved. The age of the universe and Earth are irrelevant to the Biblical story, and the scientific accuracy of Genesis evidences its Divine inspiration.

With the age of the Earth being unimportant to Genesis, let me encourage Christians to quit fighting over this issue. Or, at the very least, let us display the Spiritual fruit of love, patience, gentleness, and kindness to those with whom we disagree. Just maybe, one day the issue of the age of the Earth will be behind us, hopefully soon.

Appendix A

Word Studies in Genesis

This appendix is for the purpose of defending my definitions of the Hebrew words used in Genesis 1:1-2:4a and it concludes with a translation based upon those definitions where I have *tried* to use the *exact same* English word or phrase to translate *every use* of each Hebrew word in the account.

Many of these words have a controversial interpretation associated with them. That Genesis 1 has so many controversial words is testimony to the importance of understanding this first chapter of the Bible. Hebrew is a simple language with Strong's Exhaustive Concordance[1] numbering 8,674 words (compared to English's 160,000+). The definitions here mostly come from Strong and tracing the word's usage through the OT (mostly the Pentateuch if possible). With such a limited vocabulary Hebrew words have to have broad definitions, meaning many English words could be used to translate or interpret each word. My intent here is to produce a consistent translation where each Hebrew word has only one English equivalent to make it easy to trace a word's use through the account, and to help solve any interpretational issues.

Three items should be noted:

1. Sometimes it is not possible to choose one English word to best translate the Hebrew so I will use hyphens to indicate when multiple English words are used to translate one Hebrew word. For example, "dry-ground" translates one Hebrew word.

2. As in all translations, sometimes word choice is driven by interpretation, meaning an English word is chosen to indicate what is thought the author intended to mean. For example, "dry-ground" could be translated literally as "dry-thing" or simply "dry", but those would make the flow of the English read in ways we do not typically speak, so I chose "ground" to indicate (interpret) what I think the author meant was "dry".

3. The definition chosen for each word can have a crucial impact on one's choice of an overall view of Genesis so verify my references if you disagree with my definitions. This is particularly true for the NASB words "formless" and "expanse".

The words will be displayed using the following template:

NASB word – Hebrew transliteration: <u>Strong's #</u>   (Use locations)
My translation: simple definition
    Explanation...

Account – *toledoth*:   8435   (2:4a)
Account: an account or history of a person or event
    Scholars have long recognized Genesis is divided into 12 sections[2] by 11 uses[3] of the Hebrew word *toledoth* (2:4, 5:1, 6:9, 10:1, 11:10, 11:27, 25:12-13, 25:19, 36:1, 36:9 and 37:2). Most often translated as "account" in modern translations, it is also translated as "records", "generations", "genealogy", and "history". One author writes, "...so significant did the Septuagint translators regard it, that they gave the whole book the title 'Genesis'. This is the Greek equivalent of the Hebrew word 'generations'."[4] (Wiseman)

    Scholars differ on whether *toledoth* denotes the beginning or ending of an account however, with the vast majority saying it is a beginning. My conclusion is mixed. It seems to me some early uses of *toledoth* point back to what was before it (2:4a and 5:1a – see below) and then most uses appear to clearly point forward to what follows the *toledoth*. In one case (10:1-32), *toledoth* appears at the beginning and ending of the account (or beginning and middle depending on whether one believes 11:1-9 connects to the *toledoth* of 10:1[5]).

Genesis 2:4a is the most likely ending of the first account rather than 2:3. "This is the account of the heavens and the earth when they were created" *clearly* refers *back* to 1:1 because what follows it *is not an account of the creation of the heavens and the earth.*

Though 5:1 could refer to the genealogy that follows it I would argue that the actual "account" of Adam is before 5:1. Also, if 2:4a and 5:1a are the end of their accounts, it means the first three accounts begin in parallel fashion: 1:1 "In the beginning God created..." – 2:4b "In the day [In a timeframe] that the LORD God made..." – 5:1b "In the day [In a timeframe] when God created..."

Many conservative scholars (Collins for example[6]) disagree with splitting 2:4a and 2:4b because of the chiasm they form:

This is the account [*toledoth*] of
A   the heavens and
B   the earth when they were
C   created,
D   in the day that the LORD God
C'   made
B'   earth and
A'   heaven.

Even Collins admits, "It is certainly true that the use of (*bara'*, "create") in Genesis 2:4a, as well as the mention of 'the heavens and the earth,' links up with 1:1..."[7] Another scholar (Kitchen) says, "It is literary vandalism to break up so clear and well formed a literary mini-unit, worthy of the best of Near Eastern stylistics."[8] However, though an undeniable chiasm is formed connecting Genesis 1 and 2, no one seems to suggest the possibility the author of the second account could have intentionally connected the beginning of his account to the previous one, or vice versa. That would account for the connection *and the differences* between 2:4a and b (differences being: the exclusive use of *elohim* (God) in 1:1-2:4a vs. the regular use of the compound name *Yahweh elohim* (LORD God) in 2:4b-5:1, and the fact "the heavens and the earth" in 2:4a contain articles in Hebrew (*ha* – "the") whereas "earth and heaven" in 2:4b are missing the articles).

Later uses of *toledoth* in Genesis clearly *begin* a section rather than end it.

Beast – *chay*:   2416   (1:24, 25, 30)
Living-thing and **life**: *any* large wild animal or thing which has life (See "living creature" also)

Chay appears in the list of land animals proclaimed on Day 6: cattle, beasts, and creeping things. Cattle (*behemoth* – see below) refers to any large animal, but sometimes only livestock. Creeping things (see below) denotes any number of small creatures that scurry on the ground, including flightless bugs, reptiles, and small mammals. *Chay*, in contrast to them, denotes any living thing, but often larger *wild* animals (though it does not rule out tame ones). Some could argue *chay* refers to only carnivorous wild animals based on its clear use for that purpose (as in Gen. 37:30, Lev. 26:6, Ezek. 34:5, and Hos. 13:8). However, other uses suggest it could refer to all wild animals including herbivores (as in Gen. 9:2, Lev. 11:47, 17:13, and Ps. 104:11). That *chay* is used to describe such a wide range of wild animals is in keeping with the fact that words used in Genesis 1 are broadly generic and are meant to be exhaustive in their use. Meaning, Genesis 1 is telling us of the origin of *all* wild animals humanity would know about. Genesis 1:25 refers to the beast (*chay*) "of the earth [land]" meaning it refers to *all wild animals on dry land.* In contrast, Genesis 2:19-20 specify that Adam named all the beasts (*chay*) "of the field". The extra phrase "of the field" narrows the animals Adam named to *only those in his vicinity*, thus excluding things like walruses.

Chay, in its broadest sense, means "life" (as it is used in 1:30, 2:7, and even in 2:9 – "the tree of life [*chay*]"). Possibly the best translation of the word as it is used to describe wild animals is to translate it "livers" or "living-thing", as in "that which has life", not the internal organ. However, to consistently translate it "livers" would not read well in English. If you see the word "life" or "living" in an English Bible, it is probably *chay*. (See also "living creature" below.)

Beginning – *reshith*:   7225   (1:1)
Beginning: The first part of the whole of something, sometimes the best or chief part

As used in Genesis 1 it refers to the first part of the whole of *time* and thus "beginning" works best. Three references for *reshith* are in Chapter 2 (Job 8:7, 42:12, and Jer. 28:1) and each indicates a block of time, *not a moment or starting point*. Two other *time* references for *reshith* are: (1) Gen 10:10 says, the "beginning [*reshith*] of his [Nimrod's] kingdom was Babel and Erech and Accad and Calneh, in the land of Shinar." The "beginning" is clearly not the very first *moment* of his kingdom because of the number of places mentioned. He did not start all four cities at the same time. He then moved from those places to what he is most noted for, building Nineveh and other cities in Assyria. And (2) Hosea 9:10, "I saw [Israel's] forefathers as the earliest fruit on the fig tree in its first [*reshith*] *season*." "Season" is italicized because it is not in the original Hebrew. The end of the verse could read "in its beginning." Either way, *reshith* is referring to the first generation of Israel that wandered in the wilderness for 40 years, which is *the beginning block of time* for the nation of Israel.

The use of the word *reshith* in the Bible is much more varied than a temporal reference, but this does not change its meaning from referring to a block of time in Gen. 1:1. Not every use of the word is helpful in this determination. Some ambiguous uses include Dt. 11:12, "the beginning even to the end of the year", Eccl. 7:8, "the end of a matter is better than its beginning", and Pr. 17:14, "the beginning of strife." However, some helpful uses include Gen. 49:3, "Rueben, you are my first-born; my might and the beginning of my strength." Rueben was the first of the tribes of Israel, the first part of the whole. Proverbs 1:7, "The fear of the LORD is the beginning of knowledge." Our first knowledge of God comes through fear of consequences, but as we mature God intends for perfect love to cast out all fear (I John 4:18). The fear part occupies a significant part of the whole though. Exodus 23:19, "You shall bring the choice [*reshith*] first fruits of your soil into the house of the LORD…" The reference to a part of the whole is obvious here as it is in Num. 15:21, "From the first [*reshith*] of your dough [course grain] you shall give to the LORD an offering." And Lev. 2:12, "As an offering of first fruits [*reshith*], you shall bring them to the LORD…" And Pr. 3:9, "Honor the LORD from your wealth, and from the first [*reshith*] of all your produce." Also, I Sam. 15:21 refers to taking the "choicest" [*reshith*] of the spoils (KJV – chief, NIV and NKJV – best). And one last reference is Jer. 49:35 which comes right after one of the references to "the beginning of the reign of Zedekiak". Verse 35 refers to the "finest" (KJV – chief, NIV – mainstay) of the archers of Elam.

All of these give a clear indication that *reshith* is a reference to the first *part* of the whole of something, including time, tribe, knowledge of God, harvest, wealth, spoils, and archers. It does *not* refer to a single moment or the first of a series. It is the first part of the whole comparable in length, size, or amount to the whole. The overall meaning one gets from all the uses of the word *reshith* in the Hebrew Bible is that it refers to *the first part of the whole of something, sometimes the best or chief part*.

Birds – n. *'owph*: 5775 (1:20, 21, 22, 26, 28, 30)
Flier(s): Any flying creature, including insects, not just birds

The word "birds" is *'owph* and "fly" is *'uwph* and are related to each other. Though the word *'owph* is almost always translated as "bird" through the rest of the Hebrew Bible, it is likely its first use has a broader meaning. Mirroring "Let the waters swarm (*sharats*) with swarms (*sherets*)" is a translation of the second half of the proclamation as "and let fliers (*'owph*) fly (*'uwph*)". The use of very generic terms in Genesis 1 is common and these are some prime examples. "But here, besides, where the very broadest of class distinctions are being made, without a doubt, the expression is meant to include every type of being that has wings – the small and the large, and not only what we call birds."[9] (Leupold) Besides birds then, *'owph* includes flying insects, flying reptiles (dinosaurs), and bats, but probably not gliding creatures like flying squirrels, fish, or lizards. This interpretation of the word does not *demand* that flying reptiles (dinosaurs) were created with Adam and Eve. It only means that whatever flying animals humanity may know about, then or in the future, were created by God.

Bring forth – *yatsa*: 3318 (1:12, 24)
Produced: To bring out, bring forth, go out, or produce

This word is used very broadly in the OT. The NIV translates it as "produced" in Genesis 1. The land (earth) is said to "bring out" two things in Genesis: "vegetation" (v. 12) and "living creatures" (v. 25). Translating it as "produced" should not be taken as the land *originating* plants and animals. God had to proclaim the existence of plants and animals for them to originate. In the case of plants God proclaimed for new growth to sprout and then the land took it from there and produced more and we know how the land does its part because we see it happen all the time. In the case of animals, God proclaimed for the land to produce living creatures. We do not normally think of the land doing anything associated with animal reproduction, however, it is obvious that reproduction occurs on land and the resources of the land affect it. For the proclamation to have been fulfilled, God had to make (cause) the animals first. We are given that information out of sequence (v. 25), after the proclamation is said to have come to pass, but God had to make the animals before the land could facilitate production of more.

Cattle – *behemoth*: 930 (1:24, 25, 26)
Large-animals: *any large animal,* but often it specifies livestock (i.e. domesticated animals like sheep, goats, camels, etc. – not just cows)

The word "cattle" in Genesis 1 is *behemoth*, plural of *behemah* (Strong's 929), and is frequently translated "cattle" in most translations, while *behemah* is translated "beast". But "cattle" is far too specific. *Behemoth* refers to any number of large land creatures and probably mostly to herbivores, but does not always refer to domesticated animals (Job 40). In the KJV, for example, it is translated "beast" (*behemah*) in Gen. 6:7, "cattle" (*behemoth*) in 6:20, and "beast" (*behemah*) in 7:2. The NASB translates all these as "animals" because they refer to nearly every animal on Noah's ark. As a contrast, consider 7:21, "And all flesh that moved on the earth perished, birds and cattle (*behemah*) and beasts (*chay* – see above)…" *Behemah* and *chay* in 7:21 likely divide herbivores and carnivores. One can see how confusing an English translation can be with the Hebrew words. Two words, *behemah* and *chay*, are sometimes translated the same way, "beast". And here the NASB has translated *behemah* as "cattle" rather than "animals" like it did a few verses earlier. As cumbersome as it is, I think "large-animals" is the best way to get the meaning across when it is used to refer to nearly all animals, while "livestock" is best when it refers to domesticated flocks of animals. In Genesis 1 I believe it carries the more generic meaning as it does in the Flood account.

Appendix A – Word Studies in Genesis

Created – *bara***:**   1254   (1:1, 21, 27, 2:3-4)
Created: to make a new thing

The word "**created**" is *bara* and means to bring something into existence that did not exist before, or make something new. It is used in verse 1 to refer to bringing the universe into existence. The phrase "the heavens and the earth" is a Hebrew figure of speech for "the all" or all that exists. "Create" is also used in verse 21 in reference to the various kinds of sea creatures and birds, and then again in verse 27 in reference to man. These three uses have long been recognized by many commentators as the three major stages in creation: (1) The creation of time and space, matter and energy, from which, and in which, God made the stars and planets and plant life; (2) The creation of animate life, from which God made all creatures that move; and (3) The creation of humanity, adding the extra feature of a spirit in the image of God to a physical body made of the same materials as animate life. *Bara* is also used in Gen. 2:3 to refer to God creating the whole work for Him to do. (See Chapter 5 for why I think 2:3 should be translated as "And God blessed the seventh day and sanctified it, because on it He ceased from His whole work which God created to do.")

Norman Geisler also notes that, "*Bara* does not always mean 'to make something out of nothing' (see... Ps. 104:30; Isa. 41:20). However, used in the context of the original events of Creation, described in Genesis 1, it bears this meaning (cf. Col. 1:16; 2 Cor. 4:6)."[10] Whether Genesis 1:1 is teaching creation *ex nihilo* (out of nothing) is a controversial question these days. Did the author intend to tell us God created the universe from nothing? It is difficult to tell, but it seems fairly straight forward that the author is telling us of the origin of the universe as he knew it. The heavens and the earth *were not there* before God created them, and they were afterward. The new thing God did was the existence of the universe. Whether the author thought God used existing material is probably not possible to know. Also important to note is that "*bara*" is *never* used in the Bible to describe what man does, only God.

Creeping things – n. *remes***:**   7431   (1:24, 25, 26)
Moving-things: the verb form means to crawl, scurry away, or move with short steps therefore, the noun refers to *any* small moving creature on the ground

As a noun *remes* refers to any variety of small creatures that scurry or move away quickly, including flightless invertebrates, reptiles, and mammals. Its use is not restricted to land creatures as is evident from it being used of sea creatures in Ps. 104:25 and its verb form being used on Day 5 of sea animals (v. 21), like minnows fleeing from the sight of someone on shore. However, Genesis 1:24-25 refers to land creatures. With Genesis as an account of the origin of all things common to human experience, "creeping things" must refer to any moving thing along the ground Adam would have seen in the garden. That would have to include flightless invertebrates (like spiders and scorpions), reptiles, and small mammals. If those creatures are included in *remes*, then Genesis 1 has land invertebrates and reptiles being proclaimed on Day 6 after birds on Day 5. That creates a serious order of appearance problem in reconciling Genesis with modern science as discussed in Chapter 9. However, since the account is intentionally written topically, and the proclamations are stated in such a way that they cannot be fulfilled in a day (see Chapter 2), there is no problem between Genesis and science.

Creeps – v. *ramas***:**   7430   (1:21, 26, 28, 30)
Moves: to crawl, scurry away, or move with short steps

This word is likely defining "life" in Genesis. Defining "life" for a biologist is more difficult than one might think and today we consider plants to be alive. In Genesis plants are said to grow (2:8-9), but they are not said to be alive. The creation account definition of "life" is "that which moves", i.e. has a form of locomotion. Plants have mechanical movement like in the case of a Venus Flytrap or exploding seed pods, but plants do not locomote. Animals, on the other hand, move from one spot to another,[11] and will *instantly* recoil and/or move away from pain, damage, and predators; plants do not. This quality of animal design is why animals are called *nephesh chayah* ("living creatures/souls" – see "living creature" below). The reaction to stimuli by animals could be the Biblical "soulish" quality we all share. An amoeba moving away from heat or a predator could be seen as a primal version of fear (perhaps the simplest version of an emotional response).

Ramas (moves) is distinguished from *sharats* (see "teem" below) in that it adds speed or quickness to movement. Scurrying is a good way to picture it, like any small animal quickly moving around or away, including bugs, reptiles, rodents and fish.

Day – *yôm*:   3117   (1:5 (2x), 8, 13, 14 (2x), 16, 18, 19, 23, 31, 2:2 (2x), 3, 4)
Day: the daylight portion of a 24 hour period, or an indefinite period of time

This small word sparks what seems to be never ending controversy. However, much to the disagreement of many OEC, the controversy over the definition (at least) is easily settled because *yôm* is one of five words in the Genesis 1 account that *God defines for us*. Five times in Genesis 1 we are told God "called" or "named" something. *Yôm* is one of them. In Genesis 1:5, in its *first use* in the Bible it says, "And God called the light 'day'". "Day" is the lighted portion of what we now know to be the rotation period of Earth. "Daylight" is a simple definition anyone who can see can understand.

The controversy begins almost immediately with *yôm*'s second use in 1:5, "And there was evening and there was morning, one day." Does "day" mean the same here? There is no reason to think it does not. An ancient reader would have made that connection and it also makes sense it is what the author intended. It is really that simple.

Many see its use in 1:14 as an exception, "...let them be for signs, and for seasons, and for days and years." Surely here the word means a whole 24 hour day, not just the lighted portion. Not necessarily, earlier *in the same verse* "day" is contrasted with "night" as it frequently is in the Bible (see Gen. 8:22, Ex. 13:21, I Kings 8:59, Ps. 32:4, Is. 27:3). If it was necessary to say "day and night" to describe what we call a whole day, then "day" must mean "the lighted portion of a 24 hour period" *consistently through Genesis*, even in 1:14.

But what about Genesis 2:4b, "...in the day that the LORD God made earth and heaven"? Here it should be obvious "day" means an indefinite period of time, right? It is not that simple though. In 2:4 "day" is part of a Hebrew idiom, *b^{e}yom*, with the prefix *b^e* (in). Why does that matter? Because, some think it should be translated as "when" as it is in the NIV, "When the LORD God made the earth and the heavens..." YEC[12] (Sarfati) then use this argument to say that 2:4 cannot be used to show *yôm* means an indefinite amount of time in Genesis 1, and some OEC[13] (Collins) agree. Personally, translating *b^{e}yom* as "in the day" (or "in a timeframe") rather than "when" is still preferred because it looks more literal. Even if *b^{e}yom* forms an idiom, it still appears the meaning of *yôm* in the idiom refers to an unspecified amount of time. An idiom does not have to change the entire meaning of a word. Even in English we use the word "day" to refer to an unspecified length of time. In Hebrew, the word *yôm* can mean an indefinite amount of time, but it seems to be true only when it follows certain grammatical patterns.

However, the numbered days do not fit any of those known patterns. It should be noted that there is no distinction in Hebrew between the first and second use of *yôm* (day) in Genesis 1. Both uses are singular without any attached prepositions like *b^{e}yôm* (in the day) as it appears in 1:18 ("over the day" – KJV), or *hayôm* (*the* day) as it appears in 1:14 and 16. All uses of *yôm* at the end of each Day *are missing prepositions*. The prepositions that are there are attached to the numbers and form a unique usage of *yôm* in the OT. This uniqueness becomes inconclusive in supporting normal or long days then. Thus, except for attempting to find space for long periods of time to reconcile with great age[14], there appears to be no good textual reason to think *yôm* in Genesis 1 means anything other than "the daylight portion of a 24 hour period" *as it defines itself*. Walton concurs, "These are seven twenty-four-hour days. This has always been the best reading of the Hebrew text."[15] (See Chapter 9.II.1 and "evening" and "morning" below also)

Deep – *tehôm*:   8415   (1:2)
Deep: a deep place like a sea

The "deep" and the "waters" speak of the same place in Genesis 1:2 referring to a deep sea or ocean. However, the two should not necessarily be equated. Though "the deep" is a noun referring to a place it is also *a description of the place* and can also include underground. The use of the word "deep" to describe both fresh water (Gen. 49:25, Dt. 33:13) and salt water should be clear it does not always refer to the same place, only a similar description of a place. Proverbs 3:20 makes it clear the "deep" is more than one place because it says it is "broken up". One could argue the ancient mind believed all water came from the deep sea, including what is underground, but that is not a problem, all water did start there. Fresh water evaporates from the sea and is dumped on the land where it becomes underground water.

Finding commentators who connect *tehôm* with Tiamat, a Babylonian chaos deity who was slain and from whom Marduk made the land and sea, is not unusual. However, many other scholars do not agree the Hebrew word was borrowed from Akkadian.[16]

This word is also sometimes used metaphorically as in Psalm 36:6 and 42:7, in the same way we do today, to describe complex and difficult thinking or inner longings.

Dry land – *yabbâshâh*:   3004   (1:9, 10)
Dry-ground: a dry thing.

Other uses of this word make the definition clear as "dry ground" or "dry land" as in Ex. 14:16, 22, and 29 describing what Israel walked on through the Red Sea. The translation "dry-ground" (like the NIV) rather than "dry land" is preferred so as to distinguish this word from *erets* (earth or land – see next word).

Earth – *erets*:   776   (1:1, 2, 10, 11 (2x), 12, 15, 17, 20, 22, 24 (2x), 25 (2x), 26 (2x), 28 (2x), 29, 30 (2x), 2:1, 4 (2x))
Land: can refer to all land, land above water (dry-ground), or a specific land

Erets has multiple meanings determined by the context it is used. It can mean the whole earth (even what is covered with water – Gen. 1:1-2 and 18:25), all dry ground (Gen. 1:10), a specific land like the Promised Land or the land of Egypt (as it is used many times), or ground, as in immediately beneath one's feet (Gen. 33:3). It is important to consider *erets* the way the original audience would have seen it and not the way we think of Earth today. "We have filled the word with a meaning it clearly did not suggest to its original readers… 'Land' is a better translation than 'earth' for the Hebrew term *eretz* because the term 'land' extends only to what we see of the earth around us, what is within our horizons."[17] (Sailhamer) The original readers were not thinking of *erets* as a planet floating in space. Their perspective, and that of Genesis, is *from the surface*. However, in 1:1 "earth" does not refer only to a specific land. It refers to *all land* including that covered by water because no land was specified at that point.

Evening – *'ereb*:   6153   (1:5, 8, 13, 19, 23, 31)
Evening: the lighted portion of a 24 hour period *after sunset*, dusk

Every reference to "evening" in the Bible refers to dusk, just after sunset (though three of its uses are metaphorical – see below). Numbers 9:15-16 refers to an appearance of fire covering the tabernacle during the "night", and also describes it "from evening until morning". This clearly defines nighttime between evening and morning, which is *exactly* like Genesis 1 uses it. Other uses of "evening" and "morning" make their meanings just as evident. Ex. 27:21 and Lev. 24:3 use them as the boundaries of the nighttime. Also, Ex. 18:13 uses "morning" and "evening" (in the reverse order of Genesis) as boundaries for daytime. "Evening" refers to that period of time of light *after* sunset before dark (night). "Morning" refers to that period of time when it is light *before* sunrise. "Day" is then defined as *sunrise to sunset*, the daylight hours (see "day" above). Collins agrees, "Logically… to get a day we must describe twenty-four hours, or at least the period of daylight." Then in reference to the correct rendering of the refrain as "And there was evening and there was morning, the nth day", he says, "…if we simply allow the verbs to indicate two events, we find that they mark the end points of the nighttime."[18] One YEC commentator succinctly puts it, "For 'evening' marks the conclusion of the day, and 'morning' marks the conclusion of the night."[19] (Leupold)

Some may object and say the Jews reckoned a day to begin at sunset with the nighttime preceding the day. While that is true, it was not true until God commanded it in Ex. 12:18 and Lev. 23:32. The fact God later commanded them to reverse it implies they were previously measuring it the other way. Genesis contains no indication the Patriarchs measured a day from sunset to sunset. *The darkness before Day 1 in Gen 1:2 was not part of Day 1.* Day 1 began when God said, "Let there be light." Then evening came, then nighttime, then morning, and one daylight time passed. The time markers in Genesis (numbered days and the refrain) are the parts that are definitely in chronologic order.

Three metaphorical uses of "evening" and "morning" in the Bible are Job 4:20, Psalm 90:6, and Daniel 8:14 and 26. In Psalms sprouting grass in the morning and withering in the evening is metaphorical to the beginning and ending of a man's life as in Job 4:20. But, notice in both cases that morning refers to the beginning, whereas Genesis has evening listed first. Also, Genesis gives no indication a literal evening on Earth is being used metaphorically for an ending of a day-age. If Genesis was using morning and evening as the beginning and ending of a day-age then morning should have been listed first, or the text would have read something like, "And there was evening, one day. And there was morning, and God said…" Because of the order of the text, it reads best as normal evenings and mornings on normal Earth days.

One should also keep in mind the metaphorical uses of "evening" and "morning" in Job, Psalms, and Daniel are in poetic and apocalyptic literature which are rife for metaphors. Genesis 1 is highly structured narrative and shows no propensity to metaphor.

Expanse – *raqîa*:   7549   (1:6, 7 (3x), 8, 14, 15, 17, 20)
Expanding-clear-space: the whole sky, all that can be seen above the land from the surface, an expanded thing or an expanding clear space
   A defense of my definition required its own appendix. See Appendix B.

Fly – v. *'uwph*:   5774   (1:20)
Fly: to fly
   See "birds".

Formless – *tohu*:   8414   (1:2)
Desolate: desolate, uninhabitable, wasteland, unproductive[20]
   The Hebrew phrase *tohu wabohu* is translated as "formless and void" in the NASB, "formless and empty" in the NIV, and "without form and void" in the ESV, NKJV, and KJV. The word *tohu* (formless) is used fairly frequently in the Bible, but the word *bohu* (void or empty) is only used three times and always with *tohu* near.
   The difficulty of finding the right English word for *tohu* is evident from its many translations. In Dt. 32:10 it is "waste" in most English versions. In Job 6:18 it is

"nothing" even in the KJV, and the NIV has it as "wasteland". Job 12:24 is "waste" with the KJV as "wilderness". Job 26:7 is "empty space". Isaiah 24:10, 34:11, and 41:29 have it as "chaos", "desolation" and "emptiness" respectively and the KJV has it as "confusion" in all three. Isaiah 45:18 is important to consider, "For thus says the LORD who created the heavens (He is the God who formed the earth and made it, He established it and did not create it a waste place [*tohu*], *But* formed it to be inhabited), 'I am the LORD and there is none else.'" Notice that "formless" could not be used to translate many of these verses.

The English words used for *tohu* (formless, waste, nothing, wasteland, wilderness, empty space, chaos, desolation, emptiness, confusion, and waste place), and the contexts they are used, all have a common theme. They denote *the description of a place unfit for human life the way it was intended by God*. This is obviously the intent of Is. 45:18 where "waste place" is contrasted with "inhabited". When *tohu* is then combined with *bohu* (void or empty), not only is the place unfit for life as intended, but it is both unfit *and* empty. But, empty of what? Empty of life. Therefore, Genesis 1:2 describes the land as both desolate and lifeless.

Bohu is used in three places in the OT: Gen. 1:2, Is. 34:11 and Jer. 4:23. In Jeremiah the exact same Hebrew phrase is used as in Genesis. Isaiah 34:8a and 11b read, "For the LORD has a day of vengeance... And He shall stretch over it the line of desolation [*tohu*], and the plumb line of emptiness [*bohu*]." Because of the judgment connotation of Is. 34:11 and Jer. 4:23 (where Jeremiah sees the Earth becoming "formless and void" again), some (namely Gap View advocates) have given *tohu* and *bohu* a judgment connotation *wherever they are used*, which includes Genesis 1:2. Though the words do convey what God does not intend for man, Genesis 1:2 does not necessarily have to be read as a judgment condition. It could denote the condition of the primeval earth as a place unfit and empty of life, though this was not the condition God intended to *leave* it (Is. 45:18). The words themselves describe a condition, not the means by which Earth came to that condition. "Viewed from the perspective of the Hebrew text, the phrase 'formless and void' means simply 'uninhabitable land.'"[21] (Sailhamer) "Desolate (or uninhabitable) and lifeless" is the best way to think of the phrase.

What was "formless and void"? The earth was. What is "earth" referring to? "Earth" in verses 1 and 2 means "all land" including land covered by water (see "earth" above). Matthew Henry shows the influence of Greek philosophy on his commentary when he calls "earth" in verse 2 a "shapeless"[22] chaos of matter, but verse 2 *should not* conjure up images of what astronomers call the Nebular Hypothesis, a picture of the early solar system with a disk of gas and debris orbiting the Sun in a chaotic vortex. Unfortunately, the meaning of "formless," or "without form" (KJV), as "without a shape," could easily give that impression. However, in verse 2, "earth" could not have been *completely shapeless*, as Matthew Henry surmised above. If land existed covered with water (a deep ocean), then it could not have been without any form (shape). Astronomically speaking, a planet the size of Earth *must*, because of gravity, form a spherical shape. Genesis 1:2 is *not* teaching the whole Earth was formless in the sense of being a shapeless mass. That concept would have been completely foreign to an ancient audience.

All words have connotations. A *modern* connotation for "formless" is shapeless, but the Hebrew word cannot be translated as shapeless. Therefore, the English translation *should not be* "formless". As shown above, "waste" or "wasteland" is the most consistent translation of the word in other verses. It is precisely because the whole Earth was covered with water and dark that it was unfit for life and was an uninhabitable empty waste. In its newly created state, verse 2 says the land was desolate and lifeless. An old-English understanding of the earth as "formless" might have meant "not having any forms on it" rather than not having any form itself. In that case "formless" may be appropriate, but not with its modern connotation.

English translations of this verse suffer from an influence of Greek philosophy and cosmology because of the Septuagint (the Greek translation of the Hebrew Scriptures (ca. 250 BCE), officially abbreviated LXX).

> Since [the Greek terms used in the LXX] play an important role in the Hellenistic cosmologies at the time of the LXX translation, it is likely that the choice of these terms, and others in the LXX of Genesis, was motivated by an attempt to harmonize the biblical account with accepted views in the translators' own day rather than a strict adherence to the sense of the Hebrew text...[23] (Sailhamer)

It is because of a Greek cosmological concept of an original preexisting chaos of matter that we end up with the English word "formless" in Genesis 1:2. That concept does not come from the original Hebrew. I wish English translators would quit consistently using the word "formless" (NASB, NKJV, ESV, and NIV – in their defense, they probably do it for familiarity and traditional reasons, which is understandable). Instead, I wish they would translate it as, "And the Earth was desolate (or uninhabitable, or unfit for life, or a wasteland) and lifeless." At least the NASB footnotes it as "a waste and emptiness". Although, if the words "waste" or "wasteland" were used then it might carry the connotation God was wasteful or created the Earth a dump, and that would be wrong too. That is why the word "desolate" is best.

If the concept of a formless shapeless Earth is removed and replaced with "desolate" or "uninhabitable", then the feeling that one needs to interpret verse 2 according to a modern scientific Nebular Hypothesis, or a Greek cosmological chaotic state, disappears. The original audience would have simply understood the verse to refer to the land essentially the same as we see today, only dark and covered with water, and devoid of dry-land and life, like darkness over the open ocean.

W*hy* was Earth desolate and empty and covered with water? Was that its primeval state? Or, was it in this condition because God had destroyed Earth with a flood because of problems with a previous pre-Adamic race of people, or because of Satan's rebellion (the Gap View)? The answer could hinge on the simple translation of the verb "was". Many Gap View interpreters of Genesis would like to translate "And the earth was..." as "And the earth became..." (as footnoted in the NIV). There is no shortage of commentators who disagree with that though, mainly for two strong reasons: *First*, the Bible does not even hint of a pre-Adamic race of people. Nor, does it mention any other worldwide flood than Noah's. And even though Satan and his demons were "thrown down to the earth" after being expelled from Heaven (Rev. 12:9), there is nothing to indicate God or Satan flooded or destroyed the Earth because of this. *Second*, as one commentator succinctly put it, "**Was**. Not 'had become.'"[24] (Whitelaw) Meaning, the Hebrew structure of the verb cannot rightly be grammatically conjugated as "became" or "had become". Another commentator agrees, "Hence this does not describe an event but a state."[25] (Collins) So, verse 2 says the land "was" in that condition (state) after its creation; it did not become that way (an event).

Would God have created an uninhabitable wasteland empty of life? Possibly. That condition could simply have been a preliminary stage. Speculation about a previous judgment should be avoided. The text simply says the condition of the land sometime after its creation was desolate, lifeless, covered with water, and dark.

Fruit – *periy*:   6529   (1:11 (2x), 12, 29)   from **Fruitful** – *parah*:   6509   (1:22, 28)
Fruit: that which is produced from a plant, animal, or womb
Fruitful: to bear fruit

In Genesis "fruit" and "fruitful" both specify things desirable or beneficial for humanity that nature produces from plants, animals, or the womb. These words should not be confused with the scientific way we use the word today. In botany the word "fruit" describes what a flowering plant produces that has seed in it, edible or not. However, Biblical use of these words most often refer to something good produced as opposed to something bad. Even though they do sometimes refer to something bad produced (as in Dt. 29:18 and Is. 10:12), Genesis repeatedly calls what God did "good". Therefore, Genesis uses the words to refer to good things produced for humanity.

Also, some might think it odd to say both "fruitful and multiply" because it seems redundant, but actually there is a slight variation between them. Being fruitful, in the sense of reproducing, is possible without multiplying, i.e. increasing in total number (the meaning of the word *rabah* – "multiply"). Animals that go extinct reproduce, but their overall numbers decrease because they die faster than they replace themselves. For human population to grow couples must have more than two children on average. Any less and they are only replacing themselves or diminishing in number. God's plan, contrary to modern population control measures and environmentalist complaints, is for humanity to increase in number on Earth.

Gathered – *qavah*:   6960   (1:9)
Be-gathered: to gather together, to collect

Strong's defines *qavah* as a primitive root word meaning, "to *bind* together… i.e. *collect*; (fig.) to *expect*."[26] However, modern Hebrew dictionaries note that the trilateral root has two meanings.[27] The first sense relates to waiting patiently as in Genesis 49:18, "For Thy salvation I wait [*qavah*], O LORD." Psalm 40:1, "I WAITED patiently for the LORD; And He inclined to me, and heard my cry." *Qavah* is both words "waited patiently." The second sense of the root is "to gather" as it is used in Genesis as a verb (1:9) and a noun (1:10). The only other place in the OT the verb is used in this second sense is Jer. 3:17, "…and all the nations will be gathered to it, to Jerusalem, for the name of the LORD…" The word often translated "gathering" in verse 10 is from the same root. I used "gathering" rather than "gathered" in 1:10 to make the noun/verb distinction.

Even though the word is used in a passive sense in 1:9, meaning the waters are being *acted upon* as opposed to taking an initiative in the action (which inanimate objects obviously do not do), the action still has the connotation of *a slow process* because God is not specifically mentioned moving the waters in any unusual way. Yes, God proclaimed for the waters to gather into individual places, i.e. pools or streams and thus involved rivers, ponds, lakes, seas, and oceans, and they would not have done so unless God had said it, but the implication is God is using secondary means to accomplish the task. With the water doing its own gathering, the process took much longer than a day. Also, if it could be shown the two uses of the word are related, as Strong's suggests, then it would add further support the word refers to a long patiently anticipated process.

God – *Elohim*:   430   ("God" is used in every verse except 1:13, 15, 19, 23, 30 and 2:1)
God: God, the Hebrew word is plural but used with singular verbs

With a total of 35 uses "God" is the most frequent word in Genesis 1:1-2:4a. It even outnumbers the use of the verb "to be". The importance and preeminence of God should not be overlooked; there is nothing greater.

That the plurality of *Elohim* refers early to some kind of plurality in the nature of God is also evidenced by verse 26, "Let us make man in Our image…", compared to verse 27, "And God created man in His own image, in the image of God He created him; male and female He created them." "The singular man [*adam*] is created as a plurality, 'male and female'… Following this clue the divine plurality expressed in verse 26 is seen as an anticipation of the human plurality of the man and the woman, thus casting the human relationship between man and woman in the role of reflecting God's own personal relationship with himself."[28] (Sailhamer) Another point to note is, "Unless where it

219

[*Elohim*] refers to the angels [Ps. 8:5], or to heathen deities [Gen. 31:32, Ex. 20:3, Jer. 16:20], or to earthly rulers [Ex. 22:8-9], *Elohim* is conjoined with verbs and adjectives in the singular, an anomaly in language which has been explained as suggesting the unity of the Godhead."[29] (Whitelaw) Thus, because *Elohim* is a plural noun, used with singular verbs and adjectives, attached to plural pronouns, and analogized with humans being both singular (*adam*) and plural (male and female), the text indicates some sort of mysterious plurality existing within God. Though not understood by the Jewish captives leaving Egypt, and not well developed until the New Testament, foreshadows of the Trinity are present from the beginning.

Good – *towb*:   2896   (1:4, 10, 12, 18, 21, 25, 31)
Good: good, beneficial

This word does *not* mean perfect. Hebrew has another word for perfect that is not used in Genesis 1. The question that really needs answering here is, *good for whom*? God always does what is good and He was transforming the land to be good for something. Since we are created in His image and capable of glorifying Him, the conclusion can be drawn that what God made good was good for His purposes and good for us. If they were not good for us then we would not have been able to glorify Him. What constitutes good for us should be determined by the text however, not from some utopian idea of a perfect creation. This topic is discussed extensively in Point 1 of Chapter 6.

Govern – *memshalah*:   4475   (1:16 (2x))   **Comes from *mishal*:**   4910   (1:18)
Control: govern in the sense of having been given power already, not by taking power
    See "rule" where three Hebrew words are contrasted.

Heavens – *shamayim*:   8064   (1:1, 8, 9, 14, 15, 17, 20, 2:1, 4)
Heavens: the heights above the land, includes *all* that is up there

Heavens is plural in Hebrew and "...signifies the 'upper regions'"[30] (Leupold) or "Literally, the heights."[31] (Whitelaw) It is the upper regions or heights above the surface of the Earth. In verse 8 the "expanse" is called "heaven" (NASB, KJV, NKJV), or "sky" (NIV). Leaving it as "heavens" is best because it captures the plural better than "sky", and "skies" would sound even stranger.

Verse 8 also equates the "heavens" with the "expanse" where the waters were separated, i.e. the space between the ocean and rainclouds (see Appendix B). And verse 17 says "God placed [the Sun, Moon, and stars] in the expanse of the heavens..." Hence, "heavens" also includes outer space too. And heaven is referred to as the place where God and the angels are. Psalm 33:13-14 reads, "The LORD looks from heaven; He sees all the sons of men; From His dwelling place He looks out on all the inhabitants of the earth." Isaiah 14:12 refers to Lucifer's fall from heaven. "Heavens" is plural then because it refers to them all: the sky, outer space, and the place where God and the angels dwell.

Image – *tselem*:   6754   (1:26, 27 (2x))
Image: a resemblance of something in order to represent it to something else

"Image" means a "*resemblance*" and "*representative figure*" and is sometimes used to refer to idols.[32] It is an image in the sense of being a "stand-in" for the real thing. Therefore, the word has more of the meaning of being a representative than looking like something (which is "likeness"). As God's image bearer we represent God on Earth and are to carry out His plans.

The word "likeness" is *demuwth* and means to look like, in like manner, to be fashioned after, or "*resemblance...model, shape*."[33] This word is used to describe our likeness to God in the sense that we look like Him because *we have similar qualities*, not because we have a similar physical appearance.

Therefore, we are God's representative on Earth because we have similar qualities. This carries the responsibility of caring for Earth the way God desires. One thing is certain: these words do not mean we are an exact replica of God. God cannot replicate Himself because there cannot be two omnipotent infinite beings, and if something had a beginning it cannot be infinite. But He can create something that is analogous to Himself in the sense of possessing similar qualities and representing Him like an ambassador.

Kind – *miyn*: 4327 (1:11, 12 (2x), 21 (2x), 24 (2x), 25 (3x))
Kind: in a similar category or classification

Every time this word appears in Genesis it is part of the general phrase "after its kind" or "according to its kind" and that phrase is the most repeated phrase in Genesis 1 (10 times). The intent of stressing the word is most likely to prevent someone from believing that a plant or animal would produce anything other than what it is, so they did not have to worry about animals producing something monstrous, like folkloric griffins or cockatrices, and people should not attempt to cross-breed different animals and produce some unusual hybrid either. For the ancients it is doubtful whether they would have thought time could have made a difference to this restriction, meaning the amount of change capable over a long time would still not change the creature into anything other than something similar to itself. Thus, the meaning of the word could be a restriction meant to prevent belief in evolution, though that conclusion is not as clear as it could be.

Light – *'owr*: 216 (1:3-4 (4x), 5, 15, 17, 18) **Lights – *ma'owr*:** 3974 (1:14, 15, 16 (3x))
Light: light   **Lights:** luminous body or light-bearer

Two words for light are used in Genesis 1 though the second one is a derivative of the first. The first means simply "light". The second is "light-bearers", that which produces light. It is interesting that the first reference to light is a period of time, not just light itself. "God called the light day." The light God proclaimed to come to be was the daylight on Earth, not light in the entire universe. It makes no sense to compare light in the entire universe to darkness because no cycle of light and darkness exists in space.

Also significant is that the Sun and Moon are not called by their Hebrew names. Most commentators believe Genesis is avoiding using the proper names of the Sun and Moon to avoid anyone thinking God created lesser gods. In Ancient Near-East cultures the names of the Sun and Moon were usually identical to the names of the gods that they represented. Here, the lights are not gods; they are simply light-bearers.

Likeness – *demuwth*: 1823 (1:26)
Likeness: looking like something in the sense of having similar qualities
See "image" where the definitions of "image" and "likeness" are contrasted.

Living creature – *nephesh chayah*: 5315 and 2416 (20, 21, 24)
Living creature: a living creature/soul

The words "living creatures" are *nephesh chayah* and appear together eleven times in the Hebrew Bible (1:20, 21, 24, 2:7, 19, 9:10, 12, 15, 16, Lev. 11:10 and 11:46). In the one instance that refers exclusively to humans (2:7) it is translated as "living soul" in the KJV and "living being" in the NASB. Both translations are attempting to draw a distinction between humans and animals, but in Hebrew the terms are exactly the same. Though humans and animals are different in Genesis because humans are created in God's image, being called "living creature" is a commonality not a difference. Animals and humans share "life" and "soulishness" in common. Separately, both words are used widely in the Hebrew Bible.

Nephesh is translated as "soul" (most common), "breath", and "creature" among many others. *Chayah* is translated as "alive", "life", "live", "living", "living thing", and "beast" among a few others. *Chayah* or *chay* appears in verses 24 and 30 by itself in reference to land animals and is translated as "beast" though I prefer "large-animal".

Looking at the three uses of *nephesh chayah* in Genesis 1 shows it refers to *all living animals*. The term is never used of plants. In Genesis 1:20-21 it is used twice and applies to *all* creatures of the sea and sky, "every living creature that moves, with which the waters swarmed... [which includes many invertebrates] and every winged bird [flier]." The word translated "bird" in Genesis 1:20-21 is a generic term referring to all flying creatures (see above). The third use of the term in Genesis 1:24-25 applies to "everything that creeps on the ground."

Trying to restrict the meaning of this term in order to solve some difficulty in one's interpretation of Genesis is a losing battle. In Genesis 1, 2, and 9 it refers to a wide variety of creatures and Leviticus is the same. Like all other terms in Genesis 1, this one is very generic.

Made – *asah*: 6213 (1:7, 11, 12, 16, 25, 26, 2:2 (2x), 3)
Caused, did, and do: to do, or to cause something to happen

The word *asah* is used very broadly in the OT and is translated by a large number of words including: make (made), bearing (as it is used in 1:11-12 to refer to bearing fruit), accomplish, deal with, commit, offer, execute, keep, show, prepare, work, perform, bring to pass, get, dress, maintain, care for, and trim. But it is most often translated as a form of the very common verb "to do" (do, does, did, done, etc.). A scan of those words including "to do" reveals that *asah* generally means *to cause something to happen*, whether good or bad, whether causing order or disorder. *It is a word that shows causal responsibility.* For that reason it is used for both Divine actions *and* human actions. The first time it is used of human action is in Gen. 3:13 after Adam and Eve ate from the tree God forbade, "Then the LORD God said to the woman, 'What is this you have done [*asah*]?'" Responsibility and causality are clear subjects related to the Fall of mankind.

Care should be taken when choosing an English word to translate *asah* considering any connotations to its meaning. In English (and Hebrew), the verb "to do" has many applications, for example, "So where do you get your fingernails done?" (Even in Hebrew *asah* is used of trimming fingernails, Dt. 21:12) But unfortunately, the word "made" in English gives a connotation to any translation that may not be intended by *asah*. For example, try substituting "made" into the previous question, "So where do you get your fingernails made?" The two questions get different answers. In English "to make" something usually means to manufacture, assemble, build, or form it. But even though *asah* can sometimes be interpreted as "assemble" or "manufacture", the word has a much broader meaning than that. To avoid any connotations not intended by "made" the best way to translate *asah* in Genesis (and Ex. 20:11) is "caused" (or "did", "done", "do", etc. when that word makes more sense in English) because, like the Hebrew word, "caused" and "did" do not imply *how* God accomplished it, unlike "made".

This was the only word I was unable to translate consistently as one English word in my version of Genesis 1:1-2:4a.

Man – *'adam*: 120 (1:26, 27)
Man: man or mankind

The oddity about the use of *'adam* in Genesis 1 is that the first time it is used it appears without an article (just "man", not "the man"), and it is in association with a plural pronoun "them". The second use has an article, "the man", and then uses a singular pronoun "him". Then Genesis adds that *'adam* was also done male and female which is referred to as "them". One way to take this is to say the first time uses "man" to refer to mankind in general. God said, "Let Us make [mankind] in Our image, according to Our likeness; and let them rule..." Then the second time refers to the male specifically, "And

God created [the man] in His own image, in the image of God He created him; male and female He created them." However, on the flip side, the use of an article in Hebrew does not always refer to a specific item as opposed to a general reference. For example, Genesis 1:14 says, "Let there be lights in the expanse of the heavens to separate the day from the night..." Both day and night have the article in Hebrew, "the day" and "the night", but they do not refer to a specific day or night, only day and night in general. That is the why I think most translations do not distinguish the second use of *'adam* in 1:27 by using "the man". Only Young's Literal Translation and Green's Interlinear Bible include the article; the NASB, NIV, ESV, KJV, and NKJV all leave it off. Because it is associated with the singular pronoun "him", I prefer translating it as "the man", but the last part about "male and female He created them" refers back to mankind in general.

Monsters – *tanniym*:   8577   (1:21)
Sea-**animals:** sea or land animals feared by man

This word refers to any kind of large water or land creature man frequently fears, like snakes and crocodiles. As a land creature it is usually translated as "serpent" (three times in Ex. 7:9-12 for example). It is used 14 times in the Hebrew Bible. Here in 1:21 it is combined with "great" (large or big, same word used in verse 16 to refer to the Sun).

The NASB translating *tanniym* as "monsters" gives it an undesirable mythical connotation, but the word refers to actual living creatures. The KJV's "whale" is too specific, though whales are almost certainly included in the category. I prefer the NIV's "creature" but that could be easily confused with *nephesh* (creature) above. So, to distinguish the two words I suggest using "animal" so 1:21 would read "great sea-animals". I tagged it "*sea*-animals" because, while "*sea*" is not in the Hebrew, the context of Day 5 refers to sea creatures, not land creatures, even though some uses of *tanniym* refer to land creatures.

As a side note, some skeptics have used Ps. 74:13, "You divided the sea by Your strength; You broke the heads of the sea monsters [*tanniym*] in the waters," to say the Bible says *tanniym* sometimes had multiple heads. However, the verse does not refer to multiple heads on one creature, but multiple heads on multiple creatures.

Morning – *boqer*:   1242   (1: 5, 8, 13, 19, 23, 31)
Morning: the lighted portion of a 24 hour period *before sunset*, dawn
See "evening" where "evening" and "morning" are contrasted.

Moves – see "creeps" above. This is not to be confused with the next word "moving".

Moving – *rachaph*:   7363   (1:2)
Brooding: to nurture over something, like a bird on a nest

This word is translated as "moved" in the KJV and "hovering" in the NIV and NKJV. It is also footnoted as "hovering" in the NASB. The consensus of commentators is "hovering", but "brooding" is better because of Dt. 32:11 (*the only other place the word is used*) where God's preparation of His people (Israel) is "Like an eagle that stirs up its nest, that hovers [*rachaph*] over its young." That verse gives a picture of God preparing, protecting and nurturing Israel, not floating above them doing nothing as the English word "hovering" might imply. Therefore, the Spirit of God should be understood as preparing to transform the Earth for the main intent of His creation, i.e. humanity, like parent birds nurturing their young. "Brooding over" means brooding *above*, and should not imply God worrying. Also, because of the Hebrew verb conjugation, "This 'hovering' was not a single and instantaneous act. It rather describes a continued process."[34] (Leupold) Thus, God was not just hovering there on a particular moment. He was there working continuously on preparing the Earth for habitation.

Multiply – *rabah*:   7235   (1:22, 28)
Multiply: to increase in quantity in whatever capacity the word is used
   See "fruitful" for a comparison of "fruitful" and "multiply".

Placed – *nathan*:   5414   (1:17)
Appointed: to give, specifically in this case, for a purpose
   This word is used *very* widely in the Hebrew Bible as the primary verb "to give". In the NASB it is translated as "placed" and in the KJV and NIV it is "set". The idea is that God put (set, placed, gave) the lights in the expanse of heaven *for* a specific purpose. "Appointed" gives a fuller meaning of what God did here however. It is true God gave the lights, but they were also for a purpose. "Placed" or "put" are not good translations because they could carry the connotation God may have manufactured the lights somewhere else and then moved them into place on Day 4.

Plants – *'eseb*:   6212   (1:11, 12, 29, 30)
Plants: very generic word for plants, wild or cultivated
   See "vegetation" for a comparison between "vegetation", "plants", and "trees".

Rule – *radah*:   7287   (1:26, 28)
Rule: to rule in the sense of taking control, taking over, though it can be done positively
   The original Hebrew words and their meanings are always important and the three Hebrew words translated "govern", "rule", and "subdue" serve as excellent examples of how a verse can be misunderstood if a Hebrew dictionary is not consulted. The NASB uses three English words that are near synonyms: "govern" in 1:16 and 18, "rule" in 26 and 28, and "subdue" in 28. In Hebrew they are different.
   "Govern" is *memshalah* from a root word *mashal* which means "to rule" in the sense of having power already.[35] The Sun is said to govern the day in verses 16 and 18, meaning it has been given power to control. It did not take it, it just has it. This is not intended in any personal way as if the Sun or Moon were personal gods. The statement is intended for humility sake, *to humble us*. We do not rule them, they control us. We are at their mercy. We cannot make the Sun rise any sooner or stay longer and we have no control over the phases of the Moon. By extension, because God made these our controllers, we are subservient to Him too.
   The word for "rule" is *radah* and means, "to *tread down*, i.e. *subjugate*; [specifically] to *crumble off*."[36] The sense of the verb "rule", as opposed to "govern", is that control *is not only given, but taken*. It should be noted "rule" *is a verb, not a noun*. God told us to "rule". It does not say He made us "rulers". By proclamation (1:26), permission is given to us to rule, but we must do the subjugating and mastering. The fish, birds, cattle, and land will not bow to us automatically. They are wild and must be controlled. That paints a totally different picture of the original creation from the picture many have in their mind of the Garden of Eden. We may get the picture, especially from illustrated YEC books[37], that all the animals just walked up to Adam and Eve like pets. That is *not* the sense of the original proclamation about humanity ("let them rule over"), nor the blessing given to humanity ("subdue [the land], and rule").
   "Subdue" is *kabash* and means "to *tread* down; hence neg. to *disregard*; pos. to *conquer, subjugate, violate*."[38] "Rule" is to take authority and *kabash* adds a more negative connotation to it because of force or interference resulting from resistance. Both "rule" and "subdue" are used in negative forceful circumstances in the Bible (see Neh. 5:5, 7:28, Jer. 34:11, Zech. 9:15 to name a few). It should be noted God blessed them to "subdue" *the land, not the animals* (1:28). God blessed them to "rule" the animals. This implies the land is what would require more force. If animals are treated right, they may not need harsh measures to keep them in line, but that is not true of plants.

One YEC states, "...the type of *radah* [dominion] must be decided by the *context*. Because these words were spoken by God into an Edenic situation, before the Fall, it is especially hard to imagine any sort of destructive or ruthless implication to them."[39] (Sarfati) He is right and wrong. Context is certainly important and dominion can be done well with a result of peaceful harmony, and it can be done poorly with a result of waste and cruelty, but dominion (rule) must still be *taken*, and an "Edenic situation" does not necessarily imply those ruled will simply fall in line with no resistance. Some destruction was inevitable, like killing animals or making the landscape more hospitable for humanity. If the *whole Earth* had been an Edenic situation then God planting a special garden and placing humanity there makes no sense because anywhere humanity went would have been Eden. The boundaries of the Garden of Eden would have been impossible to discern if nothing looked as wild as we see today. God was there to train Adam and Eve how to take dominion, and it would have gone smoothly, and they could have ruled the land with minimal interference, but the land was still in need of subduing by humanity and this implies some kind of forceful application of dominance.

It is interesting that some groups of animals are left out of Gen. 1:26 and 28. Humanity is not told to rule over the large sea animals from Day 5 or the beasts from the first proclamation on Day 6. Is that because some of them cannot be ruled by us? That could be true, but there is nothing humans cannot kill. However, the ability to kill is probably not the only thing in mind here by "rule". The best leaders are not bullies, but servants. To prove we can kill something might mean we have ruled poorly. We should not forget that authority was given to us, but it can be used excessively and abused.

Separated – *badal*:   914   (1:4, 6, 7, 14, 18)
Separated: to separate or set apart for a special purpose

This word is translated as "divided" in the KJV and NKJV. The two words "separated" and "divided" are synonymous in English, but in Hebrew there are *many* words translated as "separated" and "divided" and it is helpful to see the differences in their uses to determine what the word *badal* means here in Genesis 1. One other word is *parad* as used in Gen. 10:5, 13:8-14, and Dt. 32:8 which means "to spread out", like Abram and Lot spreading out (separating) to avoid disputes. Another is *palag* as used in Gen. 10:25 and Ex. 33:16 which means "to distinguish or tell apart". Another is *chalag* as used in Gen. 14:15 and Num. 26:53-56 which means "to distribute or apportion" like you would distribute possessions in a will. Another is *chatsah* as used in Ex. 21:35 which means "to divide equally or halve". Another is *baqa* as used in Ex. 14:16 and 21 which means "to split or break", like when the Red Sea was split. Another is *bathar* as used in Gen. 15:10 which means "to cut or chop", like cutting up a sacrifice. Because none of these words were used in Gen. 1:4 and 6, we can conclude God *did not* separate the light and darkness or the waters above from the waters below by: spreading them out, making some distinguishing characteristic between them, distributing them like objects, dividing them in half, splitting or breaking them, or cutting them up.

To understand what God actually did, look at the way *badal* is used elsewhere. Exodus 26:33 says, "and the veil shall serve for you as a partition [*badal*] between the holy place and the holy of holies." Leviticus 10:10 in the NIV says, "You must distinguish [*badal*] between the holy and the common, between the unclean and the clean" in the same way that God separated [*badal*] the Israelites from other nations in Lev. 20:24, or separated the Levites from the other tribes in Num. 8:14, or told the Israelites to separate three cities of refuge in Dt. 19:2. One other reference is instructive, Isaiah 59:1-2 reads, "Behold, the LORD's hand is not so short that it cannot save; neither is His ear so dull that it cannot hear. But your iniquities have made a separation [*badal*] between you and your God, and your sins have hidden *His* face from you, so that He does not hear." The meaning one gets from these verses is that *badal* is *a moral or beneficial*

Genesis, Science, and the Beginning

separation between things reserved for special purposes and normal uses, particularly between what is holy (set apart for God's use) vs. what is common. Used in Genesis 1:4 and 6 it means God reserved light and the "waters above" for special purposes, i.e. for the benefit of humanity. Humanity needs light and fresh water, not darkness and salt water.

Spirit – *ruwach*: 7307 (1:2)
Spirit: it can mean Spirit (of God), spirit (of man), wind, or breath

The phrase "Spirit of God" in 1:2 is sometimes translated as "a wind from God" (NRSV) or "a mighty wind" (as footnoted in the NRSV). However, many conservative scholars dispute this reading because the word *rachaph* ("moving" – see above) fits better with the activity of a personal God than an impersonal wind, especially in light of Dt. 32:11. "The use of the similar image of God both at the beginning of the Pentateuch and at the end suggests that it is the picture of the Spirit of God that is intended here."[40] (Sailhamer) Can it be coincidence the only two times *rachaph* is used in the Bible is at the beginning and ending of the Pentateuch? The last use refers to the LORD so it makes sense the first use also refers to the Spirit of God, not a wind.

Sprout – v. *dasha*: 1876 (1:11)
Sprout: to begin a plant's growth, when it first sprouts green from the ground

This word is a verb and is only used one other time in the Bible. Joel 2:22, "Do not fear, beasts of the field, For the pastures of the wilderness have turned green [*dasha*, i.e. sprouted]..." The noun derivative of the word (*deshe'* – see "vegetation" below) is more common. *Dasha* refers to the very beginning of a plant's growth, when it first sprouts green from the ground. The KJV translates it as "bring forth" and the NIV has it as "produce". Unfortunately, both the KJV and NIV cause confusion between verses 11 and 12 because they both translate different Hebrew verbs (*dasha* and *yatsa* – see "bring forth" above) the same which could lead one to believe it was the same word used in both places. The KJV has it as "bring forth" and "brought forth" and the NIV has it as "produce" and produced". The NASB is more accurate with the first as "sprout" (v.11) and the second as "brought forth" (v.12).

Subdue – *kabash*: 3533 (1:28)
Subdue: to take authority by force with expected resistance
See "rule" where three Hebrew words are contrasted.

Surface – *paniym*: 6440 (1:2 (2x), 20, 29)
Face: the front or top side of something, as in the face, or side facing you

This Hebrew word is used very broadly and means forefront, front, or face among many others, including "surface". Three things in Genesis 1 are said to have a "face": the waters (twice in 1:2), the expanse (1:20), and the land (1:29). The face of the waters is understood as the surface. Seas have a top side, a clearly delineated surface. The same is true of the land. But some have taken the "face" of the sky to mean the solid surface of a hard dome over our heads. However, having a top side or front side does not have to mean the object is solid. It just means it has a side facing us. In reference to the expanse one commentator says, "The firmament is regarded as having a face, that is a side turned toward and, as we say, 'facing' the earth."[41] (Leupold) For the ancients the heavens are described as having three levels: the part where the clouds float, the part where the Sun, Moon, and stars are, and the part where angels and God are. The front side of the sky is therefore the part where the clouds are. Verse 20 restricts flying creatures to this front side which turns out to be true.[42] I would have liked to have used "surface" to translate this word, but "surface" is too specific for the sky so I used "face". (See Appendix B for much more on the idea of a solid sky and the face of the sky.)

Appendix A – Word Studies in Genesis

Swarms – n. *sherets*:   8318   (1:20)
Abundant-varieties: a swarm or variety of kinds of animals
   See "teem". Though "swarms" or "abundance" are potential good translations, "abundant-varieties" is preferred because "swarm" and "abundance" imply a large number of one kind of animal and this word refers to many kinds.

Teem – v. *sharats*:   8317   (1:20, 21)
Abound: to move about over a large area in large numbers
   This word means "to *wriggle*, i.e. (by impl.) *swarm* or *abound*."[43] (Strong) Literally, verse 20 reads, "Let the waters swarm with swarms" as in the ESV. The NKJV uses "abound." The KJV uses "bring forth abundantly", but that is confusing with the verb in verses 12 and 24 for "bring forth", *yatsa* (see "bring forth" above). *Yatsa* means "to go out or bring out" whereas *sharats* means "to wriggle or move". *Sharats* does not refer to only water animals as is evident from its use for human reproduction in Gen. 9:7, "And as for you [Noah and family], be fruitful and multiply; Populate the earth abundantly and multiply in it." *Sharats* is "populate abundantly" in the NASB. The word is very generic and in 1:20 refers to nearly all sea creatures that would abundantly reproduce and move in the water. Though the NASB uses "swarm", an incorrect connotation can result. "Swarm" should not be thought of as a swarm of one thing, like a school of one kind of fish. The word *sharats* here has a variety of creatures in mind so the swarm refers to a lot of different kinds of animals, an abundant variety of animals (because it is plural). God did not create seas *full* of many kinds of animals. He created many kinds of animals in unspecified quantities (an abundant variety) and blessed them to fill the seas.

Trees – *'ets*:   6086   (1:11, 12, 29 (2x))
Trees: any plant containing wood; plants normally seen as trees or bushes
   See "vegetation" for a comparison between "vegetation", "plants", and "trees".

Vegetation – n. *deshe'*:   1877   (1:11, 12)
Sprouts: any newly sprouted vegetation
   The words "vegetation", "plants", and "fruit trees" are *deshe'* (a derivative of *dasha* – see "sprout"), *'eseb* (plants or herb), and *periy 'ets* (fruit trees). "Literally verse 11 runs; '…Let the earth vegetate vegetation, herb seeding seed, fruit tree making fruit after its kind.'"[44] (Kidner)
   Deshe' refers to any newly sprouted vegetation. Here the NASB and NIV translate it as "vegetation", but the KJV has it too specifically as "grass". In II Samuel 23:4 David sings of God "as the light of the morning when the sun rises, A morning without clouds, *When* the tender grass *springs* out of the earth, Through sunshine after rain." *Deshe'* is all four words, "tender grass *springs* out". Proverbs 27:25, "When the grass disappears, the new growth is seen, And the herbs of the mountains are gathered in." *Deshe'* is the words "new growth" in this verse, *not* "grass". "Grass" is a different word (*chatsiyr*), translated as "hay" in the KJV (which can be appropriate). The main point here is that *deshe'* refers to *any plants' new growth*, including trees. The plants proclaimed on Day 3 sprouted naturally because that is what the word means, new growth. But the new growth began as a result of God's proclamation, so its origin was supernatural. God must have made the seeds so the land could sprout sprouts. Genesis 2:8 says God planted a garden. What did He plant? The only thing that makes sense is seeds. This first word describing plants is very generic and could refer to *any plant*.
   'Eseb is most often translated as "plant" in the NASB and is also very generic. This is even more evident when the words attached to it are considered. Here it is modified as "plants yielding seed". Genesis 1:29 and 30 specify it as "every plant yielding seed" and "every green plant", and Gen. 2:5 and 3:18 specify it as plants "of the field" (cultivated

227

field). Apparently *'eseb* covers a great many plants, even wild ones. It should be noted that *'eseb* (plant) is qualified to be a little more specific than *deshe'* (sprout) in that it refers to mature plants, not new growth. *'Eseb* also has "yielding seed" attached to it in 1:11. Technically, nearly every plant yields seed, so why does 1:11 specify "plants yielding seed"? One, early mankind may not have known almost every plant has seeds so God is giving them that information, and two, this is a reference to plants which are more beneficial for humanity, i.e. grains. Both could be true.

'Ets refers very generally to all trees, but sometimes means "stick" or "wood". In 1:11 the word "fruit" precedes it to narrow the focus, and the words "bearing fruit... with seed in them" follow it for the same reason. Though it is true that in one sense every tree produces fruit (as we define it – see "fruit" above), some fruits are more desired by humanity than others. Apples are better to eat than pine cones for example. Why did the author qualify "trees" with "fruit" and "bearing fruit with seed in them"? Because, "fruit trees" is specific to what is good for humanity like "plant yielding seed".

Are the plants proclaimed on Day 3 meant to include *all* plants or just those plants humanity would cultivate? Two of the categories listed in 1:11 seem to specify plants beneficial for humanity because they have extra descriptions, but, "vegetation" (sprouts) does not have any specifics attached to it. That seems to indicate it is more generic than the others. So I believe the verse means this, "And God said, 'Let the earth sprout [every kind of] vegetation, [specifically including the two categories meant for humanity to eat] plants yielding seed [grains] *and* fruit trees on the earth bearing fruit after their kind with seed in them." This means there are *three* categories mentioned, *one* that includes all plants, and *two* that are specific to humanity. Again, the very generic nature of Genesis 1 shines through. Genesis 1:11-12 is talking about God originating not only plants on land beneficial for humanity; it is talking about God originating all plants on land in general.

Void – *bohu*:   922   (1:2)
Lifeless: empty of life, lifeless
    See "formless".

Waters – *mayim*:   4325   (1:2, 6 (2x), 7 (2x), 9, 10, 20, 21, 22)
Waters: all waters regardless of what form they take
    This word is plural which is unusual in English, but not uncommon in Hebrew. In Hebrew it is used in a singular sense with singular verbs for example. As a plural it could be taken as referring to different kinds of water (salty, fresh, dirty, bitter, etc.), or different sources of water (springs, rain, streams, etc.) and even different states of water like vapor, snow, or ice (the ancients understood ice was water, Job 38:30). Strong's defines it as the "dual of a primitive noun (but used in a singular sense); water."[45]

Work – *melakah*:   4399   (2:2 (2x), 3)
Work: the task one was sent to do
    This word comes from the root word *malak* which is translated as "angel" (when from God) and "messenger" (when human). *Malak* is a messenger. *Melakah* is the task or ministry of the messenger, that which a messenger is supposed to do[46]. Hence it is also used of employment or "work" because what someone is supposed to do in their employment is what they are "sent" to do by their employer. Of course we understand God has no employer and cannot be sent by anyone to do anything, but He does work. However, God is the only one who can give Himself a task to do. That is what Genesis 2:3 says He did, on the seventh day "...He ceased from all His work which God created to do [for doing]." (This is my translation – see the second objection to Point 4 in Chapter 5 for a defense of it) One important point to notice in Genesis 1 is that "work" is *a noun, not a verb*. Think of "work" like "project" or "work-project".

Translation of Genesis 1:1 – 2:4a

This translation is an attempt to show the simplicity of the original Hebrew text by consistently translating the same Hebrew words exactly the same through the account and emphasizing its generic nature. The only word I was unable to accomplish the task with is *asah* (made or do) because of its wide semantic range. This translation is also an attempt to capture a major feature missing from many English translations – Five times the account uses verbs and nouns derived from one another: sprout sprouts, seeding seed, abound-with abundant-varieties, fliers fly, and moving-things that move (creepers creep). Also, remember that hyphenated words are multiple English words translating one Hebrew word, and italicized words are words not in the Hebrew but are added to clarify what I think the author meant.

Most of the words and phrases used here come from other translations, but they are combined in an attempt to make the whole sound simple. Hopefully and prayerfully this translation will help us understand better this crucial passage of God's Word.

1:[1]In the beginning God created the heavens and the land. [2]And the land was desolate and lifeless, and darkness was over the face of the deep, and the Spirit of God was brooding over the face of the waters.

[3]And God said, "Let there be light"; and there was light. [4]And God saw that the light was good; and God separated the light from the darkness. [5]And God named the light "day", and the darkness He named "night". And there was evening, and there was morning, one day.

[6]And God said, "Let there be an expanding-clear-space in the midst of the waters, and let it separate the waters from the waters." [7]And God caused the expanding-clear-space, and separated the waters which were below the expanding-clear-space from the waters which were above the expanding-clear-space; and so it came to be. [8]And God named the expanding-clear-space "heavens". And there was evening and there was morning, a second day.

[9]And God said, "Let the waters below the heavens be-gathered into one place, and let the dry-ground appear"; and so it came to be. [10]And God named the dry-ground "land", and the gathering of the waters He named "seas"; and God saw that it was good.

[11]And God said, "Let the land sprout sprouts, plants seeding seed *and* fruit trees on the land causing fruit with seed in them according to their kind"; and so it came to be. [12]And the land produced sprouts, plants seeding seed according to their kind, and trees causing fruit with seed in them, according to their kind; and God saw that it was good. [13]And there was evening and there was morning, a third day.

[14]And God said, "Let there be lights in the expanding-clear-space of the heavens, for separating the day from the night, and let them be for signs and for appointed-times and for days and years; [15]and let them be for lights in the expanding-clear-space of the heavens to give light on the land"; and so it came to be. [16]And God caused the two great lights and the stars also, the greater of the

lights to govern in the day, and the lesser of the lights to govern in the night. [17]And God appointed them in the expanding-clear-space of the heavens to give light on the land, [18]and to govern in the day and in the night, and to separate the light from the darkness; [19]and God saw that it was good. And there was evening and there was morning, a fourth day.

[20]And God said, "Let the waters abound-with abundant-varieties of living creatures, and let fliers fly above the land across the face of the expanding-clear-space of the heavens." [21]And God created the great *sea*-animals and every living creature that moves of which the waters abounded according to their kind, and every winged flier according to their kind; and God saw that it was good. [22]And God blessed them, saying, "Be fruitful and multiply, and fill the waters in the seas, and let fliers multiply on the land." [23]And there was evening and there was morning, a fifth day.

[24]And God said, "Let the land produce living creatures according to their kind: large-animals and moving-things and living-things on the land according to their kind"; and so it came to be. [25]And God caused the living-things on the land according to their kind, and the large-animals according to their kind, and every moving-thing on the ground according to their kind; and God saw that it was good.

[26]And God said, "Let Us cause man in Our image, according to Our likeness; and let them rule over the fish of the sea and over the fliers of the heavens and over the large-animals and over all the land, and over every moving-thing that moves on the land." [27]And God created the man in His own image, in the image of God He created him; male and female He created them. [28]And God blessed them; and God said to them, "Be fruitful and multiply, and fill the land, and subdue it; and rule over the fish of the seas and over the fliers of the heavens and over every living-thing that moves on the land."

[29]And God said, "Behold! I have given you every plant seeding seed that is on the face of all the land, and every tree which has fruit causing seed; they shall be food for you; [30]and to every living-thing on the land and to every flier in the heavens and to everything that moves on the land which has life, every green plant *is* for food"; and so it came to be. [31]And God saw all that He caused, and behold, it was very good. And there was evening and there was morning, the sixth day.

2:[1]And the heavens and the land, and all their hosts, were finished. [2]And God finished, on the seventh day, His work which He did; and He ceased, on the seventh day, from all His work which He did. [3]And God blessed the seventh day and sanctified it, because on it He ceased from all His work which God created to do. [4a]That was the account of the heavens and the land when they were created.

Appendix B

The Meaning of רקיע (*raqîa'*) in Genesis: Expanse or Firmament? And what are those "waters above"?

Many people may be under the impression the Hebrew word *yôm* (day) is the most controversial word in Genesis 1 because of its implications to reconciling Genesis with billions of years, but the Hebrew word רקיע (*raqîa'* or *raqiya* – translated "expanse" in the NASB, NIV, and ESV and "firmament" in the KJV, NKJV, and RSV) is far worse a problem. Why? Because *raqîa'* is understood by many liberal *and conservative* scholars to refer to a solid clear hard dome that the writer of Genesis believed separated the waters below the heavens (seas – Gen. 1:7, 10) from the waters above the heavens (a sea suspended above the dome). If Genesis really says the sky is a hard dome with an ocean above it, then a glaring scientific error exists in the first chapter of the Bible and that would have serious effects on the doctrines of Biblical inerrancy and the authority of Scripture. So, the attempt here is to sort through the various evidences from several sides of the issue and make my case *raqîa'* does not present a scientific error, but just the opposite, a scientific accuracy, and thus alleviate any scientific reconciliation issues.

Part I: What is the expanse/firmament of Genesis 1:6?

Three sides take their positions on the meaning of the expanse/firmament and still claim to maintain Biblical inerrancy:

First, many Accommodationists believe "firmament" is an accurate translation of the Hebrew and thus the Bible says the sky is a solid dome (a firm thing). However, despite the scientific error the Bible remains inerrant in their eyes because the primary purpose of the verse is theological (not scientific) telling us God made the sky. This is formally known as *Divine accommodation* (thus the reason for my label Accommodationist) where God accommodated the ignorant cosmology of the Biblical writers to make theological statements they could understand. This position redefines the traditional doctrine of inerrancy.

Second, another side believes "firmament" is a legitimate translation, but says no scientific error exists because the writer was describing the sky as it appears from a human perspective. This is referred to as *phenomenological language* and thus can be taken literally as long as the perspective is taken into account. Other examples would be the words "sunrise" and "sunset". Scientifically we know Earth spins causing the Sun to appear to rise and set from our perspective. According to this second option, Biblical inerrancy is unaffected because there is no scientific error, only a different perspective.

Third, the last side believes "firmament" is not a good translation of the Hebrew. "Expanse" is a better rendering because the word means "that which is expanded" (an expanded thing), and simply refers to an *expanded clear space*. Thus, inerrancy is unaffected because there is literally no scientific error, and an appeal to phenomenological language is not needed. This is a Concordist position.

This appendix will advocate the last one and if it is true, discussions of the legitimacy of Divine accommodation and phenomenological language become unnecessary, though some comments on them will be made near the end. On the other hand, two articles written by Paul Seely[1] compellingly present the first option and these articles, *referenced by nearly everyone* who comments on the issue, are what must be answered.

One might think a dictionary would settle the issue, but definitions of the word *raqîa'* from Hebrew dictionaries (lexicons) and commentaries vary between the two definitions listed above. Seely references five commentaries defining it as "a solid dome over the earth."[2] He then references seven more who define it as "an atmospheric expanse."[3] To these I would add Gesenius who said the firmament was "a hemisphere above the earth... to which the stars were supposed to be fixed, and over which the Hebrews believed there was a heavenly ocean."[4] And Holladay who says, "(beaten, [metal]) **plate, firmament** (i.e. vault of heaven, understood as a solid dome)."[5] And Strong who says, properly "an *expanse*, i.e. the *firmament* or (apparently) visible arch of the sky."[6] Vine says, "the 'expanse,' that which is stretched out"[7] and rejects any attempt to make it solid. Wiseman says, "It refers to the atmosphere surrounding the earth which bears up the clouds."[8] Leupold concurs with Whitelaw on the definition as "'that immense gaseous ocean, called the atmosphere'"[9] and says, "to impute to us notions of a crude view of supernatural waters stored in heavenly reservoirs would be as unjust at [sic] it is to impute such opinions to the writers of the Biblical books. The holy writers deserve at the least the benefit of the doubt, especially when poetic passages are involved."[10] And two recent scholars agree that calling it solid is "too specific" (Sailhamer[11]) and too much of a "literalism" (Collins[12]) for the Hebrew word. The bottom line is scholars of the past and present are solidly divided (pun intended) so the issue cannot easily be decided by scholarship or definition alone. Therefore, the best I can do for you is present the Biblically relevant verses, and make the issues as clear as I can, and let you decide whether or not you think the Bible contains a scientific error here, or whether my interpretations are correct.

Seely wishes to settle the issue by demonstrating ancient peoples from all over the globe had the literal historical understanding the nature of the sky was a solid dome. He impressively documents the ancient beliefs of Pacific Islanders, African tribes, Native-Americans, Europeans, Siberians, Japanese, Chinese, Indians, Sumerians, Egyptians, Hittites, Babylonians, and Greeks. He even shows that the Apocryphal writings of the Jews, and Christian beliefs, in some cases all the way up to the *sixteenth century*, affirmed the sky as a solid dome (but not including New Testament writers because the NT is silent on the subject). I will not dispute any of these (though it may be possible), and I agree that some scientifically naïve people really did believe the sky was a solid dome, including some Jews and Christians. His assessment the belief in a solid sky is the usual natural primitive conception of ancient peoples might also be true.

Add to this the fact that the Jewish people originated from nomads in a Sumerian-Babylonian world, were enslaved by the Egyptians, intermingled with the Canaanites, and were ruled by later Babylonians and Persians and one can realistically conclude the beliefs of these nations must have affected the beliefs of many Jews. That being the case Seely then asks the penetrating question, "But on what basis can it be denied that the Hebrews believed the sky was solid?"

Is there a way to deny the writer of Genesis meant the sky was a solid dome? Well, it might depend on who wrote Genesis 1:1-2:4a and when it was written.[13] However, even if Moses used sources for Genesis written before his time, he still had to put the story in the Hebrew language (or something similar) and chose to use the word *raqîa'* leaving us in the same place we are now, trying to define the word he used. So, if the word means "a firm thing" we would still have a problem, regardless of whether the author was Moses or someone else.

Is it possible the word generically means "that which is expanded" rather than specifically "an expanded hard surface"? If it does that would solve the problem because it would allow what Genesis describes as "the expanded thing" to be misunderstood as a solid surface rather than a clear space. Thus, some readers could have mistakenly believed Genesis says God expanded a solid dome over the Earth when in reality it means God expanded the "heavens" without specifying the exact nature of the sky. Therefore, my case centers on that premise: like other terms Genesis 1 uses (lights, waters, living creatures, beasts, flyers, etc.), *raqîa'* is generic enough to only mean "that which is expanded" *without specifying the nature of what was expanded.* However, I think the text does specify *what* was expanded, but not its nature.

Examining the Biblical use of *raqîa'* and its root word *raqa*

To better understand the meaning of *raqîa'*, an examination should first be made of Bible verses that use its root word *raqa*. The scholars above are just as divided on whether *raqa* primarily means "to hammer/beat out" or "to expand/spread out". If it generically means to expand or spread something out then it follows that *raqîa'* means "that which is expanded or spread out" without implying whether what was expanded was solid or not. On the other hand, if it specifically refers to hammering or beating out something solid then it follows *raqîa'* means "an expanded solid surface that was beaten or hammered out".

***Raqa* is used eleven times in the Old Testament** (italics in Bible quotes below are mine):

Exodus 39:3 says, "Then they *hammered out* [*raqa*] gold sheets and cut them into threads to be woven in with the blue and the purple and the scarlet material, and the fine linen…" By translating *raqa* as "hammered out" the NASB could give the impression that it always has that meaning, but it also could be true that the translators are being more specific than the word requires. Of course, in this case, we know gold sheets are expanded by hammering, *but not everything is expanded that way.* The translators have inserted the more specific English word "hammered" to clarify for the reader what was done, but the term may not require it. It could just as easily read, "they expand the plates of gold" (YLT) or "they expanded (spread out) gold sheets". (The same is true for Numbers 16:39, Isaiah 40:19, and Jeremiah 10:9.)

Psalm 136:6 is different however, "To Him who *spread out* [*raqa*] the earth above the waters…" Here it is the dry ground (land) that is spread out or expanded rather than metal plates. The method God used to do this is not specified, but it should be obvious ancient peoples did not believe He used a big hammer. However, one could still argue that dry ground is solid like metal plates so *raqa* could still mean "to expand a solid thing". The question is: *does it have to mean that*? One must not assume it does. Also, lest anyone accuse the verse above of saying the dry ground is floating on water, please note it simply means the land is *higher than* (above) the water, not floating over it, on it, or in it. Even the ancients could see the land extended out *under* the water. Isaiah 42:5 and 44:24 also refer to God spreading out the land, but 42:5 adds that God also "spread out" (*raqa*) the Earth's "offspring".

Mentioning the Earth's offspring introduces the topic of God's use of secondary (mediated) causes. The Earth is said to be the one producing offspring, not God. God may have caused it, but it was through secondary means. This topic can quickly go way beyond the main subject here and I bring it up only to make this point: God is said to have spread out the land and its inhabitants, but *the Bible does not specify how*. Therefore, when the Bible applies the word *raqa* to *God's actions* we are not to think that necessitates doing it the way humans would. God may act directly and He may act indirectly using secondary causes. When God spreads something out it does not mean He hammered or beat it out the way a human would spread out a gold sheet. It simply generically means He spread it out, expanded it, no matter what "it" is: dry ground, Earth's offspring, sky, or something else.

This would then apply to three other uses of *raqa*, II Samuel 22:43, "Then I [David] pulverized them [his enemies] as the dust of the earth; I crushed and *stamped* [*raqa*] them as the mire of the streets," and Ezekiel 6:11 and 25:6 which talk of people who "stamp" (*raqa*) their feet on the ground. We are not to infer from these uses of *raqa* that the Biblical authors believed God stamped or stomped out the land or the heavens with His foot. God's methods are different from ours and unspecified; therefore, these authors are using the word anthropomorphically.

The special case of Job 37:18

That leaves only one more use of *raqa*. Job 37:18 says, "Can you, with Him, *spread out* [*raqa*] the skies, Strong as a molten mirror?" This verse complicates the issue of claiming the Bible teaches a solid sky because it adds another word to the problem, and also compares the sky to a hard surface. The Hebrew word translated "skies" here is *shachaq* which is translated "clouds" in three other places in Job (35:5, 36:28, and 38:37) and elsewhere. Some may be tempted to insert "clouds" in 37:18 also and suggest the verse is only referring to spreading out the clouds. However, the NASB is correct to not translate it as "clouds" for two reasons. First, it makes no sense in context because clouds are not strong like a molten mirror. And second, the word "skies" also appears in 37:21 with the implication of a sky swept clean, meaning cloudless.

Consider also the previous chapter, Job 36:27-29 says, "For He draws up the drops of water, They distill rain from the mist, Which the clouds [*shachaq*] pour down, They drip upon man abundantly. Can anyone understand the spreading of the clouds [*'âb* – the main Hebrew word for clouds[14]]…" I never have liked it when translations use the same English word to translate two Hebrew words in the same sentence or context. These verses, like others (II Sam. 22:12), speak of clouds *and* the *shachaq* at the same time which means the *shachaq* cannot be clouds.

So, what is the *shachaq* if it is not clouds? Is it just another word for the sky? The word is sometimes used parallel with the familiar word for heavens (*shamayim*) as in Job 35:5, Psalm 36:5, and Jer. 51:9 suggesting they are synonymous. Parallel usage in Hebrew is very common, but it does not mean the words are exact synonyms. Usually, the two parallel words have different nuances that are important, and that is the case here too. The nuance of *shamayim* is that it refers to the heights above the land.[15] The nuance of *shachaq* relates to its root word *shâchaq*. The root word refers to pulverizing or grinding something to dust or miniscule pieces.[16] That leaves the most obvious meaning of *shachaq* as "that which is pulverized", i.e. basically dust (as it is translated and makes contextual sense in Isaiah 40:15). "Dust" also makes sense with Job 37:21.

Shachaq is used repeatedly in contexts where it obviously refers to the sky (like it is in the immediate context of Job 37:18, namely verse 21). That is the reason it is most frequently translated that way. The important question is: *why did the ancients use the word "dust" to refer to the sky?* What made them think the air around us *is* small particles? I do not think the answer is difficult and we would make a grave mistake if we thought the ancients were stupid. People are naturally curious and observant and so were the ancients. Think about the common human experience when a light beam shines through a hole or window into a dark room. What does it show? It shows tiny particles floating around that normally go unseen in bright light and, I might add, most people cannot help but play with it by passing their hand through it or blowing on it. To the ancients this could suggest that tiny unseen particles (pulverized bits) are floating around in the whole clear space of the sky. Thus, it makes sense to say the sky is dust, and scientifically speaking, *clear space contains tiny particles of matter*, even in outer space (how interesting?).

Relating this back to Job 37:18 puts us in an interesting position. As John Walton observes, "...it is not the *rāqī'a* that is spread out but the *šĕhāqîm* [plural of *shachaq* and another way of transliterating it]."[17] Being an Accommodationist, this leads him to suggest the *shachaq* is the Hebrew word that actually refers to the hard dome of the sky, not *raqia'*,[18] because Job 37:18 uses *shachaq*. If that is the case we are left with the same problem. Regardless of the likelihood of *shachaq* meaning "the dust particles of the sky", Job 37:18 is still saying the sky is a hard dome because it is compared to a molten mirror. In order to avoid that conclusion one scholar says, "To assert that this poetical context asserts something about physical cosmology is to accept a severe burden of proof."[19] (Collins) However, even though Job is Hebrew poetry, it still appears to clearly be saying the sky is as hard as a molten mirror. Does that clinch the Accommodationist case for a Biblical scientific error? No, consider who is speaking in Job 37. It is one of Job's "counselors", Elihu. Is it possible Elihu incorrectly believed the sky was solid? Yes. Does that mean the book of Job is advocating his position? No, Elihu was wrong and had no knowledge, as God said in Job 38:2 and 19-20.

In fact God uses the word *shachaq* in 38:37, "Who can count the clouds [*shachaq*] by wisdom...?" If that translation is retained (the NIV, ESV, KJV, and NKJV are all very similar), or if "dust" is substituted, then God is asking Job if he can count the clouds or the dust particles of the sky, which of course he cannot. However, Walton has another suggestion because of the Hebrew structure of the phrase and because he believes the *shachaq* is the hard dome. He says, "I therefore conclude that Job 38:37 is not referring to 'counting the clouds' but to 'appraising the nature of the (solid) skies.'"[20] He has interpreted "(solid)" into the verse because he believes the *shachaq* is the solid dome, but we have just seen that is not necessarily the case; the *shachaq* is more likely the pulverized dust of clear space. If he is right about the translation, think about what God is asking Job. Elihu has just said the sky was solid (37:18) and God then turns around and asks Job if he can truly appraise the nature of the sky (as He also did in verses 19-20). *God is correcting them in this case.* By asking rhetorical questions, God is telling them they did not know the true nature of the sky.

In concluding Job 37:18, one should take note that *raqa* means "to spread out", and Elihu was wrong to compare what God spread out to being strong as a molten mirror.

The conclusion of the meaning of *raqa*

The best we can do then with the meaning of the root word *raqa* by its Biblical uses is to say it generically means *to spread or expand something out*. It does not infer anything about how it was done or the *nature* of what was expanded, except that it is expandable. Its use does not specify that what was expanded has to be a hard surface because it is used to describe spreading out Earth's "offspring".

What about the word *raqia'*? The meaning of its root word only implies it means "an expanded thing", but does its use in the Bible help us determine its nature? Even if people believed the expanded thing was a solid dome, does that mean the word itself requires that definition?

***Raqîa'* is used 17 times in the Bible** (italics in Bible quotes below are mine):

Nine of its uses occur in Genesis 1:6-20 and I will say more about that below. For now, I am more interested in whether its other uses in the Bible give us clues to what it is or its nature.

Daniel 12:3, "Those who have insight will shine brightly like the brightness of the *expanse of heaven [raqîa]*..." Notice here *the whole expanse* shines brightly. It is not referring to the blue part of the sky nor the Sun, Moon, and stars shining brightly. The

235

experience of all people who attempt to look at the sky, particularly on a hazy summer day, is that not only can you not stare at the Sun for long but you also cannot stare at the sky for long either because it is too bright. (I realize that is not always the case but Daniel is referring to times when it is true for his illustration.) Assuming for a moment the Bible says that the sky is a clear firm thing separating a heavenly ocean from the seas down here, as Seely would have us believe, how does a clear firm thing shine? Common human experience is that clouds float in "front" of the blue sky and anyone can see the clouds are the real cause of the brightness of the whole sky. My point in this verse is that *the whole depth of the sky* is what is seen to shine brightly; therefore "expanse" is a reference to the whole sky here, not just a solid clear dome (the blue part).

Psalm 150:1, "Praise the LORD! Praise God in His sanctuary; Praise Him in His mighty *expanse*." Notice here we are told to praise God "in" His sanctuary and "in" His mighty expanse. "In" His sanctuary means everywhere in it, the whole of it. "In" His mighty expanse means the same, *everywhere up there*. It does not mean we or the angels are to praise God only in the limited hard surfaced part of the sky. It is saying *the whole sky* should praise Him.

Psalm 19:1, "The heavens [*shamayim* – same as Gen. 1:1] are telling of the glory of God; And their *expanse* [*raqîa'*] is declaring the work of His hands." Notice here the NASB has put "their" in front of "expanse" interpreting the expanse and the heavens as identical. Regardless of whether that is an accurate interpretation, that they are the same is expressly stated by Genesis 1:8, "And God called the expanse [*raqîa'*] heaven [*shamayim*]." This verse must be equating the two because if it does not then consistency would demand the other four times God "called" something by name (1:5 – light equals day, darkness equals night, and 1:10 – dry-ground equals land, waters equals seas) would not equate those items either.

But Seely says:

> The fact that it is named "heaven(s)" in Gen 1:8 and birds fly in the heaven(s) (Dt. 4:17) seems to imply the raqia' was not solid. But the word shamayim (heaven[s]) is broader in meaning than raqia'. It encompasses not only the raqia' (v. 8; Ps 19:6; 148:4) but the space above the raqia' (Ps 2:4; 11:4; 139:8) as well as the space below (Ps 8:8; 79:2).

Three points should be noted about his argument:

First, both words "heavens" and "expanse" can refer to the same thing and have slightly different nuances. "Heavens" is plural in Hebrew and thus can refer to the whole *and* multiple parts of the whole: i.e. the part where the birds fly, the part where the clouds are, the part where the Sun, Moon, and stars are, and the part where God and the angels are. "Expanse" refers to all of them, the whole expanse above the Earth.

Second, another article responding to Seely makes an excellent point, "he has started with the idea of the solid sky, based on the views of ancient peoples, and forced onto the text divisions in the *shamayim* that are simply not specified, and in the case of Genesis 1, not even permitted, by the text."[21] Seely has forced a division between heavens and expanse *because he has to*, otherwise the Bible says the opposite of what he claims: that the two are one and the same though slightly nuanced in their description. The better approach however is just to see that the Bible equates heavens and expanse and then go where that leads.

And *third*, the verses in Psalms he uses to support his position only specify what is in the *heavens* (*shamayim*), i.e. the Sun, waters, God, and birds. They say nothing of what is in the *expanse* (*raqîa'*), or draw a distinction between "heavens" and "expanse". Therefore, Seely has not made a good case that "heavens" and "expanse" are different, and because the textual evidence supports them being the same, *Seely's whole argument*

Appendix B – The Meaning of "expanse" and the "waters above"

collapses. If the Bible says the "expanse" and the "heavens" are the same (and it does) then, even by Seely's own admission above, the *raqîa'* is not solid.

Seely also makes much of the use of *raqîa'* in Ezekiel and makes this interesting comment:

> As for the rest of the OT, the word *raqîa'* is used a number of times usually in contexts that do not help us define the word any further than saying it means "sky." But in Ezekiel 1 the nature of a firmament is described. This is the clearest description of a *raqîa'* found in the OT... As to the composition of this firmament, it looked like "terrible crystal or ice."

Ezekiel 1:22-23 and 25-26 say:

> Now over the heads of the living beings there was something like an *expanse* [*raqîa'*], like the awesome gleam of crystal, spread out over their heads. Under the *expanse* their wings were stretched out straight... And there came a voice from above the *expanse* that was over their heads; whenever they stood still, they dropped their wings. Now above the *expanse* that was over their heads there was something resembling a throne, like lapis lazuli in appearance; and on that which resembled a throne, high up, was a figure with the appearance of a man.

We have just seen the other times the OT uses *raqîa'* helps define the word as "the whole depth of the sky" and Seely seems to agree with that by saying, "As for the rest of the OT... it means 'sky.'" These other verses are specifically talking about the sky above the Earth, but Ezekiel is talking about *visions* he saw (Ezek. 1:1) and is attempting to describe them. Visions, by their very nature, do not reflect reality as we experience it. In fact, the purpose of visions in the Bible is always theological, not for revealing the physical nature of the world on which we live. It seems Seely has chosen the most dubious Bible verses to support his position and passed over the very ones that disprove him by describing the *raqîa'* as "the whole depth of the sky".

Seely also says:

> ...there is no reason to differentiate the *raqîa'* in Ezekiel 1 from the *raqîa'* in Genesis 1. On the contrary there is good reason to identify the one with the other. For we can see in Ezekiel that above the firmament is the throne of God in glory (vv. 26-28) just as above the firmament of heaven described in Genesis is the throne of God in glory (I Kgs 22:19; Ps 2:4; 11:4; 103:19; Isa 6:1; 14:13; 66:1).

The lengthy list of verses he references all say essentially the same thing – God's throne is in *heaven*. But saying God's throne is in heaven is not the same as saying the firmament is a solid dome, especially since *none of the verses he lists even uses the word raqîa'* (except Ezekiel of course). His assertion that there is good reason to equate the *raqîa'* of Ezekiel with the *raqîa'* of Genesis is also very poorly supported. He is only asserting it is true and listing verses that have nothing to do with his assertion.

Other visions of God sitting on a throne lifted up above some kind of surface that is difficult to describe appear in the Bible: Ex. 24:9-10 where Moses and Aaron and 72 others "...saw the God of Israel; and under His feet there appeared to be a pavement of sapphire..."; Isaiah 6:1 where God is seen "...on a throne, lofty and exalted, with the train of His robe filling the temple"; and Revelation 4:6 "...before the throne there was, as it were, a sea of glass like crystal..." Even granted that the *raqîa'* that Ezekiel saw seemed solid, are we meant to understand these visions of the solid thing below God's throne is the same thing as the sky above us? If so, *that is not at all clear in the texts.*

Does the fact that God is said to be in heaven (*shamayim*) imply the Bible intended these visions to describe some physical reality above a solid dome? That conclusion does not follow, especially considering *the Bible equates the heavens and the expanse* as we saw above. If they are the same, and God is said to be in the heavens, then He is also in the expanse. Basing one's definition of *raqia'* primarily on one passage of Scripture describing a heavenly vision obviously intended to represent something beyond our normal existence is unwise hermeneutics.

As we have seen, the root word *raqa* means "to expand or spread out something" which leads us to believe *raqia'* means "something that was expanded or spread out" which is consistent with *raqia'*s uses in the Bible. Even in Ezekiel the word is describing something spread out or expanded below (or around) God's throne, *solid or not*. The other use of *raqia'* in Ezekiel at 10:1 supports it is not solid by describing the same scene later, "Then I looked, and behold, in the expanse that was over the heads of the cherubim something like a sapphire stone, in appearance resembling a throne, appeared above them." Notice here the throne is described as being *in the expanse*, not above it. It appears the expanse Ezekiel saw was more than just a solid floor below the throne. But even if it is not, *drawing the conclusion a solid floor in Ezekiel's visions is the same as the sky above us does not follow*.

And that leaves us with the nine uses of *raqia'* in Genesis. Five times it appears in 1:6-8:

> Then God said, "Let there be *an expanse* in the midst of the waters, and let it separate the waters from the waters." God made *the expanse*, and separated the waters which were below *the expanse* from the waters which were above *the expanse*; and it was so. God called *the expanse* heaven…

Three times in 1:14-17:

> Then God said, "Let there be lights in *the expanse* of the heavens to separate the day from the night, and let them be for signs and for seasons and for days and years; and let them be for lights in *the expanse* of the heavens to give light on the earth"; and it was so. God made the two great lights, the greater light to govern the day, and the lesser light to govern the night; He made the stars also. God placed them in *the expanse* of the heavens to give light on the earth…

And one last time in 1:20:

> Then God said, "Let the waters teem with swarms of living creatures, and let birds fly above the earth in the open *expanse* of the heavens."

I have five observations regarding these verses and Seely's arguments concerning them:

First, notice in verse 6 that the expanse is proclaimed to be *in the midst* of the waters (that is, in between them). I take the waters above the expanse to be nothing more than clouds, or more specifically the rain that falls from the clouds, and I will develop that thought more fully below. For now, assuming that is the case, the expanse is thus specifically defined as the *space* that was expanded *between* the seas and the clouds. Prior to the proclamation on Day 2 there was no expanse, no space between the clouds and the ocean, thus implying a fog (clouds) went all the way down to the surface. This fog was responsible for the darkness on Earth's surface mentioned in Gen. 1:2 and Job 38:9. Also, because the expanse above the Earth (the heavens) is what we see through from the surface, and God's proclamation on Day 2 limited the expanse to be *between* the waters, we can conclude that a hypothetical observer on Earth at that time would not have

Appendix B – The Meaning of "expanse" and the "waters above"

been able to see past the clouds (like an overcast day), nor could they see what was causing the light.

Second, Seely points out the statement "God made [*asah*] the expanse..." uses the verb *asah* which is "...a verb which often means 'manufacture,'" and this in conjunction with the word "separate", "...implies a tangible, i.e., solid divider." Though the word *asah* can sometimes be *interpreted* as "manufacture," that is not its primary meaning, and it can only be interpreted that way when it is commonly known the item was actually assembled somehow. Generally the word means "to cause something to happen"[22] and is most often translated as a form of the common verb "to do" (did, done, does, etc.). In this case, because we do not know *how* God "did" or "caused" the *raqîa'* between the waters, we cannot say whether it involved manufacturing something solid or not. Seely also suggests, "It would be unnatural to use [*asah*] to say God made space. Nor is it a particularly apt word for saying God made air." I do not see why not. The word is used in many locations in the sense of God making *everything*. For example, II Kings 19:15, "Thou [God] hast made [*asah*] heaven and earth" (using the merism[23] of Gen. 1:1) and Psalm 146:6, "Who [God] made heaven and earth, the sea and all that is in them..." (using the same language as Ex. 20:11). (See also II Chr. 2:12, Ps. 121:2 and 134:3 and others.) Besides, if the text had said "God made space" it would not have conveyed the idea the clear space above the Earth was *expanding*, which is the main reason for using the word *raqîa'* in the first place.

Third, Seely argues using the word "separate" with "made" implies the *raqîa'* was a solid divider. That interpretation has a major flaw involving the definition of the Hebrew word *badal* (separate) as used in Genesis 1:4 and 6-7. The word refers to a separation of something for "special" purposes as opposed to something for normal use, in this case something reserved for humanity's benefit.[24] What is so beneficial to man about a separation of waters? The answer is really quite striking: the waters above are *fresh* water and the waters below are *salt* water. God was making a "special" separation of waters for humanity's benefit because we were going to need fresh water. The same is true for the separation of light and darkness in Genesis 1:4. It was done for the benefit of life. Therefore, the word "separated" as used here in verses 6 and 7 has nothing to do with manufacturing a solid dome. It refers to a different kind of separation altogether, a separation for special purposes.

Fourth, I have already discussed in detail in Chapter 2 why the phrase "in the expanse of the heavens" is repeated three times in the text of Gen. 1:14-17. It is emphasizing that the proclamation God made on Day 4 was for the lights to come to be in *the expanding clear space* of the heavens; that is, the heavens would be expanding to become something bigger than the space between the clouds and the sea to which they were limited by the proclamation on Day 2. The expanse would now expand out to contain the sources of the lights from Day 1, and thus it could be said "it was so" that the lights came to be "in the expanse of the heavens." The Day 4 proclamation was not for the lights to be placed in a solid dome. However, that is the way Seely sees it:

> Gen 1:17 also testifies that the *raqîa'* is not air or atmosphere for it says God placed the stars (and probably the sun and moon) 'in the *raqîa'* of the heavens.' But the stars are not located in the air or atmosphere. So we know the *raqîa'* (in which 1:17 locates them) cannot be air or atmosphere.

In response I would simply point out *Genesis does not say the expanse is air or atmosphere*. The text is not that specific. The expanse is the same as the heavens and is defined after the proclamation on Day 4 to be the clear space between Earth's surface and the stars (i.e. as far out as humanity can see). Genesis only says that the Sun, Moon, and stars were appointed (set[25] – NIV, ESV) in *the expanded thing*, not in the atmosphere.

Fifth, Seely argues that the *raqîa'* is a hard surface because Gen. 1:20 says "let birds fly above the earth across the face of the firmament of the heavens" (NKJV):

> This phrase *upon the face* (surface) or in *front of* the *raqîa'* is important in that it implies the *raqîa'* was neither space nor atmosphere. For birds do not fly *upon the surface* or in *front of* space or air, but rather *in* space or air. This distinction is illustrated in the case of fish, which no one would say swim *upon the surface* or in *the front* of the water (Gen 7:18) but rather *in* the water (cf. Exod 7:18, 21).

It is true the Bible says the *raqîa'* has a front side and birds are proclaimed to be restricted to this location. But what does that mean? The Hebrew word for face/surface/front is the same word used in Gen. 1:2 in reference to the "surface of the deep" and "surface of the waters". Seely says it must mean the *raqîa'* is solid because atmosphere cannot have a surface or front side. But I say that is incorrect. From the writer of Genesis' viewpoint (i.e. the surface of the Earth[26]) the sky above was mysterious except several facts were known about it. Rain fell from it. The clouds floated in it. The Sun, Moon, and stars were up there in it. And other Biblical writers added God and the angels were up there in the heavens too. All these things were said to be in the heavens and it does not appear the writers of the Bible knew exactly where it started or how far out it extended, but the word *raqîa'* (expanse) *was used to describe it all* as we have just seen above. Because the expanse describes it all, and heavens is plural describing the sum of its parts, one could rightly say that birds fly across the face of the expanse, i.e. the front side of the heavens or the lowest part of all that is up there. The closest (lowest) part to us can be called its face and the birds are restricted to that location.[27]

The reason Genesis *limited* flying creatures to the lowest part of the heavens, the face or front side *of the whole expanse*, and limited them to reproduce "on the earth [land]" (Gen. 1:22), is because it was attempting to prevent the ancients from thinking any flying creature could reproduce on, or fly to, the Sun, Moon, or stars. Genesis 1:26, 28, and 30 refer to "birds of the sky [*shamayim* – "heavens"]" and not birds of the expanse because the proclamation on Day 4 expanded the expanse to include the Sun, Moon, and stars, and birds cannot go there. This is really quite amazingly detailed and accurate for pre-scientific times.

One more note is in order concerning Seely's reference to Gen. 7:18 which says, "the ark floated on the surface of the water." It is possible that in the case of something transparent like the "deep" or "expanse" that the "surface" (face or front) could be defined as extending into the transparent subject. As we know, ships extend down into the water upon which they float, but yet it is still described here as the "surface". The reason fish are not said to swim *only* upon the face of the deep is because they are not confined there. They go deeper than we can see.

We can conclude then: the Biblical meaning of the word *raqîa'* (expanse) in Genesis 1 is the clear space that was expanded above the Earth. John Walton has recently come to a similar conclusion, "Looking carefully at the contexts in which [*raqîa'*] is used, I agree with what has been a common understanding – that it refers to the space between heaven and earth (NIV "expanse")."[28] I think Walton is correct when he says "expanse" is a good translation and I am glad he has come that far, but he misses that the expanse is *not* the space "between heaven and earth"; *it is the clear space that is the heavens.* It refers to *the whole sky, all that can be seen above the Earth from the surface.* That is a natural human perspective of the universe. It is described as expanding because according to Genesis God expanded it from a time of total darkness when the clouds (the waters above) came all the way down to the surface of the Earth (cf. Gen. 1:2 and Job 38:9), to a clear space limited to between the waters (Gen. 1:6), and finally to a clear space that included the Sun, Moon, and stars (Gen. 1:14). Can it be coincidence that this expanding of the clear space of the heavens matches the story told by modern science? I think not. The *raqîa'* of Genesis is not a scientific blunder of the Biblical author's ancient cosmology; it is a scientific accuracy corroborating the Divine inspiration of Scripture.

Dispensing with two last Biblical arguments for a solid sky

First, according to Seely, if the author of Genesis had wanted to convey the idea the *raqîa'* was an atmospheric expanse then he could have used other Hebrew words better suited for that purpose. It is not necessary to counter all his suggestions individually. I will simply point out that all the options Seely suggests cannot convey the one crucial concept the author of Genesis wished to express. None of the other words convey the idea God *expanded the clear space of the heavens*. The main point of Genesis using the word "expanse" is to tell us God expanded our view of the heavens.

Second, Seely demonstrates that many ancient peoples believed there were literal holes in the sky. Since many people believed the sky was solid it should come as no surprise they also believed there were holes in it. The question though, as above, is not whether people believed it, but rather whether the Bible teaches it. Seely sees Biblical support for this in verses referring to "windows" in heaven and so it is those verses we must examine.

Of its nine occurrences there are three obvious literal uses of the Hebrew word "windows" (*'arubbâh*) in the Bible: a normal window (Eccl. 12:3), a nesting hole or covey for doves (Is. 60:8), and a chimney (Hos. 13:3). Because the method for making these "windows" is known and they allow observable knowledge of their nature, the verses should be taken literally.

The question is then: are there any metaphorical uses of the term? Yes, at least two uses are obviously metaphorical in the sense that one (Is. 24:18) refers to wrath that comes down from God and the other (Mal. 3:10) refers to blessings that come down from God. The Isaiah verse is obviously metaphorical unless someone wants to argue the "pits" and "snares" are literal, and the Moon and Sun can experience emotions (v. 23). The Malachi verse is obviously metaphorical unless one wants to argue God literally has to open holes in the sky to send financial blessings down to humanity. Again, as we saw above with the word *raqa* (to expand), when actions are carried out by God, the specifics of *how* that occurs are not known so in order to describe God's actions a metaphor or figure of speech is used.

Two more of the Biblical uses (II Kings 7:2 and 19) are interesting in that they express doubt on the part of the speaker that Israel's desperate circumstances at the time could be changed even *if* "the LORD should make [*asah*] windows in heaven." His doubt possibly shows that not everyone believed there even were windows in heaven because if there were, God would not have had to have *made* them. Because we are dealing with a hypothetical here it is difficult to draw any solid conclusions either way from these verses. The man did not believe God was going to do what Elisha said and it cost him his life. Whether he actually believed it was possible to make windows in heaven, or was just using a figure of speech, is unknown.

That leaves us with the last two uses of *'arubbâh* which occur in Genesis and are the main verses Seely uses to support his case. Genesis 7:11 says, "the floodgates [windows – KJV] of the sky were opened" and 8:2 says, "the floodgates of the sky were closed." The author intends to tell us God caused it to rain heavily for 40 days at the Flood and He stopped it after that. The question here is whether "floodgates" (windows) is metaphorical or not. Considering that when God's actions are referenced Biblical authors use words that describe His actions as best as possible using metaphors and anthropomorphisms, I would say these two verses in Genesis are metaphorical and not literal. The author did not know exactly how God did what He did and so he used a metaphor and thus Seely's argument falls apart.

Similarly, the one reference in the Bible to "doors of heaven" (Ps. 78:23), is also clearly metaphorical for God being generous by sending manna from heaven. I find it very difficult to believe anyone, even the Jews coming out of Egypt, would think that God must literally open doors in the heavens to get something to Earth, or that He really uses doors to keep the sea in place (Job 38:8, 10). If "doors" is literal in Job, then so is "bars", but bars cannot be literal because water obviously cannot be kept behind bars.

As a final note, one should notice the Bible speaks of windows of "heaven" (*shamayim*), but never windows of the *raqîa'* (expanse) as one might expect if the Bible taught the expanse was a solid thing with holes in it. As for these Biblical references to "windows" in heaven, they are metaphorical descriptions of God's actions when He "opens" the heavens and sends something from above. They are not meant to be understood as actual holes in the sky.

The Origin of the King James Translation of *raqîa'* as "firmament"

If all that I have said above about the Biblical definition of *raqîa'* is true, then why was it translated as "firmament" in the KJV? The answer is telling of the origin of the real problem. The English word "firmament" comes from the Latin word *firmamentum* (a firm thing) which is the Latin Vulgate translation of the Greek word *stĕrĕōma* ("something established")[29] – from another word meaning "to solidify" hence the connotation of solidity) used in the Septuagint (LXX) to translate the Hebrew word *raqîa'* ca. 250 BCE. What we have here is a chain of translation built upon a word choice made more than 2000 years ago. The LXX translators were Jewish and one might think they would have chosen a Greek word that expressed a good definition of the Hebrew. However, later Jewish scholars did not think so and have maintained the Masoretic Text of the Hebrew Bible rather than those based upon the LXX.

The most likely reason the LXX translators chose that Greek word is because *they were trying to reconcile the text to the "science" of their day*. And, as Seely has so meticulously demonstrated, some Greeks and Jews of the 3rd century BCE believed the sky was a solid dome. So, it should come as no surprise that the translators chose a word that matched their "knowledge". However, as we have just seen, the Biblical use of the word *raqîa'* does not support such a translation. This all just goes to show the importance of defining Biblical words consistently with their Biblical use, otherwise errors creep in and threaten the stability of the text, and here we are, left with the baggage of a traditional translation of *raqîa'* as "firmament" and most people do not see the problem, i.e. the potential scientific error in the translation. Thankfully, some of the best modern translations (NASB, NIV, and ESV) have corrected "firmament" to "expanse" and thus eliminated the scientific appearance of error.

Divine accommodation and phenomenological language

With the "expanse" defined as *"the whole sky, all that can be seen above the Earth from the surface,"* it is unnecessary to resort to Divine accommodation or phenomenological language to maintain Biblical inerrancy. However, there are several aspects of both that I believe need to be addressed.

Divine accommodation is the idea that God inspired humans to write Scripture but did not prevent them from including their own errant scientific or historic details. (See Chapter 10) The Bible could then be seen as theologically inerrant, but not scientifically inerrant. Thus, scientific "errors" of any sort can be dismissed while weakly (in my opinion) holding to some kind of authority structure to Scripture. Making any attempt to reconcile the Bible to modern science becomes impossible by this thinking. Four thoughts come to mind:

First, Divine accommodation calls into question any miraculous event in the Bible. Any writer describing a miracle could be accused of scientific error because miracles are scientifically impossible to many. And if the resurrection is seen as scientific error Christianity would crumble to moralistic musings rather than a personal relationship with our Creator – Jesus Christ.

Second, Divine accommodation goes against the principle that inspired Scripture corrects us. II Timothy 3:16 says, "All Scripture is inspired by God and profitable for teaching, for reproof, for correction, for training in righteousness." In what ways do scientific errors teach and correct us? Call me naïve if you wish, but I believe God is big enough to prevent ignorant humans from making mistakes if He so desires.

Third, dividing truth into categories is impossible because error in any category affects the others. What is theological truth as opposed to scientific truth? "Truth is what corresponds to its object... As applied to the world, truth is the way things really are."[30] (Geisler) Truth is what corresponds to reality regardless of whether it describes God or nature. The Bible says God made (caused) the expanse (Gen. 1:7). If, as Seely asserts, the writer of the account meant God manufactured the solid dome of the sky, and the part about the sky being a solid dome is in error, what does that say about God making it? Is that also in error? In many scientists' minds science conflicts with God miraculously making anything. But, if God really did it, would that not also be a scientific fact? In that sense, scientific truth is inseparable from theological truth. If the Bible contains errors, calling them scientific and dismissing them as human ignorance does not contribute to the case for inspired inerrancy; it weakens it, if not destroys it.

And fourth, attempting to dismiss a solid sky as human fallibility ignores one of the main points of Genesis 1:6, "Then God said, "Let there be an expanse in the midst of the waters..." We cannot ignore that the writer of Genesis is telling us *God said this*. Are we to believe God's actual fiat was in error or He did not really say those words? Then what did He say and how would we know? If He did not say that proclamation then He probably did not say the others either. Did He say or do anything? Can we say anything is accurate about the account? Only that God created everything? But, why should I even believe that if nothing else is literally accurate? And the dominos continue to fall... The way I see it, if the word *raqîa'* means a solid dome the problems for Biblical authority, Divine inspiration, and inerrancy are insurmountable.

Divine accommodation is not a slippery slope to Biblical deterioration; it is a monstrous precipice of no return.

Phenomenological language is the idea the Bible describes phenomena as they appear from a human perspective. The idea is helpful when used appropriately. The best example is sunrise and sunset. From our perspective the Sun appears to move but we know in reality it is Earth that is moving in relation to the Sun. Because the writers of the Bible were writing from a human perspective it is not error to say the Sun rises or traverses the sky because it really does *from our perspective*.

However, in the case of Genesis 1:6-7 it would be inappropriate to call this an instance of phenomenological language because the problem is more complicated. Genesis says God proclaimed the existence of the expanse. Are we to believe that means, "And God said something like (because we really do not know what He said), 'Let something that looks like a solid dome come to be in the midst of the waters...'"? Also consider there are waters above this thing that looks like a dome. Phenomenological language still puts error in God's words or leaves us not knowing what He really said.

Divine accommodation and phenomenological language are not necessary to maintain Biblical inerrancy in this instance and in fact do not help to solve the scientific errors that would occur if *raqîa'* refers to a solid dome.

Part II: What then are the waters above the expanse in Genesis 1:7?

Three sides take their positions on the meaning of the waters above the expanse/firmament:

First, one side believes "firmament" means a solid dome separates the waters below the firm thing (seas) from the waters above the firm thing (an ocean of water held in place by the dome). (Seely's position)

Second, another side believes the "expanse" refers to the intervening space between the waters, but the waters refer to the basic material building blocks (H$_2$O) that God used to make the Earth and the rest of the universe in 6 days.[31]

Third, the last side says, as I have argued above, as a result of the proclamation on Day 2 the expanse was once *limited* to being between the waters below (seas) and the waters above (rain or clouds), but has since expanded as a result of the proclamation on Day 4 beyond the waters above to include the Sun, Moon, and stars. The waters above are thus simply rain, rain clouds, or just clouds and are *no longer above the expanse*; they are in it.

First position: Are the waters above the firmament an ocean held back by a solid dome?

Before I answer Seely's arguments for a heavenly ocean I want to point out two important factors that already argue against that conclusion.

First, we have already seen the Biblical evidence that the *raqîa'* refers to the entire "expanse" of the heavens, i.e. the whole sky. With that being the case, any argument attempting to prove a Biblical heavenly ocean held back by a solid dome will have to do a better job of defining the expanse as a solid dome, otherwise there is no dome to hold back the waters.

Second, Seely does not recognize an apparent contradiction in there being a heavenly ocean above a solid dome and God's throne being above the dome. According to Seely the Ezekiel texts imply the Jews believed God's throne was sitting on the dome. So, where is the ocean of water then? Is God submerged in it? There are no Biblical texts that mention God's throne in relation to a great sea of water. Revelation 4:6 refers to a great sea of glass around the throne, but does not mention water. There is a lake of fire, but no heavenly ocean. One could speculate and say there was also heavenly land above the dome but it would be without any Biblical support. These texts attempting to describe heavenly visions are obviously not intended to describe reality as we experience it on Earth. I am not denying a heavenly reality. I am denying the textual interpretations of people who want to take them more literally than they were intended.

Seely's arguments for a heavenly ocean

Seely has three arguments he uses to support his case:

First, he says, "The concept of 'waters above the firmament'... reflects an ancient Near Eastern concept, particularly shaped by a Mesopotamian tradition found in *Enuma Elish*."[32] Again, as discussed above in relation to a solid dome, the fact that people believed in a heavenly ocean does not require the Biblical writers to believe the same unless it can be demonstrated.

This same conclusion applies to Seely's argument that later generations of Jews and early Christians believed there was a heavenly ocean. Seely shows that Jews believed it by quoting apocryphal sources, but that is my point. The Bible does not say the same as the apocryphal sources. If it did Seely would have quoted *it* and probably not bothered

Appendix B – The Meaning of "expanse" and the "waters above"

with anything else. Also, the fact these apocryphal sources have such a faulty view of the sky could be one reason (among many) they were not canonized.

Second, Seely agrees with another commentator and says, "…by not naming the waters above the firmament as he named the waters below (Gen 1:9-10) God signified that He had excluded them from the world made for man."[33] This argument is not a good one. If it were true then we could conclude that everything God did not name was excluded from man's world. Since God only named five things (day, night, heavens, earth, and seas), that would exclude a lot of creation. The truth is, the waters above the expanse are mentioned in the text of *Day 2* and *neither waters are named there*, only the space between them. "Earth" and "seas" are named after the fulfillment of the proclamation on *Day 3* which has nothing to do with the expanse, so that is why the waters above are not named there.

Seely adds that his idea is supported by the "waters above" never being mentioned again in the Bible (except Ps. 148:4).[34] I submit to you the reason they are not mentioned again is because Biblically *they are no longer above the expanse* so it is inappropriate to refer to them as the "waters above". The heavens expanded to include the Sun, Moon, and stars as a result of the Day 4 proclamation and so the "waters above" are now *within* the expanse, part of the multiple layers of the heavens, but they are still there doing what God intended them to do – watering the Earth with fresh water for humanity. Also, should someone accuse Psalm 148:4 of saying the "waters above" are above the whole heavens, I would respond the Psalm is representing praising God in *all* the "layers" of the heavens (i.e. where the angels are (vss. 1-2); where the Sun, Moon, and stars are (vs. 3); as far out as it goes – "the highest heavens" (vs. 4a); and finally where the clouds are (vs. 4b)). The reference to "the waters that are above the heavens" refers only to the lowest part where the clouds are.

Third, Seely emphatically asserts, "Genesis 1, in fact, repeatedly and from many angles makes it impossible to believe that its writer thought 'the waters above the firmament' was everyday clouds (much less a water canopy beneath the sun)."[35] The evidence he gives for this is not as good as he thinks though.

He says, "In Gen 1:1-2 the writer gives us a picture of an unformed earth immersed completely in a *tehom*."[36] I agree *tehom* (the deep) refers to a deep ocean, but I disagree that planet Earth was unformed. The phrase "formless and void" is better translated as "desolate and empty"[37] and even the NASB footnotes it as "a waste and emptiness". At best Seely can claim the Bible says the land was unformed, but the fact Genesis describes a deep ocean covered in darkness does not rule out the possibility planet Earth was already formed (even if the ancients did not understand how that was possible). It had been created in the beginning (the time before the 7 Days[38] – Gen. 1:1).

He then makes his second assertion:

> In v. 3 the creation of light dispels the darkness that was over the sea (v. 2), but there is no indication that fog or clouds were then seen covering the sea. If anything, the picture of the Spirit (or wind) of God moving upon the face of the waters implies clear visibility of the sea. In any case it would be gratuitously adding to Scripture to say that there were clouds or vapor above the sea. Consequently, the idea that the firmament in v. 6 was placed between the clouds and the sea is completely without biblical foundation.[39]

I agree that up to the point of verse 5 there is no indication of a fog, but he is already assuming the waters above the expanse are not clouds before that has been established by the text. If anything, the text through verse 5 is ambiguous about a fog. Clearly, the Spirit of God moving upon the waters *does not* imply visibility of the sea because the Spirit is mentioned in verse 2 *before Day 1 begins, when it was still dark!* Light had not appeared and the text *specifically tells us it was dark* while the Spirit was hovering over the waters. And I say that Job 38:8-9 is not "gratuitously adding to Scripture" when it says, "Or who enclosed the sea with doors When, bursting forth, it went out from the womb; When I made a cloud its garment And thick darkness its swaddling band?" I say those verses *explicitly tell us* a cloud (fog) covered the sea some time after the land's foundations were laid. Light could certainly have appeared on the surface on Day 1 while a fog covering still existed. Therefore, Seely's conclusion about verse 6 is what "is completely without biblical foundation."

He then goes into a lengthy demonstration that there must have been water on both sides of the expanse. *I agree the text clearly sets that forth.* Where I disagree with him though is when he concludes it was "sea water"[40] on both sides of the expanse. I agree the text says the waters above originated from the waters of the deep listed in verse 2, but it does not say the waters above were salty. Seely has added that detail and has missed that the separation of waters involves separating water apart from the sea for humanity's special purpose and need.[41] Water reserved for the special purpose of humanity cannot be salty, therefore the waters above the expanse must be fresh water. *The text* in no way concludes the waters above the expanse were another salty sea.

Seely also believes that proving there were waters on both sides of the expanse makes it impossible for the waters above to be clouds because the Sun, Moon, and stars were proclaimed to come to be in "the expanse of the heavens" on Day 4. According to Seely that would put them in front of the clouds (if the waters above were the clouds) because the proclamation on Day 2 said the expanse was to come to be "in the midst" of the waters, and if the expanse is between the waters, and the Sun, Moon, and stars are in the expanse, then they are below the clouds too. The problem is, he has missed that the proclamation on Day 4 was meant *to expand the heavens beyond the clouds* to include the Sun, Moon, and stars, not to put the lights in the space between the waters. That is why it is called an expanse, because it is expanding. "And God said, 'Let there be lights in the expanding-clear-space [*raqîa'*] of the heavens...'" (my translation[42] of Gen. 1:14) The Sun, Moon, and stars are not coming to be between the clouds, they are coming to be in an expanding clear space, the *raqîa'*.

Seely's arguments for the "waters above" being a heavenly ocean all fail.

Second position: Were the waters above the expanse the basic building blocks of all matter in the solar system or universe?

In response to that title question I can imagine some readers have a funny look on their face asking, "What the...?!" Obviously, that interpretation does not come from the text. No one would ever get such an idea by reading Genesis 1 by itself, especially before the modern age. So, where does it come from?

This idea arises out of some Young-Earth Creationists trying to reconcile the apparent great age of the universe with their interpretation of the Genesis account. In other words, they are reading *their* science into the text. They suggest, "...the 'waters above' are at the outer limits of the universe..."[43] or are at the "...perimeter of the solar system..."[43] Another puts it, "...it is our suggestion that these 'waters' were the originally-created, basic building blocks of matter that the earth was made from, and otherwise became all that was created outside of our atmosphere and/or our solar system... We are not told what became of these 'waters' above the *raqiya'* in Genesis."[44] He then takes a similar position to Seely in saying the "waters above" are not mentioned again in the Bible. I have four responses:

First, again, the reason the waters above are not mentioned again in the Bible is because they are no longer above the expanse. The expanse (heavens) expanded as a result of the proclamation on Day 4 to include the location of the Sun, Moon, and stars and thus extends beyond the clouds so the clouds are now *in* the expanse, not above it.

Second, the text of Genesis says nothing like the waters above were so far off the Earth they were invisible. The waters above the expanse are talked about as if a person could see and identify them *like everything else in the account*. Every other word in Genesis 1 refers to something any human at any time could understand. Why would the "waters above" be any different? Understood as clouds or rain the "waters above" are not any different. They are the plain reading of the text.

Third, notice that the waters are assumed to already be there for an expanse to separate. The proclamation is not for the waters to come to be, but for the expanse to come to be between them. Both waters, the ones above and below the expanse, are already there, and the expanse is proclaimed to come to be in their "midst" which means the two waters were joined. Are we to believe the entire substance of the solar system or universe was on the land in the dark as described in Genesis 1:2? That would look bizarre, and would mean the land would not resemble anything the ancients could envision, or even anything we would call a planet. However, because necessary rainwater falls from the clouds, the Genesis account makes much more sense explaining that God made that possible, rather than postulating unseen waters some have only recently started to *speculate* about.

And fourth, eisegesis is horrible. YEC often accuse OEC of reading science into the text and here we ironically find them doing the very thing they protest. Unlike this YEC attempt, in this book I have tried my best to let Genesis speak apart from science, and then the fact that science confirms much of the text becomes corroborating evidence for Divine inspiration. *Let the simplicity and profundity of the text shine and mean what it says*. This is a horrendous example of YEC eisegesis.

YEC's hypotheses have failed miserably on the evidence and this one fails on the exegesis too. This second option is an interpretive stretch so tight it breaks the desperate flimsy rubber band of hope attempting to hold modern science and the young-universe position together.

Third option: Rain – the "waters which were above the expanse" (Genesis 1:7)

In Chapter 1 I said *Genesis 1 was written to all humanity to declare the origins of major features of the creation common to everyone.* That is, *everyone* (who is not impaired) can understand *by experience* the definitions of the words of Genesis 1: heavens, land, deep, light, darkness, day, night, waters below (seas), dry-ground, plants with seeds, trees with fruit, the greater light, the lesser light, stars, water creatures, flying creatures, animals, living things, creeping things, male, and female. All of these are remarkably *simple* references to common human experience.

Are we to believe the "expanse" and the "waters above" are exceptions? No, the expanse is nothing more than the whole sky above us, the expanding clear space of the heavens (as I have shown above). What about the "waters above" then? Is it not the common experience of all humanity to know water falls from the sky? We all know this and need it, but how did *rain* get up there? Genesis tells us God proclaimed it to be so on Day 2. That conclusion is beautifully simple.

The idea Genesis describes common human experience has implications to both options of which I am opposed concerning the Biblical definitions of the expanse and the waters above the expanse:

As to the first option, if the waters above are an ocean held in place high above by a solid dome, there was no way for the ancients to directly confirm either the dome or the ocean, and thus, they were not the common *experience* of all humanity, even though it may have been a common belief. However, rain is a common experience of all humans. I believe Genesis is that generic, but then human speculation moved in and began to guess how that water stays up there and so they postulated some kind of heavenly reservoir which "must" require a solid barrier. But, Genesis does not tell us *how* God got the water to stay up there, only that He caused it. Just because hosts of people began to believe in a solid sky does not mean Genesis agrees. Of course, we now know how water gets up there and I submit some Biblical writers, either by observation or revelation, also knew. (See Gen. 2:6, Job 37:10-13, Ps. 135:7, and Eccl. 1:6-7 for examples.) The waters above are not some mysterious speculative ocean held back by a solid dome; they are the water we all know falls from the sky – rain. It really is that simple. And many commentators agree: "The 'waters above' the sky is likely a reference to the clouds."[45] (Sailhamer) "The *upper* waters are... the waters floating about in the higher spaces of the air."[46] (Whitelaw) "These clouds constitute the upper waters."[47] (Leupold) The simplicity of the Genesis account to speak from the human perspective on the surface of Earth comes through loud and clear.

As to the second option, the idea the "waters above" are, or were, somewhere in outer space is certainly beyond the common experience of humanity. Worse, it is eisegesis of the most egregious kind because it is taking a YEC hypothesis and reading it into the text.

The Final Conclusion

The bottom line is simple. The Bible does not say the sky is a solid dome holding back a heavenly ocean. Nor does it say the waters above the expanse became the solar system and/or universe. It says the land was dark sometime after God created it (Gen. 1:2), and it was dark because it was covered with clouds (Job 38:9). God then made light appear on the surface of the land and called it "day" (Gen. 1:3-5). But, it was still covered with clouds so God proclaimed for an expanding-clear-space (the *raqîa'*) to come to be *between* the sea and clouds (Gen. 1:6). He thus separated the salty waters below the expanse from the fresh waters above the expanse for the benefit of humanity (Gen. 1:7). But, the source of the light from Day 1 still could not be seen so God proclaimed for the expanding-clear-space (expanse) of the heavens (as seen from the land) to expand beyond the clouds to include the Sun, Moon, and stars (Gen. 1:14), the sources of the light from Day 1. This interpretation, and the Prophetic Days View in general, causes no scientific problems, neither with age nor origin. In fact, it is scientifically accurate and so simple a child can grasp it, and that is the way it was meant to be.

Bibliography:

Barnes, Albert. *Barnes' Notes on the Old & New Testament: Job Volume I.* Edited by Robert Frew. Grand Rapids, MI: Baker Book House, twelfth printing, 1974.

Behe, Michael J. *Darwin's Black Box: The Biochemical Challenge to Evolution.* New York, NY: The Free Press, a division of Simon & Schuster, Inc., 1996.

The Edge of Evolution: The Search for the Limits of Darwinism. New York, NY: The Free Press, a division of Simon & Schuster, Inc., 2007.

Botterweck, G. Johannes, editor, Helmer Ringgren, and Heinz-Joseff Fabry. *Theological Dictionary of the Old Testament.* Translated by Douglas W. Stott. Grand Rapids, MI: William B. Erdmans Publishing Co. Volume 12, 2003.

Collins, C. John. *Did Adam and Eve Really Exist?* Wheaton. IL: Crossway, 2011.

Genesis 1-4: A Linguistic, Literary, and Theological Commentary. Phillipsburg, NJ: P&R Publishing, 2006.

Science & Faith – Friends or Foes? Wheaton, IL: Crossway Books a division of Good News Publishers, 2003.

Custance, Arthur C. *Without Form and Void.* Brookville, Canada: Doorway Publications, 1970.

Davidson, Rev. A. B. *Introduction Hebrew Grammar: Hebrew Syntax.* Edinburgh: T. & T. Clark LTD., 1989.

Davies, Paul. *The Mind of God: The Scientific Basis for a Rational World.* New York, NY: A Touchstone Book published by Simon & Schuster, Inc. 1992.

Dembski, William. *The Design Revolution: Answering the Toughest Questions About Intelligent Design.* Downers Grove, IL: Inter Varsity Press, 2004.

Intelligent Design: The Bridge Between Science and Theology. Downers Grove, IL: Inter Varsity Press, 1999.

Dembski, William A. and Jonathon Wells. *the Design of Life: Discovering Signs of Intelligence in Biological Systems.* Dallas, TX: The Foundation for Thought and Ethics, 2008.

DeRemer, Frank. "Good approach misapplied to get 'analogical days.'" *Journal of Creation* 21 (2) 2007, as printed from http://creation.com/images/pdfs/tj/j21_2/j21_2_35-39.pdf from Creation Ministries International's website http://creation.com/journal-of-creation-212 (YEC website).

"Young biosphere, old universe? A review of *The Age of the Universe: What are the Biblical Limits?*" 2nd Edition by Gorman Gray, Morning Star Publications, Washougal, Washington 2002, originally printed in *Journal of Creation* **19**(2):51-57, August 2005, retrieved 9/13/12 from http://creation.com/gorman-gray-the-age-of-the-universe-what-are-the-biblical-limits)

Duncan III, J. Ligon and David W. Hall. "'The 24-Hour Response' to the Day-Age View." In *The Genesis Debate: Three Views on the Days of Creation*. Edited by David Hagopian. Mission Viejo, CA: Crux Press, Inc. 2001.

Falk, Darrel R. *Coming to Peace with Science.* Downers Grove, IL: InterVarsity Press Academic, 2004.

Friedman, Richard E. *The Bible with Sources Revealed.* New York, NY: Harper Collins, 2003.

Futato, Mark D. "Because It Had Rained: A Study of Gen 2:5-7 with Implications for Gen 2:4-25 and Gen 1:1-2:3" *Westminster Theological Journal* 60, 1998, copyright 1991 by Westminster Theological Seminary.

Geisler, Norman L. *Systematic Theology: Volume One – Introduction and Bible.* Minneapolis, MN: Bethany House, 2002.

Green, Sr., Jay P. *The Interlinear Bible.* Peabody, MA: Hendrickson Publishers, Second edition 1986.

Hagopian, David, editor. *The Genesis Debate: Three Views on the Days of Creation.* Mission Viejo, CA: Crux Press, Inc. 2001.

Ham, Ken, editor. *The New Answers Book.* Green Forest, AR: Master Books a division of New Leaf Publishing Group, 2007.

Editor. *The New Answers Book 3.* Green Forest, AR: Master Books a division of New Leaf Publishing Group, 2010.

"A young Earth - it's not the Issue!" Article on the Answers in Genesis website, page 1, printed 2/7/2005, http://www.answersingenesis.org/docs/1866.asp

"Could God Really Have Created Everything in Six Days?" *The New Answers Book.* Green Forest, AR: Master Books a division of New Leaf Publishing Group, 2007.

"Couldn't God Have Used Evolution?" *The New Answers Book.* Green Forest, AR: Master Books a division of New Leaf Publishing Group, 2007.

"Was There Death Before Adam Sinned?" *The New Answers Book 3.* Green Forest, AR: Master Books a division of New Leaf Publishing Group, 2010.

"What About the Gap & Ruin-Reconstruction Theories?" *The New Answers Book.* Green Forest, AR: Master Books a division of New Leaf Publishing Group, 2007.

Hayward, Alan. *Creation and Evolution.* Minneapolis, MN: Bethany House Publishers 1995.

Henry, Matthew. *Matthew Henry's Commentary: Volume I – Genesis to Deuteronomy.* New York, NY: Fleming H. Revell Company, 1935?

Holladay, William L. *A Concise Hebrew and Aramaic Lexicon of the Old Testament.* Grand Rapids, MI: William B. Eerdmans Publishing Company, 1988.

Horner, John R. and James Gorn an. *Digging Dinosaurs.* New York, NY: Workman Publishing Company, 1988.

Humphreys, D. Russell. *Starlight and Time.* Green Forest, AR: Master Books 1994.

Irons, Lee, and Meredith Kline. "The Framework View." In *The Genesis Debate: Three Views on the Days of Creation.* Edited by David G. Hagopian. Mission Viejo, CA: Crux Press, Inc., 2001.

Isaac, Mark. *The Counter-Creationism Handbook.* Berkeley and Los Angeles, CA, London, England: University of California Press, 2007.

Johnson, Phillip E. *Darwin on Trial.* Downers Grove, IL: InterVarsity Press, *3rd edition*, 2010.

Kelley, Page H. *Biblical Hebrew: An Introductory Grammar*. Grand Rapids, MI: William B. Erdmans Publishing Company, 1992.

Kidner, Derek. *Genesis*. Volume 1 of the *Tyndale Old Testament Commentaries*. Edited by Donald J. Wiseman. Downers Grove, IL: Intervarsity Press, 2008. © The Tyndale Press, 1967.

Kitchen, Kenneth A. *On the Reliability of the Old Testament*. Grand Rapids, MI/ Cambridge, UK: William B. Erdmans Publishing Company, 2003.

Kulikovsky, Andrew. "Unbinding the rules: A review of Genesis Unbound." In *Technical Journal* 14 (3):35-38, December 2000, printed 9/2/2009 from http://www.answersingenesis.org/tj/v14/i3/rules.asp?vPrint=1

Lamoureux, Denis O. "No Historical Adam: Evolutionary Creation View." In *Four Views on the Historical Adam*. Edited by Matthew Barrett and Ardel B. Caneday. Grand Rapids, MI: Zondervan, 2013.

Lennox, John C. *Seven Days that Divide the World*. Grand Rapids, MI: Zondervan, 2011.

Leupold, H. C. *Exposition of Genesis* in *Barnes Notes on the Old & New Testaments*. Grand Rapids, MI: Baker Book House, 1978.

Lewis, C. S. *The Complete C. S. Lewis Signature Classics*. San Francisco, CA: Harpers San Francisco, a division of Harper Collins Publishers, 2002, 41, from *Mere Christianity*, 1952.

MacArthur, John. *The Battle for the Beginning*. Nelson Books, a division of Thomas Nelson Publishers, 2001.

MacDonald, William. *Believer's Bible Commentary*. Nashville, TN: Thomas Nelson, 1995.

Maxwell, Arthur S. *The Bible Story*. Hagerstown, MD: Review and Herald Publishing Associates, 1994.

McCabe, Robert V. "A Critique of the Framework View Interpretation of the Creation Account (Part 1 of 2)." In *Detroit Baptist Seminary Journal*, vol. 10 (2005): 19-67, as printed 9/2/2009 from http://www.answersingenesis.org/articles/aid/v2/n1/framework-interpretation-critique-part-one

McIntosh, Andy, and Bodie Hodge. "How Did Defense/Attack Structures Come About?" In *The New Answers Book*. Edited by Ken Ham. Green Forest, AR: Master Books a division of New Leaf Publishing Group, 2007.

Meyer, Stephen C. *Darwin's Doubt: The Explosive Origin of Animal Life and the Case for Intelligent Design.* New York, NY: Harper One, An Imprint of HarperCollinsPublishers, 2013.

Miller, Johnny V. and John M. Soden. *In the Beginning... We Misunderstood.* Grand Rapids, MI: Kregel Publications, a division of Kregel, Inc. 2012.

Mitchell, Tommy. "Why Does God's Creation Include Death and Suffering?" from *The New Answers Book.* Edited by Ken Ham. Green Forest, AR: Master Books a division of New Leaf Publishing Group, 2007.

Morris, Henry M. *The Henry Morris Study Bible.* Green Forest, AR: Master Books, a division of New Leaf Publishing Group, Inc. 2012.

Mortenson, Terry. "Why Shouldn't Christians Accept Millions of Years?" from *The New Answers Book.* Edited by Ken Ham. Green Forest, AR: Master Books a division of New Leaf Publishing Group, 2007.

Muncaster, Ralph O. *Examine the Evidence.* Eugene, OR: Harvest House Publishers, 2004.

Nakarai, Toyozo W. *Biblical Hebrew.* Johnson City, TN: Don and Mignon Printing Company, 1976.

Newman, Robert C. "Progressive Creationism." In *Three Views on Creation and Evolution.* Edited by J. P. Moreland and John Mark Reynolds. Grand Rapids, MI: Zondervan, 1999.

Newman, Robert C. and Herman J. Eckelmann Jr. *Genesis One & the Origin of the Earth.* Downers Grove, IL: InterVarsity Press, 1977.

Oard, Michael. "Where Does the Ice Age Fit?" in *The New Answers Book.* Edited by Ken Ham. Green Forest, AR: Master Books a division of New Leaf Publishing Group, 2007.

Oard, Mike, and John K. Reed, editors. *Rock Solid Answers: The Biblical Truth Behind 14 Geological Questions.* Green Forest, AR: Master Books a division of New Leaf Publishing Group, Inc. 2009.

Piper, John. *Desiring God.* Sisters, OR: Multnomah Publishers, Inc., 2003.

Rana, Fazale, and Hugh Ross. *Who Was Adam?* Colorado Springs, CO: NavPress, 2005.

Ross, Hugh. *A Matter of Days.* Colorado Springs, CO: NavPress, 2004.

The Creator and the Cosmos. Colorado Springs, CO: NavPress Publishing Group, 2001.

> *The Genesis Question*. Colorado Springs, CO: NavPress Publishing Group, 1998.
>
> *Improbable Planet*. Grand Rapids, MI: Baker Books, 2016.
>
> *Navigating Genesis*. Covina, CA: RTB Press, 2014.
>
> *Why The Universe Is The Way It Is*. Grand Rapids, MI: Baker Books, 2008.

Ross, Hugh, and Fazale Rana. *Origins of Life*. Colorado Springs, CO: NavPress, 2004.

Ross, Hugh, and Gleason Archer. "The Day-Age View." In *The Genesis Debate: Three Views on the Days of Creation*. Edited by David Hagopian. Mission Viejo, CA: Crux Press, Inc. 2001.

Sailhamer, John H. *Genesis: Text and Exposition in The Expositors Bible Commentary: Volume 2 Genesis – Numbers*. Grand rapids, MI: Zondervan Publishing House, a division of Harper Collins Publishers, 1990.

> *Genesis Unbound*. Sisters, OR: Multnomah Books, Questor Publishers Inc., 1996.
>
> *The Pentateuch as Narrative*. Grand Rapids, MI: Zondervan Publishing House, 1992.

Samples, Kenneth Richard. *7 Truths That Changed the World: Discovering Christianity's Most Dangerous Ideas*. Grand Rapids, MI: Baker Books a division of Baker Publishing Group, 2012.

> *A World of Difference*. Grand Rapids, MI: Baker Books a division of Baker Publishing Group, 2007.

Sarfati, Jonathan. D. *The Genesis Account: A theological, historical, and scientific commentary on Genesis 1-11*. Powder Springs, GA: Creation Book Publishers, 2015.

> *Refuting Compromise: A Biblical and Scientific Refutation of "Progressive Creationism" (Billions of Years), As Popularized by Astronomer Hugh Ross*. Green Forest, AR: Master Books, Inc., 2004.

Schroeder, Gerald. *The Science of God*. New York, NY: Free Press a division of Simon and Schuster, Inc, 1997.

Seely, Paul. "The Firmament and the Water Above – Part I: The Meaning of *raqîaʿ* in Gen 1:6-8." In *Westminster Theological Journal* 53:2, Fall 1991.

"The Firmament and the Water Above – Part II: The Meaning of the Water above the Firmament" in Gen 1:6-8." In *Westminster Theological Journal* 54:1, Spring 1992.

"The Geographical Meaning of 'Earth' and 'Seas' in Genesis 1:10." In *Westminster Theological Journal* 59:2, Fall 1997.

"Noah's Flood: Its Date, Extent, And Divine Accommodation." In *Westminster Theological Journal* 66:2, Fall 2004.

Smith, George H. *Atheism: The Case Against God*. Amherst, NY: Prometheus Books, 1989.

Snelling, Andrew A. "What Are Some of the Best Flood Evidences?" In *The New Answers Book 3*. Edited by Ken Ham. Green Forest, AR: Master Books a division of New Leaf Publishing Group, 2010.

Strobel, Lee. *The Case for Faith*. Grand Rapids, MI: Zondervan, 2000.

Strong, James. *The Exhaustive Concordance of the Bible: with Dictionaries of the Hebrew and Greek Words*. McLean, VA: MacDonald Publishing Company.

Tortura, Gerard J., Berdell R. Funke, and Christine L. Case. *Microbiology: an introduction – ninth edition*. San Francisco, CA: Pearson Benjamin Cummings, 2007.

Tsumura, David. *Creation and Destruction*. Winona Lake, IN: Eisenbrauns, 2005.

Tyson, Neil DeGrasse, and Donald Goldsmith. *Origins: Fourteen Billion Years of Cosmic Evolution*. New York, NY: W. W. Norton & Company, 2004.

Vine, W. E. *Vine's Expository Dictionary of Old & New Testament Words*. Nashville, TN: Thomas Nelson Publishers, Inc., 1997.

Waltke, Bruce K. and M. O'Conner. *An Introduction to Biblical Hebrew Syntax*. Winona Lake, IN: Eisenbrauns, 1990.

Genesis: A Commentary. Grand Rapids, MI: Zondervan, 2001.

Walton, John. *Genesis 1 as Ancient Cosmology*. Winona Lake, IN: Eisenbrauns, 2011.

The Lost World of Genesis One. Downers Grove, IL: InterVarsity Press, 2009.

Ward, Peter D. and Donald Brownlee. *Rare Earth: Why Complex Life is Uncommon in the Universe*. New York, NY: Copernicus Books, 2004.

Whitefield, Rodney. *Reading Genesis One – Comparing Biblical Hebrew with English Translation*. San Jose, CA: R. Whitefield Publisher, 2009.

Whitelaw, Rev. Thomas. *The Pulpit Commentary: Volume 1 – Genesis and Exodus*. Grand Rapids, MI: Wm. B. Eerdmans Publishing Company, 1958.

Williams, Alex, and John Hartnett. *Dismantling the Big Bang: God's Universe Rediscovered*. Green Forest, AR: Master Books, Inc. a division of New Leaf Publishing Group, 2005.

Wiseman, P. J. *Clues to Creation in Genesis*. Edited by Donald J. Wiseman. London: Marshall, Morgan & Scott, 1977.

Young, Davis A. and Ralph F. Stearley. *The Bible, Rocks and Time*. Downers Grove, IL: InterVarsity Press, 2008.

Footnotes

Introduction
1. Smith, *Atheism: The Case Against God*, 117.
2. Ibid, 195.

Chapter 1 – The Big Pictures of Genesis One
1. This use of "all" is not absolute. "All" comes with the understanding it refers to everything about the land and sea normally seen by humans. Thus, angels and demons are not included in the account. Nor does the "all" refer to God Himself. Obviously, the account does not tell us the origin of God because God does not have an origin. God's existence is assumed in Genesis 1:1 to be ontologically before "the beginning". Categories questionably not appearing in the account include: distant galaxies only visible by telescope (though these are likely included in the generic word "stars" – 1:16, especially because galaxies are made of stars), microscopic life like dust mites, one-celled creatures, and bacteria (though these could very loosely be included in "everything that creeps on the ground" – 1:25), and the most likely missing category is sea plants (and algae) of which it is difficult to include in any term used in Genesis 1. In Genesis, Day 3 specifically refers to plants growing on dry-ground, even though it could be said sea plants grow in earth/land that is underwater. However, because humans do not generally eat sea plants, their absence from the account does not eliminate the universal human nature of the account.
2. See Chapter 7 and 9 for more detail on the Framework View.
3. Frank DeRemer (pp. 35-39 – a YEC) argues for a chiastic arrangement of the Days. He says, "On Day 3 God forms and *names* the dry land 'earth' and the gathered waters 'seas'. Only then is the dry land ready for birds and the seas for fish. The birds fly above the earth (verse 20), were made from the ground (verse 2:19), and multiply on the earth, not in the air (verse 22). The seas are not ready for the fish on Day 2 as needed by this version of the framework scheme. Hence, Day 5 relates to Day 3, not Day 2." (p. 36) I agree with his historical assessment the dry land must precede the birds but to conclude Day 5 relates to Day 3 is missing the simple point the birds fly in the heavens (*shamayim* - Gen 1:26 and 28), i.e. what the "expanse" was named (Gen 1:8) even though they are restricted to the lowest level (the face or front side) of the expanse (Gen 1:20). The point is the birds from Day 5 fly in the expanse from Day 2 and the sea creatures from Day 5 swim in the waters below the expanse from Day 2. The topical arrangement stands. Also, DeRemer's suggestion of a chiasm to the 6 Days (p. 37) is *destroyed* by the land animals which *he leaves out of his scheme*. The chiasm falls apart if you add them to his outline. Ironically however, DeRemer and I agree the Days remain literal, chronological, and historical despite their topical arrangement and despite our disagreement why it is so.
4. Some may object to me saying there is only one proclamation on Day 4 because *hâyâh* ("to be" translated as "let there be" in 1:14) is actually used three times in verses 14-15. While that is true the second and third uses are prefixed by ו (*waw* – "and") which negates a jussive translation (command – "let there be") for a future translation ("and they will be for..." - See Rodney Whitefield, *Reading Genesis One*, 102). Also, all three uses of *hâyâh* are with nouns prefixed by ל ("for" or "to") and are like no other uses in Genesis 1. Thus, all uses of *hâyâh* in Gen. 1:14-15 are one proclamation declaring three purposes, as the NASB translates it.
5. These Hebrew terms are English transliterations. Actual Hebrew is read from right to left and looks like ראשית (*reshith* – beginning).
6. Hugh Ross, *The Genesis Question*, 49, 52-53.

257

7. Consult nearly any Hebrew grammar textbook, for example: Davidson, 71, Kelley, 145, or Nakarai, 27.
8. See Appendix A under "evening" and "morning".

Chapter 2 – The Prophetic Days View
1. Alan Hayward, *Creation and Evolution*: This book introduced me to the Prophetic Days View, only Hayward calls it the "Days of Divine Fiat" (p. 167) as do many others. I just do not like that title because the word "fiat" is not commonly understood outside formal theological settings. So, I changed it to help the average Bible reader understand the basic concept behind the view. Much later I found the name "prophetic-day view" in Young and Stearley (144), though I had renamed my view by then and they used it in reference to the Revelatory Days View. They also mistakenly say Hayward supported the Day-Age View (157). Hayward credits the Days of Divine Fiat to two sources: one, a late friend of his, Peter Watkins who "evidently thought of it himself some thirty years ago" (ca. 1955 since Hayward's first edition was 1985), and two, F. H. Capron who published a book containing the idea in 1902, *The Conflict of Truth* (London: Hodder & Stoughton, 169-199).
2. Sailhamer, *Genesis Unbound*: There is a major difference between the way Sailhamer and I interpret Gen. 1:1. He believes 1:1 refers to the creation of all creatures on Earth except those created in the Promised Land on the 6 Days, and that only the Promised Land was desolate and lifeless as described in 1:2, not the whole Earth. Whereas, I believe that 1:1 refers only to the creation of the primeval heavens and Earth ending (or beginning so to speak) with the *entire* Earth being desolate and lifeless. Then the 7 Days refer to a work God did to cause the Earth to be the way it is today. The difference is significant.
3. Ross, *The Creator and the Cosmos*, 19.
4. Hayward, 167-172.
5. The original author and audience are difficult to identify but I consider Moses to have been the compiler/editor of Genesis. However, whether Moses wrote Genesis himself or used sources does not change the fact he is primarily responsible for what we have today in that he gave to the people of Israel before they entered the Promised Land what was to become our copy of Genesis. Joshua 8:30-32 says, "Then Joshua built an altar to the LORD, the God of Israel, in Mount Ebal, just as Moses the servant of the LORD had commanded the sons of Israel, as it is written in the book of the law of Moses... He [Joshua] wrote there on the stones a copy of the law of Moses, which he [Moses] had written, in the presence of the sons of Israel." The writer of these verses intended us to believe Joshua and the "sons of Israel" knew Moses wrote the Law which included Genesis.
6. For definitions of the words "formless and void" see Appendix A.
7. Collins, *Genesis 1-4*, p. 42. The whole quote reads, "Since the backbone of the narrative, as we have already discussed, uses the *wayyiqtol*, and since Genesis 1:1-2 does not use the *wayyiqtol*, we conclude that these verses stand outside the main stream of the narrative." The *wayyiqtol*, also frequently called the *waw* (or *vav*) consecutive, is a verb structure in Hebrew whereby an imperfect verb is preceded by the Hebrew letter ו (*waw* – often written as *vav*) effectively changing the verb to perfect (almost always translated in the past tense). According to Collins the *wayyiqtol* is "improperly" called the *waw* consecutive (see his footnote 20 on page 21) and *many* commentators agree the *waw* consecutive is not always consecutive, i.e. chronological, so it seems calling it consecutive is misleading (See also Davidson p. 71 and Kelley p. 145). Genesis 1:3 begins with the *wayyiqtol*. In Hebrew the order is "and said God". But, Gen 1:2 is a *waw* disjunctive (noun

precedes verb), "and earth was". The *wayyiqtol* is intended to move a narrative along to the next thought *though it may or may not be in chronological order*, whereas the *waw* disjunctive is intended to give extra information about what has been said previously. The *waw* disjunctive "…introduces a parenthetic statement… a descriptive phrase about the previous noun." (Sarfati, *RC*, 103)

8. See Appendix A under "beginning".
9. Sailhamer, *Genesis Unbound*, 38.
10. Sailhamer, *EBC*, 23.
11. See Appendix A under "heavens" and "earth".
12. It was necessary to write an entire appendix to defend this claim. See Appendix B. I highly encourage you to read that appendix before continuing with Chapter 2 *IF* you disagree with me that the expanse is an expanding clear space.
13. Leupold, 59-60.
14. Whitelaw, 10. Whitelaw takes a Day-Age View, despite seeing Day 1 referring to all light everywhere. Most Day-Agers would disagree with him now. He represents an older version of the DAV (1958 and before).
15. Walton, *The Lost World of Genesis One*, 53. Though I agree Genesis 1 is referring to the function of light, I do not agree with Walton that is *all* it means. I believe the author of Genesis would have said the account includes the material origins of the light makers/bearers also (1:1 and 16). See Chapter 9 for more on my disagreements with the Cosmic Temple View of Walton.
16. Ibid, 54.
17. Again, see Appendix B if you question this.
18. Williams and Hartnett, 180.
19. Even though many OEC have arrived at the conclusion the Sun, Moon, and stars became visible as a result of the proclamation of Day 4, at the time of writing this I have in my possession over 40 books specifically commenting on the Genesis 1 account, including six commentaries, and I have perused two local Christian bookstores and my seminary library and scanned through at least four more commentaries, and many online articles, and *none of them* contain what I saw about the "expanse of the heavens" phrase. And many of them (the OEC ones) would have benefited from using my argument. So, I do not know why none of them use it. I have even searched diligently for any glaring contradictions with this interpretation of the phrase thinking that maybe I am missing something obvious but I cannot find any. Surely, I cannot be the first to see the importance of the phrase. One possible reason for few, if any, seeing this is because of the poor translation of the Hebrew word *raqîa'* as "firmament" in the KJV, rather than "expanse" as in the NASB. (See Appendix B) I suppose it is possible because of the dominance of the KJV for hundreds of years no one has seen the importance of this phrase until now.
20. I argued for this in Chapter 1, but more detail is in Chapter 9 and Appendix A under "day".
21. See Appendix A under "gathered".
22. Day 3 has God naming "land" and "seas" and also seeing the fulfillments as good, but these actions are not directly related to fulfilling the proclamations. By asserting that God's actions are missing from Day 3 I am not including the proclamations. I am referring to actions mentioned after the proclamations. I am also not suggesting God did not do anything to fulfill the Day 3 proclamations, only that none of His actions are mentioned in the Day 3 text. In Chapter 3 I will show that the absence of God's actions reveals an emphasis for Day 3.
23. The NIV, KJV, and NKJV are particularly confusing here translating two *different* Hebrew verbs *exactly* the same as "produced" (NIV) and "bring/brought forth" (KJV and NKJV).

Genesis, Science, and the Beginning

24. See Appendix A under "sprout".
25. See Appendix A under "brought forth".
26. See Appendix A under "signs".
27. In Chapter 1 I discussed how Hebrew verb structure is not as concerned about sequence as English (See footnote 7 above again also). Hebrew narrative is often a series of past tense (completed) phrases that are not always in chronological order. Chronology must be determined by logic and context and here on Day 4 this proclamation cannot logically be fulfilled until humanity arrives much later, but that is not a problem for the Hebrew reader. The fact remains that the proclamation was already fulfilled when the account was written even though it was fulfilled after the second Day 6 proclamation despite being listed before Day 6.
28. See Appendix A respectively on "beasts", "cattle", and "creeping things".
29. Refer back to Chapter 1 and Figure 1.1.
30. I have occasionally stepped on some Christian's "raging dogma nerve" (as I call it) just by mentioning my position on controversial doctrines. People in that condition, *especially* those who represent Christ's name, should be highly discouraged from trying to convince anyone of anything. The fruit of the Spirit includes love, gentleness, kindness, patience, and self-control. Spirit-filled discussions are a joy. The others, well...

Chapter 3 – A Beautiful Picture of Our Creator

1. Refer again to Chapter 2 under the heading "The Five Points of the Prophetic-Days View" for more on the meaning of the phrase "the heavens and the earth".
2. The Septuagint (LXX: Greek translation of the Hebrew text – ca. 250 BCE) inserted "and God saw that it was good" in verse 8 apparently thinking it belonged there. The LXX made two other changes to the text (see footnote 51 of Chapter 5), however no evidence exists of earlier manuscripts containing the phrases the LXX added or moved. As Whitelaw (p. 15) has said, the additions to the text by the Septuagint are "unsupported by any ancient version." Sailhamer adds, "...the LXX readings are an attempt to correct the imbalance of the MT [Masoretic Text]... The overall impression given by the LXX in these instances is of a secondary attempt to provide a balanced, consistent text. Thus the MT is to be taken as the more original." (Sailhamer, *EBC*, 30f)
3. See Appendix A under "separated" for a further explanation.
4. Day 3 has God naming "land" and "seas" and also seeing the fulfillments as good, but these actions are not directly related to fulfilling the proclamations. By asserting that God's actions are missing from Day 3, I am not excluding the proclamations as actions of God. Of course God's actions included Him making proclamations on each Day. I am referring to actions mentioned after the proclamations. I am also not suggesting God did not do anything to fulfill the proclamations on Day 3, only that none of His actions are mentioned in the text of Day 3.
5. From a deeper perspective some might argue the Biblical view of God's actions is that He directly controls *everything*. Verses like Psalm 104:14, "He causes the grass to grow for the cattle," and Matthew 5:45, "He causes His sun to rise on *the* evil and *the* good, and sends rain..." could be used to support such an idea. A complete refutation of that claim would take considerable length and is outside the scope of this book. I will suffice it to say my responses would include my observations of the Day 3 text, the many places in the Bible God's creation is the subject of the actions, not God Himself (like Psalm 104:22, "the sun rises", and Eccl 11:3, "If the clouds are full, they pour out rain..."), and the fact that the Bible can describe God causing something without always explaining *how* He does it. Meaning, secondary causes are *how* God causes the sun to rise or the clouds to rain. Also, taking God as the

cause of everything could eventually lead to the conclusion God causes sin, which the Bible explicitly states God does not do (James 1:13-15).
6. See Chapter 9.II.3.5 for more.
7. See Appendix A under "image".
8. See Appendix A under "likeness".
9. Piper, 10.

Chapter 4 – The Beginning and you – What now?
1. See Ross, *The Creator and the Cosmos* and *A Matter of Days*.
2. Davies, *The Mind of God*, 57. Davies is not a Christian by his own admission in his book, pp. 16 and 191.
3. Ward and Brownlee, *Rare Earth*, 163, 227, and 233.
4. Ross, *The Genesis Question*, 42-43.
5. Tyson and Goldsmith, *Origins*, 248.
6. See Ross and Rana, *Origins of Life*.
7. Ward and Brownlee, xxiii.
8. See Samples, *7 Truths*, 179-184 and *A World of Difference*, 181-185.
9. Johnson, *Darwin on Trial*, 114.
10. See Michael Behe, *Darwin's Black Box* and *The Edge of Evolution*, Stephen Meyer, *Darwin's Doubt*, William Dembski and Jonathon Wells, *the Design of Life*, and a host of other books by the Discovery Institute.

Chapter 5 – Objections to the Prophetic Days View
1. Duncan and Hall, *The 24-Hour Response*, 171.
2. See Appendix A under "work".
3. See https://www.biblegateway.com/passage/?search=Genesis%202&version=NASB where the footnote reads, "Lit [literally] to make".
4. Whitefield, 132.
5. See http://www.breslov.com/bible/Genesis2.htm of the Jewish Publication Society website.
6. See https://www.biblegateway.com/passage/?search=Genesis%202&version=HCSB which is from *Holman Christian Standard Bible*. Nashville, TN: Holman Bible Publishers, Copyright © 1999, 2000, 2002, 2003, 2009.
7. Green, 2.
8. Whitelaw, 36.
9. Whitefield, 134.
10. In Hebrew *asah* is prefixed by the letter *lamed* (ל). This prefix denotes the preposition "for" or "to" (Nakarai, p. 20 and Leupold, p. 72).
11. See Appendix A under "made".
12. From a personal correspondence I am indebted to Rodney Whitefield for this example and other scholarly and personal advice he gave on translating Hebrew and my original book draft.
13. Mortenson, *Why Shouldn't Christians Accept Millions of Years?* 27.
14. Ham, *What About the Gap & Ruin-Reconstruction Theories?* 53.
15. Collins, *Science & Faith*, 363.
16. MacArthur, 91.
17. Leupold, 61.
18. The verb is actually used 6 times in the first creation account (Gen. 1:1-2:4a), but three uses refer to the same event (v. 27 – the creation of mankind), thus really only four different times.
19. Collins, *Genesis 1-4*, p. 67.

20. Mortenson, 28. YEC's jabs are really quite unbecoming of Christ-like behavior. To say that only YEC are faithful followers of Jesus is completely unnecessary and arrogant, especially since their proof-text is extremely weak.
21. Sarfati, *Refuting Compromise*, 298.
22. Ross, *A Matter of Days*, 93.
23. Sarfati, *Refuting Compromise*, 298. To be thorough I must respond to four other verses this author uses to support his position. (1) and (2), he quotes Mk 13:19 and II Pet 3:4 to show the phrase "the beginning of the creation" refers to the whole creation. However, Mark 13 refers to "tribulation" that has not happened since the beginning of creation and must also refer to events regarding humanity only because it refers to disaster experienced by humans; therefore the phrase refers to the beginning of the creation of humanity. II Peter 3 speaks of scoffers that say "*ever since the fathers fell asleep, all continues just as it was from the beginning of creation.*" Their accusation refers to human events also referring to a time "since the fathers fell asleep", and so the phrase refers to the beginning of humanity. That means in every case the phrase "the beginning of creation" references the beginning of humanity, not the whole creation. On a side note, that interpretation also relieves II Peter 3:4 from a faulty interpretation referencing uniformitarian geology, as it is often used by YEC. Also, are YEC saying they agree with scoffers? (3) Luke 11:50-51 talks about how the blood of Abel was shed "from the foundation of the world", but this phrase references God's foreknowledge of the event as it does in Eph. 1:4, I Pet. 1:20, Rev. 13:8, and 17:8, and has nothing to do with actually placing Abel's death at the time of the forming of the Earth. (4) Rom 1:20 says in the NASB, "For since the creation of the world His invisible attributes, His eternal power and divine nature, have been clearly seen, being understood through what has been made..." Sarfati suggests the verse means people were there to see the creation from the start, but the NASB translation is not the best. A literal rendering from Jay P. Green (Greek Interlinear also backed by the KJV and YLT) reads, "for the unseen things of Him from the creation of the world are clearly seen, being understood by the things made..." and means just the opposite of what YEC are trying to say. What was done at the creation of the world was *unseen*. Now, qualities of God are seen because of what was done unseen ("invisible" – NASB). Instead of supporting Sarfati's position, Rms. 1:20 says what was done at the creation of the world was unseen. Humans were not there to see what God did.
24. I have not seen this objection in print but I am anticipating hearing it.
25. Duncan and Hall, *The 24-Hour View*, both quotes p. 40.
26. Robert V. McCabe, *A Critique of the Framework View Interpretation of the Creation Account* (Part 1 of 2), p. 15. His quote is from John D. Currid, *A Study Commentary on Genesis, Volume 1: Genesis 1:1-25:18* (Darlington, England: Evangelical Press, 2003), 72.
27. MacArthur, 141.
28. In direct opposition, consider two other commentators referencing "and it was so", "Not immediateness, but certainty of execution, is implied in the 'it was so' appended to the fiat." (Whitelaw, 17) And, "The account has no comment on how long it took for God's wish to be carried out; it rather focuses on the way that God's wish alone determines what happens." (Collins, *Genesis 1-4*, 76) What "indicates" something to one person does not always indicate the same thing to someone else, especially when presuppositions cloud one's judgment. Collins (ibid) responds directly to the claim from Currid that the account teaches "instantaneous" creation saying, "the text says no such thing."
29. Whitefield, 95. He estimates at least 320 times the verb is translated elsewhere as "and it came to pass".

30. Leupold, 64.
31. Duncan and Hall, 32.
32. Ibid, 41.
33. Leupold, 66.
34. Duncan and Hall, 53.
35. Formally, various chemicals are the *material cause* of plants, God was the *formal cause* of what *defines* a plant, God was the *efficient* cause of plant *origination*, but soil, water, and sunlight are the *efficient cause* of plant *growth* (what God proclaimed on Day 3), and finally, God was the *final cause* of plant design and purpose. The Earth was not the cause of anything related to the miracle of creation. The Earth was the cause of plant *growth* and *reproduction*, but not plant origination.
36. Two Hebrew verbs are used. See footnote 23 of Chapter 2 and Appendix A.
37. McCabe, 15.
38. Sarfati, *Genesis*, 236. Sarfati's newest book was published April 2015 and when I saw it I knew it would be necessary to add it to this work which was basically complete then. His book adds nothing new to the Genesis 1 interpretation debate nor challenges any of my arguments here. It does rehash the complete current YEC position, science and all. Even though it is nearly 800 pages long it spends more space on YEC science and history arguments than exposition of Genesis 1-11. In many ways it is *Refuting Compromise* in a different order with updated arguments.
39. The Bible does not specify the quantity of each animal God made. It could have only been two of each (of some animals). All that can be said is that He told sea creatures to fill the sea so we know *the sea was not made full of animals*. He told flying creatures to multiply on the land so we know the land was not made full of birds. By extension it makes sense God did not make the land full of animals. He let them multiply the way He proclaimed. It is interesting to note that neither flying creatures nor land animals were blessed to *fill* the land, and the reason is God blessed humanity to do it (1:28). For humanity to fulfill God's command, some animals were going to have to be displaced so it would appear God sanctioned the death of animals before the Fall (more on that in Chapter 6).
40. I know micro-evolution is the most common term to describe it but I prefer to avoid the term because of the connotation it carries of progression. Everything in this creation runs down with time and I do not believe life is an exception even when minor adaptive variations to environmental changes occur. The progression of life on this planet from less complex to more complex is not the result of blind random chance. Common sense understands accidents do not create organized complexity. Increased complexity of the magnitude evident by living creatures can only come from the input of intelligence. When left to run on its own life decays, changes (evolves) toward less order, i.e. devolves.
41. Leupold, 82.
42. Ibid, 85.
43. Ibid, 92.
44. Ibid, 103. The reference in the quote is from, "Procksch, Otto, *Kommentar zum Alten Testament* (Genesis), Ernst Sellin, editor. Liepzig: Deichert. 1913."
45. Duncan and Hall, 40 and 98 respectively.
46. Ibid, 98.
47. McCabe, p. 15 quoting Currid.
48. Duncan and Hall, 46-47.
49. Sarfati, *Refuting Compromise*, 139.
50. Some of the evidence for interpreting the Days as normal daylight on Earth was covered in Chapter 1 but more is in Chapter 9 and Appendix A. Also, Day-Age View arguments for long "days" are covered in Chapter 9.

51. The translators of the Septuagint (LXX – ca. 250 BCE) saw some of the peculiarities of the text and changed parts of the textual order, moving "and it was so" from the end of 1:7 to the end of 1:6, which may indicate they saw the potential out-of-sequence problem. They also added the "and it was so" phrase to the end of 1:20 and added another phrase, "and God saw that it was good", to 1:8 where they are missing in the Masoretic Text (MT) indicating they saw the parallel structure of the account. Responding to these changes one commentator says, "The overall impression given by the LXX in these instances is of a secondary attempt to provide a balanced, consistent text. Thus the MT is to be taken as the more original." (Sailhamer, *EBC*, p. 30 ftnt. 7) These changes by the LXX were completely unnecessary because the parallel structure of the account is already consistent without the changes and the account was not meant to be perfectly symmetrical. The chronological changes miss the fact the information after the fulfillment phrases is parenthetical, whereas on Day 2 that may not be the case. Day 2 is the only Day the fulfillment phrase is duplicated (See Chapter 3 for a possible explanation). The point here is that the nuances of the text have been seen for more than two thousand years, which means people have struggled to interpret it for a long time.
52. This is formally known as phenomenological language. The Bible describes most (maybe all) phenomenon as they appear from a human perspective on the Earth.
53. Duncan and Hall, 107.
54. MacArthur, 26.
55. Leupold, 45. Please do not think the use of the word "geocentric" means Genesis, or Leupold, teach the Sun revolves around the Earth or that Earth is the center of the universe. It simply means the perspective of the text is from the Earth's surface.
56. MacArthur, 78.
57. Leupold, 47.
58. MacArthur, 76.
59. Whitelaw, 10. Whitelaw takes a Day-Age View, despite seeing Day 1 referring to all light everywhere. Most Day-Agers would disagree with him now. From personal conversation, I know Hugh Ross believes Day 1 refers only to light on the Earth. Whitelaw represents an older version of the DAV.
60. Sarfati. *Genesis*, 106.
61. Ibid, 165.
62. Ibid, 166. For more on the meaning of the "water above" the expanse, see the latter part of Appendix B under the heading, "What then are the waters above the expanse in Genesis 1:7?"
63. Sailhamer, *EBC*, 29.
64. Whitelaw, 15.
65. Leupold. 60.
66. See footnote 19 in Chapter 2 again.
67. Leupold, 71. The reference in this quote is from Robert Jamieson, *A Commentary Critical and Explanatory*, (Jamieson, Fausett and Brown: New York, NY: George H. Doran, no date or page).
68. Sarfati, *Refuting Compromise*, 143.
69. Irons and Kline, 229.
70. Ibid, 294.
71. Williams and Hartnett, 231.
72. Leupold, 75.
73. McCabe, 16.
74. Close attention should be paid to what *is* listed after the fulfillment phrases of each Day. In Genesis 1 statements made *after* the fulfillment phrase are extra information not directly related to fulfilling the proclamation made on that Day. Follow me here

on each Day: **Day 1** – The proclamation is "Let there be light." The fulfillment is "and there was light." The phrase *after* the fulfillment is "God separated" day and night, but has nothing to do with fulfilling the production of light, nor does God naming the day and night. **Day 2** – The proclamation is "Let there be an expanse..." An action phrase *precedes* the fulfillment, "God made the expanse..." and this phrase is directly related to the fulfillment. The fulfillment is next, "and it was so." Then God naming the heavens is unrelated to the fulfillment. **Day 3** – The first proclamation is "Let the waters...be gathered... and let dry ground appear." The fulfillment is "and it was so." There is no action phrase after the fulfillment. The second proclamation is "Let the earth sprout vegetation [sprouts]..." The fulfillment is "and it was so." The action phrase *after* the fulfillment is "the earth brought forth vegetation [sprouts]..." which does not fulfill the proclamation because the proclamation was for new growth to sprout, not for plants to reproduce (bring forth). The fulfillment happened when the plants first sprouted, not when the Earth produced more plants by natural means. **Day 4** – The proclamation is "Let there be lights in the expanse of the heavens for..." The fulfillment is "and it was so." The actions are God "made" and "appointed [set, gave]" the lights. Do these relate directly to the fulfillment? God making the lights does not; the fulfillment happened when the expanse expanded to include the lights, not when the lights were made. God appointing the lights presents the strongest case against my argument. One could argue God appointing (placing/giving – See Appendix A under "placed") the lights for their purposes fulfilled the proclamation. However, verse 17 has a change of verb to "appoint" instead of "to be" and is meant to give us extra information beyond just the lights coming to be in the expanse. The fact verse 17 has extra information shows it is not the fulfillment of the proclamation. Therefore, verse 17 is not an exception to this pattern. **Day 5** – The proclamation is "Let the waters teem with swarms of living creatures... and let birds fly..." The fulfillment is "God created... every living creature that moves..." in the water and sky. The action is "God blessed them..." and does not fulfill the proclamation. **Day 6** – The first proclamation is "Let the earth bring forth living creatures." The fulfillment is "and it was so." The action phrase is "God made..." the land animals. Here again this may look like the direct fulfillment but it is not. The proclamation is for *the land* to produce animals, but it cannot do this until land animals are there. So, the action phrase made it possible for the fulfillment, but the fulfillment did not happen until the animals actually started reproducing. The proclamation was not fulfilled when the animals were made; it was fulfilled when they reproduced, which had to take longer than a day. The second proclamation on Day 6 is "Let us make man..." All the other phrases precede the fulfillment phrase of "and it was so" which is at the end (1:30). There is no action phrase to relate to the proclamation after the fulfillment. **Conclusion** – I said all that in response to the incorrect idea that these out-of-sequence phrases are added details about how the fulfillment of the proclamation was done. They are not. If God had meant for verses 16 and 25 to refer to how the fulfillment was accomplished, they would have come before the "and it was so" phrase. *The pattern of the text tells us that the statement "God made the lights" is not an account of the fulfillment of the proclamation.*

75. Sailhamer, *EBC* and *Genesis Unbound*.
76. See Appendix A under "beginning".
77. Andrew Kulikovsky, *Unbinding the rules: A review of Genesis Unbound*, page 1.
78. Ibid.
79. Ibid.
80. Ibid, 1-2.

81. According to astronomy and the Day-Age View, Analogical Days View, Intermittent-Days View, Prophetic Days View and maybe some versions of the Framework View, the "beginning" lasted approximately 9.7 billion years compared to the approximate 4 billion years since. These figures are comparable even though the beginning is longer than the ending.
82. They have no response defending a position the Earth was created on Day 1 other than to assert it is true or assume it is true because they believe all was completed in seven days, but they do have responses to some of my five points where they advocate the Earth was created on Day 3.
83. Leupold, 42.
84. See Chapter 1.
85. See Appendix A under "evening" and "morning". Also, my interpretation of the evening and morning phrase answers the argument that the "darkness" from verse 2 is *equated* with "the darkness" of verses 4-5. One YEC in reference to verse 5 argues, "What darkness is being called 'night' here? The only darkness mentioned so far, in v. 2, as separated from 'day' in v. 4. The first day consists of that first night and the following first daytime, as marked by the first evening and the first morning, the complete cycle." (Frank DeRemer, *Young biosphere, old universe?* p. 2) DeRemer is saying the darkness in verse 2 is the *exact same* darkness in verses 4-5 which makes the darkness of Day 1 occur *before* the daylight of Day 1. In another article he contradicts himself by saying, "verse 5 brackets that first night between evening and morning as it defines the notion of (a full) 'day'." (DeRemer, *Good approach misapplied to get 'analogical days'*, 36) The contradiction is in saying, on the one hand, the darkness was before the day and then saying the evening and morning phrase brackets the first darkness. It is a contradiction because the evening of Day 1 occurs *after* the daylight according to the text (first daylight, then evening, then morning, and night is between evening and morning, therefore after the day). DeRemer also points to the fact the Hebrew text contains a definite article (the) before "darkness" in verses 4-5 thus referring to a specific darkness ("the darkness", not just a darkness), but the article is missing from verse 2. He says the use of the article equates the two by pointing the latter back to the former. However, the definite article could refer to "the" specific darkness on Earth without equating verses 2 and 5 as *the exact same time.* In other words, it is dark on Earth every day and in one sense that is the same darkness because it is the darkness on Earth, but it occurs at different times. Therefore, "the" darkness from verses 4-5 can be the same darkness from verse 2 without being at the same time. Regardless, the use of the definite article could also refer to "the" day ("day" also has the article) and "the" darkness of Day 1 without having anything to do with verse 2 because "the day" can only refer to the light on Day 1. Either way, the darkness of verse 2 is not part of Day 1 because the darkness of Day 1 occurs after the daylight between evening and morning as the text literally reads. Therefore, DeRemer's arguments fail.
86. In Hebrew the cardinal number (one, two, three, etc.) is used at the end of 1:5, not the ordinal number (first, second, third, etc.) like it does on the other days. This fact is mentioned by many commentators and is used by YEC (Sarfati, *Refuting Compromise,* 76-77) to say Genesis 1 defines the Days as 24-hour days, not long periods of time. The NASB and Amplified Bible render it as "one day" and that translation is considered by many to be best, rather than "the first day" as the KJV, NKJV, ESV, and NIV have it. However, YEC need to consider one interesting point. If the text had said "first day" instead of "one day" it would have strengthened their case. Why? Because by using "one day" the text is likely pointing out the fact that *this is not the very first 24 hour period on Earth.* There were others before this one (the Earth was there before the 7 Days began), but not that an observer on Earth

could measure. This *is* the first day of the 6 Days, and it is *the first measurable day* on the surface of Earth, but it *is not* the first time the Earth spun on its axis. "In his conception of the narrative of chapter 1, the author may not have wanted to convey the idea that the day that begins in v. 3 was actually... [the first day]. He may have wanted to reserve the notion of 'the first day' for the day that began... in v.1." (Sailhamer, *EBC*, 28)
87. Sarfati, *Genesis*, 288.
88. The Greek influences are evident by translating *tohu* as "formless" or "without form" from a belief the universe began in chaos. See Appendix A under "formless".
89. Matthew Henry, 3.
90. DeRemer, *Young biosphere*, 2.
91. Ibid.
92. Ibid.
93. Frank DeRemer's reply to Gorman Gray's letter to Journal of Creation **20**(1) 2006, 38. DeRemer says, "Every Bible I can find translates *tohu* in v.2 as 'formless', 'unformed', or 'without form'. It seems the translation experts disagree with Mr. Gray." DeRemer would of course say they all disagree with me too, but again, see Appendix A for my defense of the definition of *tohu* as "desolate".
94. Gorman Gray's letter to Journal of Creation **20**(1) 2006, 37.
95. The definitions of *tohu* and *bohu* (formless and void) greatly affect the way DeRemer and I interpret Genesis 1. If I am right DeRemer cannot be, and vice versa. Please see Appendix A for more info to resolve this issue.
96. See Appendix A under "dry land".
97. The narrowing of focal location should be obvious in Genesis. It starts with "the all" (the heavens and the earth) which included all land, even underwater. Then it moves to dry land, i.e. what humanity needs. Then finally it moves to a specific land prepared by God for humanity, i.e. the Garden in Eden.
98. DeRemer, *Young biosphere*, 1
99. See Appendix A under "heavens" and "earth".

Chapter 6 – The Main Objection: Death *Before* the Fall
1. Sarfati, *Refuting Compromise*, 195.
2. This was expressed to me in a private conversation where the speaker wished to remain anonymous.
3. Theistic Evolutionists believe humanity would have died physically regardless of the Fall, meaning the body was mortal. Some OEC agree, but I am inclined to disagree.
4. Ham, "Was There Death Before Adam Sinned?" from *The New Answers Book 3*, 112.
5. Mortenson, 28-29.
6. Sarfati, *Refuting Compromise*, 195.
7. Ibid, 196.
8. Andy McIntosh and Bodie Hodge, *How Did Defense/Attack Structures Come About?* from *The New Answers Book*, Ken Ham general editor, 263.
9. Ibid
10. Ibid, 269.
11. Sarfati, *Refuting Compromise*, 211.
12. Ibid, 206-207.
13. Whitelaw, 31. His sources are: Macdonald, *Creation and the Fall, a Defense and Exposition* (London and Edinburgh, 1856); Murphy, *Commentary on Genesis* (Edinburgh, 1863); Calvin, *Commentarii in Genesin* (Geneva, 1563); Kalisch, *Historical and Critical Commentary on the Old Testament* ((London, 1858); Knobel, (?); and Alford, *Genesis, and Part of Exodus, for English Readers* (London, 1877).

14. Sarfati, *Refuting Compromise*, 207.
15. Ibid, 209.
16. Ibid
17. John Wesley, "God's Approbation of His Work," Sermon 56 (Gen 1:31), 1872; http://gbgm-umc.org/UMhistory/Wesley/sermons/serm-056.stm. as cited in Sarfati, *Refuting Compromise*, 206.
18. Sarfati, *Refuting Compromise*, 205.
19. McIntosh and Hodge, 267. It is difficult to believe they actually suggested this.
20. See Appendix A under "moves".
21. See Appendix A under "birds".
22. Sarfati, *Refuting Compromise*, 212.
23. McIntosh and Hodge, 267.
24. Sarfati, *Refuting Compromise*, 212.
25. Ibid, 205.
26. Ibid, 201.
27. I use the word "relevant" here because I do not intend to discuss everything God addressed in Gen 3:14-19, only the parts relevant to misinterpretations by YEC that no animal death occurred prior to the Fall or was present in God's original "very good" creation. So I have left out the prophetic reference to Eve's seed bruising Satan's head, the effect of Satan having to crawl on his belly, Eve's "desire" for her husband, and the part about men ruling over women.
28. Sarfati, *Refuting Compromise*, 166.
29. See Appendix A under "account" for more on how Genesis is divided into sections by the use of the word *toledoth* (usually translated "generations").
30. Sarfati, *Refuting Compromise*, 204.
31. Ibid.
32. Collins, *Genesis 1-4*, footnote on 159.
33. Mitchell, "Why Does God's Creation Include Death and Suffering?" from *The New Answers Book*, Ken Ham general editor, 329.
34. Ham, "Could God Really Have Created Everything in Six Days?" 100.
35. A nightly rest is implied in the word "separated" used in 1:4. It was a holy separation for the benefit of humanity. See "separated" in Appendix A for more.
36. The popular doctor's waiting room book by Arthur S. Maxwell (p. 42) shows Adam standing in the midst of a lion, sheep, goat, cow, wolf, deer, cat, rabbits, horse, zebra, chickens, and a parrot all living in smiling harmony. And Ken Ham's, *The New Answers Book*, illustrations on pages 105, 157, 266, and 328, depict humans standing next to tyrannosaurs, crocodiles, bears, and lions, in some cases with the animals having smiling faces. These are good examples of the fairly-tale fantasy-like images I am talking about.
37. Tommy Mitchell, 330-331.
38. Collins, *Genesis 1-4*, 182-184. Collins attempts to interpret the "corruption" experienced by the creation in Romans 8 to be nothing more than the moral corruption of man, but I disagree because of the way the word is used in Romans 1. There the "corruptible" *creation* is contrasted with the "incorruptible" God and has more to do with our physical nature than our moral nature, and so does the word's use in I Corinthians 15.
39. The "problem" was caused by God intentionally. It is only a problem *for us* we must look to God to solve. That is, we will all die one day, but God originated the problem of decay for His own glory, because by us accepting the solution, it glorifies Him, and benefits us. Even the original creation had to have choices between what the creation offered and what a relationship with God offered. If it had not then loving God would be impossible. So, some level of discontent, i.e.

suffering, albeit minor, compared to after the Curse, must have existed in the original "very good" creation to balance the desire for contentment from the creation with contentment from the Creator so real free-choice could exist.

40. Paul Davies, *The Mind of God*, 46. I chose Davies' definition of the Second Law out of many candidates because of its simplicity and because he is a respected secular mathematician. Davies is not a Christian by his own admission in his book, pages 16 and 191.
41. Sarfati, *Refuting Compromise*, 213.
42. Collins takes the Isaiah verses figuratively. (Collins, *Science & Faith*, 152-157)
43. Sorry Reformers, no belief in Limited Atonement here.
44. Sarfati, *Refuting Compromise*, 216.
45. Ham, *Couldn't God Have Used Evolution?* 37
46. Ibid.
47. Sarfati, *Refuting Compromise*, 215-216. I agree with him that animal sacrifice is an archetype of Christ's atonement, but animal sacrifice and animal predation are different. Just because one animal sheds another's blood does not mean an atoning sacrifice was made. Atonement was done by a priest on an altar in a prescribed manner. Animal predation does not fit that description at all.
48. The three Biblical exceptions are Enoch, who "walked with God, and he was not, for God took him" (Gen. 5:24) and Elijah, who "went up by a whirlwind to heaven" (II Kings 2:11) and in the future, those raptured, "Then we who are alive and remain shall be caught up together with them in the clouds to meet the Lord in the air, and thus we will always be with the Lord" (I Th. 4:17).
49. That which is good is not an arbitrary choice by God however. Being good flows from the goodness of God's nature (what He is) and He cannot be something He is not. He is, was, and always will be what He is. For example, rape is evil not because God arbitrarily said it is evil (as if God could have defined rape as good). Rape is evil because it is contrary to the good nature of God. Goodness does not force the unwilling to participate in an act reserved for consensual marriage partners.
50. Charles Templeton, *A Farewell to God* (Toronto: McLelland and Stewart, 1996), pages 197-199 as cited in Sarfati, *RC*, 220. Templeton was a friend and colleague of Billy Graham, but later left the Christian faith. As a side note, I agree with Sarfati that the response given by Norman Geisler as interviewed by Lee Strobel in *The Case for Faith* (176-177) is inconsistent and "totally contradicts his [Geisler's] old-earth belief." (Sarfati, *RC*, 220) However, I disagree with Sarfati when he says all death originating after sin is the "only way" to answer the skeptics (Ibid).
51. M. Buchanan, "Wild, Wild Life," *Sydney Morning Herald*, The Guide (March 24, 2003): p. 6 quoting Sir David Attenborough as cited in Sarfati, *RC*, 221.
52. Carl Sagan, *Contact* (New York, NY: Pocket Books, Simon & Schuster, Inc., 1985) as cited in Sarfati, *RC*, 222.
53. C. S. Lewis, *The Complete C. S. Lewis Signature Classics* p. 41 from *Mere Christianity* (1952 – end of Chapter 1 in Book Two for those with a single copy).
54. The Gap View is an exception. The GV says God's re-creation of the Earth after a previous destruction did not involve animal death before the Fall. However, the GV has other well known problems (See Chapter 9).
55. I am not necessarily referring to global warming. Whether humans have contributed to that, or whether it is the natural cycles of Earth, or both, does not negate other bad things we have done to the Earth.
56. Peter D. Ward and Donald Brownlee, *Rare Earth*. This book is not Christian but concludes on page 275, "…it appears that Earth indeed may be extraordinarily rare." It is dedicated to Carl Sagan, ironic then that I use it to refute one of his arguments.

57. Ross, *Why the Universe is the Way It Is*, and Rana and Ross, *Origins of Life*: Both books show the fine-tuning of the conditions of the universe necessary for life to originate and exist and how life appears on Earth in its various stages at the exact times when the conditions of the Earth could support it. Also, because of the direction the universe is evolving, advanced life can only exist for a relatively short time before the conditions of our solar system will make it impossible for us to exist.
58. Ibid.
59. Whether *absolutely every* dinosaur died 65 million years ago is debatable, and even if some survived (most likely smaller versions if so) to live along side humans, *it is actually irrelevant to the age of the Earth*. If one was found alive today, though exciting, it would not cause countless skeptics and atheists to repent of their naturalistic evolutionary thinking and turn to the creationism of Christianity. All they would say is, "Well what do you know? Some did survive, just like alligators, coelacanths, and turtles." It would solve nothing between the creation/evolution or old-Earth/young-Earth debates.
60. Sarfati, *Refuting Compromise*, 218-219.
61. Ham, *Couldn't God Have Used Evolution?* from *The New Answers Book*, 36-37.
62. Ross, Improbable Planet.
63. Waltke, *Genesis: A Commentary*, 68.

Chapter 7 – The Top Ten Views of Genesis One

1. Some YEC, like nearly all OEC, believe there are gaps in the Genesis 5 and 11 genealogies and those YEC extend the age of the Earth beyond 6000 years, but not usually beyond 10 to 15,000 years.
2. Ham, *A young Earth - it's not the Issue!* p. 1.
3. Ross, *A Matter of Days* or *The Genesis Question* (now entitled *Navigating Genesis*)
4. Go to www.reasons.org the website for Reasons To Believe, Hugh Ross's ministry.
5. MacDonald, *Believer's Bible Commentary*, 33-34.
6. Custance, *Without Form and Void*.
7. Irons and Kline, *The Framework View*, p. 217
8. Ibid, but his FV dates at least 50 years earlier than this book and elements of the view (the recognition of the parallel structure of Days 1-3 with 4-6) predate Kline himself by as much as 200 years in Johann Gottfried von Herder (1744-1803), *The Spirit of Hebrew Poetry*, translation by James Marsh (Burlington, Ontario: Edward Smith, 1833).
9. Collins, *Genesis 1-4*, 124-125.
10. Examples include: a continuing Sabbath (Ibid, 125), and the events of the 6th Day being too long to happen in 24 hours (Ibid, 121). See Chapter 9 for more.
11. A summary of the PCA findings is available at http://www.reasons.org/report-creation-study-committee
12. Collins, *Genesis 1-4*, 124.
13. Young and Stearley, 210.
14. Newman, "Progressive Creationism" and Newman and Eckelmann, *Genesis One & the Origin of the Earth*.
15. Lennox, *Seven Days that Divide the World*, 55 and 157.
16. Sailhamer, *Genesis Unbound*, 27, 44-45.
17. Collins, *Science & Faith*, 363. See also the PCA findings (footnote 11, p. 28).
18. P. J. Wiseman, *Clues to Creation in Genesis*: Despite disagreeing with the RDV I recommend this book as an archaeological resource. As a side note, Donald Wiseman (the son) does not share his father's view and believes a more Theistic Evolution/ Accommodationist/ theological significance/ phenomenological language view. (See Kidner, 58-62)

19. Walton, *The Lost World of Genesis One*, see his comments on p. 111 on the Framework View.
20. Ibid, 91.
21. Ibid, 131.
22. Ibid, 97-98.
23. Ibid, 161.
24. Hayward, *Creation and Evolution*: This book introduced me to the Prophetic Days View, only Hayward calls it the "Days of Divine Fiat" (p. 167) as do many others. I just do not like that title because the word "fiat" is not commonly understood outside formal theological settings. So, I changed it to help the average Bible reader understand the basic concept behind the view. Much later I found the name "prophetic-day view" in Young and Stearley (144), though I had renamed my view by then and they used it to reference the Revelatory Days View. They also mistakenly say Hayward supported the Day-Age View (157). Hayward credits the Days of Divine Fiat to two sources: one, a late friend of his, Peter Watkins who "evidently thought of it himself some thirty years ago" (ca. 1955 since Hayward's first edition was 1985), and two, F. H. Capron who published a book containing the idea in 1902, *The Conflict of Truth* (London: Hodder & Stoughton, 169-199).
25. Some YEC point to Hayward's heretical beliefs to discredit him before his arguments are ever presented. For example, Jonathon Sarfati refers to him as, "Some skeptics, such as the Christadelphian heretic…" (*RC*, 338) Despite agreeing with Sarfati that Hayward's Christology was heresy, why does he find it necessary to introduce Hayward's argument with a personal attack? It can only be an attempt to make someone take Hayward less seriously. Just because someone is wrong sometimes (even if it is a big error), does not mean they are wrong every time, otherwise we are all wrong. Unfortunately, personal attacks are not uncommon in much of the popular YEC literature. I find it un-Christ-like, unnecessary, and generally disgusting when those claiming Christ's name use such tactics.
26. For definitions of the words "formless and void" see Appendix A.
27. I actually am not sure whether the CTV advocates the week was before or after billions of years. John Walton does not specifically address that issue but, best I can tell from his book, he falls in category two, though there is a chance he may be in category one. See Chapter 9 for more.
28. Two excellent Christian sources for scientific age evidence are: astronomy – Ross's *A Matter of Days*, and geology – Young and Stearley's *The Bible, Rocks and Time*.
29. Muncaster, 67.
30. PCA report, see footnote 11 above, p. 2.
31. Ibid, 6.
32. Ibid, 28. The PCA's 10 views do not exactly match mine. The Days of Divine Fiat View (i.e. the Prophetic Days View of this book) receives little more than a mention and brief definition in the report, and they do not include the Cosmic Temple View of John Walton, maybe because the CTV did not exist before their meeting, or the PCA did not consider the CTV evangelical. They list Gerald Schroeder's view as their tenth view.

Gerald Schroeder presents a view of Genesis that is like a combination of the Day-Age and Young-Earth Views. He says Genesis can be understood in such a way that the Days of Genesis 1 can be both normal 24-hour days from one perspective (on Earth), but ages long from another (God's). This is accomplished by time dilation predicted by Einstein's Theory of Relativity, a concept also used by some YEC to explain the appearance of great age for objects in the universe (See Chapter 8 under Supernova Remnants for a brief explanation). Essentially, Schroeder has the time represented by each "day" as reducing by half each day. So Day 1 represents 8 billion years, Day 2 – 4 billion, Day 3 – 2 billion, Day 4 – 1 billion, Day 5 – 500 million, and Day 6 – 250 million for a total of 15.75 billion years which Schroeder says is roughly the age of the universe. Each Day represents a major stage of the history of the universe. On Day 1 God creates the universe 15.75 bya (billion years ago). On Day 2 the Solar System begins to form 7.75 bya. On Day 3 land and plants appear approximately 3.75 bya. On Day 4 the sky became clear enough for the sun and moon to be visible 1.75 bya. On day 5 sea creatures appear approx. 750 mya (million) and on Day 6 land animals and man appear within the last 250 million years. A number of problems exist with his view. Scientifically the dates are wrong. The latest age estimate for the universe is 13.73 billion. When Schroeder wrote his book estimates put the age at 15 billion but better measurements refined it lower. The Cambrian explosion represented by Day 5 was more like 543 mya, not 750. Time dilation of this magnitude lacks support of any kind. The timing of supernovae at great distances show the time dilation expected by the Big Bang Theory, but nothing like the magnitude required by this view or the YEV (See Ross's *A Matter of Days*). Schroeder's view also runs into exegetical issues as well. The Earth does not appear until Day 3 in direct contradiction to the Genesis text which places the origin of the Earth before the 7 Days and tells a much simpler story (See Chapter 2). Also Genesis mentions fruit trees on Day 3 and birds on Day 5, neither of which fit Schroeder's time scale.

Chapter 8 – Why I Repented of the Young-Earth View
1. Isaac, 166, citing Kitagawa, H., and J. van der Plicht. 1998. "Atmospheric radiocarbon calibration to 45,000 yr B.P.: Late glacial fluctuations and cosmogenic isotope production". *Science* 279: 1187-1190.
2. Sarfati, *Refuting Compromise*, 367-371.
3. Ibid, 368, citing H.A. Makse, S. Halvin, P.R. King, and H.E. Stanley, "Spontaneous Stratification in Granular Mixtures", *Nature* 386 (6623): 379-382 (March 27, 1997).
4. Isaac, 148, again citing Kitagawa. A very simplified explanation of radiocarbon dating is as follows: Carbon dating is only done on material that was once living, meaning it is only done on Carbon based materials, and it is only accurate to approximately 45-50,000 years because after that the amounts of ^{14}C are so small the material being dated is indistinguishable from background contamination which is *always* present. When things are alive the amount of ^{14}C in their body is in equilibrium with their environment. After they die they quit taking in ^{14}C and the total amount of ^{14}C in their makeup begins to decay to ^{14}N. By measuring the amount of ^{14}C in a dead thing, like wood or diatoms, scientists can determine how long it has been dead (when they know contamination has not occurred). The varves in Lake Suigetsu give scientists a chance to calibrate Carbon dating because they can see how well the Carbon decay correlates to the number of layers. Radiocarbon has a half life of 5730 years, which means any given amount of ^{14}C in a sample will be reduced by half after 5730 years have passed. By simple physics, radiocarbon is an accurate means of measuring the age of nearly any once living thing and its accuracy has been verified by independent means repeatedly.
5. Oard and Reed, 131.
6. Ibid.
7. Oard, "Where Does the Ice Age Fit?" 214. If the Earth is only about 6000 years old, as many YEC say, then it was created in roughly 4000 BCE. The Flood would have occurred 1654 years later (the sum of the ages in Gen. 5 plus Shem's age in 11:10) in about 2350 BCE. Thus, according to YEC, the Ice Age lasted from approximately 2350 to 1650 BCE.

8. Young and Stearley, 272. Why do YEC think the strata below and above these fossils were formed by the Flood? Because, according to YEC, no death occurred before the Fall, and fossils are a record of death, and the strata above and below the dinosaur fossils all contain other fossils. Therefore, all of the strata had to be formed by the Flood because the geologic formations are too thick to have been formed by some other process since the Flood ended, and the Flood is the only Biblical event that could have formed them between the Fall and Noah.
9. Snelling, 283. The waters increased for 150 days (Gen 7:24) and then receded after that (Gen 8:3).
10. Horner, 108, 145, and 193.
11. Ibid, 126-133.
12. Ibid, 147.
13. Young and Stearley, 272.
14. Oard and Reed, 245.
15. Ibid, 246.
16. Ibid, 248.
17. Horner, 107 and 152.
18. Ibid, 163.
19. Ibid, 53.
20. Ibid, 104 and 152.
21. Ibid, 151.
22. Oard and Reed, 253.
23. YEC often imply uniformitarian geological processes are always slow which is then pitted against the fast catastrophic processes required by the Flood. The comparison is entirely too simplistic. Geologists let the evidence of the *wide variety of formations* dictate the method by which those formations formed. Scientists readily admit that some formations show evidence of rapid deposition (a fact happily seized upon by YEC for their own benefit). However, strong evidence exists that some formations were caused by slow processes, facts that do not fit the YEC model.
24. Ross, *A Matter of Days*, 204 citing P. R. McCullough, Brian D. Fields, and Vasiliki Pavlidou, "Discovery of an Old, Nearby, and Overlooked Supernova Remnant Centered on the Southern Constellation of Antlia Pnuematica," *Astrophysical Journal Letters* 576 (2002): L41-L44.
25. See Humphreys, *Starlight and Time*.
26. At the National Conference of Christian Apologetics in Charlotte, NC on October 11th, 2013 I attended a debate between Hugh Ross (OEC astronomer) and Jason Lisle (YEC astronomer). During the Q&A I asked a question to Lisle about what he thought of his colleague's (Humphreys) hypothesis of time dilation since it was not the position Lisle had taken in his presentation. Part of his response was "I'm just not convinced the math works out."
27. Ross, *A Matter of Days*, 166-169.
28. Sarfati, *Genesis*, 217.
29. My book is not about defining Christianity, but in the introduction I said at the very least Christianity can be defined as *believing and following the teachings of Jesus Christ*. Those teachings are found in the Bible. Logically it follows that who Jesus is, what He taught, and what He did must be important to defining Christianity and for the most part OEC and YEC agree on the fundamentals. However, one's interpretation of the Days of Genesis 1, despite its importance to the authority of the Bible, *is not one of those fundamentals*, but I do believe it is a major piece of the theological foundation those fundamentals rest upon. The fundamentals rest upon the authority of Scripture, and authority rests on inerrancy, and one's view of inerrancy is affected by potential scientific errors in the Bible; therefore, how

reconciliation is accomplished (one's view of Genesis 1) is part of the foundation upon which our faith rests, and is more important than most non-essential doctrines.
30. Macroevolution is the idea micro (small) changes in animals add up to macro (large) changes over long periods of time. While OEC and YEC do not have a problem with micro-evolution, they agree it has its limits (like changing the populations of finches with various beaks, or maybe causing speciation). They also agree it cannot account for major changes like fish becoming reptiles, or reptiles becoming birds, or something ape-like becoming human, etc., thus both reject macroevolution.
31. Morris, *The Henry Morris Study Bible*, 9. See the commentary on Genesis 1:7.
32. Williams and Hartnett, 180.

Chapter 9 – Evaluating Other Creationist Views
1. Because most (if not all) of these views have come about because of a modern scientific belief the Earth is old, many people conclude these views cannot be correct because they believe the views are reading modern science into Scripture rather than taking the text for what it says. I have already covered this unfounded objection in Chapter 5 as the seventh objection to Point 4, but it is also possible some people in the past may have seen some of these views and rejected them because of their own faulty science. Traditional views are not correct just because they have been traditional for a long time.
2. Some have wanted to say Genesis 5:1-2 specifies mankind was made within one day because it says "in the day". However, the phrase "in the day" is a translation of $b^e y\hat{o}m$ (*be* – the preposition "in" and *yôm* – day) and does not always literally mean within the timeframe of 24 hours. It often means "in a time" or "in a timeframe" and refers to an unspecified amount of time as in Genesis 2:4. (See footnote 10 below and Appendix A under "day" also)
3. It would have to be in real-time *after* time had begun and the universe existed, i.e. after Genesis 1:1. Also, because the account is written from an anthropomorphic perspective, it must be in real time because that is how we experience the universe.
4. One should note there is no distinction in Hebrew between the first and second use of *yôm* (day) in Genesis 1. Both uses are singular without any attached prepositions like $b^e y\hat{o}m$ (in the day) as it appears in 1:18 ("over the day" – NKJV), or *hayôm* (the day) as it appears in 1:14 and 16. All uses of *yôm* at the end of each Day *are missing prepositions*. The prepositions that are there are attached to the numbers.
5. See Appendix A under "evening".
6. See Appendix A under "morning".
7. Leupold, 57.
8. In a one-on-one lengthy conversation I was privileged to have with Hugh Ross (Day-Age View advocate) I made this same claim that the most natural way to understand the Days was as normal Earth daylight times. He disagreed and responded that was not the most natural way he took them the first time he read them. Despite my admiration for the man and his ministry (which I am part of and support), I believe he is an exception. I believe the general impression most people get from reading Genesis 1 is that the Days are normal Earth days. Ross's first impression of long periods of time may have occurred because of his early astronomy training from a modern scientific perspective, not an ancient cosmological or exegetical conclusion.
9. Ross, *A Matter of Days*, 74.
10. Some disagree (Sarfati, *RC*, 70-72) $b^e y\hat{o}m$ in Gen. 2:4 means a longer period of time than "day" because *yôm* is part of a Hebrew idiom meaning "when" as it is translated in the NIV, "When the LORD God made the earth and the heavens..." That is then used to say that 2:4 cannot be used to show *yôm* means an indefinite

amount of time in Genesis 1 and some OEC agree (Collins, *Genesis 1-4*, 104) though Collins points out that every use of *bᵉyôm* does not qualify as the idiom, only those uses "followed by an infinitive construct". *bᵉyôm* is used in Gen. 1:18, "to rule over the day [*bᵉyôm*]" (NKJV) and could just as easily read "to rule in the day" so it is not always translated as "when". Regardless of these arguments, there are good reasons to believe "day" used at the end of each Day means "daylight" even if *bᵉyôm*, translated as "in the day" in 2:4, means longer than a day. And *bᵉyôm* as used in 1:18 supports that even *yôm* with a prefix can mean daylight.

11. Though I have not personally reviewed every reference (there are over 2200) I have read an extensive amount of books and articles on Genesis, many of which support a Day-Age View, and in all that there have only been two exceptions offered, Hosea 6:2 and Zech. 14:6-8. However, Hosea 6:2 is not an exception. It uses "For two days" (plural and prefixed by "for") and "on the third day" (*bᵉyôm* – literally "in the day the third"). Zechariah 14:6-8 comes the closest to a case where a singular use of *yôm* attached to a number may mean a long period of time. These verses are in the context of "the day of the LORD" which must be longer than a 24 hour day, but the specific use in verse 7 may refer to a single day within the larger time. The passage is difficult. It should also be noted this verse uses *echad* (one) in a similar structure to Gen. 1:5 which says "one day", not "the first day" (see footnote 86 in Chapter 5). From such limited examples it is difficult to insist the Days in Genesis are long periods of time. One might say it is possible the Days are long because no "rule" says they must be 24 hour days, however, the evidence still leans heavily in favor of letting Genesis define "day" as the daylight portion of a 24 hour period, unless some *textual* reason occurs to cause a different meaning to be sought, but no such textual reason exists, especially when combined with the evening and morning phrase.
12. Ross, *A Matter of Days*, 81.
13. Collins, *Genesis 1-4*, 125.
14. See Appendix A under "account" for why 2:4a is the end of the first account.
15. Hugh Ross argues that a continuing 7th Day helps explain why the fossil record does not show the introduction of any new animal species on Earth since humanity arrived (Ross, "The Day-Age View" in *The Genesis Debate*, 141.). Ross says this is because God is still ceasing from creative activity because He is still in His Sabbath rest since finishing His creation after creating humanity. However, I would point out that God does not have to be in a continual state of rest to explain His lack of new species creation. Genesis 2:1 plainly tells us God is *finished* with "the heavens and the earth" and "all their hosts" which accounts for the lack of any new animal creative activity by God without postulating a continuing Sabbath. God says He is finished with the heavens and Earth, therefore we should not expect Him to be creating new animals, but that does not have to mean we are still in the 7th Day.
16. Ross, *A Matter of Days*, 81.
17. Irons and Kline, 87.
18. Ibid. 245.
19. Ibid.
20. See footnote 7 of Chapter 2 again. Most verbs in the Genesis 1 and 2 accounts are *wayyiqtol* verbs (*waw-consecutives*). *All commentators agree* the so-called *waw-consecutive* is not always consecutive. For example, Leupold (p. 108) speaking of the order of Genesis 2 says, "Rather, those supplementary facts... are given in a sequence which is entirely logical. In other words, the connective 'and' (*waw*) is not to be taken in the sense of 'next' (e.g. next God did thus and so) but rather in the sense of a loose 'also' without thought of time-sequence... The logical sequence will, however, have to be explained..."
21. Irons and Kline, 231-232. Two important distinctions appear in their translation:

(1) "Mist" in the NASB is changed to "rain-cloud" to which they say,

> 'mist'... is a rare word that occurs only one other time in the Hebrew Bible [Job 36:27]. The difficulty with such obscure words is that scholars often disagree on their meanings. In a situation like this, students of lexical semantics determine meaning by using two complementary methods: by studying cognate languages – Semitic languages such as Ugaritic, Akkadian, and Eblaite; and by examining the context – ultimately the most important test. In this case, both methods lead to the same conclusion: the word should be translated 'rain-cloud' rather than 'mist' or 'streams'. [NIV]

Leupold, Collins, and Whitelaw agree with this conclusion (Leupold, p. 114, Collins, *Genesis 1-4*, p. 104, and Whitelaw, p. 41). Personally I think a translation of "vapor" is even more literal because its use in Job 36:27 refers to it as what *becomes rain*, not rain itself. However, I agree with "rain-cloud" as an *interpretation* because that is what the vapor becomes. The word apparently refers to the process of evaporation that leads to rain, and some Biblical writers semi-understood that process (Job 37:10-13, Ps. 135:7, and Eccl. 1:6-7).

And (2) "Used to rise" in the NASB is changed to an inceptive action, "began to arise", to which Collins says "is possible" (p. 104). Irons and Kline (p. 231) say of the change,

> ...the verb 'to rise' can be translated in one of two ways, defining either durative action in the past ("used to rise") or inceptive action in the past ("began to arise"). The first option must be rejected because it makes nonsense out of the flow of thought. According to the NASB, verse 6 would be affirming the *presence* of an ample supply of water at the very time when, according to verse 5, the *lack* of such a water supply is stated as the reason for the absence of vegetation.

Against many translations, Irons and Kline's changes make sense of the flow of Gen 2, so I used theirs. The YEV idea that no rain ever fell on Earth until the Flood is a ridiculous conclusion to draw from Gen. 2:5, especially from such an obscure word that refers to water vapor *becoming rain* in Job. In their defense, many YEC no longer say rain began at the Flood.

22. What many authors do not mention about Gen 2:5-6 is the fact that *two categories* of plants are specified "of the field". The word "field" in Hebrew (*sâday*) in Strong's Hebrew Dictionary is a root word meaning "to *spread* out; a *field* (as *flat*)". It is used many times in the OT and generically means a flat place or plain (thus not mountains, hills, or a dense forest). It refers to *both a cultivated field and a wild field*. Fields are a preferred place for settlement because, as everyone knows, gardening in the mountains is more difficult because of trees, slope, and rocks.

Thus, Genesis 2 has *two plant types missing* ("shrub of the field" ("shrub" is not mentioned in Genesis 1 but its other three uses in the Bible suggest it is *wild shrubs* – Gen. 21:15, Job 30:4 and 7) and "plant of the field" ("herb" – same as Gen. 1:11 and 29 leaning towards plants for humanity's food)). We have two reasons why they were missing and two solutions. This 2/2/2 pattern suggests the first and last of each series correspond to one another. Therefore, Genesis 2 is referring to both wild and cultivated plants as missing and could thus be describing not only events of the proclamation from Day 6, but also events from the proclamation of Day 3, even though "of the field" refers to locations primarily for humanity.

Many commentators disagree with that assessment because it further complicates the order of creation differences between Genesis 1 and 2, but I have already explained that neither account is in strict chronological order so no contradiction exists. Also, some commentators (Collins, *Genesis*, 110) disagree because they believe all activities in Genesis 2 refer to events on Day 6, but that is an assumption on his part necessary for his method of reconciling Genesis 1 and 2.

Notice the text of Genesis 2:5 specifies "no shrub of the field was yet in the earth" meaning the *wild plants* were not *"on the land"*, and then it says, "no plant of the field had yet sprouted [grown – same as 2:9]" meaning no cultivated plant had been planted and grown. The lack of rain and humanity are listed as the reasons for the missing plants and then rain fixes the first and the formation of humanity fixes the second. Genesis 2 thus refers to activities from the proclamations on Day 3 and 6, *and Day 2* also because the formation of rain was begun as a result of the separation of the fresh and salt waters (see Appendix B). It also refers to activities related to the proclamation on Day 5 because that is when God proclaimed for flyers to fly (i.e. birds and all flying creatures). Genesis 2:19 says, "And out of the ground the LORD God formed every beast of the field and every bird of the sky..." Did He form *every* "bird of the sky" *on the 6th Day*? No, so obviously Genesis 2 is referring to more than just Day 6 and thus could include events related to Days 2, 5, and probably 3 also. One could argue Genesis 2 does not refer to activities related to Day 3 because the specification "of the field" refers to locations humanity is most likely to live. However, even though "of the field" is more specific to humanity, 2:5 still specifies *wild plants* were missing and the presence of humanity to cultivate the ground has nothing to do with their absence, nor solves it.

I think the textual evidence leans in favor of Genesis 2:5 referring to a situation where no plants existed (i.e. like the situation prior to Day 3), not where Genesis is describing a situation "...in some land [the western Levant], at the end of the dry season..." (Collins, *Genesis*, 111).

23. The primary differences of opinion between the FV and ADV involve: (1) whether Genesis 2 has any reference to Day 3 (the original creation of plants as described in the previous footnote); (2) whether Genesis supports Days 4-6 recapping Days 1-3; and (3) whether the 7 Days are a metaphorical framework and thus not a real week, or whether they are a real series of God-days (long periods of time) analogous to a human week. As to those three: (1) As I just defended in the previous footnote, I agree with the FV over the ADV that Gen. 2:5, "no shrub of the field was yet in the earth [on the land]," refers to wild plants and thus back to the Day 3 proclamation. (2) However, in agreement with the ADV over the FV, I see no recapitulation of Day 3 on Day 6. The previous footnote showed Genesis 2 also contains references to Days 2 and 5 and thus the idea Days 4-6 recap Days 1-3 is not supported by Genesis 2. And (3) I disagree with both metaphorical and analogical Days as supported in the main body of my book.

24. Newman, "Progressive Creationism: Conclusion", 155. Newman cites Capron from Dallas E. Cain, "Creation and Capron's Explanatory Interpretation: A Literature Search," *IBRI Research Report* 27 (1986). See also footnote 24 of Chapter 7.

25. Walton, *The Lost World of Genesis One*, 90-91. I think one of the reasons a Framework View advocate can get so excited about the Cosmic Temple View is because it adds a real week to their view of Genesis. Hence, an author like Davis Young (having "sympathy for aspects of the last two views" – i.e. the ADV and FV (Young, p. 210)) can write this endorsement on the back of John Walton's book, "*Every theologian, every pastor, every Christian in the natural sciences... must put aside all other reading material this minute and immediately begin to absorb the*

contents of John Walton's The Lost World of Genesis One." [emphasis his] Apparently he is very excited about Walton's work.
26. Irons and Kline, 217.
27. Waltke, *Genesis*, 76.
28. Sailhamer, *EBC*, 28. See footnote 86 in Chapter 5 again.
29. Walton, *The Lost World of Genesis One*, 68.
30. Technically the Sun is the only source of light on Earth (relatively speaking). Obviously, we know moonlight is caused by the Sun, and starlight is negligible, and manmade light is miniscule compared to the Sun. That moonlight is caused by the Sun is not out the realm of deduction even for the ancients, yet they still believed light came before the Sun, Moon, or stars (Egyptian and Mesopotamian cosmogonies both have light before the Sun – see next footnote). They most likely did not understand how that was possible, but they believed it anyway. The interpretation of Day 4 in Chapter 2 offers the perfect solution to how it can be believed light was before the Sun, and yet maintain scientific credibility because the Sun was the cause all along, but could not be seen from the perspective of the surface of Earth on Day 1. From an Earthbound observer's point of view, even though no one was actually there to see it, light came before the Sun was visible.
31. Johnny V. Miller and John M. Soden, *In the Beginning... We Misunderstood*, 125.
32. Strong, 80
33. Waltke, *Genesis*, 77.
34. See Chapter 7 again for definitions of Accommodationists and Concordists.
35. Hugh Ross once said to me that having many views of Genesis was good because, just like science, it is always good to have competing hypotheses because it eventually brings out the truth and the best hypothesis stands through the scrutiny of time. I must admit I had not looked at it positively until he said that. The situation does create a sense of humility (or should) when examining all the options because many sincere very intelligent Christians see things so differently, and the details of the text are abundant. Someone wanting to take a dogmatic stand (like me) must be very careful to examine all sides.
36. See Appendix A under "birds".
37. I said it before and I will say it again, I respect Hugh Ross greatly and applaud him for taking a stand for truth and remaining faithful and mature through all of the attacks against him over the years. And I support his ministry, and love his heart for the lost, a fact anyone who knows him will testify to. He was instrumental in converting me to an old-Earth position, but I have never been convinced the Day-Age View is exegetically correct. My intent is not to be harsh on Hugh Ross, only to disagree with his arguments for a view of Genesis I believe does not work scientifically or exegetically.
38. Ross, *The Genesis Question*, 39.
39. See Appendix A under "tree".
40. See Appendix A under "vegetation".
41. Ross, *Navigating Genesis*, 92.
42. Ross, *The Genesis Question*, 49.
43. Ibid, 52-53.
44. Ross, *Navigating Genesis*, 65.
45. See Appendix A under "creature" for the references.
46. Ross, *The Genesis Question*, 48.
47. Newman, *Genesis One & the Origin of the Earth*, see his chart on page 84.
48. Collins, *Genesis 1-4*, 129.
49. See Appendix A under "birds".
50. Walton, *Genesis 1 as Ancient Cosmology*, 165.

51. Ibid, p. 162. Technically Walton points out that Day 4 mentions separating the day from night, but sees it as just a reference back to the separating done on Day 1 and "…no additional separation takes place on Day 4."
52. PDV Point 4 –see Chapter 2
53. See the first objection to Point 4 in Chapter 5.
54. Collins, *Genesis 1-4*, 56.
55. Ibid, 129.
56. Ibid, 56.
57. Ibid, 128.
58. Leupold, 46.
59. Whitelaw, 4.
60. See Appendix A under "formless".
61. Sailhamer, *Genesis Unbound*, 110.
62. Ibid, 112.
63. John Sailhamer wrote a very good introduction and commentary on Genesis in *The Expositor's Bible Commentary* and has written other excellent books like, *The Pentateuch as Narrative*. Even *Genesis Unbound*, despite my overall disagreement with the LCV, contains many insightful and scholarly points worth reading, including Point 2 of the PDV which I got from him.
64. Walton, *The Lost World of Genesis One*, 90.
65. Ibid, his book is laid out in 18 propositions which he expounds upon.
66. Ibid, 92-93.
67. Ibid, 54.
68. Ibid, 93.
69. Ibid, 94.

Chapter 10 – Does Biblical Scientific Inerrancy Exist?
1. Conservative and liberal are often labels with blurred distinctions and they are used rhetorically to illicit an emotional response. That is not my intent here. For those who want to rush out and label Accommodationists "liberal" so we can all know they are "bad", I simply wish to point out that someone could take a high view of Scripture, believe it is the inspired word of God, trust Jesus as their Savior, worship and praise the same God, and be very conservative morally and politically, but yet believe the Bible accommodates scientific errors. So, even though I am about to argue that divine accommodation erodes the philosophical foundation of Christianity, my argument is against the idea, not the people who espouse it. I do wish they would change their mind though. And it is necessary to label the belief by some name in order to deal with it.
2. Geisler, 248.
3. Miller and Soden, 36-37.
4. Ibid, 37.
5. Ibid.
6. Ibid, 40.
7. Walton, *The Lost World of Genesis 1*, 14
8. Ibid.
9. Ibid, 15.
10. Miller and Soden, 40.
11. See Dembski, *Intelligent Design: The Bridge Between Science and Theology* and *The Design Revolution: Answering the Toughest Questions About Intelligent Design*.
12. See Appendix A under "made".
13. Tortora, Funke, and Case, *Microbiology*, 387.
14. Ibid, 16.

15. Walton, *The Lost World of Genesis One*, 16.
16. The two words most often translated "heart" (*lêb* – 3820 and *lêbâb* – 3824) are used over 750 times in the OT.
17. From Strong's "Hebrew and Chaldee Dictionary", they are *mê'âh* (4578 – p. 69) translated "stomach" (Num 5:22), "inward parts" (II Sam 20:10), and "bowels" (II Chr. 21:15, 18, 19, 32:21) among others; and *beten* (990 – p. 20) translated "womb" (Gen. 25:23-24, 30:2, 38:27), "abdomen" (Num. 5:21-22, 27), or "belly" (Judg. 3:21-22) among others.
18. A list of authors I consider to be Accommodationists would at least contain John Walton, Johnny Miller, John Soden, Davis Young, Ralph Stearley, Denis Lamoureux, and Darrell Faulk (I am sure there are many more). However, *all* of these authors have a common source and quote from at least two articles by Paul Seely to support their position, "The Firmament and the Water Above – Part I" and "The Firmament and the Water Above – Part II". Seely's articles seem to be taken as indisputable. I will agree they are well documented, but I disagree they are conclusive. I deal specifically with both articles in depth in Appendix B.
19. Paul Seely, "The Geographical Meaning of 'Earth' and 'Seas' in Genesis 1:10", 238.
20. Ibid, 239.
21. Set, appoint, and decree are other meanings of the Hebrew word *châqaq* (2710) from Strong's "Hebrew and Chaldee Dictionary", page 43, translated "inscribed" in the NASB.
22. Three Hebrew words are used to describe the "ends" of the land. From Strong's "Hebrew and Chaldee Dictionary", they are: *'ephec* (657) meaning the end point of something, like an extremity or appendage or the end of a pole (p. 15); *kânâph* (3671) the Hebrew word for "wing" also meaning the tips or outer parts like English would use the word "wingspan" (p. 56); and *qâtsâh* (7098) meaning the cutoff points or a place where something is determined to end (p. 104). All three words have the effect of describing the edges or ends of something with slight nuances.
23. Seely, "The Geographical Meaning of 'Earth' and 'Seas' in Genesis 1:10", 239-240.
24. Ibid, 240.
25. Ibid, 239.
26. Ward and Brownlee, *Rare Earth*, 49-53.
27. Ibid, 163, 227, and 233.
28. Seely, "The Geographical Meaning of 'Earth' and 'Seas' in Genesis 1:10", 252.
29. Ibid, 255. For more on the "deep" see Appendix A.
30. Multiple Hebrew words are translated "foundation" though three of them are related and they are the most common ones used. From Strong's "Hebrew and Chaldee Dictionary", they are: *yâcad* (3245 – p. 50) which is a root word meaning to set or found, thus, implying settling an issue or establishing something (it is also the root word for two other words translated "foundation" – *môwcâd* and *môwcâdâh* (4144 and 4146 respectively – p. 63)). Two other words are *'eden* (134 – p. 8) meaning a base, used of the earth only in Job 38:6, and *mâkôwn* (4349 – p. 66) meaning a fixture, particularly a dwelling place, used of the earth only in Psalm 104:5.
31. See http://earthquake.usgs.gov/earthquakes/world/index.php?region=Israel for some basic info.
32. The Hebrew word is *mâtsûwq* (4690) from Strong's "Hebrew and Chaldee Dictionary", 71. The more common word translated "pillar" is *'ammûwd* (5982 – see note 35). It is the one used in Job 9:6, 26:11, and Ps. 75:3.
33. The Hebrew word translated "world" is *têbêl* (8398) from Strong's "Hebrew and Chaldee Dictionary", 122. It generally refers to the inhabited land or a specific nation, not the land (*erets* – earth) itself.
34. Collins, *Genesis 1-4*, p. 264.

35. The Hebrew word is *'ammûwd* (5982) from Strong's "Hebrew and Chaldee Dictionary", 89. The word refers to something standing erect like a column.
36. For visual examples do an image search for "geologic pillars of the earth".
37. Lamoureux, 48-49.
38. Ibid, 49 f19.

Appendix A – Defending definitions: Word studies in Genesis
1. James Strong, *Strong's Exhaustive Concordance of the Bible:* Strong finished the concordance in 1890 and provided a continually valuable source for Biblical study. He numbered every Hebrew and Greek word in the Bible and the numbering system is still used today.
2. Some commentators number the sections as 11 divided by 10 uses of *toledoth* (Kitchen, 314, Leupold, 21-23, Sarfati, *RC*, 98, and Whitelaw, lxxxiv) and some think it is 12 sections divided by 11 uses of *toledoth* (Collins, *Genesis 1-4*, p. 36, Wiseman, 34-35, and Walton, *The Lost World of Genesis One*, 44). All those who advocate 11 divisions drop 36:9 because it seems redundant to 36:1 because both say these are "*the records of* the generations of Esau." However, it would seem strange that the use of *toledoth* divides Genesis at every place except one. It makes more sense to me, and seems more consistent, to say that each use divides the text rather than saying one sits in the middle of one of the divisions. Both sections, 36:1-8 and 36:9-43 contain nothing more than descendant lists of Esau. No particular history is added for Esau in contrast to Abraham, Isaac, Jacob, and Joseph. Because a consistent theme runs through Genesis concerning to whom God's promise to Abraham would be fulfilled, and to whom the land of Canaan was given, it comes as no surprise little detail is given for Esau, except as it relates to Jacob in 25:19-34, 27:1-41, and 33:1-16. Also, the possibility exists Moses cut out as irrelevant any other stories of Esau that may have originally been included with 36:1 or 36:9. That might also explain why 36:1-8 and 36:9-43 are so short right in the middle of two lengthy sections (25:19-35:29 and 37:1-50:26 the end of Genesis).
3. There are actually 13 uses of *toledoth* in Genesis but all agree the other two (10:32 and 25:13) correspond with 10:1 and 25:12 respectively. In other words, 10:1 and 10:32 both reference the sons of Noah and bracket the genealogies of Noah's sons. And 25:12-13 use the word twice in roughly the same breath and obviously do not form a one sentence account. Besides, 10:32 and 25:13 are not exactly the same in Hebrew as the other 11 uses.
4. Wiseman, 34.
5. The possibility exists that 11:1-9 (the story of the tower of Babel which has nothing to do with the previous account of Noah's sons – 10:1-32) may stand alone as a 13th section of Genesis not corresponding to any use of *toledoth* because 11:10 refers to the record of Shem which also has nothing to do with Babel and is followed by Shem's descendants. It could then be said Genesis is divided into 13 sections by 12 uses of *toledoth* with 10:32 marking the end of the 10:1-32 account thus dividing it from 11:1-9. Biblically, as a number, 12 divisions makes more sense though.
6. Collins, *Genesis 1-4*, pp. 40-41.
7. Ibid, 41.
8. Kitchen, 428.
9. Leupold, 80.
10. Geisler, 441.
11. I am aware that some creatures may not *appear* to fit nicely into this separation between animals and plants. Corals and barnacles come to mind, but even these sessile animals have several larval stages that swim.

12. Sarfati, *Refuting Compromise*, 70-72.
13. Collins, *Genesis 1-4*, p. 104.
14. Some people think we must read the days as long periods of time *because* scientists say the universe and Earth are billions of years old. They equate this situation with using science to read Scriptures about geocentricity as phenomenological language in order to avoid scientific error. Though I realize that interpreting Scripture in light of extra-biblical knowledge is not necessarily bad, because, as many say, all truth is God's truth, and the author of both nature and Scripture would not contradict Himself, but the situation with "day" is different. Interpreting it as long periods of time *does not solve the whole problem*. It still leaves the scientific order of appearance problem. It also creates more exegetical problems, like with the "evening and morning" phrase. (See Chapter 9 on both counts) Interpreting Scriptural descriptions of the Sun rising and setting as the way they appear to us on Earth helps. Interpreting "day" as a long period of time does not, and the evidence is much stronger the Days of Genesis were normal daylight periods on Earth.
15. Walton, *The Lost World of Genesis One*, 90.
16. See Collins, *Genesis 1-4*, p. 45n16, and Walton, *Genesis 1 as Ancient Cosmology*, 145 for examples. Walton references Tsumura, *Creation and Destruction*, 46-57, and says, "Not much can be added to Tsumura's thorough analysis of *těhôm*."
17. Sailhamer, *Genesis Unbound*, 47 and 49.
18. Collins, *Genesis 1-4*, 56.
19. Leupold, 57.
20. Walton, *The Lost World of Genesis One*, 47, citing a word study by David Tsumura, *Creation and Destruction*, 35. I agree unproductivity is contained in the definition of *tohu*. Walton stresses this to support his idea Genesis 1 is primarily about functional rather than material origins. However, *the reason* the land was unproductive is because of its material condition and I do not think the author of Genesis was overlooking that. So, I prefer the word "desolate" to translate *tohu* because it describes its physical condition and also retains the idea of unproductivity.
21. Sailhamer, *Genesis Unbound*, 60.
22. Henry, 3.
23. Sailhamer, *EBC*, 27.
24. Whitelaw, 4.
25. Collins, *Genesis 1-4*, 128.
26. Strong, from the "Hebrew and Chaldee Dictionary", 102.
27. Botterweck, 565.
28. Sailhamer, *EBC*, 38.
29. Whitelaw, 2-3.
30. Leupold, 10. Leupold cites Eduard Koenig, *Woerterbuch zum Alten Testament* (Leipzig: Dieterich, 1922, 2nd and 3rd edition) for the definition.
31. Whitelaw, 15.
32. Strong, from the "Hebrew and Chaldee Dictionary", 99.
33. Ibid, 31.
34. Leupold, 51.
35. Strong, from the "Hebrew and Chaldee Dictionary", 67 and 74.
36. Ibid, 107. Leupold has *radah* as, "signifying 'to trample down' or 'to master,'" 91.
37. See footnote 36 of Chapter 6 for examples of a very wrong interpretation of Genesis.
38. Strong, from the "Hebrew and Chaldee Dictionary", 54.
39. Sarfati, *Refuting Compromise*, 203.
40. Sailhamer, *EBC*, 25.
41. Leupold, 79.
42. See footnote 27 of Appendix B.

43. Strong, from the "Hebrew and Chaldee Dictionary", 121.
44. Kidner, 52.
45. Strong, from the "Hebrew and Chaldee Dictionary", 65.
46. Ibid, 66.

Appendix B – The meaning of *Raqîa'* in Genesis: Expanse or Firmament?
1. Seely, "The Firmament and the Water Above – Part I" and "The Firmament and the Water Above – Part II"
2. Seely only lists his sources as commentaries on Genesis by S. P. Driver, H. Gunkel, J. Skinner, G. von Rad, and C. Westermann
3. Seely lists John Calvin, *Genesis* (Grand Rapids: Eerdmans, 1948) 78-79, A. Clarke, *The Old Testament* (New York: Hunt & Eaton, n.d.) 1.31, G. Bush, *Notes on the Book of Genesis* (New York: Ivison, Phinney, 1860) 33, R. S. Candlish, *Commentary on Genesis* (1868; reprint Grand Rapids: Zondervan) 25, C. F. Keil and F. Delitzsch, *Biblical Commentary on the Old Testament, The Pentateuch* (Grand Rapids: Eerdmans, 1949) 1.52, A. R. Faussett and D. Brown, *A Commentary on the Old and New Testaments* (Grand Rapids: Eerdmans, 1948) 5, and H. L. Ellison and D. F. Payne, "Genesis," in *The International Bible Commentary* (ed. F. F. Bruce; Grand Rapids: Zondervan, 1979) 115.
4. Wilhelm Gesenius (1786-1842), *Gesenius's Lexicon* from a public copy translated by H. P. Tragelles as quoted 2/13/2012 at
http://www.blueletterbible.org/lang/lexicon/lexicon.cfm?Strongs=H7549&t=KJV
5. Holladay, 347. (bold and brackets in the original)
6. Strong, from the "Hebrew and Chaldee Dictionary", 110.
7. Vine, 67.
8. Wiseman, 193.
9. Leupold, 59, citing Whitelaw, 15.
10. Ibid, 60.
11. Sailhamer, *EBC*, 29.
12. Collins, 46.
13. I believe that Moses compiled records of the Genesis stories from earlier writers and thus Genesis was not originally written by him, but by the people whose events they document. It is currently not possible to know what source Moses used for Genesis 1:1-2:4a. It is possible Genesis 1 was given directly to him by God, but it also could have been the first revelation given by God to humanity (even as early as Adam) that was given in such a way as to make it very easy to memorize and pass along orally for many years before it was finally written down. If it was written that long ago, or at least before civilizations, then it is possible the author did not believe in a solid sky, or had no opinion on the subject, and simply believed God expanded the heavens above without saying how or with what materials. Authorship of Genesis 1 is not easily solved except to say Moses gave the Israelites its current form, and even that is disputed by liberal scholars.
14. The Hebrew word most often translated "clouds" is *'âb* (Strong's #5645, p. 84) which is a derivative of *'ûwb* (Strong's #5743, p. 86) which is a root word referring to covering with darkness as with a cloud. *'âb* is used 33 times in the OT and is mostly translated as "cloud" or "thick cloud" and clearly indicates from its use in context that "clouds" is the best way to translate it, and many times "thick clouds" or "rain clouds" are good ways to interpret it.
15. *Strong's*, rfrom the Hebrew and Chaldee Dictionary p. 114, and reference its four uses: Ex 30:36, II Sam 22:43, Job 14:19, and Psalm 18:42.
16. See Appendix A under "heavens".
17. Walton, *Genesis 1 as Ancient Cosmology*, 156.

18. Ibid, 157.
19. Collins, 264f.
20. Walton, *Genesis 1 as Ancient Cosmology*, 158. He says Job 38:37 uses *shachaq* in the Piel form and that combined with a similar structure to Job 28:27 means "count" should mean "appraise".
21. James Patrick Holding, "Is the *Raqiya'* ('Firmament') a Solid Dome? – Equivocal Language in the Cosmology of Genesis 1 and the Old Testament: *a Response to Paul H. Seely*" (Nov 1, 1999), page 5 as printed 10/28/2011 from http://www.answersingenesis.org/articles/tj/v13/n2/firmament&vPrint=1
22. See Appendix A under "made".
23. Hebrew scholars agree the phrase "the heavens and the earth" is a Hebrew figure of speech (merism) for "the all" or "the universe". It describes the universe from a human perspective as everything up there (the heavens) and everything down here (the surface of the Earth).
24. See Appendix A under "separated".
25. See Appendix A under "placed".
26. Refer again to Point 3 in Chapter 2.
27. Scientifically speaking the lowest part of Earth's atmosphere is the troposphere which extends to a maximum height of about 56,000 ft at the Equator. For the most part clouds are restricted to this layer and the highest recorded flight of birds is the bar-headed goose which migrates across the Himalayas at elevations just over 21,000 ft. Thus, birds *cannot* fly higher than the front side of the expanse and mostly stay below the clouds, just as God restricted them.
28. Walton, *Genesis 1 as Ancient Cosmology*, 159.
29. Strong, from the Greek Dictionary, 66.
30. Geisler, 114.
31. Holding, 10. This is only one Young-Earth view of the "waters above". Not every YEC takes this position.
32. Seely, "The Water and the Firmament – Part II", 31. *Enuma Elish* is a Babylonian creation myth ca. 2nd millennium BCE.
33. Ibid, 34.
34. Ibid.
35. Ibid, 39.
36. Ibid.
37. See Appendix A under "formless".
38. See Points 1 and 2 in Chapter 2.
39. Seely, "The Water and the Firmament – Part II", 39.
40. Ibid, 40.
41. See Appendix A under "separated".
42. See my translation of Genesis 1 at the end of Appendix A.
43. Williams and Hartnett, 180.
44. Holding, 10.
45. Sailhamer, *EBC*, 29.
46. Whitelaw, 15.
47. Leupold, 60.

Scripture Index

Genesis
1:1 – **22-24**, 33, 34, 41, 53, 55, 61, 66-67, **85-88**, 90-91, 107, 131, 133, 148, 172, 180-181, 185, **211**, 236, 239, 245, 257, 258
1:1-5 – 19
1:1-31 – 9, 60-61
1:1-2:4a – 7, 10, 11, 34, 43, 56, 66, 183, 194, 225, 238, **Appendix A**, 232, 261, 283
1:2 – 22-24, **25-26**, 41, 53, 67, **80-81**, 82, 87, **89-90**, 107, 131, 133, 148-149, 156, 170, 180-181, 185, 202, **216-218**, 238, 240, 245-248, 258
1:3 – **26-27, 81**, 148, 151, 245, 258
1:3-5 – 33, **44, 157-159**, 184, 248
1:4 – 111, 239, 268
1:5 – 79, 147, **168-169, 214**, 236
1:6 – 82, 154, 182, **Appendix B**, 263
1:6-8 – **45, Appendix B**
1:7 – **27-28**, 182, 185, 203, **247-248**, 263
1:8 – 26, 29, 214, **236**, 257, 264
1:9 – **34**, 81, 83, 90, 154, 185, 193, 202, 215, 245
1:9-13 – **46**, 107
1:10 – 71, 89, 90, 133, 199, 202, 215, 231, 236, 245
1:11-12 – **35**, 37, 65, **72-73**, 75, 78, 107, 154, 163, 171, 173, 175, 185, 193, 212, 215
1:14 – 67, 74, 83, 150, 154, 185, 240, 246, 248, 274

1:14-19 – **28-33, 36, 47, 84-85**, 238, 239
1:15 – 25, 29, 30, 61, 67, 74, 150, 185, 257
1:16 – 61, 67, 81, 83, 84, 150, 163, 185, 257, 274
1:17 – 25, 215
1:18 – 214, 274
1:20 – 154, 212, 215, 221, 238, 239, 257, 264
1:20-21 – 102, 171, 173, 175
1:20-23 – **48**
1:21 – 55, 66, 163, 221
1:22 – 25, **37**, 39, 98, 109, 155, 240, 257
1:24-25 – **37-38**, 61, 66, 73, **74-75**, 77, 79, 102-103, 150, 154, 163, 172-174, 193-194, 221, 257
1:26 – 25, **38-39**, 66, **76**, 122, 154, 155, 240, 257
1:27 – 55, 66, 69, 122, 155, 163, **169**, 213
1:28 – 25, 39, 76, 98, 109, 118, 155, 180, 240, 257, 263
1:28-30 – 94, **98-101**, 118, 154
1:29 – 108, 111, 173, 276
1:29-30 – 100-101, **105-109**, 129
1:30 – 25, 76, 100, 240
1:31 – 94, **95-98**, 117, 214
2:1-4a – 50, **60-64**, 76, 91
2:1 – 61, 88, 215, 275
2:2 – **60-62**, 151, 214
2:3 – 39, **62-64**, 66, 111, 155, 210, 213, 214
2:4 – 159, **210**, 274
2:4a – 160
2:4b – **214**
2:4-7 – **167**
2:4b-5:1 – 55, 108, 163

2:5 – 276
2:5-6 – 159, **165**, 204, **226-227**,
2:6 – 28, 248
2:7 – 163, 174, 211, 221
2:8-9 – 36, **73**, 79, 108, 111, 163, **164**, 173, 211, 213, 277
2:15 – 110
2:16-17 – 73
2:17 – 57, 105, 106, 118
2:18 – 123, 164
2:19 – 47, 75, 72, 163, 164, 170, 176, 194, 211, 221, 257
2:19-20 – 186, 243
2:20 – 108, 164, 176, 211
2:21 – 111, 163
2:22 – 163
2:24 – 69
3:1 – 108
3:2-6 – 173
3:4-5 – 196, 200
3:8 – 36, 111, 164, 170
3:13 – 65, 222
3:14-19 – 94, **107-111**, 118, 268
3:16 – 113
3:17-19 – 105, 118
3:19 – 57, 106
3:21 – 100, 170
3:23 – 108
4:4 – 100
5:1 – 209-210, 274
5:2 – 156, 274
5:5 – 111
5:24 – 269
6:5 – 197
6:6 – 198
6:7 – 212
6:9 – 209
6:20 – 212
7:2 – 99-100, 118, 212
7:8 – 99-100, 118
7:11 – 204, **241-242**
7:18 – 240
7:19-24 – 143
7:21 – 212
7:24 – 273

285

8:2 – 204, **241-242**
8:3 – 273
8:21 – 198
8:22 – 214
9:1-4 – 99-100
9:2 – 210
9:10, 12, 15, 16 – 221
10:1 – 209, 210, 281
10:5 – 225
10:10 – 86, 211
10:25 – 225
10:32 – 210, 281
11:1-9 – 210, 281
11:10 – 209, 281
11:27 – 209
12:9 – 196
13:3-4 – 22-23
13:8-14 – 225
14:15 – 225
15:10 – 225
17:17 – 198
18:25 – 215
21:15 – 276
24:16 – 96
25:12-13 – 209, 281
25:19 – 209, 281
25:32 – 280
31:32 – 220
33:3 – 215
36:1 – 209, 281
36:9 – 209, 281
37:2 – 209
37:30 – 210
37:35 – 207
42:28 – 188
45:26 – 198
49:3 – 211
49:18 – 219
49:25 – 204, 215

Exodus
4:14 – 198
7:9-12 – 223
7:18 – 240
7:21 – 240
8:32 – 198
12:18 – 88, 157, 216
13:21 – 214
14:16 – 215, 225
14:21 – 225
14:22 – 215
14:29 – 215
15:8 – 198
15:10 – 225
16:22-30 – 51, 155
18:13 – 157, 166, 216
20:3 – 220
20:4 – 203
20:8-11 – **64-68**, 79, 85, 87, 155, 239
21:35 – 225
22:8-9 – 220
23:12 – 169
23:19 – 211
24:9-10 – 237
24:18 – 155
25:2 – 198
26:33 – 225
27:21 – 157, 166, 215
31:17 – 65, 66, 68, 79, 85, 87, **169-170**
33:16 – 225
33:20 – 170
35:29 – 64
35:34 – 198
39:3 – 233

Leviticus
2:12 – 211
10:10 – 225
11:6 – **197**
11:10 – 221
11:46-47 – 103, 173-174, 210, 221
17:13 – 210
20:24 – 225
23:32 – 88, 157, 216
24:3 – 157, 166, 216
25:1-12 – 110
26:6 – 210

Numbers
5:22 – 279
8:14 – 225
9:15-16 – 178, 215
14:7 – 96
15:21 – 211
16:39 – 233

Deuteronomy
4:17 – 236
4:18 – 203-204
6:4-5 – 197
10:16 – 198
11:12 – 211
19:2 – 225
21:12 – 65, 222
29:18 – 218
30:6 – 198
32:8 – 225
32:10 – 216
32:11 – 116, 223, 226
33:13 – 204, 215
33:17 – 201

Joshua
8:30-32 – 258
10:12-13 – 79

Judges
3:21-22 – 280
18:9 – 96

I Samuel
2:8 – 205
4:13 – 198
14:5 – 205
15:21 – 211

II Samuel
11:2 – 96
16:14 – 169
18:14 – 198
20:10 – 279
22:12 – 234
22:43 – 234, 283
23:3-4 – 194, 227

I Kings
1:6 – 96
8:27 – 200
8:59 – 214
17:1 – 192
18:1 – 192
22:19 – 237

II Kings
2:11 – 269
5:22 – 196
7:2 – 241
7:19 – 241
15:12 – 71
19:15 – 66-67, 239

Scripture Index

19:29 – 194

I Chronicles
16:30 – 203

II Chronicles
2:12 – 67, 239
21:15 – 18, 19, 279
32:21 – 279

Nehemiah
5:5 – 224
7:28 – 224

Job
1:2 – 33
1:6 – 155, 170
2:1 – 155
2:9 – 33
4:20 – 216
6:18 – 216
8:7 – 22, 86, 211
9:5-6 – 205, 280
12:24 – 217
14:19 – 283
22:14 – 199-200, 206
26:7 – 217
26:10-11 – 199, 205, 280
28:24 – 201
28:27 – 283
30:4, 7 – 276
35:5 – 234
36:27-29 – 234, 276
37:3 – 201-202
37:10-13 – 248, 276
37:18 – 234-235
37:21 – 234
38:2 – 200-201, 206, 235
38:4 – 21, 33, 154, 205
38:4-12 – **80-81**, 87, 181, 205
38:6 – 280
38:7 – 33, 154
38:8-11 – **26**, 204, 242, 246
38:9 – 21, 54, 82, 238, 240, 246, 248
38:12-13 – 21, 182, 201
38:16 – 204
38:19-20 – 235
38:30 – 228
38:33 – 205
38:37 – 234-235, 283
42:7-8 – 200
42:12 – 22, 86, 211

Psalms
2:4 – 236-237
8:5 – 220
8:8 – 236
11:4 – 236-237
14:1 – 196
18:7 – 205
19:1-6 – 195, 236
24:2 – 203
32:4 – 214
33:6 – 70, 154
33:9 – 70, 154
33:13-14 – 220
36:5 – 234
40:1 – 219
51:10 – 184
59:13 – 201
74:13 – 223
75:3 – 205-206, 280
75:8 – 206
78:23 – 242
79:2 – 236
84:11 – 116
90:6 – 216
93:1 – 203, 205
95:5 – 35
95:10-11 – 161
96:10 – 203
99:1 – 203
103:19 – 237
104:5 – 79, 203
104:5-9 – 71, 90, 181, 204
104:11 – 210
104:14 – 193, 260
104:21 – **100-101**, 104, 105, 118
104:22 – 194, 260
104:25 – 213
104:30 – 213
113:3 – 79
114:3-4 – 72
119:128 – 145, 187
119:142 – 187
119:163 – 187
121:2 – 67, 239
134:3 – 67, 239
135:7 – 28, 248, 276
136:6 – 203, **233**
139:8 – 236
146:6 – 66-67, 239
147:8 – 36, 164
148:1-4 – 236, 245
148:5 – 67
150:1 – 236

Proverbs
1:7 – 211
3:9 – 211
3:20 – 28, 204, 215
8:22-27 – 23
8:24-29 – 204
8:27 – 199
8:28 – 204
8:29 – 204, 205
9:18 – 207
12:17 – 145
17:14 – 211
27:25 – 227

Ecclesiastes
1:6-7 – 28, 248, 276
7:8 – 211
8:11 – 111
11:3 – 28, 194, 260
11:4-6 – 194
12:3 – 241

Isaiah
5:6 – 28
5:20-21 – 123
6:1 – 237
11:1-10 – 114-115
11:6-9 – 94
11:12 – 79
14:12-13 – 155, 220, 237
22:18 – 200
23:15 – 159
24:10 – 217
24:18-20 – 205, 241
24:19 – 203
24:23 – 241
27:3 – 214
29:3 – 200
34:8 – 159, 217
34:11 – 217
40:12 – 200

287

40:15 – 234
40:19 – 233
40:22 – 199, 260
40:26 – 67
40:28-29 – 170, 201
41:20 – 213
41:29 – 217
42:5 – 67, 204, 233
44:24 – 204, 233
45:18 – 180, 217
46:9-10 – 34
51:10 – 204
55:10 – 36, 164
59:1-2 – 225
60:8 – 241
63:13 – 204
65:17 – 67
65:17-25 – 114-115
66:1 – 237

Jeremiah
3:17 – 219
4:23 – 90, 180, 211
10:9 – 233
16:20 – 220
17:9 – 93
24:2-3 – 96
28:1 – 22, 86, 211
34:11 – 224
49:35 – 211
51:9 – 234

Ezekiel
1:1-28 – 237-238
6:11 – 234
10:1 – 238
24:5 – 200
25:6 – 234
26:19 – 204
30:3 – 159
31:4 – 204
34:5 – 210

Daniel
4:8 – 201
4:10-11 – 201
8:14, 26 – 216
12:3 – 235

Hosea
6:2 – 275

9:10 – 86, 211
13:3 – 241
13:8 – 210

Joel
2:22 – 226

Amos
4:13 – 184

Jonah
4:6 – 36

Zechariah
9:15 – 224
14:6-8 – 275

Malachi
3:10 – 241

Matthew
5:45 – 192, 260
7:24 – 205
13:31-32 – 195
19:4 – 68-69
19:8 – 68-69
20:28 – 58
23:37 – 116
24:36 – 196

Mark
2:27 – 39, 155, 161
4:30-32 – 195-197
10:2-9 – 68
10:6 – 68-69
13:19 – 262

Luke
1:1-4 – 190
2:1 – 112
2:52 – 196
8:45 – 196
10:6 – 98
11:50-51 – 262
16:19-31 – 207
23:43 – 207
24:27 – 190

John
1:1-3 – 57, 154
1:3 – 86

5:16-17 – 161
8:26-29 – 196
8:32 – 187
10:10 – 106
11:16 – 196
12:23-25 – 195-197
14:6 – 157
16:13 – 18
17:17 – 187

Acts
1:3 – 190
2:23 – 116
2:32 – 190
3:18-21 – 115
3:21 – 94
16:25-26 – 192
17:11 – 59, 190
17:17 – 190
17:31 – 190
19:27 – 112
26:24-29 – 190

Romans
1:8 – 112
1:18-23 – 44, 112, 190
1:20 – 262
3:22-24 – 58
5:12 – 98, 105-106
5:17-19 – 105-106
7:14-25 – 93
8:18-23 – 94, **112-114**, 118
8:28 – 122
10:9 – 58
15:12 – 115

I Corinthians
8:1-2 – 5
10:13 – 122
15:3-8 – 190
15:21-22 – 98, 105-106
15:26 – 106, 116
15:42 – 56
15:50-54 – 113

II Corinthians
4:6 – 182, 213
5:8 – 207
5:10 – 122
5:21 – 196

Scripture Index

11:4 – 125
12:3-4 – 207

Ephesians
1:3-5 – 116, 262
1:9-12 – 50
2:1-5 – 106
3:20-21 – 58
4:8-10 – 207

Philippians
2:9-10 – 206

Colossians
1:16-17 – 192, 213
1:20 – 94

I Thessalonians
4:17 – 106, 269
5:21 – 190

II Thessalonians
2:6-7 – 122

I Timothy
1:15 – 117

II Timothy
2:15 – 5
3:16 – 243

Hebrews
3:18-19 – 161-162
4:3-6 – 161-162
4:9-10 – 161-162
4:15 – 196
5:8 – 196
6:1 – 162
7:26-27 – 196
9:23 – 117
11:3 – 154
11:6 – 46
12:25-29 – 145

James
1:13-15 – 261
2:26 – 207

I Peter
1:20 – 262
3:15 – 190
3:18-20 – 207
5:5 – 5

II Peter
1:16 – 190
3:4 – 262
3:5 – 81

I John
3:5 – 196

4:18 – 211
5:12 – 106

Jude
3 – 56-57

Revelation
2:11 – 106
4:6 – 237, 244
5:3 – 206
5:13 – 206
7:1 – 79
12:9 – 218
13:8 – 116, 262
17:8 – 262
20:14 – 106, 207
21:1 – 56
21:3-5 – 94
21:4 – 122
21:8 – 106
22:3 – 94
22:5 – 32

Subject Index

Accommodationists – **128**, 132-4, 171, 179, 182-3, 186, **Chap. 10**, App. B, 270, 279-80
Adam and/or Eve – 9, 39, 41-2, 51, 57, 65, 68-9, 73, 89, most of **Chap. 6**, 131, 134-5, 155, 162, 164-5, 170, 173-4, 176, 180, 210-13, 218, 222, 225, 268, 283
Analogical Days View (ADV) – 131, **132-3**, 136, 137, 153, 159-61, 164-65, 171, **174-5**, **178-9**, 181, 265, **277**
ancient cosmology – 128, 132, 134, 185, 188-90, 195, **199-208**, Appendix B, 274
"and it was so" phrase – 10, 30-1, 36, 47, 48-9, 61, **70-7**, 149, 262-5
angels – 33, 80, 86, **154-6**, 170, 182, 192, 220, 226, 236, 240, 245, 257
anthropomorphic language – 147, 156, **170**, 234, 241, 274
appearance of age – **145**, 271
Atonement, the – **116-7**, 151, 269
Attenborough, Sir David – 119
author
    intent – 8-9, 12, 23, 18, 27, 38, 55, 58, 91, 132-3, 135, 147, 154, 160, 166-9, 178, 194, 209, 241, **258**
    of Genesis – 7, 12, 15-19, 58, 132, 137, 155, 163-4, **232**, **258**, **283**
authority, Biblical – 42-3, 53, 95, 124-5, 127-9, **147**, 177, **187-90**, 192, **207-8**, 231, **241-3**, 273

"beginning", the – 19-21, **22-24**, 33, 34, 40-42, 56, **85-6**, 88, 91, 133-4, 148, 180-1, **211**, 257
Big Bang – 23, 53, 272

blessing – 39, 49, 74, 76, 98, 118, 149, **154-5**, 167

Calendar Day View – 129
Carbon dating – 141, 272
chiasm – 210, 257
chronology/dischronology – 9-14, 16, **31-2**, 37-41, 61-2, **84-85**, 131-2, 150, 163-4, 167-8, 171, 175-80, 216, 258-60, 264, 276
Collins, C. John (Jack) – 21, 65, 67, 109, 113, 132-3, 153, 160, 174, 178-180, 205-6, 210, 214, 216, 218, 232, 235, 258, 262, 268, 274, 276
Concordists – 128, 130, 133, 171, 182, **187-8**
Cosmic Temple View (CTV) – **134-5**, 136, 153, 167, **182-186**, 271, 277
Curse, the – 94, 96, **106-11**, 114, 116, 118-9, 268
Custance, Arthur C. – 131

Darwin, Charles – 55, 117, 124
Day
    1 – 9-10, 15-16, 20-1, 25, **26-7**, **32-3**, **44-5**, 48, 50, 61, 67, 69-70, **80-1**, 85, **87-89**, 148-9, 157-9, 166-7, **169**, 176, 181, 184-5, 216, 239, 245-6, 264-5, 266
    2 – 9-10, 13, 16, **25-7**, 30, 46, **45-6**, 50, 67, **81-5**, 89, 91, 158-9, 166, 176, 182, 185, 202-3, **App. B**, 257, 264-5, 277
    3 – 9-10, 12, 25, **34-6**, **46-7**, 50, 54, **71-74**, 84, **89-91**, 149, **172-4**, 175-6, 185, 193, **227-8**, 257, 259, 265, 276-7
    4 – 9-10, **28-33**, **36-7**, **47-8**, 50, 67, 74, **82-5**, 89, 149-50, 167, 169, 176, 185, 224, 239-40, 244-47, 257, 259-60, 265, 278

291

5 – 9-10, 12, 25, **37**, **48-9**, 50, 54-5, **74**, 149, 173-6, 213, 223, 225, 257, 265, 277
6 – 9-10, 12-13, 25, **37-9**, **49**, 50, 69, 84, 98, 149-50, 159, **162**, 165, 169, 173-6, 210, 213, 225, 260, 265, **276-7**
7 – **39**, **51-2**, **59-64**, 76, 79, 149-50, 155, **160-2**, 168, 178, 275
Day-Age View (DAV) – 15, 18, **130-1**, 132, 136-7, 153-4, **158-66**, 171, **172-4**, **178**, 181, 216, 259, 265, 275, 278
days
   God's days – 60, **131**, **136**, 178
   length of – 2, **14-16**, **41**, 78, 88, **136**, **147**, **156-66**, 177, **214-5**, **274-5**
   metaphorical/figurative – 41, 60, **131-2**, **136**, **167-71**, **179**, 216
   overlapping – 173, **174-76**
Days of Divine Fiat View – 17-18, 135, 166, 258, 271
death and disease
   animal – **Chap. 6**, 150-1
   human – 93-4, **106**, 118, 121-2
deep, the great – 25, 89-90, 199, 203-4, **215**
dinosaurs – 105, 122, 139, **142-4**, 174, 212, 268, **270**, 272
disease – see death
dischronology – see chronology
divine accommodation – see Accommodationists

Earth
   age of – 1-2, **21**, **40-2**, 56, 127-30, 136-7, **151**, 154, 177
   creation of – **21-24**, 33, 85-91
Eden – see Garden of Eden
evening and morning phrase – 8, 10, **15-16**, 19-21, 61, 79, **88**, 90, 147, **156-60**, **166-8**, 175, 178-9, **215-6**, 266, 275

evolution – 1, **42**, **55-6**, 74-5, 77, 117-8, 128, 141, **147**, 195, 208, 221, 263, 270, **273-4**
ex nihilo – 67, 86, 184, 213
expanse – 11, **25-33**, 45-7, 67, **82-5**, 149, 185, **203**, 216, **App. B**

Fall of man – 4, 57, 65, **Chap. 6**, 129-30, 150-1, 222, 225, 263, 267-9, 272-3
fifth Day – see Day 5
firmament – see expanse, **Appendix B**
first Day – see Day 1
flat Earth – 199-202
Flood of Noah, the – 99, 127, 129, **142-4**, 149, **151**, 172, 181, 204, 212, 241, 272-3, 276
Focus-on-Palestine View – see Limited-Creation View
"formless and void" phrase – 25-6, 89-90, 131, 148, 180, **216-8**, 245, 267
fossils – 24, 55, 93, 95, 106, 120, 124-5, 129, 142, 151, 172, 175, 181, 276, 275
foundations of the earth – 21, 33, 80, 87, 154-5, 181, 199, 203-5, 246, 280
fourth Day – see Day 4
Framework View (FV) – 41, **131-2**, 134, 136-7, 153, 159-62, 165, **167-71**, **179**, 265, 270, 277
fulfillments – **8**, 13, 20, **31-2**, **34-42**, 44, 46-49, **56**, **59-80**, **84-5**, 87, 92, **135-6**, **149-51**, 166, 168, 173-80, 186, **264-65**

Gap View (GV) – **24**, **130-3**, 136, 153-4, 172, **180-1**, **217-8**, 269
Garden of Eden – 36, 41, 104, **108-10**, 116, 131, 134, 150, 164, **224-5**, 267
genealogies – 129, 151, 209-10, 270, 281

Subject Index

generic nature – 7, **8-9**,16, 102, 173, 186, 210, 212, 221-2, 227-8, 229, 233-5
Gish, Duane – 1
God of the gaps – 193

Ham, Ken – 64, 94, 116-7, 125, 129-30, 268
Harryhausen, Ray – 139
Hayward, Alan – 2, 18, 135, 258, 271
heart – 197-8
"heavens and earth" phrase – **19, 22-4**, 61, **66-8, 85-92**, 210, 213
historical narrative – 4, **7**, 9, 16, 41-2, 131, 167-71, 179

Ice-Age, the – 141-2, 272
image of God – 38-9, 43, **49**, 51, **55**, 69, 155, **169**, 213, 219, **220**, 222-3
inerrancy – 1, 42, 56, 124, **127-8**, 145-6, **147**, 163, 168, **177, Chap. 10**, 231, 242-3, **277**
insects – **12**, 96, **101-3**, 141, 143, 171, 173-4, **212**, see invertebrates also
Institute for Creation Research (ICR) – 1
Intelligent Design – 55-6, 191, 193
Intermittent-Days View (IDV) – **133**, 136, 153, 158, **166-7**, 171, 174, **179**, 181, 265
Invertebrates – **101-3**, 106, 124, **213, 222**, see insects also

kinds – 37-8, 74, 77, **147, 221**
Kline, Meredith – 83, 84, **132**, 165, 270, 276
Lennox, John – 133, 153
Leupold, H. C. – 26, 66, 72, 75-6, 80, 82, 84, 87, 158, 180, 212, 216, 220, 223, 226, 232, 248, 261, 275-6
Lewis, C. S. – 119

life
    definition of – 102, 195-7
    origin of – 54-55
light
    first light – **26-7, 80-82**, 149
    lights, appearance of – **28-33, 67-8, 82-5**
Limited-Creation View (LCV) – 86, **133-4**, 136, 153, 172, **181-182**

mediated creation – 35, 63, **72**, 75, **192-4**, 233
merism – see "heavens and earth" phrase
miracles – 42-3, 77, 150, 164, 190-1, 243, 263
Moon – see lights
Morris, Henry – 1, 149
Moses – 51, 64, 68-9, 110, 134, 155, 232, 237, 258, 281, 283
Mustard seed – 195-7
myth – 3-4, 41, 130, 147, 223, 255

naming – 10, 27, 29, 33, 108, **156**, 162, 176, 211, 214, 245
narrative – see historical narrative
naturalism
    methodological – 191
    philosophical – 191
nephesh chayah – **101-5, 173-4**, 214, **221-2**, 223
Newman, Robert – 133, 166, 174
Noah – see the Flood

Old-Earth Creationists (OEC) – 1, 3, 18, **128-30, Chapter 9**
order of appearance problem – see scientific order problem
parallel structure of Genesis 1 – **9-10**, 41, 160, **168, 176**, 264, 270
patterns – 7, **8, 10**, 16, 20, 31, 38, 44, 61, 85, 87, 186
Pentateuch – 133, 181, 209, 226
phenomenological language – 137, 203-4, **231-2, 242-3**, 264, 281

pillars of the earth – 199, 203, 205+6
poetry – 7, 41, 72, 181, 200, 205-7, 232, 235
polemic – 170
pre-Adamic race – 131, 218
Presbyterian Church in America (PCA) – 137, 270-1
proclamations – **8-10**, 13, 16, **20**, **31**, **34-40**, 41-2, 44, 59-69, **69-77**, **135-6**, 149-50, 154-6, 173, 176, **177-8**, **264-5**
Progressive Creationists – 35, 57, **128**
prophecy – **34**, 79, **136**, 189-90
Prophetic Days View (PDV) – the whole book (humor intended)
providence – 72, 165, 192-4

Reasons To Believe (RTB) – 2, 57, 131, 172
reptiles – 12, 101, 172-4, 210, 212-214
Revelatory-Days View (RDV) – 134, 136, 153, **155**, **182**, 258
Ross, Hugh – 2, 18, 57, 69, 124, 131, 140, 153, 158, 160, 172-5, 274, 275, **278**
Ruin-Reconstruction View – 131

Sabbath – 39, 51, 59, 64-5, 76, 110-11, **161-2**, 275, see Day 7 also
Sagan, Carl – 119, 122
Sailhamer, John – 18, 22, 82, 85, 133, 153, 172, **181-2**, 215, 217-8, 226, 232, 248, 258, 260, 264, 279
Sarfati, Jonathon – 69, 74, 78, 81-3, 88, 93, 95-6, 98, 101, 105-6, 114, 116, 124, 140, 145, 214, 225, 259, 262-3, 266, 269, 271, 274
Satan – 96, 104, 107, 107, 109, 118-9, 131, 200, 218, 268
Schaefer, Francis – 95
Schroeder, Gerald – 271-272

science, definition – 189-190
scientific order problem – 9, **12**, 168, **171-77**, 179
second Day – see Day 2
Second Law of Thermodynamics – 114
secondary causes – 35, 44, 47, 50, 63, 72, 86, **192-4**, 233-4, 260
Septuagint – 113, 209, 218, 242, 260, 263-4
seventh Day – see Day 7
sixth Day – see Day 6
stars – see lights
Sun – see lights
supernova remnants – 144-145
surface perspective – 15, **24-33**, 41, 47, 54, 61, 64, 67-8, 79, **80-85**, 149, 215, 226, 248, 264

Templeton, Charles – 119-120
Theistic Evolution – 74, 117, 128, 146, 267
third Day – see Day 3
toledoth – 209-210, 281
topical arrangement – **9**, **12**, 40-1, 61, 132, 135, 163, 167-8, **176-177**, 179, 186, 257

underworld – 199, 206-207
universe
    age of – 1-2, 21, 28, **40-2**, 43, 53, **56**, 58, 92, **127-8**, 130, 136, **144-146**
    creation of – 19, **22-5**, 53, 55, 66-7, 85-9, 213

vav consecutive – see waw consecutive
varves – 140-142
vegetarianism – 94, **98-101**, 104, 107, 151
"very good" – 93-4, **95-8**, 106, 108, 117-8, 126, 268
void – see "formless and void" phrase

294

Subject Index

Waltke, Bruce – 126, 167, 170
Walton, John – 27, **134-5**, 153, 169, 176, **182-6**, 189, 198, 215, 235, 240, 271, 280
waw consecutive – 257, 258-9, 275
wayyiqtol – see waw consecutive
whales – 12, 103, 118, **223**
Wiseman, Donald J. – 134, 270
Wiseman, P. J. – 134, 209, 232
work – 7, 15, 21, **39**, 40-1, 45, 51-2, **59-68**, 76, 88, 91, 148, **160-162**, **177-178**, **228**

Young-Earth Creationist/View (YEC)/(YEV) – 1-2, **17**, 18, 21, 41-2, most of Chapter 5, **Chapter 6**, **127**, **129-30**, 136, **Chapter 8**, 159, 171, **172**, 246

295